Kant's *Critique of Pure Reason*
Background Source Materials

This volume offers English translations of texts that form the essential background to Kant's *Critique of Pure Reason*. Presenting the projects of Kant's predecessors and contemporaries in eighteenth-century Germany, it enables readers to understand the positions that Kant might have identified with "pure reason," the criticisms of pure reason that had been developed prior to Kant's, and alternative attempts at synthesizing empiricist elements within a rationalist framework. The volume contains chapters on Christian Wolff, Martin Knutzen, Alexander Baumgarten, Christian Crusius, Leonhard Euler, Johann Lambert, Marcus Herz, Johann Eberhard, and Johann Tetens. Each chapter includes a brief introduction that provides succinct biographical and bibliographical information on these authors, a concise account of their projects, and information on the importance of these projects to Kant's first *Critique*. Extensive references to the first *Critique*, brought together in a concordance, highlight the potential relevance of each text.

Eric Watkins is Professor of Philosophy at the University of California, San Diego. The recipient of grants from the Fulbright Foundation, the National Endowment for the Humanities, the National Science Foundation, the Max Planck Institute for the History of Science, and the Alexander von Humboldt Foundation, he is the author of *Kant and the Metaphysics of Causality*, which won the Book Prize in 2005 from the *Journal of the History of Philosophy*.

Kant's *Critique of Pure Reason*

Background Source Materials

Edited and translated by

ERIC WATKINS
University of California, San Diego

CAMBRIDGE
UNIVERSITY PRESS

CAMBRIDGE UNIVERSITY PRESS
Cambridge, New York, Melbourne, Madrid, Cape Town, Singapore,
São Paulo, Delhi, Dubai, Tokyo

Cambridge University Press
32 Avenue of the Americas, New York, NY 10013-2473, USA

www.cambridge.org
Information on this title: www.cambridge.org/9780521787017

First published 2009

Printed in the United States of America

A catalog record for this publication is available from the British Library.

Library of Congress Cataloging in Publication Data
Kant's *Critique of pure reason* : background source materials /
[compiled by] Eric Watkins.
p.   cm.
Includes bibliographical references (p.) and index.
ISBN 978-0-521-78162-6 (hardback) – ISBN 978-0-521-78701-7 (pbk.)
1. Kant, Immanuel, 1724–1804. Kritik der reinen Vernunft.
2. Knowledge, Theory of – History – 18th century – Sources.
3. Causation – History – 18th century – Sources.
4. Reason – History – 18th century – Sources.   I. Watkins, Eric, 1964–
B2779.K364   2009
121–dc22   2008036423

ISBN 978-0-521-78162-6 Hardback
ISBN 978-0-521-78701-7 Paperback

Für Jürgen und Michael
Aus Dankbarkeit für unsere langjährige Freundschaft.

Contents

Preface

It is obviously impossible to produce a single volume that includes all of the background texts that are minimally necessary for a reader to attain even a basic understanding of Kant's *Critique of Pure Reason*. For when composing the first *Critique*, Kant was undoubtedly aware of and reacting to the views of numerous major thinkers such as Plato, Descartes, Locke, Newton, Leibniz, and Hume, and one must also keep in mind, especially in the cases of Newton, Leibniz, and Hume, that how their views were received and interpreted in eighteenth-century Germany may have been very different from our understanding today. Moreover, there are myriad "minor" figures whose views Kant would have been intimately familiar with. The scope of the relevant texts is simply too vast for all of them to be included in a single volume. Insofar as the texts of the major philosophers are currently available in high-quality English editions, readers of Kant are, comparatively speaking, already well served. The same cannot be said, however, of Kant's immediate predecessors and contemporaries, that is, eighteenth-century philosophers in Germany who wrote in Latin, French, or German.

The present volume thus represents a first attempt at providing English translations of selections of those German, French, and Latin works that would most help us to put the *Critique of Pure Reason* in its fuller historical context. It would naturally be highly desirable if all of the major works of all of the relevant authors were translated in their entirety. Instead, I have chosen those figures whose works are least available in English while also being the most relevant to understanding Kant's first *Critique*. As a result, I have not included authors of only tangential relevance to the Critical Kant (such as Boscovich and Maupertuis), even though they are interesting in their own right, and Moses Mendelssohn, who was extremely influential at the time, was not selected for this volume because Cambridge University Press has already made his most important philosophical works readily available in a recent volume. Insofar as many authors who were not included in this volume deserve to be, I gladly invite others to rectify on other occasions the injustices I have committed. For each author included in this volume, I have selected and translated those passages that either give a sense of the author's overall project or are most directly relevant to specific passages in the first *Critique*.

I have attempted to indicate the relevance of the texts translated below to Kant's thought by inserting footnotes that suggest which passages they would be related to in some way, whether it be by comparison or contrast. I have focused primarily on references to the *Critique of Pure Reason*, though not in a comprehensive and exhaustive way, which would have been neither possible (in light of the scope) nor even desirable (in light of the different views that readers might take on this issue). References will be either to specific passages, indicated by the standard A/B pagination of the first and second editions of the first *Critique*, or to sections of the first *Critique*, or, where appropriate, to both. The concordance provides a handy way to identify which passages are relevant to which particular sections in the first *Critique*. In addition, I have occasionally made reference to several of Kant's pre-Critical publications when the passage in question was especially pertinent. If the texts translated herein help us to appreciate their significance as well, this is a welcome bonus, but insofar as Kant's pre-Critical works shed light on the *Critique of Pure Reason*, their indirect contribution may be crucial too. All editorial actions are indicated with brackets. All footnotes marked by a number are the editor's. Any footnote marked by something other than a number is the author's.

For those looking for discussions that draw on the historical background to Kant's *Critique of Pure Reason* in attempting to determine his mature thought, the following books are especially helpful: Karl Ameriks's *Kant's Theory of Mind*, Michael Friedman's *Kant and the Exact Sciences*, Paul Guyer's *Kant and the Claims of Knowledge*, Manfred Kuehn's *Kant: A Biography*, Béatrice Longuenesse's *Kant and the Capacity to Judge*, Eric Watkins's *Kant and the Metaphysics of Causality*, and Allen Wood's *Kant's Rational Theology*.

I am grateful to James Messina and Tim Jankowiak for their help with proofreading the translations and to James for help with the references to the first *Critique* as well as with the preparation of the concordance.

I am indebted to Kimberly Brewer for assembling the index. I thank several of my German Philosophy Translation classes at the University of California, San Diego, for their input on select passages from Lambert and Herz. I thank Brandon Look for a series of helpful suggestions on the translation of one of Knutzen's difficult texts, and Manfred Kuehn, who was instrumental in helping to formulate the original project and get it started. I am also happy to acknowledge the general advice and particular suggestions of Daniel Garber, John Cottingham, Karl Ameriks, Paul Guyer, and Allen Wood.

Abbreviations

Abbreviations of Kant's works are as follows:

Dreams of a Spirit-Seer	*Dreams of a spirit-seer elucidated by dreams of metaphysics*
False Subtlety	*The false subtlety of the four syllogistic figures*
Inaugural Dissertation	*On the form and principles of the sensible and the intelligible world*
Inquiry	*Inquiry concerning the distinctness of the principles of natural theology and morality*
Metaphysical Foundations	*The metaphysical foundations of natural science*
New Elucidation	*A new elucidation of the first principles of metaphysical cognition*
The Only Possible Argument	*The only possible argument in support of a demonstration of the existence of God*
Physical Monadology	*The employment in natural philosophy of metaphysics combined with geometry, of which sample I contains the physical monadology*

Other abbreviations are as follows:

GW	*The Critique of Pure Reason*, edited and translated by Paul Guyer and Allen Wood

| (number:number) | The first number refers to the volume of the Academy Edition of Kant's works (*Gesammelte Schriften*), the second to the page number. |
| A[number]/B[number] | A refers to the first edition pagination of the *Critique of Pure Reason*, B refers to the second edition pagination. |

Introduction

Before undertaking the arduous task of trying to understand Kant's *Critique of Pure Reason,* it is helpful to consider briefly two preliminary questions. The first question is: Who was Kant's intended audience for this work? Whom did he hope to win over with its main argument? Given that Kant wrote the first *Critique* in German when it still would have been possible for him to have written it in Latin, just as he had his *Inaugural Dissertation* and several other earlier works, it is clear that he was writing primarily, even if not exclusively, for German-speaking philosophers in the second half of the eighteenth century. Who are these philosophers, and what views do they hold? Unfortunately, Kant's own text gives us very little explicit information on these points. However, this lack of information should not be thought particularly surprising, since it would be natural for Kant to assume that given his choice of audience, his readers would be in a position to identify who was coming under attack, on what point, and for what reason. At the same time, this situation does present an extra obstacle for contemporary readers, given that we do not, as a rule, know simply from reading his texts who his opponents are, what views they hold, and on what grounds.

The second, much more difficult question is: What would Kant's intended audience have understood the overall project and significance of the first *Critique* to be? On the one hand, one might think that Kant, like philosophers before him and, for that matter, ever since, is simply attempting to answer the eternal questions of philosophy. What is knowledge? What is reality? How should I act? etc. On the other hand, even if one grants the idea, contested by some, that there are eternal questions, which the great philosophers simply answer in powerful and radically different ways, it is still the case that these questions are both posed and answered in specific ways under particular historical conditions, with different background assumptions in place. As a result, it cannot simply be taken for granted that one immediately knows, in light of the eternal questions, what project a given philosopher has chosen to undertake and what the significance of that project is supposed to be. The situation with the *Critique of Pure Reason* is no different. Even if Kant does develop an account of the nature of knowledge and explain what is real and what is not, he must be doing so in some specific context, at the very least with some particular understanding of what "pure reason" is, what it would mean to "critique" it, what method one could use to undertake such a critical project, and what pure reason could be replaced by. While Kant is not entirely mute on these points, one can fully appreciate what he took the nature and import of his undertaking to be only if one understands the projects and views of his immediate predecessors and contemporaries that he could have expected his intended audience to be familiar with. For knowing what they would have viewed as controversial and what beyond dispute as well as what projects had already been undertaken and with what success is indispensable to an accurate assessment of the contribution Kant was trying to make, of what new perspectives and options he hoped to be offering. In a very general way, the following, extremely brief characterizations of the figures whose texts have been translated below can provide a basic orientation to their significance for Kant's first *Critique*.

Christian Wolff and Alexander Baumgarten, who are often credited with systematizing and popularizing Leibniz's rationalist position in Germany starting in the 1720s and 1730s, are particularly important in the present context insofar as they offer specific formulations of and arguments for the kinds of positions that Kant would clearly associate with "pure reason." Martin Knutzen, perhaps the most prominent of Kant's teachers at the university he attended in Königsberg, provides an example of how one could deny certain Leibnizian conclusions, especially regarding causality, without, however, also rejecting the Leibnizian-Wolffian principles on which they were alleged to rest. As a result, familiarity with the views of Wolff, Baumgarten, and Knutzen promises to help us to understand some of the very specific forms that the object of Kant's criticisms of metaphysics takes in the first *Critique*.

Christian August Crusius and Leonhard Euler took much more critical positions toward the dominant Leibnizian-Wolffian position in the 1740s and 1750s. Crusius, whose Pietist background influenced his basic orientation, was motivated by metaphysical and theological issues to relentlessly criticize the rationalist and putatively necessitarian positions of Wolff and to work out in creative ways a position that leaves room for contingency in both the divine and human cases. Euler, whose expertise in mathematics and rational mechanics was unparalleled in the eighteenth century, criticized Wolff's metaphysics on grounds stemming from a sophisticated understanding of nature as represented by the physical and mathematical sciences (Newtonian physics in particular). Accordingly, Crusius and Euler are both valuable insofar as they represent importantly different ways in which one could be critical of pure reason at the time. Knowledge of their views is thus crucial to an appropriate assessment of the critical dimension of Kant's project, since only on the basis of this knowledge can one judge the extent to which Kant is simply adopting or adapting in subtle ways criticisms that others had already developed and the extent to which he is articulating original objections from a genuinely novel standpoint.

Johann Heinrich Lambert and Marcus Herz provide important insights into Kant's development in the 1760s and early 1770s. Lambert, another important mathematician and scientist, was somewhat less critical of Leibniz and Wolff, devoting his attention instead to the more positive project of seeking the proper method in science, mathematics, and metaphysics and attempting to establish an adequate epistemological foundation for these branches of knowledge. Insofar as Kant's first *Critique* similarly calls into question the philosophical methodology of his predecessors, Lambert's reflections provide an important point of comparison. Herz, the student whom Kant selected to publicly defend his *Inaugural Dissertation,* carefully examines Kant's position in the *Inaugural Dissertation* in detail in his main philosophical publication, and carries on a correspondence with Kant. While Herz does not offer a general perspective that is independent of Kant's at this time, he does have an excellent sense of how careful yet sympathetic readers of Kant's works at the time would have been reacting to the position he was staking out and developing further in the Critical period. In addition, his correspondence with Kant provides us with direct access to Kant's thinking in the crucial period when he was writing the first *Critique*. In different ways, therefore, Lambert and Herz offer particularly useful perspectives on what issues were of special interest to Kant in the decades prior to the publication of the first *Critique*.

Johann August Eberhard and Johann Nicolaus Tetens, despite radical differences in their philosophical orientations, both undertook the project of synthesizing various empirical phenomena within a broadly rationalist framework in the mid-1770s, during the heart of Kant's so-called silent decade. Eberhard, whose basic sympathies lie with Leibniz, attempts to show how thinking and sensing, in the face of their fundamental contrasts, are nonetheless compatible with the soul having only one basic power, namely, that of representation. Tetens, who is generally sympathetic to both Locke's position and elements of Hume's empiricism, though certainly not in an uncritical way, similarly argues that the various mental phenomena we encounter are consistent with a single representative power, and then develops a sophisticated account of rational and sensitive cognition. Knowledge of the views of Eberhard and Tetens is thus important insofar as they are engaged in a project that is similar in fundamental ways to Kant's such that one can profitably compare and contrast their ways of synthesizing empiricist and rationalist elements.

Each of the following nine chapters fills out this cursory general introduction with selections from the most important works of each of these figures, roughly in chronological order. Brief introductions to each chapter have been limited to providing the barest of essentials – basic biographic and bibliographic information as well as a quick sketch of each author's main project and relevance for Kant – so as to maximize the quantity of primary texts provided. It is hoped that these primary texts will allow readers to attain a much more historically accurate and philosophically sophisticated understanding of Kant's position in the *Critique of Pure Reason*.

1

Christian Wolff

Christian Wolff was born in Breslau in 1679 and received his initial education there; he studied theology at Jena, then mathematics at Leipzig, where he received his master's degree. He was appointed professor of mathematics and natural science in Halle in 1706, at the recommendation of Leibniz, with whom he corresponded until the latter's death in 1716. Through his engaging teaching style and clear systematic prose, Wolff established himself as an important proponent of Enlightenment ideals at what was then the leading university in Prussia. In 1723 he was expelled by King Frederick William I, ostensibly because of the Pietists' accusations that his adherence to preestablished harmony committed him to fatalism, Spinozism, and atheism. Wolff fled to Marburg, where he continued to lecture and publish as a professor of mathematics and philosophy. In 1740 he returned to Halle at the request of Fredrick the Great, who had since taken over the throne from his father. Wolff remained in Halle until his death in 1754.

Wolff was an extraordinarily prolific writer, publishing, among many other things, a series of lengthy German textbooks from 1713 to 1725 – on logic, metaphysics, ethics, politics, physics (including cosmology), and teleology – and then reworking many of these into longer Latin versions in the 1730s and 1740s in order to gain a wider European audience, though he also penned voluminous polemical tracts on the side in his debates with the Pietists. The most important and influential of these works is his so-called German Metaphysics, or *Vernünfftige Gedancken von Gott, der Welt und der Seele des Menschen, auch allen Dingen überhaupt* (Rational Thoughts on God, the World and the Soul of Human Beings, Also All Things in General), first published in 1720 (but reprinted in twelve editions by 1752). It establishes a basic philosophical terminology and framework for his thought and for the generations of students who would use it throughout the eighteenth century in Germany. Specifically, it lays the foundation for his views in other disciplines such as physics, ethics, teleology, and politics, providing support for the view that philosophy – metaphysics in particular – is the queen of the sciences.

Rational Thoughts on God, the World and the Soul of Human Beings, Also All Things in General, contains six chapters, which reflect his understanding of the systematic structure of metaphysics. After an introductory first chapter, which contains a brief discussion of certainty and how to attain it, Wolff introduces his general ontology, concerning "all things in general," in a second chapter, where the basic concepts of his ontology are laid out and his fundamental principles, the principle of contradiction and the principle of sufficient reason, are established. In the remaining chapters he then draws on these ontological concepts and principles to provide his accounts of the more specific kinds of objects listed in the title of the work. Accordingly, Chapter Three and Chapter Five discuss the soul in the context of his accounts of empirical and rational psychology, Chapter Four develops an account of the primary features of the world in his cosmology, and Chapter Six concludes with a discussion of God in his natural theology.

Wolff's importance for Kant is considerable and plays out in both positive and negative ways. On the positive score, not only does Kant adopt much of the German philosophical vocabulary Wolff had introduced (in fact, building on it with his own distinctive terminology), but he also accepts Wolff's basic division of metaphysics into rational psychology, rational cosmology, and rational theology (such as in the division of the Transcendental Dialectic's three main chapters). At the same time, and on the negative side, he of course criticizes Wolff's position and arguments on many occasions (as indefensibly dogmatic), though he never cites particular passages in which these positions and arguments are stated in Wolff's works. The selections translated below are intended to remedy this defect by indicating how Wolff develops his overall position and by providing detailed passages that are directly relevant to particular arguments and criticisms in the *Critique of Pure Reason.*

RATIONAL THOUGHTS ON GOD, THE WORLD AND THE SOUL OF HUMAN BEINGS, ALSO ALL THINGS IN GENERAL (1720)[1]

CHAPTER ONE. HOW WE COGNIZE THAT WE EXIST AND OF WHAT USE THIS COGNITION IS FOR US

§1.[2] *How we cognize that we exist.* We are conscious of ourselves and of other things. No one who is not completely out of his mind can doubt that, and should someone want to deny it by pretending, through his words, that things are other than he finds within himself, that person could quickly be shown that his pretense is absurd. For how could he deny something or call something into doubt if he were not conscious of himself and other things? But whoever is conscious of what he denies or calls into doubt, exists. And consequently it is clear that we exist.

§2. *Whether one has reason to question it.* Some will perhaps be surprised, while others who, due to a lack of deep insight, are unable to deal with explanations and proofs, will even laugh that I must first prove that we exist. For no human being under the sun has ever denied this, and if someone were to go this far, it would not be worthwhile to refute him, because he would either be robbed of his understanding and thus not know what he is saying, or have to be so obstinate that, against his own better judgment, he would deny everything on principle. For this reason even the most unusual sects of egoists who recently arose in Paris and denied the existence of all things have admitted: **I exist.**

§3. *The first reason.* I hope that they will soon stop being surprised when I tell them the reasons that have inclined me to do this. In the preface to the philosophy that is found at the beginning of my *Rational Thoughts on the Powers of the Human Understanding* (§5), I remarked that philosophers must not only know that something is possible or occurs, but also be able to indicate the reason why it is possible or occurs. Because we have such certainty about our own existence that we cannot call it into doubt in any way (§1), it is also incumbent upon us to show where this certainty

---

[1] Translated from *Vernünfftige Gedancken von Gott, der Welt und der Seele des Menschen, auch allen Dingen überhaupt* (Halle, 1751, 11th ed.).
[2] §§1–7 are relevant to the Paralogisms (A338–A405/B396–B432), especially A341–A348/B399–B406.

comes from. And because we intend to deal with philosophy here, we must inquire where such a great certainty comes from.

§4. *The second reason.* And (which is the second reason) this investigation has a great value of its own. For if I know why we have such great certainty about our own existence, then I am aware of how something must be constituted so that I can cognize it with as much certainty as I do that I myself exist. It is a great thing when I can say of important truths without fear: "They are as certain as that I exist," or also, "I cognize that they exist with the same certainty as I have when I know that I exist." And quite a bit rests on this because we are attempting to explain our natural cognition of God and the soul as well as of the world and all things in general with indubitable certainty.

§5. *Consideration of the way in which we cognize that we exist.* For us to obtain this benefit we must consider a bit more precisely in what way we cognize that we exist. Now when we do this, we find that our cognition in this case is constituted as follows: (1) We undeniably experience that we are conscious of ourselves and of other things (§1 above & §1 c. 5 of *Logic*). (2) It is clear to us that whoever is conscious of himself and other things exists. Consequently, we are (3) certain that we exist.

§6.[3] *By means of which syllogism this occurs.* If we want to cognize distinctly how these reasons convince us that we exist, we shall find that the following syllogism is contained in these thoughts:

Whoever is conscious of himself and other things, exists.
We are conscious of ourselves and other things.
Therefore, we exist.

§7. *How this syllogism is constituted.* In this syllogism the minor premise is [supported by] an indubitable experience, whereas the major premise belongs to those [propositions] that one admits without any proof as soon as one understands the words that arise in it, that is, it is a fundamental principle (§2 c. 6 *Logic*). For who would want to doubt the existence of a thing of which we cognize that it exists in a certain way? Everyone sees that if specific [*besondere*] things are to exist, they can exist in none other than a certain way (§27 c. 1 *Logic*).

---

[3] See B422–B423 (Paralogisms), where Kant appears to deny the soundness of such an inference.

§8.[4] *What certainty a demonstration has.* A proof of this sort is a demonstration (§21 c. 4 *Logic*) and accordingly makes clear that everything that is properly demonstrated is just as certain as our existence because what is demonstrated is proven in just the same way as our existence is.

§9. *With what certainty geometrical truths are proven.* Not only have I noted [as much] in my *Thoughts on the Powers of the Human Understanding* (§23 & 24 c. 4), but anyone who would aim to analyze proofs in geometry precisely will realize that proofs in geometry are likewise carried out through syllogisms in which the premises are of undoubted certainty, and require no further proof. Therefore, one sees that geometrical truths are proven with the same certainty as our own existence and, consequently, everything that is proven in geometrical fashion is as certain as our own existence is.

CHAPTER TWO. ON THE FIRST PRINCIPLES OF OUR COGNITION AND OF ALL THINGS IN GENERAL

§10.[5] *Principle* [Grund] *of contradiction.* When we cognize that we are conscious of ourselves and other things, and take this to be certain, this occurs because it is in fact impossible for us to comprehend that we should be conscious of ourselves and at the same time not be conscious of ourselves. Similarly, in all other cases we find that it is impossible for us to comprehend that something does not exist when it does. And in this way we acknowledge without any reservation at all this universal proposition: **Something cannot at the same time be and also not be**. We call this proposition the **principle of contradiction** and not only do syllogisms have their certainty through it (§5 c. 4 *Logic*), but it also places any proposition that we experience beyond all doubt, just as we experience this in our own case, [namely] that we are conscious of ourselves.

§11. *Constitution of contradiction.* Accordingly, a contradiction requires that what is affirmed is also denied at the same time. And in this fashion it is necessary that the thing of which something is affirmed is not only the one of which something is denied, but also that in both cases this one thing is taken in the same circumstances and viewed in the same way. E.g., if two people do not take a word in the same meaning, the one

---

4 See A734/B762 (Discipline of Pure Reason).
5 §§10–12 are relevant to On the Highest Principle of all Analytic Judgments (A150/ B189ff.). §§10–12 are also relevant to Section 1 of *New Elucidation* (1:388ff.).

can verbally deny of this thing what the other affirms (§15 c. 2 *Logic*) and still no contradiction arises insofar as what the one person is affirming is not the same as what the other person is denying.

§12. *What is possible and impossible.* Because nothing can be and not be at same time (§10), we recognize that something is impossible if it contradicts something else of which we already know that it is or can be, as when it follows that a part is equal to or greater than the whole, or also when one thing contradicts another that is supposed to be subsumed under it. And in this way what contains something contradictory in itself is impossible, as, for example, iron wood is or two circles that intersect each other and have the same middle point. For whatever is iron cannot be wood and when two circles intersect each other they cannot have the same middle point, as is proven in geometry. Hence one can see further that whatever contains nothing contradictory in itself is possible, that is, whatever not only can itself exist next to other things that are or can be, but also contains in itself only those things that can exist next to each other is possible, as, for example, a wooden plate is. For being a plate and being wooden do not oppose each other; rather, both can exist at the same time.

§17.[6] *What identity and difference are.* If I can posit thing B for thing A and everything remains as it was, A and B are **identical**. [...] But if I posit B for A and not everything remains the same, A and B are **distinct** or are **different things**.

§18. *What similarity and dissimilarity are.* Two things are **similar** to each other, if that by which one is to cognize them and distinguish them from each other, or through which they are determined in their kind [*Art*], is identical in both. By contrast, A and B are **dissimilar things** if that by which one is to cognize them and distinguish them from each other is different in both. [...]

§20. *How similar things are distinguished.* Accordingly, similar things cannot be distinguished from each other unless one either actually brings them together or does so in thought by means of a third thing, e.g., when one places two similar clocks next to each other or represents two similar buildings in their different positions, for which reason we also

---

[6] §§17–21 are relevant to On the Amphiboly of the Concepts of Reflection (A260/B316ff.).

assume in the example given that whoever is to judge of the similarity will be led blindfolded from the one to the other. But when one brings together things that are to have a similarity, one distinguishes them either through their size or through their position. For although size is indeed an internal difference, it cannot be reckoned among those things by means of which one cognizes and distinguishes things, because it cannot be comprehended as such by the understanding, but rather is only given and thus must be grasped merely by the senses. For if I am supposed to tell someone how large something is, I must tell him what relation it has to a certain measure that he is familiar with.

§21. *What size is.* Because similar things, without detracting from their similarity, can have nothing in themselves other than the size by which they are distinguished, this can serve as an explanation of size: that it is the internal difference of similar things (41 c. 1 *Logic*), namely, that through which similar things can be distinguished from each other.

§29.⁷ *What a ground is and what is called grounded.* If a thing A contains in itself something from which one can understand why B is – B can be either something in A or outside A – one calls that which is to be found in A the **ground** of B. A itself is called the cause, and one says of B that it is grounded in A. The ground is that by which one can understand why something is, and the cause is a thing that contains the ground of another in itself. I want to illustrate this with an example. If I investigate how it happens that everything in a garden grows quickly, and find that this is to be ascribed to the warmth of the air, warmth is the ground of the rapid growth, and the air, insofar as it is warm, is the cause. But the rapid growth is grounded in the warm air. One can also call the warmth a cause and its efficacy in the growth the ground. Again, if I want to go outside because the weather is beautiful, the representation of the beautiful weather is the ground of my desire, and the soul, insofar as it makes this representation, is the cause of the desire. The beauty of the weather is the ground of my going outside, and the weather, insofar as it is beautiful, is the cause of my going outside.

§30. *Principle of sufficient reason.* When something is present from which one can comprehend why something exists, that [thing] has a sufficient

---

7 §§29–32 are relevant to the Second Analogy of Experience (A189–A211/B232–B256). §§29–32 are also relevant to Section 2 of *New Elucidation* (1:392ff.), especially 1:391–393 and 1:396–397.

ground (§29). For this reason, when no such thing is present, there is nothing from which one can comprehend why something exists, namely, why it can become actual, and thus it must arise out of nothing. Accordingly, what cannot arise out of nothing must have a sufficient ground for why it exists, as it must be possible in itself and have a cause that can make it actual if we are talking of things that do not exist necessarily. Now, since it is impossible that something can arise out of nothing (§28), everything that exists must have its sufficient ground for why it exists, that is, there must always be something from which one can understand why it can become actual (§29). We wish to call this proposition the principle of sufficient reason. *Historical information about it.* The importance of this proposition, upon which, long ago, Archimedes rested his doctrine of the balance or the balanced state of heavy bodies and which Confucius had seen previously in his ethics and politics, Herr von Leibniz revealed in our days by means of glorious proofs in his *Theodicy* as well as in the letters that he exchanged with the Englishman Clarke about several disputed points.[8] He assumed it as a proposition grounded in experience against which no counter-example can be raised, and he therefore gave no proof of it, although Clarke demanded it. It can be enough of a proof if we show below (§143) that the difference between truth and dreams, even between the true world and the land of milk and honey, arises through it.

§31. *Further proof thereof.* I establish this proposition in the following way as well. Assume two things, A and B, that are identical. If something can exist that has a sufficient ground neither in the thing nor outside it for why it exists, then a change can occur in A that does not take place in B if B is put in the place of A. In this fashion B is not identical to A (§17). Now since it follows from assuming A to be identical to B that if one does not grant the principle of sufficient reason, it is not identical to B, but it is impossible that something can be and not be at the same time (§10), the same proposition must have its indisputable correctness, that is, it is true: Everything has its sufficient ground for why it exists.

§32. *How what is attributed to an object is constituted.* Accordingly, if one can distinguish various [determinations] in a thing from each other, one of them must contain the ground within itself for why the rest are attributed to it [i.e., the thing], and because this cannot in turn have its

---

[8] Wolff is referring to the Leibniz-Clarke correspondence, where the principle of sufficient reason is discussed in several passages (starting with Leibniz's Second Letter).

ground for why they are attributed to it in one of the rest, as can easily be comprehended through the principle of contradiction (§10), they must necessarily be attributed to it. For what necessarily exists in this way requires no further ground for why it exists in this way. Namely, in every thing there is something necessary through which it is determined in its kind and the rest have their ground in it.

§33.⁹ *What essence is.* That in which the ground of the [remaining determinations] that are attributed to the thing is to be found is called the **essence**. Thus, whoever cognizes the essence of a thing can point out the ground of everything that is attributed to it. Yet one cognizes the essence of a thing when one understands how [*wodurch*] it is determined in its kind (§32).

§34. *The essence is primary in a thing.* What contains within itself the ground of the rest is the first [principle] that can be thought in a thing. Whatever is grounded in it cannot be posited beforehand. For one must begin with that from which I can cognize why the other exists. Thus the essence is the first [principle] that can be thought in a thing.

§35. *What it consists in.* However, nothing can be thought in a thing prior to thinking how it is possible. For it is a thing precisely because it can be, and it can be, because it is possible (§16). Hence the essence of a thing is its possibility, and whoever understands in what way a thing is possible understands the essence. But one knows how something is possible if one understands how it is determined in its kind.

§36. *What is necessary.* When what is contrary to a thing contains in itself something contradictory, the thing is **necessary**. Now since what contains something contradictory in itself is impossible (§12), what is contrary to something necessary is impossible. And if what is contrary to a thing is impossible, that same thing is necessary. It is also clear that what is necessary can be determined in only one way and thus can also exist in only one way.

§38.¹⁰ *The essence of things is necessary.* What is possible cannot be impossible at the same time (§10), and if something is possible in a certain

---

⁹ §§33–36, 38, and 42–43 are relevant to *The Only Possible Argument* (esp. 2:86–133 passim).
¹⁰ See *New Elucidation* (1:395–396).

way, it cannot be impossible in that way at the same time, and is therefore necessarily possible (§36). Now since possibility is intrinsically [*an
sich*] something necessary, but the essence of a thing consists in it being
possible in a certain way (§35), its essence is necessary.

§42. *Essence is immutable.* For this reason, since the essence of a thing
is necessary (§38), it is also immutable. But if I can think of a possible
change in the essence of a thing, the essence of the thing is not thereby
changed; rather, by cognizing it I have attained cognition of the essence
of another thing. E.g., the essence of a triangle consists in enclosing
space within three sides. It is possible that one can take four rather
than three sides and enclose a space. However, this does not change the
essence of a triangle. For if four sides enclose a space, one has a rectangle and thus another thing.

§43. *Nothing foreign can be communicated to an essence.* Because the essence
of a thing is immutable and does not remain the same if something in its
essence is changed (§42), one can comprehend that the essence of one
thing cannot be communicated to another, that is, it is not possible that
a thing receive, in addition to its own essence, the essence of another
thing and still remain the same thing. E.g., it would be absurd if one
wanted to imagine that a rectangle could be a triangle at the same time,
or else that a body could be a spirit at the same time. Indeed, because
everything that is constantly attributed to a thing and is distinct from its
essence must have its sufficient ground in its essence (§33), nothing can
be added to a thing that is grounded not in its own essence, but in the
essence of another thing. E.g., one can in no way add the properties of
a triangle to a rectangle, nor the properties of a spirit to a body or the
properties of an animal, such as memory, to a plant.

§44. *What an attribute is.* What is grounded solely in the essence of a
thing is called an **attribute**. E.g., sight is grounded in the essence of an
animal that has eyes, and is thus an attribute of it. Thus attributes cannot be separated from a thing, are immutable just as the essence itself
is (§42), and are what are necessarily and thus continually attributed to
a thing (§38).

§45.[11] *What is external* [ausser] *to us and external* [ausser] *to each other.*
When we pay attention to ourselves, we find that we are conscious of

---

[11] §§45–50 are relevant to the Transcendental Aesthetic (esp. A22–A30/B37–B45).

many things as external to us. But we posit them [as] external to us when we cognize that they are distinct from us just as we also posit them [as] external to each other when we cognize that they are distinct from each other. Everyone will find in his own case that as soon as he assumes that different things are supposed to exist at the same time, he represents to himself one [as] external to the other, just because it seems impossible to him to think that two different things could be only one (§10, 17), and it seems also impossible to him to represent the one in the other.

§46. *What space is.* Now when many things that exist at the same time and are not identical are represented as external to one another (§45), a certain order among them thereby arises such that when I take one of them as the first, I take another as the second, another as the third, yet another as the fourth, and so on. And as soon as we represent this order to ourselves, we represent **space** to ourselves. For this reason, if we do not want to consider the object differently from how we cognize it, we must take **space** to be the order of those things that exist at the same time.[12] And thus no **space** can exist if things are not present to fill it, although it is still distinct from these things (§17).

§47. *What place is.* In this way, each thing has a certain [*gewisse*] mode of coexistence with others such that none of the rest exists in precisely that way with the others. And it is precisely this that we are accustomed to calling the place of a thing. Namely, the place is the way in which a thing is present at the same time next to others. We are aiming here only for what can be comprehended distinctly (§13 c. 1 *Logic*).

§49. *How place and space are constituted.* But from what has been said of place, it is easy to judge that place and space change nothing in a thing, as they have nothing at all to do with its internal [state]. Sometimes, however, the latter is still distinct from the place of the thing as well as from the place of another thing (§17), but in the latter case merely according to its number and size (§18, 20).

§50. *Why a thing is in this place.* And hence it is possible that each thing can occupy the place of another. For neither in the one nor in the other is it grounded why it must be in precisely this place. But since nothing can exist without its sufficient ground for why it exists (§30), it must be found somewhere else, which is to be investigated in the following.

[12] See *New Elucidation* (1:414) for a similar claim.

§51.[13] *What composite things are.* All things that we are conscious of as external to us consist of many parts. For in each thing we find many things that we can distinguish from each other, yet these many things, taken together, still constitute only one thing because the parts are connected [*verknüpft*] with each other (§24). We call that which consists of many parts that are distinct from each other, but that follow upon each other in a certain order and are connected with each other, a **composite thing**.

§52. *Why they fill a space.* Each composite thing must necessarily fill a space. For it consists of parts each one of which is distinct from every other one (§51). Now since one part is external to the other (§45), they are next [*bei*] to each other in a certain order in such a fashion that if one takes one part for the first, [then] one takes another as the next, yet another as the third, and so on. For this reason, they fill a space (§46) and each one of them has its special place (§47); consequently, since the parts, taken together, are the whole (§24), the whole, that is, the thing composed of them, fills a space too.

§72. *What kinds of changes can occur in a composite thing.* No changes can occur in a composite thing other than in its size and shape, in the location of its parts, in its internal motion and in the place of the whole thing. For a composite thing has nothing further in itself [*an sich*] other than its parts, whose sum constitutes its size (§61), while its limits constitute its shape (§54), the order of its parts constitutes space and extension (§46, 55), and every part as well as the whole thing has its own special place (§47). Accordingly, if a change is to occur, either the size or the shape or the place of its parts or the place of the whole must be changed. That such changes can occur has been established above (§65, 68, 57).

§73. *Size, shape, [and] filling space are attributes of composite things.* Because size, shape, filling space, and the possibility of internal motion take place in a composite being given that it consists of many parts (§61, 54, 52), they are thus grounded in its essence (§29, 59) and are for this reason attributes of composite things (§44).

§74. *Internal constitution of a composite thing.* A composite thing has its essence by means of the composition of its parts (§59). Now since

---

[13] §§51–52, 72–76, and 81–82 are relevant to the Second Antinomy (A434/B462ff.). See also Section 1 of the *Physical Monadology* (1:477ff.).

everything that can be attributed to it is grounded in its essence (§33), it has the ground of its changes in many things.

§75. *What is called a simple being.* Since whatever has parts is called a composite thing, one conversely calls whatever does not have parts a **simple thing**. But we must now investigate what the simple things are and how they are different from composite things.

§76. *That there are simple things.* If there are composite things, there must also be simple beings. For if no simple beings were present, then all parts – they can be taken to be as small as you might ever like, even inconceivably small parts – would have to consist of other parts. But then, since one could provide no reason where the composite parts would ultimately come from, just as little as one could comprehend where a composite number would arise from if it contained no unities in itself, and yet nothing can be without a sufficient ground (§30), one must ultimately admit simple things from which the composites arise. Whoever has proper insight into the principle of sufficient reason comprehends that one does not arrive at such a ground until one has no more questions and does not receive the same answer, as happens when one admits parts to infinity.

§81.[14] *Simple things have no shape, size, and internal motion, and also fill no space.* Accordingly, it is established that there must be simple things through whose composition the parts of others arise. But then, because these simple things have no parts (§75) and are thus not composed any further of others (§51), yet size, shape, filling of a space, and internal motion are attributes of composite things (§73), simple things can have no shape and size, they can fill no space, and no internal motion can be found in them (§43, 44).

§82. *Simple things are completely different from composites.* In this way simple things are completely different from composite things (§17), and since all things we are conscious of as external to us are composite things (§51), we can attribute nothing that we find in them to the simples.

§104. *What an action* [Thun] *and a passion* [Leidenschaft] *are.* If something is changed, the ground of the change is to be found either in it or external to it. One of the two is necessary (§30). A change whose ground

---

[14] See *Physical Monadology* (1:480).

is to be found in the object that is changed is called an **act** [*That*] or an **action** [*Thun*]. By contrast, a change whose ground is to be found in an object other than the one that is changed is called a passion. [...]

§114.[15] *Distinction between things that subsist by themselves* [vor sich bestehen] *and those that subsist through others.* Now it can also be understood how it is that things that subsist by themselves actually differ from those that subsist only through others. Namely, a thing that **subsists by itself**, or a **substance**, is that which has in itself the source of its own changes, whereas a thing that subsists through another is nothing other than a limitation of the former. E.g., our soul has a power by which it brings about its thoughts successively in an uninterrupted order, and for that reason it is a thing that subsists by itself. By contrast, the concepts that it brings about as well as the appetites that grow out of it are nothing other than limitations of this power that arise when it is determined with respect to something certain, since as such it could be directed toward infinitely many things [*unendlich vielem*]. For this reason its concepts and appetites are things that subsist through another. I provide this only as an elucidation so that the present explanations, which would remain obscure without any example, can be understood better. The matter should not yet be accepted as true; it will be established in its proper place. [...] Here, in any case, we are explaining only words, and are not yet asking which things subsist by themselves.

§115. *What power is, and in what things it is to be found.* The source of changes is called a **power** [*Kraft*]. In this fashion one finds in every thing that subsists by itself a power that is not to be met with in things that subsist through others.

§116.[16] *Self-subsisting things can do something.* Now since the changes that occur in a self-subsisting thing are grounded in it (§29) by means of this power, they are acts [*Thaten*] of the same thing (§104), and in this fashion one sees that every self-subsisting thing can do something and one can thus cognize it on this basis and distinguish it from other things. Consequently, this is its proper feature, as Herr von Leibniz[*] remarked long ago without proof. What is said here of self-subsisting things can be

---

[15] §§114–119 are relevant to the First Analogy of Experience (A182–A189/B224–B232). §114 is also relevant to Section 3 of *New Elucidation* (1:410ff.).

[16] See A204–A205/B249–B250 (Second Analogy).

[*] In *Actis Erudit.* A. 1694, pp. 111–112. [Wolff is referring here to Leibniz's "De Primae Philosophiae Emendatione, et de Notione substantiae," which is reprinted in *Die*

illustrated with the example of our soul. It can do something, namely, think, and it is cognized through its thoughts and is also thereby distinguished from other things in which we do not sense any thoughts. And for this reason one can also say that a self-subsisting thing is what can do something.

§117. *How a power is distinct from a capacity* [Vermögen]. But a power must not be conflated with a mere capacity, for a **capacity** is only a possibility of doing something, whereas since power is a source of changes (§115), a striving [*Bemühung*] to do something must be found in it. E.g., when I sit, I have the capacity to stand up, for it is merely possible that I can stand up. But if I actually want to stand up and someone holds me back against my will, a power of standing up is expressed in me. A change is merely possible according to a capacity; through power it becomes actual. And for that reason a self-subsisting thing can bring about something that was merely possible (§114, 115).

§118. *Self-subsisting things are striving* [sind bemüht] *to do something.* Now since a power is to be found in a self-subsisting thing (§115), it must also contain a striving to do something (§117), that is, to change its limits (§104, 107).

§119. *How action is different from striving.* If this striving continues without interruption, action arises out of it. Now insofar as nothing is present why it should not continue, that is, if nothing resists it, it continues (§30), and accordingly action always follows if no resistance is present. E.g., if I attempt to stand up and no one is present to hold me back or resist me otherwise, then I stand up.

§120.[17] *What an effect and an efficacious cause are.* Accordingly, what was only merely possible attains its fulfillment through a power, that is, the possible is brought to actuality (§14). But now, what attains its actuality by an action is called an **effect**. By contrast, that thing that helps the possible to actuality through its action, that is, brings something about, is called an **efficacious cause**. E.g., if the sun melts the wax, it occurs through continued warming. And thus the sun's warming is its **action**, the melting the **effect**, and it is itself the **efficacious cause** by which it

---

Philosophischen Schriften von Leibniz, ed. C. I. Gerhardt, 7 vols. (Berlin: Weidmann, 1875–1890), vol. 4, pp. 468–470.]

[17] §§120–121 are relevant to the Second Analogy of Experience (A189–A211/B232–B256).

accomplishes this. But the warming arises out of its repeated striving to warm, whose constitution should be explained intelligibly in its proper place in physics.

§121. *The state of a thing.* A way of being limited [*Die Art der Einschränckung*] is what we call the **state** of a thing. If the limitation occurs in that through which the object subsists, it is called the internal state of a thing, but if it pertains to what is external to a thing, that is, to that by which it relates to other things, it is called the external state thereof. E.g., the concepts that the soul brings about and its appetites are limitations of its power (§114), and accordingly they constitute its state, [and] in fact, its internal state. By contrast, the size of our fortune, our honor, and the number of our friends and enemies constitute the external state of a human being.

§175.[18] *That there are contingent things and where they come from.* Now because things of one kind can be very different from one another due to differences in their degrees of perfection (§172), it is clear that if a thing of a certain kind has a certain degree of perfection, it could just as easily have had a different one. One degree of perfection is just as possible as another because the one contradicts the essence of the thing as little as the other does (§12). Thus, if an object could have been different from how it is, its opposite contains nothing contradictory in itself (§12) and is therefore not necessary (§36). Now, since one typically calls an object that is not necessary contingent, it is clear that that whose opposite can be or whose opposite is not contradictory is contingent. [...]

§176. *What is grounded in the essence is necessary.* Since the essence of a thing is necessary (§38), everything that is grounded in it alone must also be necessary. For what is grounded in another subsists as long as its ground subsists and for that reason cannot be changed as long as its ground is not changed. Now the essence of things is immutable (§42). Therefore, whatever is grounded in the essence of things alone must also be immutable. Now since it is such and cannot be otherwise, what is contrary to it (§11) contradicts what is grounded in the essence of a thing and is for that reason necessary (§36). Hence it is also clear that the essence of things is the source of what is necessary.

---

[18] §§175–176 are relevant to *The Only Possible Argument,* especially the Third Reflection (2:81ff.).

§177. *The constitution and origin of things of one kind.* Because what is necessary cannot be otherwise (§41), all things that have one essence have this in common (§176). To this extent they are called things of one kind. Whence it is clear that the similarity between essences is the ground of the kinds of things (§18, 29). [...]

§178. *How they can be different.* By contrast, things of one kind can also differ with respect to what can exist in more than one way [*Art*]. Now, since everything that is grounded in the essence alone is necessary (§176), this [way of existing] cannot be grounded in the essence alone and must therefore have its ground partially in its essence (§32, 33) and partially in something else (§30). Namely, whatever can exist in different ways is not determined by the essence of the thing. However, if a thing is not supposed to be incomplete [*unvollkommen*], it must be determined in such fashion that it agrees with its essence (as that from which the ground of its completeness is taken) (§152). [...]

§179. *Where particular* [besonderen] *kinds of things come from.* Now one can comprehend how things that have one and the same essence can still be distinguished into different kinds, [and] in fact, several of these kinds can probably still be distinguished further into yet other kinds. Namely, some of what the essence leaves undetermined can be determined in one way and yet the rest in another. Now since things are similar to each other through what was determined in one way (§18), yet similarity constitutes a particular kind, which is one ground of the kinds of things, there are as many **particular kinds** as there are similarities that can exist among the remaining differences. [...]

§180. *The constitution of individual things.* What makes something into one individual thing is no less conceivable [than what constitutes a kind of thing]. Namely, in an individual thing everything that can merely be perceived and is different from all else is determined in a certain way, whether it be considered for itself alone or also with respect to the other things with which it coexists and upon which it follows, or else that follow upon it. [...] Sometimes everyone will be able to explain for himself this ground of individual things, which one calls **thisness**. [...] It is difficult to give examples for natural things, because they contain infinitely many parts that are all determined in a particular way (§84, 85). And from this one sees why it is that one cannot completely comprehend individual things in nature if one looks only to what is essential about them, that is, to what possibilities they have in themselves (§35).

CHAPTER THREE. ON THE SOUL IN GENERAL, NAMELY, WHAT WE PERCEIVE OF IT

§191.[19] *Plan.* I do not yet wish to show what the soul is and how changes occur in it; rather, my plan right now is merely to report what we perceive of it through daily experience. And I do not want to present anything further here than what anyone who pays attention to himself can cognize. This will serve as a ground for us to derive other things that not everyone can immediately see for himself. Namely, we want to seek out distinct concepts of what we perceive of the soul, and occasionally note several important truths that can be proven from them. And these truths, which are confirmed by infallible experience, are the ground of the laws according to which the powers [*Kräfte*] of the soul are controlled in cognition as well as in willing and not willing, consequently by logic, morality, and politics (§10, 13 *Proleg. Logic*).[20]

§192. *What one understands here by the soul.* Yet so that one knows what one is to perceive, it should be noted that I understand by the soul that thing which is conscious of itself and other things external to it insofar as we are conscious of ourselves and of other things as external to us.

§193. *Warning about a misunderstanding.* But it would be off the mark if someone were to hold that I sought the essence of the soul in the fact that we are conscious of ourselves and other things, and wanted to claim with the Cartesians that nothing could be in the soul of which it was not conscious. For the opposite will be shown below. For right now, I cannot go on anything other than what we are conscious of in ourselves, because I am intent on speaking of what we perceive of ourselves. For wherever more is to be found in us than we are conscious of, we must draw it out by means of inferences, and, in fact, from inferences based on what we are conscious of, because we have no ground for them otherwise. Namely, what I want to attribute to the soul of those things that it perceives must occur because of what I have noticed about it in experience (§30).

---

[19] The paragraphs selected from this chapter, on empirical psychology, are relevant throughout the entire *Critique of Pure Reason*, but especially to A50–A83/B74–B116 (Introduction to the Transcendental Logic and Analytic and Metaphysical Deduction).

[20] See A347/B405–B406 (Paralogisms) for a cautionary remark on such empirical psychology.

§194. *When we do and do not think.* I have already noted above (§45) what the first thing is that we perceive in our soul when we pay attention to it, namely, that we are conscious of many things as external to us. When this occurs, we say that we **think**, and accordingly call changes in the soul of which it is conscious **thoughts** (§2 c. 1 *Logic*). By contrast, when we are not conscious of ourselves, as we take ourselves to be, e.g., during sleep, or even sometimes while we are awake, we typically say that we are **not thinking**.

§195. *On what basis* [Woraus] *we cognize thoughts.* In this fashion we posit being conscious as a feature on the basis of which we cognize that we are thinking. And thus it brings with it the habit of saying that being conscious cannot be separated from thought. But there is no reason why we would want to depart from our customary way of speaking, provided that we take care that we do not, for that reason, posit that the soul can have no further effect than having thoughts (§193).

§196. *Difference between thoughts.* But we find a difference between the thoughts that we think of things external to us and those of things within us, namely, precisely that difference that I assigned to concepts in *Thoughts on the Powers of the Understanding* (§9 & ff. c. 1). Although I could rely on this now, I do not think it unhelpful if I briefly repeat this difference here, because it turns out that a few things will need to be remembered.

§197.[21] *On what basis* [Woher] *we cognize what is in us.* However, because I said that this difference occurs, [i.e.,] we can think of things external to us or of things in us, it is requisite that prior to all else I explain the basis on which we cognize that something is in us. For the basis upon which we take it that something is external to us has already been shown above (§45). Namely, when we are conscious of several things, e.g., see a building or persons, we cognize, by means of the principle of contradiction established above (§10), that I, who am conscious of a thing, am not the same thing of which I am conscious. And hence I cognize it as distinct from me (§17). But because I find in myself nothing beyond consciousness, that is, my thoughts (§194), so I ascribe nothing further to myself than thinking, and accordingly what belongs to it I see as [being] in me. And hence the Cartesians have mistakenly held

---

[21] See the Refutation of Idealism (B274–B279).

that consciousness constitutes the entire essence of the soul and that nothing could occur in it of which we would not be conscious.

§198.[22] *What clear thoughts are.* Some thoughts are constituted such that we know very well what we are thinking and [that we] can distinguish them from others. In such cases we say that they are **clear**. E.g., right now I see buildings, human beings, and other objects. I am quite conscious of what I see, I can cognize each one, and distinguish it from others. For this reason I say that my present thoughts are clear.

§199.[23] *What obscure thoughts are.* By contrast, when we ourselves do not quite know what we are to make of what we are thinking, our thoughts are **obscure**. E.g., from afar I see something white in the field, but do not know what I should make of it because I cannot quite distinguish one part from another; in this case, the thought that I have of it is obscure.

§201. *Where clarity comes from.* Clarity thus arises from noticing the difference in a manifold, whereas obscurity arises from failing to notice this [difference].

§206. *When thoughts are distinct.* Sometimes it happens that we can determine a difference in what we are thinking and thus can also report it to others upon demand. And in this case our **thoughts** are **distinct.** [...]

§276. *When we understand something. What understandable* [verständlich] *is.* As soon as we have distinct thoughts or concepts of a thing, we understand it. And whatever we can cognize distinctly is understandable. In everyday life one typically also says that one understands an object if one has only a clear concept of it, but in the sciences it is necessary to distinguish the mere cognition of an object from understanding it.

§277.[24] *What the understanding is.* The faculty of distinctly representing what is possible is the understanding. And the understanding is distinguished from the senses and the imagination in that when the latter occur by themselves, representations are at best only clear and not distinct, whereas when the understanding is added, they become distinct. For that reason, when someone does not know how to tell us anything

---

[22] §§198–199, 201, and 206 are relevant to B414–B416 (Paralogisms).
[23] See *Inquiry* (2:290).
[24] See *False Subtlety* (2:59).

about an object, even if he can immediately imagine it to himself, that is, if he has no distinctness in his thoughts (§206), we typically say: he has no **understanding of it**, or he does not **understand** it. By contrast, if he can tell us what he represents of an object, we say that he has an **understanding of it**, or he **understands** it. And meanwhile we even distinctly cite **distinctness** as the ground that someone does not understand an object, namely, when we say: **how can he say it, he understands nothing of it**, although we are aware that he has sensed the object and can imagine it again.

§278. *When we cognize something.* As soon as we can represent an object to ourselves, we **cognize** it. And if our concepts are distinct, then **our cognition** is also **distinct**, whereas if they are **obscure**, then the **cognition** is **obscure** as well. Distinct cognition is the understanding of an object (§276).

§279. *Degrees of cognition.* Thus the more distinctness there is in our cognition, the better we understand the object (§276) and the more we know to say about it (§206). And hence the degree of cognition increases (§106).

§280. *Which cognition is the greatest.* Thus if someone distinctly comprehends everything that can be cognized of a thing, then he has attained the highest degree of cognition of this thing and it is not possible to attain a greater cognition.

§281. *Where a cognition's imperfection comes from.* By contrast, where indistinctness and obscurity remain, cognition has not yet been brought to the highest degree, and according to how much or how little indistinctness and obscurity remain, it is far or not far away from it. And thus the degrees of imperfect cognition stem from indistinctness and obscurity (§106).

§282. *When the understanding is pure, when it is impure.* Because distinctness of cognition belongs to the understanding, while indistinctness belongs to the senses and the imagination (§277), the understanding is separate from the senses and the imagination when we have completely distinct cognition. However, if we can still identify indistinctness and obscurity in our cognition, it is still united with the senses and the imagination. In the first case, the **understanding** is called **pure**, in the second **impure**.

§283. *Pure understanding is not an empty illusion* [Einbildung]. Since we can now cite a distinct difference between pure and impure understanding, which we also find grounded in experience (§282), those who hold that pure understanding is an empty illusion of mathematicians (§242) are deceived, and they deceive themselves because they do not understand the difference between pure and impure understanding (§276), or sometimes have barely even cognized it indistinctly (§278).

§284. *Why the understanding should not be taken more broadly.* I know quite well that the understanding in general has recently been taken as a power to represent what is possible, whether it occurs distinctly or indistinctly, or even completely obscurely, in which case the power to sense and the imagination are also comprehended under it. However, why must we render a word ambiguous unnecessarily due to an instability in our way of speaking, given that we have enough words to put us in a position to distinguish all faculties or all powers of the soul from each other, and, in fact, so that we can retain the customary meanings that the words once had?

§285. *Our understanding is never pure.* Sometimes experience shows, and in its proper place we shall establish, that our understanding is never completely pure; rather, much indistinctness and obscurity always remain along with any distinctness. But despite this, one can attribute to the soul each faculty that belongs to it and thereby avoid misunderstanding arising from ambiguous ways of speaking.

§286. *The understanding brings us to universal cognition.* Accordingly, the understanding manifests itself in concepts when we differentiate from each other what is to be found in one thing, as we represent it, and when we hold [these determinations] up against the different [determinations] of other things, so as to determine the differences between these things. This allows us to provide explanations (§36 c. 1 *Logic*) and cognize the genera [*Arten*] and species of things (§182). Thus, that we have universal concepts (§28 c. 1 *Logic*), and therefore universal cognition at all, stems from the understanding.

§287. *When the understanding judges.* As soon as we distinguish the kinds of things and their species, as well as their attributes and changes, and their behavior toward each other, we cognize that this or that thing has, or at least could have, this or that intrinsically [*an sich*], or also that something could stem from it, that is, that one could find in it the ground of a change in something else; by contrast, [we also cognize that] another thing does not have, or could not have, this or that intrinsically [*an sich*], that is, that something could not stem from it. And we call this activity [*Verrichtung*] of the understanding **judging**. One can find examples of this in *Thoughts on the Powers of the Understanding* (§1 c. 3).

§288.[25] *What judging depends on.* We see from this that it is not enough for a judgment if one represents a thing with its attribute, or change, or else with its effects, but rather requires beyond this that we distinguish the attribute, or change, or else effect from the thing and view them as two different things that exist at the same time as each other, and such that one of them is connected with the other. In this fashion judgment aims at the representation of the connection of two things with each other. And the same is true for the separation of two things.

§316. *Difference between figurative and intuitive cognition.* It is to be noted, namely, that words are the ground of a special kind of cognition that we call **figurative**. For we represent objects either themselves, or through words, or through other signs. E.g., when I think of a man who is not present and whose image is none the less floating before my eyes, I am representing the person himself. But when I think to myself these words about virtue "It is the skill of directing one's actions according to the law of nature" then I represent virtue through words. The first is called intuitive cognition, the second is figurative cognition.

§325. *What experience is.* Cognition that we obtain by attending to our sensations and changes in the soul we are accustomed to calling **experience**. *Difference between common experience and experiments.* And we call it **common experience** if the sensations are given by themselves, but **experiments** if we obtain experience through our efforts. E.g., the sky is covered by clouds without our help, and we see the dark clouds without having previously formed an intention to see them. Accordingly, when I pay attention to what I see and am conscious that the sky is covered with dark clouds, this is a common experience. By contrast, when I pump the air out of a large copper or glass sphere in order to see whether it weighs less than when it is full of air, this is an experiment. For I obtain this cognition through my efforts. Without our help we shall never be able to see such a thing, because nature never brings together spheres, air pumps, and scales, much less does it pump out the sphere and hang it on the scale.

[25] See B93 (Metaphysical Deduction) and B140–B141 (Transcendental Deduction).

§326. *What we have to do for experience.* Thus for experience we can do nothing further than carefully take note of everything that can be distinguished from each other either in the sensation of what is external to us or in the state of our soul, and call each thing by its proper name so that we do not conflate our illusions [*Einbildungen*] and preconceived opinions with experience and attempt to obtain in such fraudulent fashion any grounds of cognition that are not grounded in the things. Below, in the case of the correspondence of the body with the soul (§529, 534), we shall have a clear example of this.

§329. *What kind of cognition one obtains through experience.* But through experience we obtain concepts and judgments. And in *Thoughts on the Powers of the Understanding* (c. 1. & 5) I have explained what to attend to in both cases so that one does not become lost, just as one should not imagine that this matter has already been exhaustively treated there. The **art of experience** and **experiments** is so rich in rules that one can make a special part of the sciences out of it. And it would not be without great value if this were to happen, because we obtain much cognition through experience. Not only from astronomers but also from several careful natural historians do we have glorious examples of experience and experiments from which one who is intent upon it can discern universal rules that give occasion to further thoughts. This purpose can also be served by my own experiments, which clear a path for the thorough observation of nature and art and in which I have undertaken, among other things, to present objects in such a fashion that one can both see and learn how to set up experiments skillfully.

§330. *Where the certainty of experience comes from.* Although I do not intend to remedy prior deficiencies in the art of experience and experiments here, I must still point out where the certainty of experience comes from. For whoever wants to be acquainted with [*kennen*] the soul must know [how] to indicate the ground if one is speaking of something that pertains to it. Concepts are certain when we cognize their possibility (§5 c. 9 *Logic*). Now since experience shows us that the things for which it affords us a concept exist, we also cognize that they are possible (§15). Judgments are certain when we attribute to things (§6 c. 9 *Logic*) what does or can pertain to them. Now if we reach a judgment by means of experience, then we have cognized that this or that does pertain to a thing, and it is accordingly clear once again that it *can* pertain to it (§15). However, because everything in a judgment is asserted of a thing under certain conditions (§6 c. 3 *Logic*), it is not certain that something will occur again unless the same conditions occur again, that is, in **similar cases** (§18). E.g., I see that iron starts to glow in the blacksmith's workshop if it is placed in glowing coals that are strongly fanned by bellows. From this I judge: The iron can begin to glow. However, this judgment is not true *simpliciter*. For I cannot begin to hope that it will happen [again] unless I see the iron lying in blazing coals.

§331. *What kind of certainty is in the actions of those who look to experience.* This is why those who merely look to experience and pay attention to it, will wait for similar cases, and **the expectation of similar cases** is the ground of all their actions. If they knew how to distinguish these cases properly, that is, at least had a clear concept of them (§198), then they would be certain in their belief [*Vornehmen*]. For it is correct that the same thing happens in similar cases (§10). Often, however, because one's concept [of similar cases] is for the most part very obscure, sometimes even downright incorrect, if one determines a case by means of unusual circumstances that appear to be true to the naked eye, the result of the undertaking is often very questionable and it leads astray those who hold their views to be the most certain. Examples of this occur daily in human life.

§340.[26] *What syllogisms* [Schlüsse] *are.* When we draw one proposition out of two others, we call it **to infer**, and the kind of inference **a syllogism.** [...]

§347. *What a demonstration and a proof in general is.* From this one can see what a demonstration actually is, namely, a constant connection of many syllogisms in which no premises are accepted unless we remember having previously cognized their correctness. [...] What I understand by a connection of syllogisms is to be determined from the preceding. One syllogism is connected to another when its conclusion is made into one of the premises of the other syllogism. One connects two syllogisms with a third when by comparing their conclusions one produces a third proposition that can be made into a premise of a new syllogism.

§361. *What knowledge* [Wissen] *and science* [Wissenschaft] *are.* We typically say that we **know** something if it can be deduced from undoubted grounds through correct syllogisms. And one calls **science** the skill of

---

[26] See A303–A304/B359–B361 (Introduction to Transcendental Dialectic) and *False Subtlety* (2:49).

deducing what one asserts from undoubted grounds through correct syllogisms. [...]

§368.[27] *What reason* [Vernunft] *is*. The art of inferring shows that truths are connected to each other, which should also be demonstrated in its proper place. The insight that we have into the connection of truths, or the faculty of seeing into the connection of truths is called **reason**. That this explanation of reason is in accordance with our customary way of speaking, I show (§16 c. 2 *Logic*) in what follows. [...]

§369. *What is in accordance with reason*. Accordingly, whatever is connected to cognized truths is **in accordance with reason**. Now since one deduces by demonstration what is connected to cognized truths (§346), what one has demonstrated is in accordance with reason. By contrast, since without a demonstration one cannot see whether or not something is connected to cognized truths, in such a case it is uncertain whether or not it is in accordance with reason. [...]

§370. *Degrees of reason*. The more insight one has into the connection of truths, the more one has reason (§368). For this reason one has that much less reason, the less one has insight into the connection of truths. And wherever one has no insight at all into how things hang together, there is no reason at all.

§371. *Experience is opposed to reason*. Now because one does not have insight into how something whose existence is cognized through mere experience is connected to other truths (§325), no reason at all is [involved] in this cognition (§370) and, in that case, experience is opposed to reason. However, science comes from reason, as will be established below.

§372. *Paths for cognizing the truth*. Accordingly, we have two paths by which we can obtain knowledge of the truth, experience and reason. The former is grounded in the senses (§220, 325), the latter in the understanding (§277, 368). [...]

§373. *Why syllogisms are called inferences of reason*. Because the formal syllogisms that we described above (§340) distinctly laid before our eyes the connection of truths (§206), and we thus attained insight into it by this means, they are properly called **inferences of reason**.

[27] See A293–A309/B349–B366 (Introduction to Transcendental Dialectic).

§374. *Expectation of similar cases is similar to reason.* The expectation of similar cases (§331) has a similarity with reason. For if we notice that something has happened under certain circumstances and we expect, on seeing the very same circumstances again, that it will happen again, it appears as if one had insight into the nature of things and knew how to infer from the one to the other. And thus this expectation is to some extent similar to reason (§368, 18).

§375. *When it comes close to reason.* However, in the greatest part of human actions it not only takes the place of reason, but can also become neutral to reason (§17) or even in accordance with it (§369), if one properly determines the circumstances under which something occurs. For in this way one cognizes that the result is connected to the circumstances, although one does not comprehend how this happens and thus has no distinct insight into the connection (§206).

§376. *When it is without reason.* Still, sometimes the expectation of similar cases can also be without any reason. For if we have only a clear, but thereby indistinct, more often completely obscure, concept of the circumstances by which the case is determined, and we look at these circumstances anew, the imagination also immediately represents what happened previously (§238), and our memory assures us that they both accompanied each other (§249), and for that reason one looks for it there again.

§381. *What kind of cognition arises out of reason.* Because reason is an insight into the connection of truths (§368), yet truth is cognized when one understands the ground why this or that can be (§144), reason shows us why this or that can be. And thus the philosophical cognition that I was thinking of in the preface to *Thoughts on the Powers of the Understanding* (§5, 6) arises from it, just as common cognition, which was being reported on there as well, comes from experience.

§382. *When reason is pure* [lauter]. When one has insight into the connection of things in such fashion that one can connect the truths to each other without assuming a single proposition from experience, reason is pure. By contrast, when one receives aid from experiential propositions, reason and experience are combined with each other and we do not have complete insight into the connection of truths with each other. For when we come to a proposition from experience, we are standing still and our reason cannot proceed further. *Whether it is pure in our cognition of nature.*

We find it sufficient in the sciences that our reason is not always pure,
especially in our cognition of nature and ourselves. And I also take it to
be the most secure path that we do not assume anything in the cognition of nature other than what is grounded in infallible experiences. For
those who want to attribute more to reason than is proper have taken
recourse to fabricated things and have thereby strayed from truth into
error. *Of mathematics.* In arithmetic and geometry just as in algebra we
have examples of pure reason. For here all syllogisms proceed from distinct concepts and only from grounds that have been separated from the
senses.

§383. *Science comes from reason.* Since science is the skill of establishing
everything that one asserts on undoubted grounds, or, in one word, of
demonstrating (§361, 347), but in demonstration truths are connected
to each other (§347), one thus cognizes the connection of truths through
the sciences, and thus it comes from reason (§368).

§384.[28] *What an opinion is.* When we deduce a proposition from assumptions (§347) of whose correctness we are not completely certain, our
cognition is called an **opinion**.

§389. *What certainty is.* The **certainty of our cognition** is the concept of
the possibility, or even the actuality, of a judgment. Namely, in the case
of universal judgments we look merely to possibility because the universal has no actuality other than in the individual things of one genus and
species (§182), whereas in the case of judgments about individual things
we also sometimes direct our thoughts to actuality. E.g., I am certain
that the rapid growth of plants can be promoted through skill if I represent its possibility. I am certain that a father loves his son if I represent
the actuality of it to myself.

§390. *Where certainty comes from.* But we obtain this concept either
through experience or through reason (§372). How experience brings
it about has already been explained above (§330). Through reason it
happens when we cognize the connection of our judgment with other
truths (§368). Now since this connection is discovered by syllogisms
(§340), yet with syllogisms one is to look in part to the correctness of the
propositions and in part to their connection with each other, that is, as

---

[28] §384, 389–390, and 395 are relevant to On the Canon of Pure Reason, Third Section
(A820/B848ff.).

one typically puts it quite succinctly, in part to the form and in part to the matter, certainty arises in this case when we have insight into both the correctness of the propositions with which we connect our judgment and the correctness of the inference.

§395. *What true and false are.* When a judgment is possible, whether we cognize it or not, it is called **true**, but when it is impossible, it is called **false**. Now since everything either is or is not, all judgments must be either true or false.

§396. *What error is.* Whoever holds a true judgment to be false or a false judgment to be true **errs**. And a false illusion of the truth and falsity of a judgment is an **error**.

§397. *How error arises.* When our senses represent different things as identical and we therefore judge that they are identical, or also if, out of haste, we hold different things to be identical, we hold a false judgment to be true (§395) and thus we err (§396). If we nonetheless believe that we are certain that the things are identical, we have a false illusion of the truth of our judgment (§394, 395). And accordingly we entertain an error (§396). Most errors stem from this source.

§422. *What is good.* What makes us and our state more perfect is good. [...]

§492.[29] *What the will is.* When we represent an object as good, our mind is inclined toward it. This inclination of the mind toward an object for the sake of the good that we believe to perceive in it is what we typically call the **will**. E.g., someone sees a book lying in a bookstore, leafs through it a bit, and believes to find in it matters that are useful for him to know, that is, he represents the book as good (§422). When this happens, he gets a desire [*Lust*] to buy the book. This inclination that he gets toward the book, because he holds it to be good, is called the will. And one then says: He wants to buy the book. Since the sensible desire [*Begierde*] arises from an indistinct representation of the good (§404) and I am now proceeding from what comes from indistinct cognition to what stems from distinct cognition, everyone sees that we are talking of distinct representations of the good. And the example given, in addition to the citation, proves it as well.

[29] §§492–496 and 514–522 are relevant to the Third Antinomy (A444/B472ff.).

§493. *What not willing is.* By contrast, our mind withdraws from an object that we represent to ourselves as evil [*böse*]. This withdrawal of our mind from an object for the sake of the evil that we believe to perceive in it is what we typically call **not willing**. [...]

§494. *How not willing is different from the omission of willing.* From this it is clear that not willing is something more than refraining from willing. For one refrains from willing when one sees nothing good in an object [...], whereas one does not will it if one finds evil in it. [...]

§496. *What motives are and that the will cannot exist without them.* On the basis of the explanation of the will just given, one sees that we must always have a ground why we will something, namely, **the representation of good** (§492), similarly, a ground why we do not will something, namely, **the representation of evil** (§493). And that this is the case is sufficiently clear from the principle of sufficient reason (§30). For if everything must have its sufficient ground, why it is rather than is not, there must also be a sufficient ground why we will and do not will, just as it is impossible that a scale can register an imbalance if there is no weight to cause it. These grounds of willing and not willing are typically called motives.

§514.[30] *We understand free actions.* Accordingly, we find (1) that we understand or comprehend distinctly the constitution of these actions (§276). E.g., the question arises whether I should buy a book or not. I am aware of what kind of book it is and what I should pay for it. I know whether or not such a book can be useful for my purposes and whether I can afford [to spend] as much money as it will cost.

§515. *They are not intrinsically* [an sich] *necessary.* We find (2) that the actions that we call free are not necessary *simpliciter*, because what is contrary to them is just as possible (§36). [...]

§516. *The motives do not make them necessary either.* Now although motives are present for why the action is favored, they still do not for that reason make it intrinsically [*an sich*] necessary. For they leave the constitution of the object and the faculty of executing it in the one case as in the other, and cannot make a change in it. E.g., although I take into account that the book is useful to me and thereby I get the desire [*Lust*] to buy

---

[30] §§514–522 are relevant to Section 2 of *New Elucidation* (esp. 1:398–407), where Kant offers a similar compatibilist account of freedom.

it, this still does not change anything in the book or in the motions in the parts of the body that are required for the purchase or in the other circumstances that are required for it; rather, everything remains as it was before. Namely, it can happen and it can not happen. The one is just as possible as the other.

§517. *But rather only certain*. It of course remains true sometimes that they are what make the possible actual (§414), and insofar as they are sufficient for this, they produce certainty. E.g., if one asks why I am buying the book, since I could have refrained from it just as easily, I cite as the ground, because I consider it to be useful and it is not onerous for me to spend the money on it. And as soon as I draw the conclusion [*Schluß*] for the sake of this motive, it becomes certain that I will buy the book, but not necessary, for it remains possible now as beforehand that I refrain from the purchase (§516). [...]

§518. *Its ground is in the soul*. Finally, we find (3) that the soul has within itself the ground of those of its actions that we typically call voluntary [*freiwillig*]. For the representations that it needs for its motives (§496) are in it and derive from it, and by its own power it tends toward the object that pleases it, and withdraws from what displeases it, because the motives do not necessitate or determine it. *What is arbitrary*. As in our example we determine ourselves to buy the book, or else to do something else, namely, to refrain from the purchase. For what the second ground prescribes cannot coerce us to refrain from it. It itself does not want to coerce us. Now insofar as the soul has within itself the ground of its actions, one attributes choice [*Willkühr*] to it and for that reason calls action and passion arbitrary [*willkührliches Tun und Lassen*] if its ground is to be found in the soul.

§519. *What freedom is*. If we gather all of this together, it is clear that freedom is nothing other than the faculty of the soul to decide, by means of its own power of choice, between two equally possible things whatever pleases it the most, such as a book that we see in a bookstore, either to buy or refrain from its purchase, or (which is the same thing) to determine itself toward whatever it is determined to neither by its nature nor by something external to it.

§520. *What it is grounded in*. Now since insight into the connection of things shows us what is good and evil, what is better and worse (§422, 426), reason is the ground of freedom (§368).

§521. *What kind of necessity is in freedom.* It is not to be denied that it is impossible for a human being who cognizes something as better [than something else] to prefer what is worse, and in this fashion it happens necessarily that he chooses the better. However, this necessity is not contrary to freedom. For a human being is not coerced to choose the better, because he could have chosen the worse instead, had he so desired, given that the one is just as intrinsically possible as the other (§516). [...] And from my *Thoughts on Human Action and Passion,* where I explained the actions of human beings in particular, one can see that without this kind of necessity (which one had called moral necessity) one could not hope for certainty in morality. [...]

§522. *The human will cannot be coerced.* Despite this necessity, it still remains true that the human will cannot be coerced. For, because we cannot will anything that we do not hold to be good, and cannot not will without what we view as evil (§506), yet the understanding cannot be coerced in its representations, it is also in no way possible to coerce the will. And in this fashion the will is free from all external coercion. I assume that the understanding cannot be coerced in its representation because it is a claim that no one cares to call into doubt, given that it is grounded in daily experience.

CHAPTER FOUR. ON THE WORLD

§540.[31] *Why the world is treated here.* Before we can understand what the soul actually is and what the reason is for what has been attributed to it so far, we must first come to know what a world is. For later we shall see that one can comprehend neither the essence of a spirit in general nor that of a soul in particular before understanding what a world is and how it is constituted.

§541. *To what extent it will be treated here.* Right now, however, we do not want to be concerned with those changes that occur in our universe, and especially on earth, because an extensive report on such matters should be provided when my *Rational Thoughts on Nature and its Effects* is published.[32] Here we want to teach only what belongs to the universal

---

[31] The paragraphs selected from this chapter, on cosmology, are relevant to the Analogies of Experience (A182–A215/B224–B262) and the First and Second Antinomies.

[32] Wolff published *Rational Thoughts on the Effects of Nature* (*Vernünfftige Gedancken von den Würkungen der Natur*) in 1723.

cognition of the world, which has previously been almost entirely lost from sight, despite being one of the most important truths that we can cognize, because cognition of God and of natural religion depends on it and [because] the most difficult puzzles that have been raised against it can be happily resolved by means of it, as can be seen sufficiently from the last chapter.

§542. *How we obtain our concept of the world.* So that we can obtain an adequate concept of the world now, we may only attend to the one that stands before us, consider what we can distinguish from each other in it (§7 c. 1 *Log.*), and also compare the things that we perceive against each other (§19, cap. cit.).

§543.[33] *How our world is constituted.* When this happens, we find (1) many composite things on our earth (§51) that are next to each other, and in the heavens we discover, in addition to the earth, yet other large bodies that are similar, in part, to our earth and, in part, to our sun (§291, 318 *Astron.*). We perceive (2) that of the things we find on the earth several precede, while others, by contrast, come [later], and thus one thing follows another. Yes, even if the things themselves subsist, many changes still occur in them, with one [change] following another, and we also find this in the stars, at least in their position with respect to the earth and each other, which is testified to not only by daily experience, but primarily by the observations of astronomers. [...] If one compares against each other things that are next to each other as well as follow upon each other, along with their changes, one cognizes (3) that one always has its ground in another, and each one is for the sake of the other, that is, both things that are next to each other and things that follow upon each other are grounded in each other (§29). And that is what we can in general notice of things that constitute a world together.

§544.[34] *What a world is.* Now since the actuality of things does not belong to their essence (§35), while explanations of matters portray only the essence of a thing (§48 c. 1 *Log*), it follows from what he have already noted that the **world** is a series of changeable things that are next to each other and follow upon each other, but, in general, are connected to each other.

---

[33] Wolff's definition of the world is particularly relevant to Kant's distinction between world and nature at A418/B446. §§543–550 are also relevant to Section 3 of *New Elucidation* (1:410ff.). See also Inaugural Dissertation (esp. 2:389–392 and 2:406–409).

[34] See *Inaugural Dissertation* 2:387.

§545. *When things are connected to each other.* I say that things are **connected** to each other if each one of them contains in itself the ground why the other exists next to it at the same time, or follows upon it (§543). [...]

§546. *When they are connected spatially.* When two things coexist and the one contains in itself the ground why the other exists next to it at the same time, each one of them has its own special way in which it coexists with the rest. For this reason each one has its own special place (§47), and they are thus connected to each other (§545) spatially (§46).

§547. *When they are connected temporally.* When two things follow each other and the preceding one contains in itself the ground why the other follows, and, by contrast, the following one contains the ground why the former precedes it, they follow each other in an order (§132, 134) and are thus connected to each other temporally.

§548. *Everything in the world is connected spatially and temporally.* Now since things in the world are connected to each other insofar as they coexist as well as insofar as they follow each other (§544), they are connected to each other spatially and temporally (§546, 547).

§549. *The world is something singular* [etwas eines]. Whatever is connected together temporally and spatially constitutes one. For from the spatial and temporal connection of different [matters] one cognizes that it is only one thing. Now since everything in the world is connected temporally and spatially (§548), the world is to be viewed as one thing.

§550. *The world is a whole, consisting of parts.* For this reason the world is a whole, and the things that exist next to each other, like those that follow upon each other, are its parts (§24).

§551. *It is a composite thing.* What consists of parts is a composite thing (§51). Now since each world is a whole that consists of different parts (§550), each world must be a composite thing.

§582. *What elements are.* Because a world is a composite thing (§551), simple things must exist of which its parts are composed (§76). One typically calls these simple things **elements**.

§583. *Common mistake about the elements.* Now since simple things can have no parts (§75), the elements, too, can have no parts (§582). Yes, since simple things do not have, for themselves, a size and shape, nor even an internal motion (§81), the elements, too, can have neither a size nor a shape nor an internal motion. [...]

§584. *Constitution of the elements.* Because the elements are simple things (§582), everything is true of them that was discussed above in detail about simple things. They have a power (§125) by which they continuously change their internal state (§126), and are something self-subsisting (§127), and so cannot perish except through annihilation (§102).

§585.[35] *Difference between simple things.* Accordingly, those simples that constitute the elements of the world can be distinguished from each other only by their internal states (§584, 17). The state of a thing is its way of being limited (§124). Accordingly, they are distinguished from each other through their way of being limited.

§586. *Nothing [simple] in the world can be identical* [ähnlich] *to anything else.* Two things cannot exist in the world that are identical to each other. For, since identical things agree with each other about everything by which one is supposed to know and distinguish them from each other (§18), one cannot find in them anything [that would explain] why the one would be in this rather than in another place and why the other would be in that rather than this place. But nothing can exist without a sufficient ground (§30), and thus it is not possible [*es gehet nicht an*] that identical things exist in different places at the same time. Precisely this also remains true regarding time.

§587. *Nor can a composite thing be identical to any other.* One easily comprehends that no composite thing in the world can be identical to any other. For the proof that we presented for simples remains unchanged for composites. [...]

§592. *Internal state of simple things in each moment.* Since two simple things cannot be identical to each other (§586), something must at all times be found in the one, and accordingly, be perceived by whomever cognizes it (§278), that is not found in the other and, by the same token, something must be revealed in the other that is not present in the one (§18).

---

[35] §§585–587 and 592–594 are relevant to the Transcendental Aesthetic and the Amphiboly chapter (esp. A263/B319ff. and A271/B327ff.). They are also relevant to Section 2 of *New Elucidation* (esp. 1:409–410).

Because no difference can be found in simple things other than in their internal states (§585), the internal state of each simple state must be distinct at every moment from the internal state of all the rest.

§593. *Why each of the simple things exists here now and not elsewhere.* Because everything must have its ground for its existence (§30), there must also be a sufficient ground why each of the simple things exists here rather than elsewhere. But now, since space and time contain nothing in themselves from which one could understand why this or that simple thing exists at this or that time, or here rather than elsewhere, because the parts both of space and of time have nothing in themselves by which they could be distinguished from each other insofar, namely, as they are viewed as empty of the things that are to be found in them (§46, 94), the desired ground cannot be found in them either (§29). Accordingly, if it is not to be found external to the simple things, it must be found within them; consequently, we must find it in the internal state of each simple thing (§585).

§594. *Also why these and not others are next to each other.* Since everything has its sufficient ground why it exists rather than does not exist (§30), there must also be a sufficient ground why each of them is to be found next to this one and not next to others. But because here, too, the ground is to be sought neither in space nor in time insofar, namely, as they are to be viewed as empty of the things that are to be found in them (§46, 94), by the same token, it must be found in those things that are next to each other, and thus in the internal states of simple things (§58).

§595. *Origin of perfection in composite things.* According to this, the internal state of each simple thing is oriented toward [*richtet sich nach*] the remaining ones that are around it. Accordingly, they all correspond to each other (§593, 594), which maintains the perfection in the composite (§152).

§596. *In the whole world.* Because all composite things in the world are connected to each other (§544) and the simples are connected to the rest of the simples so that, together, they constitute a composite thing (§595), the internal state of each simple thing must be oriented toward all composites that are around it as if around a focal point. And in this fashion each of the simple things harmonizes with the whole world and from this the perfection of the world arises (§152).

§597. *What simple things bring about* [würken]. The internal state of a simple thing is nothing other than the kind of limitation of that through which it subsists (§121); the alternations of its limitations are its changes (§107); its changes are nothing other than the alternations of the degrees (§106) of its power (§115). Now, since simple things are constantly efficacious [*würcken*] in this fashion (§120), something must be produced by its efficacy that refers not only to all remaining simple things that are around it, but also to all composites in the whole world.

§598.[36] *Its efficacy is deferred for further investigation.* We want to defer for further investigation [consideration of] what is actually brought about by the efficacy of the simple things. Herr von Leibniz has in mind that the whole world is represented in every simple thing, which allows for a comprehensible explanation of how each one can be distinct from each other and refer to the whole world in a special way, even of how it refers to the things that are around it differently from how it refers to those that are further away. However, I still have reservations about accepting this.

§599. *Unities of nature.* And hence one understands what Herr von Leibniz wants to have with his *monadibus* or **unities of nature**, which he also typically calls the **indivisible of nature**. It is to be noted, however, that, according to him, they are not aware of everything that is being represented in them. Accordingly, one could say that every one of Leibniz's unities is a mirror of the whole world that is represented in it according to the point where it is. However, because we still want to defer this investigation at present (§598), it is enough for us that we have presented a distinct concept of Leibniz's unities of nature and at the same time have shown how they are not opposed to what we have established about the simple things in the world (§597). And if Herr von Leibniz had wanted to establish that he did not ascribe impossible things to his unities of nature, he would have had to have established it in just the way that we established the constitution of the elements. Below (§742) we shall establish that the soul belongs among the simple things and that it has a power of representing the world according to the state of its body in the world (§753). We shall also show that many other simple things are also possible that represent the world in a way less perfect than does the soul

---

[36] §§598–600 are relevant to the Amphiboly Chapter (esp. A266–A268/B322–B324 and A274–A276/B330–B332).

(§900). Accordingly, things such as **Leibnizian unities of nature** are possible. Everything that we established about the elements of things is attributed to them, and if one turns the elements into these unities, all simple things remain similar to each other just as the composites are, and constitute one kind of thing (§177).

§600. *Universal harmony of things.* Now that I have distinctly established that the internal state of every simple thing refers to all the rest that exist in the world (§596) and Herr von Leibniz explains this in such a way that the whole world is represented in each simple thing according to the point where it is (§599), one can also understand further how, according to his opinion, everything in the world down to the smallest thing harmonizes with every other, and accordingly what he advances with his universal harmony of things, which, like all the rest that he has presented in this regard, appears to many as a puzzle that they believe to be unsolvable, since he has neither explained nor proved it sufficiently. However, because at the present time we do not want to decide what it really means for the inner state of simple things to refer to everything in the world, we shall let it remain undecided for the present in what the universal harmony of things consists, and it is enough for us that we have shown that it is present and that it can be explained in an intelligible manner according to the sense of Herr von Leibniz.

§601. *Its size.* Since every simple thing is distinct from the rest according to its internal state at every moment (§592), one can cognize from this the size of the universal harmony of things.

§602.[37] *How simple things fill space.* By the same token, since each one of them refers to the rest in a special way according to its internal state (§595), it coexists with the rest in a special way such that none of them can exist with the rest in precisely this way. And thus not only is each one external to the others (§45), but many, taken together, also follow each other in an order (§132, 133), and thus many, taken together, fill a space (§46), although each one of them does not actually fill a space, but rather only has a certain point in it.

§603. *How composite things come from simples.* Now it is time that I explain how it is possible that composites, which have parts, can nonetheless

---

[37] §§602–610 are relevant to the *Physical Monadology* and the Second Antinomy.

come from simple things that have no parts at all by which they touch each other. If one understands properly the constitution of simple things, it is not difficult to comprehend this. For, because each one of them coexists with the rest in such a fashion that none of them can exist with the others in precisely this way (§602), it is not possible that many can exist at the same time in one point, but rather each one requires its own [point]. Since each one is connected to the others that are around it (§594, 545), many simple things, together, constitute one (§549), and for that reason the composite acquires an extension in length, breadth, and width (§53).

§604. *Where the difficulties come from in this matter and how to remove them.* That one has sensed difficulties [concerning] how a divisible thing could arise from indivisible things arose because one assumed, as is [actually] the case in mathematics, that all indivisible points are identical to each other, and wanted to compose what is extended in length, breadth, and width from them just as we see that coarse parts are glued together or otherwise attached to each other in art. Since we have now shown that the points of nature are indivisible, but not identical to each other (§586), and also have a power that is constantly efficacious in them (§584) and, for this reason, each one must be external to the other (§45), the first source of difficulties has been blocked. By the same token, since it is not necessary that elements be glued or sewn together in order for extension and the continuity in this extension to result, but rather it is enough that they are different from each other, while still constituting one, and having such an order among them that others can no longer be posited between them in another order (§53, 58), a second source of difficulties is blocked as well. Simple things are completely different from their composites, and one can attribute nothing of what we perceive of the latter to the former (§82). Therefore, they cannot be combined with each other in the same way as composites are. They are not matter and for that reason also cannot be connected in such a way as the parts of matter are. As they are now comprehended by the understanding, so, too, their connection with each other must be merely understandable. Everything retains its correctness in reason (§369), but we cannot imagine the internal and external state of the simple things and their connection with each other. For what we imagine are composite things, since we bring a lot together in one image that we cannot distinguish from each other distinctly.

§605. *How simple things cohere.* It is also evident from what has been said that simple things do not need to be anchored to each other as composites do. For each one of them is different from the others and continually remains different from it, and since nothing can occur in the world without a sufficient ground (§30), none can dislodge another from its point. For the internal state of each one is oriented toward those that are around it (§596). Accordingly, in order for simple things to cohere, nothing is required other than the connection that the internal state of one thing has toward the internal state of the others, which we comprehend with the understanding, but certainly cannot grasp through either the senses or the imagination (§604).

§606. *Constitution of bodies.* After having considered simple things, we must also come to composites. Now, whatever has been established about them in general must also be valid for those that we find in every world. In our world we call composite things **bodies**, or also **corporeal things**, and accordingly it is clear that a body necessarily fills a space (§52), and is extended in length, breadth, and width (§53); that it has a shape (§54), can be divided (§55) and moved (§57); that its essence consists in its mode of composition (§59); that it has a measured size (§59); that it can neither arise nor perish (§64); that it can undergo changes in its size and shape without a change in its essence (§65, 66, 68), and, notwithstanding this, even has internal motion (§71).

§607. *What matter is.* Yet let us investigate properly a bit more what the constitution of a body is and how much we can actually investigate it so that we can find the proper ground of everything that is ascribed to it. We have seen that every body is extended and for that reason can be divided into many parts (§606), and experience reinforces this for the bodies of our world as well. Besides, we find that every body has a power of resisting motion so that it cannot be put into motion unless its resistance is overcome. Suppose one places a weight on a scale that hangs from a beam and lets the pan rest so that the weight is not pulled down too far. If one wanted to pull this weight up high by pressing down with one's hand on the other, free-standing pan, it would resist by means of its gravity. For this reason, one needs great power to press down on the one pan and thereby raise the other up high with its weight. However, if one places a counterweight on the other pan that is equal to that of the first pan, the resistance is thereby removed. And in that case one needs little power to lift the weight in the other pan. Now, what gives a body extension with its resisting force is called **matter**. However, from the preceding we know that extension, along with persistence in a place, comes from the simples things as elements (§603, 605), and matter, accordingly, is not a messy lump, that is, is not a heap of identical parts that are thrown together in which nothing other than size could be distinguished, but rather everything in it is distinguished from everything else in a wholly special way. And the vulgar concept of matter – since one represents it as a powerless lump whose parts, taken together, can be assumed to be as large or small as one likes – arises merely from the imagination, which represents the matter indistinctly and, for this reason, overlooks what is in it (§214).

§608.[38] *No body moves itself.* Since matter has a power of resisting motion (§607), no body can move itself, and accordingly it must have an external cause, if it is to be moved (§30, 29).

§609. *No body impedes its motion that it was put into [from without].* By the same token, because nothing can occur that does not have its sufficient ground for why it exists rather than does not exist (§30), once a body has been put in motion, it cannot cease again unless an external cause is found for why it occurs. And in this way it is evident that it must continue to move itself constantly in one direction, if nothing changes its bearing.

§610. *Constancy in rest and motion.* In this fashion every body remains either at rest or in its motion, and retains one direction in its motion, until it is put into a different state by another, all of which one also finds thus in experience, and is taken as an immutable law of nature by those who investigate the rules of motion.[*]

§615. *Changes in bodies occur through motion.* By the same token, in bodies just as in composite things (§606), no change can occur except in the size, shape, or place of either the parts or the whole (§72). Now since none of these can occur without a change of place (§65, 68, 47), all changes occur through motion (§57).

---

[38] §§608–610 and 615 are relevant to the Second Analogy of Experience (A189/B232ff.) and the *Metaphysical Foundations'* Mechanics (4:543–544).

[*] *Newton in Princip. Phil. Nat. Math.* p. 12 edit. sec. [Wolff is referring here to Newton's first law of motion, on page 12 of the second edition of the *Principia*.]

CHAPTER FIVE. ON THE ESSENCE OF THE SOUL AND OF A SPIRIT IN GENERAL

§727.[39] *Present intention.* I already treated the soul extensively above in the third chapter, but only insofar as we can perceive its effects and attain a distinct concept of it (§191). We must now investigate what the essence of the soul and of a spirit in general consists in, and how it grounds what we perceive of it and have noted about it above. In this [investigation], various aspects of the soul can be treated to which experience does not immediately lead us. And in this fashion one can see that what was cited above about the soul on the basis of experience is the touchstone of what is taught here of its nature and essence and of the effects that are grounded in it; what is taught here, however, is in no way at all the touchstone of what experience teaches us.

§728.[40] *Why we start with consciousness.* The first thing that we noted about ourselves is that we are conscious of ourselves and of other things external to us (§1), that is, we know that we currently represent many things as external to us. [...] For this reason let us now investigate how it happens that we are aware of that.

§730. *When we are aware of ourselves.* From this it is clear when we are aware of ourselves, namely, when we notice the difference between ourselves and other things of which we are aware. However, this difference is immediately revealed as soon as we are aware of other things. For if we are to be aware of what we cognize through our senses, then we must notice the differences between what we perceive in it, and even immediately distinguish that which we cognize thereby from other things (§729). Yet the representation of things as well as this [act of] distinguishing (which seems to be even clearer) is an activity [*Würckung*] of the soul, and we accordingly cognize thereby the difference between the soul and those things that are represented and that it distinguishes. And accordingly, we are also conscious of ourselves (§729). [...]

§735.[41] *How it actually occurs that we are conscious.* And now we comprehend how it actually occurs that we are conscious, that is, that we know what we

---

[39] This entire chapter is relevant to the Paralogisms.
[40] §§728, 730, and 735–736 are relevant to the Transcendental Deduction (A84–A130/ B116–B169).
[41] See A99–A104 (Transcendental Deduction), where Kant makes a similar claim.

are thinking, or why our thoughts bring consciousness along with them (§194). Namely, when I think something, I hold onto a thought through a noticeable time and, as it were, distinguish it from itself through the parts of time that we distinguish from each other, albeit only indistinctly (§214). We hold it up against itself and cognize that it is still the same (§17), and in this way we think at the same time that we have had it from this time forth. And thus memory and reflection [*Überdenken*] produce consciousness (§733, 734).

§736.[42] *Every thought has its measured* [abgemessene] *time*. Because various [thoughts] in the soul must take place successively in this fashion if it is to be conscious of a thing (§735), consciousness requires time (§94). Now since our thoughts are changes in the soul that we are conscious of (§194), every thought occurs in time, or every thought has its measured time.

§738.[43] *No body can think*. All changes in a body occur through motion (§615) and have their ground in the size, shape, and position of its parts (§614). Therefore, if a body were to think, thoughts would have to be a change that occurred in the position of several parts of a certain size and shape through a determinate motion. Now if a thought is to be held onto for a certain time, either the parts would have to be held in their position and thus their motion impeded, or other, similar parts would have to be put in their place through a similar motion. Further, if the body is supposed to be conscious of this change, the two similar states of the body (§18) would have to be compared to each other, and one would have to note their intrinsic similarity, but [also] their differences according to time as well as with respect to its body (§733). Now since this cannot be achieved through the motion of parts, given that they can represent nothing further than something composed by its size, shape, and place, a body cannot be conscious of this change and of the representation that is thereby brought about (§735). Thus, because thoughts bring consciousness along with it (§194), no body can think.

§741. *A body cannot receive a power to think*. I know perfectly well that some are of the opinion that God could give bodies or, as they sometimes put it more crudely, matter the power to think. We have seen (§738) that no thought can come from the essence and nature of a body and, when

---

[42] See A99.
[43] §738 and 741–742 are relevant to the Second Paralogism (A351/B407ff.).

they desire that God should give such a power to bodies, they themselves cognize the point. In this way, God would have to make it be the case that something could follow from the essence of a body that cannot follow from it, and accordingly change its essence, or at the same time give it the essence of another thing from which the thoughts could come. Now, however, it is well known that the essence of a thing is immutable (§42) just as it is that the essence of one thing cannot be given to another thing (§43). And accordingly, saying that God should give matter the power to think is tantamount to desiring that God should at the same time turn iron into gold so that it would be iron and gold at the same time.

§742. *The soul is a simple thing.* Because a body cannot think according to its essence and its nature (§738, 739), and because neither a body nor matter can be given the power to think (§741), the soul cannot be anything corporeal and cannot consist of matter (§192). And since it is clear from the proofs of the stated grounds that thoughts cannot be attributed to a composite thing, the soul must be a simple thing (§75).

§743.[44] *It subsists by itself.* Since all simple things are things that subsist by themselves (§127), the soul, too, must be a self-subsisting thing (§742).

§744.[45] *Has a power.* Again, since every self-subsisting thing has a power from which its changes flow as from a source (§114, 115), the soul, too, must have such a power from which its changes flow, which we have determined from experience above in the third chapter.

§745. *And only a single one.* Further, since it is a simple thing (§742), but there can be no parts in a simple thing (§75), a plurality of powers distinct from each other cannot be found in the soul either, because otherwise every power would require a self-subsisting thing to which it would be ascribed (§127). Namely, a power consists in a striving to do something (§117) and thus different powers require different strivings. It is not possible that a simple thing can have different strivings at the same time, because it would be as if a body, which is to be viewed in its motion as an indivisible thing (§667), should move in different directions at the same time. And thus there exists in the soul only a single power

[44] §§743–748 are relevant to the First Paralogism (A348/B407ff.).
[45] §§744–747 are relevant to A648–A649/B676–B677 (Appendix to the Transcendental Dialectic), where Kant discusses the attempt to seek some one fundamental power of the human mind.

from which all its changes derive, even if we typically attribute different names to it due to its different changes.

§746. *This is illustrated with an analogy.* We even find it to be such in corporeal things. E.g., there is nothing more in the flame of a burning light than one single power, namely, the motive power due to which the flame moves. However, we give this single power several names because of the differences in its effects. For if we see that a light shines, we attribute a shining power to it. If we perceive that the flame heats, we say that it has a heating power. In the same fashion one posits in it an igniting power when it ignites something, a burning power when it burns, a scorching power when it scorches, and so on.

§747. *A single power in the soul brings about different effects.* Accordingly, the senses (§220), the imagination (§235), memory (§249), the faculty of reflection (§272), the understanding (§277), sensuous desires (§434), the will (§492), and whatever else one can distinguish by changes perceived in the soul cannot be different powers (§745). For this reason the single power of the soul must bring about sensations, images, distinct concepts, syllogisms, desires, willing and not willing, and yet other changes. And we shall have the task of investigating where this difference in effects comes from in the single efficacious power.

§748. *How one comes to cognize it.* In order to learn how to cognize this power, we must reflect on [*nachdenken*] those changes that occur in the soul. For, since the soul is the source of changes (§115), it presents itself to cognition only through the changes that it brings about.

§753. *The soul has a power of representing the world.* I already remarked above that sensations are oriented toward the changes that occur in sense organs (§219), and represent those mundane bodies that touch our senses (§217, 220). But these bodies are a part of the world (§606). And thus the soul represents part of the world, or as much of the world as is allowed by the position of its body in the world; consequently, since the effects of the soul derive from its power (§744), the soul has the power of representing the world according to the state of its body in the world.

§769. *Sensations are similar to the things sensed.* Accordingly, because the soul has a power of representing the world (§753), these representations must also be similar to the things that exist in the world. For if they were not similar, the soul would represent not the world, but rather something else. A picture that is not similar to the object that it is to represent is a picture not of it, but of another thing (§17, 18).

§770. *Represent only sizes, shapes, and motions.* Now since the world consists solely of composite things, yet nothing other than shapes, sizes, and motions can be distinguished in them (§72), all sensations of corporeal things must represent nothing other than shapes, sizes, and motions (§769).

§878. *How desires and willing arise in the soul.* And hence we can understand how sensuous desires and the will do not require a special power of the representing power of the soul. Namely, we saw above that sensuous desires as well as the will stem from representations of the good (§434, 492). Now, since we have pleasure in the good that we represent (§404, 422), the soul is thereby determined to strive to bring about the sensation of it or (which is the same) it thereby determines itself to bring about this sensation. And the inclination that is sometimes called sensuous desire and sometimes called the will consists in this striving, but, accordingly, is still nothing other than a striving to bring about a sensation that we cognize or, as it were, see previously.

§906. *Human beings do not have perfect reason.* Since it is not possible that a human being can have insight into the connection of all truths, because he does not comprehend everything distinctly (§285), he also does not have perfect reason (§905).

§907. *Most perfect will.* However, the will is perfect if each and every willing corresponds with each other and none conflicts with any other (§152). But this cannot happen unless its motive is the representation of the best. For if we represent the best completely, it is not possible that we could want something once that we did not want at another time (§496). Accordingly, the most perfect will is one that has a complete representation of the best as its motive.

§909. *A human being does not have a perfect will.* Now since a human being cannot have an overview of his whole life, he is also not in a position to judge what is best; rather, if he proceeds quite a ways, he can judge what is better among what he cognizes. For this reason, human beings do not have a perfect will in the highest degree (§907).

CHAPTER SIX. ON GOD

§928.[46] *It is a necessary being.* We exist (§1). Everything that exists has its sufficient ground why it exists rather than does not exist (§30) and, therefore, we must have a sufficient ground why we exist. If we have a sufficient ground why we exist, that ground must be found either within us or external to us. If it is to be found within us, then we exist necessarily (§32), but if it is to be found in something else, then that something else must have in itself its ground why it exists and thus exists necessarily. Accordingly, there is a necessary being. Whoever might object that the ground for our existence could be found in something that does not have in itself the ground for its existence does not understand what a sufficient ground is. For one must in turn ask further of such a thing what has the ground for its existence, and one must ultimately arrive at something that needs no external ground for its existence. But in order to learn now whether we ourselves are such a being or whether it is some-thing else, we intend to investigate its properties to see whether they can be attributed to our soul or not.

§989. *If and how one can appeal to the will of God.* Now since the divine understanding is the source of essences, or of what is possible (§975), whereas the divine will is the source of actuality (§988), one can never appeal to the will of God when asking about how something is possible, but rather only when one desires to know why something is actual, and even here, one cannot appeal to the divine will *simpliciter* due to his motive, namely, the greater perfection of things (§981). Besides this, since one state of the world comes from another (§544) and, for this reason, is itself also a sufficient ground of actuality in the world in par-ticular cases (§29), one can never appeal to the divine will unless one is talking about the whole world in general. I am speaking here only of those things that happen naturally, as is the case in this whole book.

§1026. *[God] acts according to intentions.* Accordingly, God does not actu-alize everything indiscriminately, but rather only what he has previously thought should occur (§988). Now since he lets the perfection of the world move him (§981), but this comes from the coherence of things and their events (§152), he thus sought to retain these events and the

---

[46] See the Third and Fourth Antinomies and On the Impossibility of a Cosmological Proof (A603/B631ff.).

perfections that thereby arise in the world, and accordingly they are all to be viewed as his intentions (§910). And in such fashion it is clear that God acts according to intentions. One can also establish this in another way. Every rational being acts according to intentions (§911). God is the most rational being (§974) and, therefore, he must act completely according to intentions. I say, God acts completely according to intentions. For we human beings act according to intentions too, but because we do not have a perfect reason (§906) and for that reason do not have complete insight into the connection with other things that we seek (§368), many of our actions get conflated with things that we did not propose to do, and accordingly much occurs without our intentions. However, because God completely comprehends all connection (§972), there is nothing in the least that he did not foresee (§968) and incorporate into his intentions.

§1027. *That intentions [are] everywhere in nature.* And hence it is evident that nature is full of divine intentions that God seeks to retain through the essences of things. [...]

§1067. *What the divine essence consists in.* Everything that we have previously established about God comes from [the fact] that he can distinctly represent all at once everything that is possible. And accordingly the divine essence consists in the power to represent distinctly [and] all at once everything that is possible, that is, all worlds (§33). And accordingly, the divine essence is somewhat similar to the essence of our soul in this respect (§755).

§1076.[47] *Whence we have a concept of God and his properties.* Because the divine essence is similar to the essence of our soul (§1067), but the soul cognizes itself (§730) and thus has a concept of itself (§273), we thereby also have a concept of God. For since our essence and the properties grounded in it are limited (§783), whereas God is infinite in everything (§1072), if we only leave off the limitations of our essence and our properties, we get concepts of the essence and properties of God.

§1077. *Elucidated by an example.* The essence of the soul consists in the power of representing the world according to the state of its body in the world

---

[47] §§1076–1079 are relevant to The Transcendental Ideal (A571/B599ff., esp. A580/B608) and the Critique of All Speculative Theology (A695/B724).

and the changes that occur, for that reason, in its sense organs (§755). The limitations of this power are (1) that the soul represents only this and no other world; (2) that this representation is oriented toward the state of its body and, for that reason, represents only few things clearly, little of it distinctly, and even this only in succession. Accordingly, if one leaves off these limitations and accordingly puts all worlds in place of the one world, if one further extends distinctness to everything that is to be found in them, if, finally, one leaves time out so that everything is represented all at once, the result is a power that represents all worlds simultaneously with complete distinctness, that is, the divine essence or its first concept, from which the rest can be derived (§1067). One can attempt this in similar fashion with the remaining properties.

§1078. *How concepts of God are possible.* And hence we understand why it is possible that we can proceed from cognition of our soul to concepts of the divine essence and perfections. Namely, it is proper, because we have a figurative cognition (§316) by means of which we can distinguish what is found next to and within each other in intuitive cognition. For we may leave out only those words or signs that indicate limitations, and posit those in their stead that signify the liberation of all limits; accordingly, the words or other signs represent the unlimited in God.

§1079.[48] *Constitution of cognition of God.* Accordingly, it is clear that in this world we do not have an intuitive, but rather only a figurative cognition of God (§1078). Whatever intuitive [element] is found in this case belongs to our soul (§1076), and in such a fashion that we now see God only through our soul (§1076) and the world (§1046) as if in a mirror.

---

[48] See *Inaugural Dissertation* (2:396).

Martin Knutzen

Martin Knutzen was born in Königsberg in 1713 and, like Kant, lived there his entire life, attending first a traditional elementary school (though not the Collegium Fridericianum, as Kant did) and then the university, from which he graduated in 1734. Supported by Friedrich Albert Schultz, who was one of his professors and a leading Pietist at the university, he was offered and accepted the extraordinary professorship of logic and metaphysics at the early age of twenty-one. Over the next seventeen years Knutzen forged a distinctive synthesis of religious Pietism, Leibnizian-Wolffian metaphysics, and Lockean epistemology, while lecturing and publishing with considerable popularity on a wide range of topics in logic, philosophy, and mathematics. Historical evidence suggests that Kant attended his lectures and even received personal attention from him outside of class. Knutzen's death in 1751, at the age of thirty-eight, cut short a fairly distinguished, even if not exceptional, academic career.

Despite his early death, Knutzen established himself as the best and most influential philosopher in Königsberg in the 1730s and 1740s by publishing a number of substantive works in natural theology, logic, astronomy, and metaphysics. In 1740 he published an extremely popular work in natural theology, *Philosophischer Beweis von der Wahrheit der christlichen Religion* (Philosophical Proof of the Truth of the Christian Religion), a work that was directed primarily against English deists and went through five editions before 1763. In 1747 he published a textbook in logic (*Elementa philosophiae rationalis seu logicae;* Elements of Rational Philosophy or Logic), which displays a Lockean epistemology in its insistence that internal and external experience is the source of all of our cognition. In astronomy Knutzen received considerable attention for having predicted that a comet would appear in

1744 and that it would be the same as one that had last been visible in 1698. This interest in comets is documented in the publication of *Vernünftige Gedanken von den Cometen* (Rational Thoughts on Comets) in 1744. Knutzen's fame in astronomy was severely tarnished when Euler demonstrated that the comet that did in fact appear in 1744 could not be identical to the 1698 comet given that the former would require an orbit of over 400 years rather than a mere forty-six. This should not, however, detract from Knutzen's importance, since his greatest significance stems from his contributions to metaphysics. His first dissertation, which he defended in 1733, was on the impossibility of the eternity of the world and was followed, in 1735, by his most important philosophical work, *Commentatio philosophica de commercio mentis et corporis per influxum physicum explicando* (Philosophical Commentary on the Commerce of the Body and the Mind Explained by Physical Influx), which presented a defense of "physical influx" against preestablished harmony and occasionalism. Due to its importance, this work was reprinted in 1745 as *Systema Causarum Efficientium* (System of Efficient Causes) along with *Commentatio philosophica de humanae mentis individua natura sive immaterialitate* (Philosophical Commentary on the Individual Nature or Immortality of the Human Mind) a treatise that was originally published in 1741 and then translated into German in 1744 as *Philosophische Abhandlung von der immateriellen Natur der Seele* (Philosophical Treatise on the Immaterial Nature of the Soul).

Knutzen's *System of Efficient Causes* divides into three parts. Part One sets up the basic philosophical framework by laying out the three different causal theories at issue, namely, physical influx (which asserts intersubstantial causation), occasionalism (which denies all finite causation), and preestablished harmony (which denies intersubstantial in favor of intrasubstantial causation), and by arguing that each of these theories is fully consistent with our observation of the *commercium*, or commerce, of mind and body, that is, the correlations that hold between the mind's representations and the body's motions. Part Two contains a series of detailed arguments in support of physical influx, arguments that are of particular note because of the way in which Knutzen presses a point that was perceived at the time to be especially difficult for Leibniz and Wolff, namely, how to explain in a precise way the relationship between the fundamental metaphysical level (of monads or elements) and the level of physical bodies that we perceive. Accordingly, Knutzen argues that one monad ought to be able to act on other monads if monads are ultimately to be held responsible for the physical properties of bodies. In Part Three Knutzen then develops detailed responses to a number of (at the time, well-known) objections to physical influx. Against the background of Leibniz and Wolff, what is particularly significant is not that Knutzen argues for a position that is opposed to Leibniz's and Wolff's views, but rather that he does so on the basis of Leibnizian-Wolffian principles. Knutzen's views on causality are also of tremendous importance for Kant insofar as they are highly relevant not only to several of his pre-Critical publications (e.g., the *New Elucidation, Physical Monadology,* and *Inaugural Dissertation*), but also to the first *Critique,* since these issues are discussed in the Second and Third Analogies of Experience, the Amphiboly, and the Second and Third Antinomies, and also bear on his doctrine of Transcendental Idealism, insofar as it can be seen as a reaction to Knutzen's way of explicating the relationship between fundamental reality and what appears to us in the physical world.

In his *Philosophical Treatise on the Immaterial Nature of the Human Soul,* Knutzen presents an extended argument for the immateriality and simplicity of the soul, noting that our knowledge of the existence of God as well as of the soul's immortality and freedom depends on our cognition of the nature of the human soul, a point that is reminiscent of Kant's characterization of traditional metaphysics in the second edition Preface of the first *Critique.* Knutzen's main argument, which is directed primarily against materialists who attempted to exploit Locke's suggestion that matter might be able to think (should God desire it to be so), rests on the claim that matter, which essentially involves a plurality of beings, is incompatible with the unity and simplicity that is required for conscious thought. Knutzen's argument thus differs significantly from Wolff's, which depends – as we saw above at §738 and §741 of his *Rational Thoughts* – on the assumption that the only changes that matter can undergo are changes in motion. In the course of this argument, Knutzen thus raises a number of considerations that are very closely related to Kant's discussion of the self in both the Transcendental Deduction (especially in the second edition) and the Paralogisms (where Kant explicitly considers what is often referred to as the "unity argument"). Knutzen's argument is also based on an understanding of what a substance is (insofar as he equates the subject of thought with a thinking substance) so that his discussion is also relevant to Kant's First Analogy of Experience.

SYSTEM OF EFFICIENT CAUSES (1735)[1]

SECTION I ON THE COMMERCE OF THE MIND AND THE HUMAN BODY, AND THE VARIOUS WAYS OF EXPLAINING IT IN GENERAL

§1. *What the commerce of the mind and the body is.*

The commerce of the mind and the human body is the dependence of those perceptions through which things are represented as located external to us on the changes of our body, especially on those that occur in the sensory organs of the body, and no less the dependence of certain motions in the body on the desires of the mind with respect to the determination of their kind and coexistence (or, if you prefer, immediate succession).

[...]

§7. *The reality of commerce between the mind and the body is established.*

The commerce of the mind and the human body is supported by the indubitable testimony of experience. For we are said to experience whatever we observe when attending to our perceptions (§664 of Wolff's *Logic. Lat.*). But when we attend to our perceptions, we observe that certain mental perceptions are always joined with motions that are caused by external objects in our sense organs (§2) and by other conditions in our body (§3). Similarly, we observe that determinate motions are aroused in the body as soon as either the mind's will or the sensitive appetite requires such things (§5). These observations support the dependence of representations on motions in the sense organs and on other conditions in the body (§4) and the dependence of motions on mental passions (§6) with respect to the determination of their kind and either their coexistence or their immediate succession. Therefore, it has been shown by the indubitable testimony of experience that there is commerce of the mind and the body (§1).

[...]

---

[1] Translated from *Systema Causarum Efficientium* (Leipzig, 1745). Knutzen's text is divided up into a series of points (§§) that have a heading, a main text, and then a detailed commentary on the main text, which is often quite lengthy, single spaced, and in a smaller font. The same sort of textual structure is repeated in his work on the immaterial nature of the soul.

§10.[2] *What is the system of physical influx or of efficient causes?*

There is no *physical influx of the mind on the body and of the body on the mind* unless there is a real action of the mind on the body or of the body on the mind. *The system of physical influx or of efficient causes,* however, is where the commerce between the mind and the body is explained through the physical influx of the mind on the body and of the body on the mind.

[...]

§11. *There are various kinds of physical influx.*

There are as many kinds of physical influx of the mind on the body and of the body on the mind as there are special ways of conceiving of the action of the mind on the body and in turn of the body on the mind: and whoever admits physical influx in a general sense, for the purpose of [admitting] a single kind, surely is not required to defend the other ones. Undoubtedly, from a given general notion specific notions are discovered – if those which are contained indeterminately in the general notions are determined (§712 Log.). Surely no mode of action is determinate in the general concept of influx (§10). Therefore, if the latter is determined, particular kinds of physical influx appear, and indeed there are as many [such kinds] as there are ways in which the reason for acting (which was first) is determined.

§12.[3] *The system of occasional causes is defined.*

The system of occasional causes is a ground for explaining the commerce of the mind and the body, according to which it is asserted that those changes that depend on others in commerce, with respect to their kind or co-existence, are harmoniously produced by a Being distinct from

---

[2] For an apparent dig at Knutzen's version of physical influx, see *New Elucidation* (1:415–416) and *Inaugural Dissertation* (2:407). For Kant's acceptance of (a version of) physical influx during the pre-Critical period, see Section 3 of *New Elucidation* and *Inaugural Dissertation*, especially 2:389–391 and 2:406–409. In the first *Critique*, Kant explicitly discusses physical influx as applied to the mind–body relationship at A381–A394 (Observations on the Paralogisms).

[3] See A390–A391 (Observations on the Paralogisms). See also the *Inaugural Dissertation* (2:409).

the mind and the body, undoubtedly God thrice greatest and most powerful, according to the presence of directives.[4]

[...]

§13.[5] *What is the system of pre-established harmony or harmonious causes?*

The system of pre-established harmony is a way of explaining the commerce of the mind and body according to which it is supposed that the changes of the mind that depend on the body follow from its own power of mind according to logical-moral laws, and according to which the motions of the body that are dependent on the mind follow from the structure and motive force of the body according to physico-mechanical rules, in such a way, however, that they correspond to its directives from the most wise pre-ordination of God.

[...]

§15. *Experience is insufficient to distinguish the truth of the system of commerce of the mind and the body.*

None of the systems mentioned is established immediately through experience. For however much we direct the mind to our perceptions, even if the coexistence of one kind of change of determinations of the mind and the body is observed in the commerce of the mind and the body (§7), we by no means perceive actions. Therefore, we experience no action of the mind on the body or vice versa (§664 Log.). For that reason the system of physical influx is not established through experience (§10). Much less do we observe the immediate action of God on the mind and the body, namely, the production of voluntary motions in the body and of sensual representations in the mind by intrinsic powers, merely by observing the attention [we pay] to those things that we perceive. Therefore, no subject is pre-established before our perceptions. Therefore, neither the system of occasional causes (§12) nor the system of pre-established harmony (§13) is established through experience.

[...]

---

[4] In §1 Knutzen introduces a distinction between directives and dependents in order to distinguish between those changes in the mind and body that depend on others from those that do not, but rather on which the others depend. Dependents are the former, directives the latter.

[5] See A390–A391 (Observations on the Paralogisms) and B331 (The Amphiboly Chapter). See also *Inaugural Dissertation* (2:409).

SECTION II ON THE SYSTEM OF PHYSICAL INFLUX AS
THE TRUE GROUND FOR EXPLAINING THE COMMERCE OF
THE MIND AND THE BODY

§17. *What is the human mind?*

The human mind is a spirit that represents the world to itself in accordance with those changes that occur in a certain organic *body* that it calls *its* or *its own*.

Because I now undertake the demonstration of physical influx, the laws of method demand that I develop more distinct concepts of those things whose mutual action on each other I want to demonstrate, although as long as I consider them in general, the ideas of these things seem sufficiently clear to me. Therefore I now assert definitions of the mind and the body along with their connections to others, which I limit to the concepts of motion and representation, since they are effects or consequences of its action. Finally, I turn to the *other* ones that are necessary for carrying out the demonstration. [...]

§18.[6] *Definition of a spirit and monad.*

A *spirit* is a simple substance endowed with an intellect and a free will. A *simple substance or monad* is a substance lacking parts. Hence it is clear that the mind *takes pleasure in its intellect and free will* (§17), and because what lacks parts is immaterial, the *soul* is an *immaterial substance*.
   [...]

§19. *What are composites and bodies?*

Composites are those things that consist of parts. Yet those composite or extended entities that exist in the world are called *bodies*.
   [...]

§20.[7] *The existence of monads in bodies or the composition of bodies from monads is established.*

Bodies consist of simples or monads. Bodies are composite entities (§19) and therefore consist of parts (according to the same §). Either these parts

---

[6] See *Dreams of a Spirit-Seer* (2:319–322).
[7] See the Second Antinomy. See also *Physical Monadology* (1:477).

will be in turn composite, that is, they will have other parts that again have others and so on to infinity, or one must at last reach parts that do not consist of others. If the former, there will be an infinite number of parts the existence of which implies a contradiction (as is demonstrated in the diss. *de Aeternitate Mundi impossibili* §21). Therefore, a body is composed of parts that do not have other parts. Therefore, it consists of simples, or monads (§18).

[...]

§21. *What is action?*

A being is said to *act* when it contains in itself the reason for the existence (or change) of a certain thing.

[...]

§22. *What is force* [vis][8] *and principle? The canon concerning forces.*

A *force* is that which contains the sufficient reason for the actuality of an action or is the striving [*conatus*] for action. A *principle* is that which contains in itself the reason for another thing and therefore force is the principle of changes (§21). Because it cannot be, however, that after having posited the sufficient reason of the actuality of an action it not attain its act, unless something stands in the way, *a certain action arises from a continuous force as long as no hindrance intervenes.*

[...]

§23.[9] *What is space, what fills space, what are place and position?*

Space is the order of coexistent things insofar as they coexist. An entity in which there is an order of coexistents as such is said to fill space. *Place* is a finite and determinate mode of coexisting with *other* coexisting things, i.e., it is the order of continuous coexistent things. *Position* is the order of non-continuous coexistent things. *Therefore, whatever has a place or is in a place is also in space. However, diverse entities (I speak of finite substances) cannot be in one place at the same time.* (§610 of Wolff's *Ontol.*).

[...]

---

[8] In other works in this volume, *vis* is often translated as power rather than force. Force is preferred in the present case, however, because Knutzen's discussion focuses on physics, where force sounds more natural in most contexts.

[9] See the Transcendental Aesthetic (esp. A22/B37ff.).

§24. *What in particular are internal and total motion, and motive, primitive, and derivative force?*

Motion is the continuous and successive change of place. The change of position that the parts in an entity maintain with respect to each other is *internal motion*. The motion of all this is in fact called the *total motion*. A *moving force* is that which contains in itself the reason for the actuality of some motion or is a striving [*conatus*] to move. A *primitive moving* force is what is inherent in the movable per se. A *derivative* moving force is what results through a modification of the primitive force. From what has been said it follows that because nothing is without a sufficient reason *a being that moves itself or other things takes pleasure in the force of moving.*
   [...]

§25. *Motion changes nothing intrinsically in what is moved. What is real in motion?*

Insofar as we regard motion as change with respect to place or we consider motion in itself, that which moves introduces no intrinsic change to itself. But even if you wished to turn your attention to what is intrinsic to what is moved while it is moved, or to what is real in motion, you would surely find an instantaneous striving to change its own place. For since place does not exist except as a mode of coexisting with other things (§23), it surely does not exist except as a relation to other coexisting things, and therefore is nothing unless it involves a being extrinsically, it therefore follows that its change as such brings about no change intrinsic to what is moved. Therefore, motion such as it is changes nothing of what is intrinsic to a being (§24). Since, however, the moveable that changes place is also endowed with a motive force (§24) and no one has denied that this same force is something intrinsic, because it is intelligible per se and it is, therefore, something real, it follows that the real in motion or what is intrinsic to the moveable is the instantaneous striving to move or the striving to change its place.
   [...]

§26.[10] *What is completely determined?*

I call *completely* determined that in which nothing a thing can-not exist without ought still to be posited or determined. However,

---

[10] See A571/B599ff.

because everyone understands that a thing cannot exist without those things it is impossible for it to exist without, *all things are completely determined.*

[...]

§27.[11] *It is demonstrated that simple elements are in a place and are moved, although they do not fill a space.*

The simples of which bodies consist, I demonstrated above (§19), and that I will henceforth call **elements** *are in a place and are moved. Still, they do not fill up a place or a space.* Since everything that exists is completely determinate (§26), even simples will be completely determinate as long as they coexist; and they will, therefore, have a determinate way of coexisting with other things, i.e., a place, because there is no doubt about the finitude of these things (§23). However, ordinary experience clearly shows anyone that bodies, which are encountered in the world by the senses, change their place or are moved, yet these surely consist of the simple elements as parts (§20), and to this extent simples change their places or are moved, unless you wish to concede that a whole whose parts have remained in their previous place can be moved. Nevertheless, the simples do not consist of parts as bodies do, but are rather destitute of all parts (§19). Therefore, it is impossible that there be an order of coexistent things in them: For this reason they do not fill a space, although they are in space (§23).

[...]

§28. A *force [of something] to move itself involves in reality a force of moving another as well.*

A force of moving that brings it about that any thing changes its own proper place without the force of moving other things that surround it cannot be conceived, but rather it is necessary that when the one is posited, the other is posited at the same time. For a force of moving that brings it about that a thing changes its own place does not exist except as a striving to change its own place (§24), i.e., to occupy a place that is distinct from the one that it now occupies, yet one that is still continuous to it (§ cit.). But since two distinct beings cannot be in one place at the same time (§23), other coexistent things that surround that movable thing on all sides

[11] See the Second Antinomy and *Physical Monadology* (1:480ff).

occupy a place distinct from the place of the moveable thing. Therefore, a thing endowed with the force of moving itself strives to push things to another place, if they resist. But if in fact they are also supposed to yield spontaneously, nevertheless, what is already participating in progressive motion exerts itself in the way that is required to complete the motion beyond itself or to push things to another place. Because resistance is to such a degree the occasional cause of motion, it does not add anything to the intrinsic force. Therefore, a thing that moves itself enjoys the striving to change the place of coexistents or the force of moving other things (§24). Therefore, the force of moving itself without the force of moving other things cannot be conceived, but after the one has been posited, the other is posited at the same time.

[…]

§29. *The real, mutual action of simple elements on each other is demonstrated.*

Simple elements not only can act mutually on each other, but they also act on each other mutually in reality, [and] not merely apparently. For assume simples do not act mutually on each other. Since it was demonstrated that simple elements are moved (§27) and nothing exists without a sufficient reason, it is necessary that a sufficient reason for this motion be present. It is surely impossible that this reason be contained in the other simples, contiguous or external to the simple that is moved. For the other simples act mutually on each other (§21), which is contrary to the hypothesis. Therefore, the reason for the motion of the simples is contained in those very simples that are moved. Therefore, they enjoy the force of moving themselves (§22), and since there is no force by which a being that moves itself without the force of moving other coexistent and contiguous things (§28), simple elements have a force of moving other simples that surround it, and to that extent they are powerful in this force of acting on these other simples (§22). And because a force posits not only the potentiality or mere possibility of acting, but a certain continuous action is also then produced unless hindrance intervenes (§22), surely no hindrance of this kind can be conceived now and the pre-established running through of other simples on account of the most skilled internal divine pre-determination would be assumed without reason, because the possibility or rather the striving to bring about or determine the motions of other things is already present in the simples which would then be useless. Simple elements act on each other mutually and they really do so, not [merely] apparently. The same can also be demonstrated another way. Simple elements are impenetrable, according to the opinion of the illustrious Leibniz, who asserts that all finite substances are impenetrable. See his Letter to the celebrated **Wagner** p. 201. Tom. I. Epist. Edit. Kortholtianae.[12] Hence, it cannot be the case that one substance is in the place of another. Therefore, there is something real, by whose force one simple excludes another and pushes up against [it], lest the other invade its place. Since it is most certain that simples are moved (§27) and that distinct simples are not moved along a contrary line of direction, it is consequently impossible that they mutually resist each other; and indeed what we may gather from the conflict of bodies and their collision is that they are in fact carried in a contrary direction mutually away from each other. It follows in this case that one must hold that either simples penetrate each other mutually, which goes against Leibniz's assertions, or if they resist each other mutually, they must act on each other mutually. Q.E.D.

[…]

§30. *What are perception and representation?*

Perception is the representation of external things in a simple thing. Now in general a thing is said *to represent external* things if, on the basis of what is observed or is present in it, one can understand what external things are like.

[…]

---

[12] This letter, from Leibniz to Rudolph Christian Wagner, dated June 4, 1710, is reprinted in *Die Philosophischen Schriften von Leibniz*, ed. C. I. Gerhardt, 7 vols. (Berlin: Weidmann, 1875–1890), vol. 7, pp. 528–532. Leibniz does not explicitly assert that monads are impenetrable, but he does make a series of remarks that could naturally be interpreted that way. For example, he says: "I respond, secondly, that the resistance of bare [or prime] matter is not an action, but a mere passion, as long, of course, as it has antitypy or impenetrability by which in fact it resists the thing about to penetrate, but it does not make that thing rebound unless an elastic force is added that must be derived from what is moved and therefore from an active force that is superadded to matter." While it is not absolutely necessary to assume that impenetrability is to be identified with the resistance of prime matter, one can certainly excuse Knutzen for reading Leibniz in this way. Moreover, later, Leibniz concludes: "Only God is a substance truly separate from matter, because he is pure act, is not at all endowed with the capability of being acted on, that is everywhere, and constitutes matter. And in fact all created substances have antitypy by means of which it naturally occurs that one is outside [*extra*] another, and therefore penetration is excluded." Knutzen could easily take the "one" referred to in the last sentence as referring to "created substances," which are implicitly characterized in the previous sentence merely as being capable of being acted on.

§31. *Simple elements or elementary monads perceive.*

Simple substances that constitute a certain body, or individual elements, perceive external things or have perceptions of external things. For simple elements act on each other mutually (§29), and accordingly contain in themselves the reason for the existence of the changes that occur in those things on which they act or in which they produce changes (§21); and accordingly the simples are the extrinsic, efficient causes of changes that occur in other simples (§886 of Wolff's *Ontol.*), and accordingly changes of this sort are their effects (§ cit.). But from the effect it is understood what sort of cause might have existed (§886 *Coll.* 881 *Ontol.*). Therefore, from the internal changes of the simples it can be gathered of what sort or in what state the external simples will have been, and therefore there is perception of external things in elementary simples (§30).

   [...]

§32. *Physical influx occurs by the action of one simple substance on others.*

The action of the mind on the simples of the body and of those simples in which bodies consist on the mind suffices for physical influx. For physical influx consists in the action of the mind on the body, and of the body on the mind (§10). But a body consists of the simples of which it is composed as of its parts (§20). Therefore, no one will deny that the mind acts on the body, if it acts on simples or on the body's parts. Nor will one be able to doubt the action of the body on the mind, if only one will have been convinced of the action of the simples of which the body is composed on the mind. Therefore, the action of the mind on corporeal simples and of the simples out of which bodies consist on the mind suffices for physical influx.

   [...]

§33. *Of what sort is absolute perfection? In God all perfections are absolute.*

Perfection which implies no limitation per se, that is, which can exist together with any other possible (as the Scholastics say) is called *perfection absolutely* or *simpliciter.* But in natural theology it is demonstrated that whatever is truly attributable to God, thrice greatest and most powerful, is a simple perfection simpliciter and it involves no contradiction except with limitations and imperfections.

   [...]

§34. *The possibility of physical influx is demonstrated.*

Physical influx is possible. Physical influx of the mind on corporeal simples and of those simples in turn on the mind is completed by an act (§32). Therefore, if physical influx is to be shown to be possible, then it must be shown in what way the action of the mind on other simples external to itself does not involve a contradiction (§85 *Ontol.*). Therefore, let us investigate whether one can discover anything in the mind that contradicts the mind's action on external things. We discover in the mind those things that primarily amount to this: that the mind is a simple thing and surely that this thing perceives or is a perceiver, and in a far greater degree of eminence than that of simple elements, since it perceives distinctly or is endowed with an intellect and a will (§17, 18). The action of the mind on external things cannot contradict [the] simplicity [of the mind] because not only does God, thrice greatest and most powerful, act outside himself (according to the *Princ. of Nat. Theol.*), but also the simple elements act on each other mutually (§29). Nor can this action contradict the mind insofar as it is a being that perceives or is perceiving, because simple elements take pleasure in the perception of external things (§31); yet an action of this kind cannot be denied to these simples. Therefore, nothing remains other than that eminent perfection by which the human mind is separated from simples that have inferior perceptions, and that places the faculties of understanding and willing in the mind, and if the external action of the mind does not contradict this, then the possibility of physical influx will have been established beyond doubt. But action on external things is a simple perfection because it can be ascribed to God, thrice greatest and most powerful (§33), and it cannot, therefore, be inconsistent except with limitation and imperfection (§ cit.). Therefore, it cannot be inconsistent with intellect and volition, which exceed the faculty of mere perception, and which at the same time confer a greater perfection on the thing, since, as was already shown, this kind of action is agreeable with a merely perceptive being and a more perfect being. Therefore, who could doubt that the mind can act on the body? However, because it was demonstrated above (§29) that action on other simples must be attributed to the simples of which the body consists, surely the mind, insofar as it is a simple substance, can act on such simples (according to the demonstr.). There will be no reason why anyone should judge the action of the body's simples on the mind to be impossible. Therefore, it is established that physical influx is possible.

[...]

§35. *The probability of the system of influx is shown.*

The system of physical influx is quite probable. Quite probable is that in which we notice hardly a few conditions or characteristics of the truth (§578 of Wolff's *Logic*). However, if we consider the system of physical influx, we detect various conditions of the truth in it, the distinguished ones of which will suffice here, since it would take too long to describe them all. Indeed, at the start it answers exactly to all the phenomena of the commerce of the mind and body, so that even the celebrated Wolff determines this commerce in this step, as it were, as the norm of all systems and he admonishes that it must be presupposed in any system that perceptions of sensible things in the mind and voluntary motions in the body arise in such a way as if the body and soul mutually influenced each other (§537 *Psych. Rational.*). Accordingly, the first condition of the true system is present in influx. There is the additional fact that nothing is discovered and presupposed in this system that is impossible, because the possibility of physical influx has already been established above (§34). You have the second condition of truth. The system of physical influx agrees with divine wisdom no less than what is maximal. For it is shown in natural theology that God, thrice greatest most powerful, in conformity with his greatest and infinite wisdom, chooses the natural, shortest path, i.e., if other effects can be produced abundantly through the forces of natural things and at the same time according to the order established by his total wisdom, no miracles are wasted, nor will those things that can come about naturally through a select few occur through many or by the longer path. If whoever actually weighs the system of physical influx more carefully discovers not only that all phenomena of commerce can be explained according to it naturally and without miracles, he will also learn that the true path of all things, to the extent that it exists, is also the shortest by which this commerce can be brought about, which will easily become evident from comparing any other systems. The Kind Reader will not acknowledge new conditions of truth without [due] consideration. Therefore, it cannot be doubted that the system of physical influx is quite probable.

[...]

§36. *The system of influx or of efficient causes is superior to all the rest.*

The system of physical influx must be preferred to the other systems and, though it has not yet been established concerning its actuality, it should be embraced, if any other should be. The system of physical influx is quite probable, because it is not only possible, but it also corresponds to the phenomena and agrees exactly with the conditions of the wisest divine attributes (§35). But as for what concerns the system of pre-established harmony, as the celebrated Wolff himself has acknowledged (§638 *Psych. Rational.*), its possibility has not yet been shown. He supposes that whatever things are capable of being made through shortcuts have been made by the wisest God through roundabout ways, because so many skills are necessary for producing this harmony both in the body and in the mind that they may overcome every form of comprehension (just as Bayle or the acknowledged celebr. Bilfinger have splendidly shown). But even admitting that physical influx or a shorter path (§35) is quite possible (§34), there is no reason why a material world should have been produced by God, thrice greatest and most powerful (§13 note); so I may pass over the remaining theories taught by others. And, therefore, since the conditions of truth which are necessary are hardly present, it is less probable. The same is true for the system of occasional causes, since it not only contradicts the divine wisdom by imputing continuous miracles to the rule of nature, but is also absolutely injurious to the sanctity of God, thrice greatest most powerful. Finally, this way of explaining the phenomena, namely, summoning Deus ex machina, in the style of poets, without the necessary investigation into the nature of things is very unworthy of a philosopher, as was shown in many ways above (§12 note). But since it is certain that the probable and the more probable are to be preferred to that which is not probable or less probable, the system of physical influx should be preferred over the systems of occasional causes and pre-established harmony. However, other than these three mentioned simple systems no more are possible (§14). Therefore, the system of physical influx must be preferred to every possible system, and embraced, if any other is.

[...]

§37.[13] *The existence of the soul in a place is demonstrated.*

The soul or human mind is in a place and is present and participates in its body, although it does not fill a space. For whatever exists, exists completely determined (§26). Therefore, it is necessary that the human mind has a determinate mode of coexisting along with other things. Thus, it has its place and is in space, because no one doubts that it is finite (§23).

---

[13] §§37–38 are relevant to *Dreams of a Spirit-Seer* (2:321–328).

But the human mind does not refer to other coexistent things or has
no communion with these, except through the mediation of the body,
according to whose position and changes it represents external things
to itself and not unless it acts through the organs of the body due to the
position that it maintains, whether actually or merely apparently (§7).
And, therefore, the mode of coexisting with other coexisting things that
pertains to the mind, i.e., its place, is determined according to the place
of the body (§23). Therefore, there is no reason why one must think of
the mind in another place remote from the body. For it is present and
participates in its body (§10 *Ontol.*). But since the human soul is a simple
being and therefore lacks parts (§18), there is no order in the mind of
things existing at the same time outside of themselves. Therefore, it cannot fill a space, although it is in a place and is present and participates
in its body (§23).

[...]

§38. *It is shown that the soul is moved together with the body.*

*The soul or human mind changes place or is moved together with the body, with
respect to [its] total motion. Nonetheless, no internal motion must be admitted in
it.* For any ordinary experience you wish teaches that our body is constantly changing its place. For whenever it pleases us, we pass over from
one place to another; we walk; we run; and so on – provided that sick-
ness does not hinder us and our powers do not fail. But the mind always
participates in the body and it is always present and participates in the
place where the body exists (§37). Therefore, if I change the place of
the body, it is necessary that the place of the mind also be changed.
Therefore, the human soul is moved together with the body (§24).
However, because the mind is an immaterial substance and lacks parts
(§18), the position of parts in it cannot be changed. Therefore, there is
no internal motion in the mind, but if it is moved, it cannot be moved
except with respect to [its] total motion (§24).

[...]

§39. *The action of the mind on the body and of that, in turn, on the mind is
established.*

The human mind acts on its body and the body, in turn, acts on the mind. Let's
assume that the mind does not act on the body and that the body does not
act on the mind. Because the soul is moved together with the body (§38),

it is necessary that a reason for the existence of this motion be given (§70 *Ontol.*). It cannot be contained within the simple elements in its body, for otherwise the body would act on the mind, which is contrary to the hypothesis (§21). The mind itself ought to contain in itself the reason for its motion, when it changes its place along with the body. Therefore, the mind is endowed with a force of moving itself (§24), a force that, because it already involves the force of moving other surrounding things and cannot be separated from the mind (§28), shows sufficiently clearly that the mind, by its force, is capable of moving other things that surround it, i.e., its body (§37) and its parts. However, because this force has been presupposed, action is presupposed, unless some other external hindrance intervenes (§22). But one cannot think of a hindrance of this kind contrary to the continuous striving of the mind. No one who perceives accurately what has been established can assert that the mind never exercises its action on the body. Therefore, the human mind acts on its body, and because it consists in simples (§20), it acts on the elements or simples of the body. But the simples of which it consists act on other simples contiguous to themselves and they take pleasure in the force of acting on it (§29) and, therefore, they resist the mind that acts on them (according to the demonstr.) and act on the mind. Therefore, it cannot be doubted that the body, as an aggregate of these simples, acts on the mind. Therefore, it is false that the mind does not act on the body and the body does not, in turn, act on the mind, and therefore it is shown and, moreover, it is certain that the mind or the human soul acts on its body and the body in turn on the mind. *In other words.* The mind is an impenetrable substance or has resistance in the same manner as all finite substances (cf. the letters of the ill. Leibniz). But the human mind is surrounded in space by the body's monads (§37). Therefore, there will be something in the mind that excludes from its place or resists the monads or simple bodies that, as we showed above, are moved. But resistance is an action of the patient (passive element) on the agent (active element). Therefore, the mind acts on corporeal simples and these act on the mind, i.e., there is mutual action between the mind and body. Q.E.D.

[...]

§40. *The existence or actuality of influx is demonstrated and the truth of this system is shown.*

There is physical influx of the mind on the body and of the body on the mind, and the system of physical influx is true and is a sufficient reason for explaining the commerce of the mind and the body. For since the mind acts on the body and the body in turn acts on the mind (§39), and in fact the action of the body on the mind and of the mind on the body is physical influx (§10), it is therefore certain that there is physical influx of the mind on the body and vice versa. However, because the system of physical influx is that by which the commerce of mind and body is explained through physical influx (§10), having already shown the truth of physical influx, it cannot be doubted that this system is the true reason for explaining the commerce of the mind and body, which is surely sufficient, whence one can infer why it corresponds to all the phenomena of this commerce and everything appears in such a manner as if they act in turn on themselves. For this is what the great Wolff himself has observed, who, though calling the truth of the system of influx into doubt, still concedes its sufficiency by demonstrating (*Psych. Rational.* §537) that each system (if it is truly to be sufficient) presupposes that perceptions of sensible things and voluntary motions occur in the body in such a way as if the soul and the body influence each other mutually. And thus because nothing is presupposed in the system of physical influx except for what is given in an act and everything that can be explained from this supposition [of an act], the system of physical influx is the true and genuine and in fact sufficient reason for explaining the commerce of the mind and the body.

[…]

§41. *Physical influx is vindicated of reproach of empty terms.*

Physical influx is not an empty term, nor an occult quality. For physical influx occurs in the mutual action of the mind on the body and of the body on the mind (§32). Therefore, because it was shown above (§39) that the mind in fact acts on the body and the body in turn on the mind, there is no reason why anyone should doubt the reality of the concept of physical influx. But we call a term empty to which no concept corresponds, even though it might seem to correspond to one (§38 *Logic*). Therefore, the term physical influx is not empty. Similarly, it is shown that the physical influx of the mind on the body and vice versa is not an occult quality. For an occult quality is what lacks a sufficient reason why it is present in a subject or at least could be present (§189 *Cosmol.*). But physical influx lacks a sufficient reason neither for its possibility (§34) nor for its actuality (§39). Therefore, one can hardly count it among the occult qualities.

[…]

§42.[14] *It is shown that the most specific mode of influx cannot be comprehended distinctly by us on account of the nature of things.*

The most specific mode of physical influx, or action, by which the mind influences its body and the body in turn influences the mind cannot be distinctly compre-hended by us on account of the very nature of the thing. For physical influx occurs in the action of the mind, which is a simple substance, on sim-ples or elements of the body and of these elements on the mind (§22), and thus the action of a simple substance on another simple substance comes to be considered only in this way. But every simple lacks parts (§18), and so change that is introduced into it by another external to it cannot penetrate one part after another at length and arise successively in it. Therefore, it is necessary that it appear instantaneously from the start (§693 *Ontol.*). And because the past, present, and future cannot be distinguished from each other in such a beginning (§ cit.), there-fore, those that succeed each other mutually or exist together one after another cannot be distinguished (§584 *Ontol.*). If a distinct concept of a thing is truly to be formed, those things that we can mutually distin-guish from each other should be present in that same concept (§682 *Logic*). Therefore, the beginning of this change, or the very specific mode of action through which physical influx is brought about, is not understood distinctly by us.
[...]

§43. *The human mind is not really passive according to the opinion of the system of influx.*

According to the system of physical influx the human mind is not to be conceived of as really passive in every respect nor specifically in thinking. For since the mind acts on the body in the system of physical influx (§10), it is abso-lutely opposed to this system to be conceived as purely passive in every respect. It is clear from our system or from what follows from it that, when thinking, the mind is not in fact really passive and that it is only truly passive (§714 *Ontol.*) insofar as a body in fact acts on it, modi-fying it in a certain way [*ratione*] so that a representation arises (§39). But since it was shown above (§1 note) that with respect to the mind there are a variety of faculties of thought that hardly depend immedi-ately on the body, e.g., consciousness of oneself, judgment, reasoning

---

[14] See the Phenomena and Noumena (A235/B294ff.).

and so on, physical influx, which is only a way of explaining commerce, changes nothing in the phenomena thereof, but leaving it entirely aside, these faculties can be included among the actions of the mind and even deservedly so. Therefore, the mind is not to be conceived as completely passive in thinking according to the system of physical influx.

[...]

§44. *True influx or its more specific idea is explained by which the flowing out and metamorphosis of motion and ideas is excluded.*

While the body acts on the mind according to the system of physical influx, it does not pour ideas of external things into the mind, nor the force of representation. Rather, it modifies only the force of the mind and its substance in such a way that a representation arises in the mind. To be sure, the mind, when it acts on the body, does not pour a moving force into it, but rather, with its actions, only modifies and directs a force to the extent that it is present in corporeal elements, in such a way that motion is finally produced in the body. For ideas and the force of representation are either accidents or substances. If they are accidents, they cannot flow into the mind from the body and be transferred out of the body into the mind by a certain local motion. For accidents do not migrate from subject to subject (§791 *Ontol.*). But if you suppose that they are really substances, it is similarly impossible to allow such a transition, because the mind is a simple substance (§18) and such a substance cannot really be the receptacle of another substance or of a plurality of other substances. Therefore, neither ideas nor the force of representation can flow from the body into the mind. However, because representations of external things appear in the mind through the action of the body (§40 note), nothing remains to be said but that when the body acts on the mind, it modifies its force and substance so that representations of external things in fact appear or are caused in the mind. For a similar reason it can be shown that no moving force can be transferred from the mind to the body, and thus only those forces that were recently demonstrated as being present in its elements (§196 *Cosmol.*) are modified and directed through the action of the mind according to certain reasons so that determinate motion is finally produced in the body through the determination of these forces.

[...]

§45.[15] *Two forces of the mind flow from one spring.*

---

[15] See the Paralogisms (A338–A405/B396–B432) and *New Elucidation* (1:412).

The forces of representation and motion in the human mind either flow from a certain common spring and principle, i.e., a certain primitive force, or the one is the foundation of the other. In fact, it even seems to me that one can easily derive the force of moving from the force of representing. For the mind is a simple substance (§18) and so it cannot have many forces together (§57 *Psych. Rat.*). Therefore the forces of representing and moving cannot be forces absolutely and really distinct from each other, but rather one ought to derive either both of them from a common spring or the one from the other. But if in fact we examine more carefully which of those things is most in agreement with the truth, it does not seem impossible to me that the force of motion is derived from the force of representing. For the celeb. Wolff has already demonstrated in the *Psychol. Rational.* (§497) that the effort of producing perceptions even of external things that I see and sensations flows from the force of representing. But sensations do not appear in the mind unless certain changes occur in the body and the state of the body assists it in such a way that it is required for a certain sensation (§484 and 485 *Psych. Rat.*) and so the mind, too, focuses on and strives to produce such a state of the body, i.e., strives to produce motion in it, the reality of whose striving has already been shown above (§39), where it was demonstrated that the mind acts on the body, which is something one cannot at all conceive without the force of acting (§22) and is confirmed by the fact that this striving and its effect reveal themselves at the time when there are appetites or volitions present in the mind (§1 note). Therefore, the force of moving flows from the force of representing.

[...]

PHILOSOPHICAL TREATISE ON THE IMMATERIAL NATURE OF THE SOUL (1744)[16]

Preface[17]

[...] Many truths that are resplendent with the greatest weight and standing are constituted such that they depend on the rigorously known, that is, simple, nature of souls. For the **nature** of the **infinite divinity**, which is exempt from all matter and not subject to mortality, since nothing composite is to be found in it, is at once placed in a brighter light as soon

---

[16] Translated from *Philosophische Abhandlung von der immateriellen Natur der Seele* (Königsberg, 1744).

[17] All the selections here are relevant to the Paralogisms (A338–A405/B396–B432). The Preface is also relevant to the Third Antinomy.

as matter's incapacity to think and the simple nature of the human soul are grounded by and attached to a secure proof. For this reason learned men whose sharp intellects and rich erudition have already attracted the most glorious praise have not judged unreasonably, holding that one can hardly ever successfully refute people of such absurd scholarship who are not ashamed to deny the existence of God, and in particular, from among them, Benedict Spinoza, unless one had already irrefutably proved that it is impossible for a thinking power to subsist at the same time along with extension. The most magnificent adornment of rational nature that raises our exceptional precedence over animals even more and that alone makes us capable of happiness, I mean **the freedom of our human soul**, rests on this too. [That is,] it is grounded on its simple nature no less [than is its immateriality]. For if someone wanted to deny that the nature of the soul were completely different from a coarse and awkward matter that is unable to move itself, he would have to dispute our freedom no less than, e.g., that of clocks and other such machines that are moved by internal workings. Additionally, we have what I easily could have stated first, namely, the natural immortality of our souls, which one could rightly call the foundation of true virtue and all religion. Now this could hardly be demonstrated properly and as reasonableness requires if the simple and imperishable nature of the soul had not been proved and established. At the same time nothing is so attached to the entirety of humankind, true religion, and also to happiness than that the following propositions rest on secure ground: that a God, a creator of all things, exists, whose nature is completely different from that of this corporeal world; that our soul possesses a true freedom, is thus capable of rewards as well as punishments, and that it is created eternal, and for that reason will not be destroyed at the death of the body. [. . .]

Part One In Which the Simple Nature of the Human Soul Is Presented and Established through Distinct Syllogisms

§1. *An explanation of what is to be understood by thinking and the human soul.* Experience convinces us with irrefutable certainty that something can be found in us that is conscious both of itself and of different representations of other things, or even of the things themselves. This thing may be of whatever kind and constitution one likes, but the consensus of almost all philosophers, even the most common way of speaking, typically gives it the name of the human soul. However, if and to the extent that this soul is conscious of itself and other things, then and to that extent one says of it, according to the common way of speaking, that it is **thinking**. The **human soul** is thus nothing other than that thing that thinks in us, or, more precisely, which is endowed with a faculty of thinking.

[...]

§2.[18] *What consciousness of oneself and of other things consists in.* The laws of reason not only teach, but also require that if one wants to undertake an investigation into the true nature of our soul, one must first strive to penetrate into the inner nature and constitution of human thinking. We already showed above in the preceding how consciousness of ourselves and of other things is required for thinking, but this remark does not yet suffice to lead us to our goal. Accordingly, we shall proceed further in our analysis of concepts and must investigate what actually constitutes consciousness of ourselves and of other things. This investigation is not of such great difficulty that our observations, if we direct them properly toward ourselves, should miss their mark. Animated attention shall convince us with moving clarity that we are conscious of ourselves when we distinguish ourselves from other things, and that we notice a consciousness of other things only when we cognize the distinctions among them.

[...]

§3. *What is required to distinguish, or to intuit the distinction of, things.* Because consciousness of both oneself and other things and, consequently, every thought contains an intuition of a distinction and an attentiveness to distinguishing, we shall derive no small use from penetrating deeper into the mysteries of distinguishing and investigating further what actually belongs to it necessarily. Sharper observation of the matter will convince anyone who directs his attention to himself at the same time that no distinction of objects can be made, nor even a distinction perceived in them unless (1) **several** things are represented **in a single subject** and (2) the comparison of these representations is undertaken **by the same subject**, in virtue of which something can be noticed in one thing that

---

[18] §§2–3 and 6–7 are relevant to the Transcendental Deduction.

neither is present nor can be found in another.[19] Here you have a real definition that follows and is built upon prior reasons! **Distinguishing or intuiting the distinction of things** consists in a comparison of different representations of things that are found not in many, but in a single subject and that are compared to each other not by many but by a single subject in such a way that, due to this comparison, something can be found in several representations that neither is nor can be found in others.

[…]

§4. *An explanation of what matter, material, and immaterial are.* Now that we have explained the inner nature and constitution of our thoughts, we must also investigate further what the true subject of our thoughts actually is, in which, namely, they occur and by which they are brought into being. But because, above all, the question is raised as to whether thoughts, too, must be derived from **matter**, as it is typically held to be the subject of things that enter into our senses, or rather from something that is completely distinct from it, what is especially required here is that the idea of matter be elucidated and placed at the foundation of our proof. By the term **matter** I understand nothing other than the sum or connection of parts of which the composite things of the world consist. I call something **a composite thing** if it consists of actual parts, or of parts that are posited external to each other. Accordingly, one can easily see what one should take material and immaterial to be. **Material** is that which consists of parts that are actually distinct from each other or are placed external to each other. By contrast, that which is completely devoid of all parts is typically called **immaterial** or **a simple thing**.

[…]

§5.[20] *What a substance and subject are and that matter is a set of substances.* A substance is an enduring subject that is subject to the change of accidents, or rather, it is a thing that is not to be found in another as a subject, or in such a way that it could not subsist any more after being separated from it. Something is called an accident if it is not the subject

---

[19] See B132–B133 (B-Transcendental Deduction) and A103–A110 (A-Transcendental Deduction) for a somewhat similar claim.

[20] This is relevant to the First Analogy (A182–A189/B224–B232ff.).

of changes, or, more precisely, is not found in another thing as in a subject, i.e., in such a manner that when it is separated from that thing it is not in a position to subsist [by itself]. One understands by a subject, however, a thing insofar as one can view it as something that has an essence and, moreover, is capable of other properties. The explanation of substance that the famous Herr von Leibniz gives, namely, that it is a thing that is endowed with a power of activity, can even be easily reconciled with that of the famous Herr von Wolff's and ours. If one distinctly represents the idea of substance in such a way, it must be more than abundantly clear that **matter is a connection of substances, hence also of many subjects**. This shines all the more brightly, the less we let ourselves be annoyed by seeking the coherence of the explanation of matter from §4 with this one of substances, which is in accord with the typical way of speaking. Since all individual parts of matter are actually distinct from each other and are posited external to each other, but are not to be found in other things as in subjects, no doubt remains that therefore each and every part of matter also earns the name of substance and that matter itself could be called a connection or sum of many substances.

[...]

§6.[21] *First proof that matter cannot think*. **Matter cannot think**. For whatever thinks must be conscious of itself and of other things (§1). This consciousness of itself and of other things includes an intuition of the distinction [between itself and others] and a task in drawing the distinction without which it could not occur or be exercised (§2). But this intuition of the distinction of things can only be the achievement of a single subject, by no means a matter that stems from several or many, namely, because it requires in part that the representations of the distinguished things must be pictured in a single subject, and in part that their connection must be brought about by the very same efficacious subject, or come from the first source of them, and by their efficacious power (§3). Now, since matter is nothing other than a connection of many substances and subjects, and consists of several such things that have special powers (§4), nothing will be more apparent and obvious than that the intuition of the distinction of things, thus also every thought, is not the achievement of matter and, consequently, also cannot possibly be undertaken

---

[21] §§6–7 are relevant to the Second Paralogism.

by matter to the extent that it is that. Accordingly, we rightly claim that matter is completely incapable of thinking. Q.E.D.[22]

[…]

§7. *Second proof that matter cannot think.* Matter's complete incapacity to think can also be proved in the following way due to precisely the reasons [given] against those who take the famous Herr von Leibniz's doctrine of monads in an improper sense and want to misuse it to confirm the corrupt mistake of materialism. If the power of thinking, thus also the intuition of the distinction of things, is supposed to owe its origin to, or must be derived from, the powers of monads or the individual simplest parts of matter, one and the same [conclusion] can certainly be determined from the following three possibilities: (1) either only one individual part of matter, a single monad in a bunch of matter, will be endowed with the perfection of thinking, or (2) all individual parts will possess the special skill of collecting thoughts and of being conscious of itself and of other things, or finally, (3) all **individual** monads, or several monads **together**, will produce thoughts with their **combined powers**, for whose exertion each one is not particularly suited, i.e., it must be presupposed that a thought or consciousness of itself and other things is a joint venture, which several or all monads and simple parts must exert with combined powers. One may choose whichever of these [possibilities] one likes – thoughts by material things is what is at issue. Let's start by assuming the **first** case. If a monad, [that is] if, according to their opinion, only a part of matter is resplendent with the perfection of thinking, I have already attained my goal. What is thinking in matter will be a thing with a simple and individual nature. It will not constitute a connection of parts or matter (§4). In fact, it will be quite different from the other parts of matter, those namely that are robbed of the perfection of thinking. In one word, in this case something will be in matter, or have its seat therein, that will be thinking, but matter itself could never be held capable of thinking. Let us consider the **second** case. Let the **individual** parts of matter, the individual monads themselves, be endowed especially with consciousness of themselves and of other

---

[22] In the ensuing discussion, Knutzen distinguishes his proof from Wolff's, which presupposes, as we saw above, that all change occurs through motion, and argues that his own proof is not subject to doubts that one might raise about Wolff's, namely, whether motion (or motive powers) can be derived from representation (or representative powers).

things, and thus with a capacity for thinking. In that case, too, one will not be able to attribute the least thought to matter without committing a great absurdity. For in this case the parts of matter will all be thinking either of the same thing or of different things. If they are thinking of the same thing, then, especially if we apply it to our own case, many thinking souls that nonetheless always represent exactly the same thing will live in us, which contains a great absurdity. If they are thinking of different things, then there will be nothing that compares them all against each other and distinguishes them, for which a single subject would be required (§3). In the **third** case, finally, a thought cannot be produced by the combined powers of several individual monads, or of the simplest parts of matter insofar as the task of distinguishing [things] (§3) and thus every thought (§§1–2) inevitably requires the unity of the subject in which it occurs, and the unity of the forces by which it is taken up.[23] Therefore, one can think of and view the matter however one likes, in no case will it be possible that one could ascribe the faculty of thinking to matter. Accordingly, in light of the most important reason, we again infer from all of this, the conclusion that any matter – it may be as small and subtle as one likes – is nevertheless completely unsuited for thinking. Q.E.D.

§8. *The impossibility of thinking is unconditional in matter and is also not altered by divine omnipotence.* Now from what was just demonstrated, one can also easily draw the conclusion (1) that **matter's incapacity** for **thinking**, which we clearly established, is not merely something that is supposed in matter, but is rather something that is connected with its essence so precisely that it could in no way be separated from it or, put differently, that it is not merely impossible that matter could think, but rather that this is a great and unconditional impossibility. What contradicts the first and essential concept of a thing we call unconditionally impossible (according to reasons [given] in *Ontol.*), but thought is completely opposed to the first and essential concept of matter, because thought requires a proper and indivisible unity and, at the same time, the essence of matter consists in a plurality (due to what was already proved). Accordingly, it is clearer than daylight that representing matter endowed with the perfection of thinking means nothing other than fitting together something that is obviously contradictory and imagining something absolutely impossible under the appearance of possibility.

---

[23] See A352 (Second Paralogism). See also *Dreams of a Spirit-Seer* (2:328).

Further, the conclusion can also be inferred from the preceding (2) that matter's inability to think is so great that not even the divine and unlimited omnipotence of the exalted God could give it the capacity to distinguish itself from other things and thus to think. For the unlimited power of God is a faculty to produce everything that can happen, or what is not unconditionally impossible and contains no contradiction in itself (§347 of Wolff's *Nat. Theol.*). But since it has already been proved that it is simply impossible that matter could think, it follows immediately that not even through divine omnipotence could matter receive a faculty for thinking. Q.E.D.

[…]

§9. *The soul is immaterial.* **The human soul is immaterial**, or a **thing** with an **individual** and **simple nature**. For our soul is what is conscious of itself and of other things in itself, or is what thinks in us (§1). But since matter cannot at all think (§6) and its incapacity to think is of such unconditional necessity that it could not even be raised by divine and infinite powers (§8), no longer will anyone claim that our soul could be matter or material, unless, that is, one wanted to defy the most distinct statements of reason with complete hardheadedness. However, what is not material and thus devoid of a plurality of parts we call immaterial or a thing with an individual and simple nature (§4). Consequently, no doubt remains that we should rightly count our soul, too, among the order of immaterial or simple things. Q.E.D.

§10. *What figure and extension as well as invisibility are.* We shall not be acting contrary to our undertaking if we also take into account here those properties that are connected to an immaterial soul, so that we can form a concept of its simple and individual nature that is all the more complete and perfect. And to this end, we are presupposing the following explanations. **A figure** is nothing other than the continuous limit of extension. But we call **an extended thing** whatever consists of parts that are posited external to each other, but are also connected to each other, or it is any composite thing insofar as it is viewed as one thing that is constantly continuous. Further, we say that something is **invisible** if its surface cannot bring about a change in the eye with the help of light, either mediately or immediately, through reflected light rays. And on the basis of these explanations it can very easily be proved now that the human soul is free from all extension, completely devoid of all figure or shape, and is invisible in every respect.

[...]

§11. *No extension occurs in the soul, i.e., it is not extended.* **The human soul is free of all extension**. For the human soul is immaterial and of a simple nature (§9), thus it lacks a plurality of parts (§4). But since we call something extended only if it consists of parts that are posited external to each other and are connected to each other (§10), our soul can in no way be held to be extended. Q.E.D.

[...]

§12. *The soul is invisible and has no shape.* The human soul is neither shaped nor visible and cannot be constituted in this way due to its nature. For the human soul cannot be extended (§10) and thus cannot be enclosed within the limits of extension. But since we call the continuous limit of extension a figure (§11), it is already beyond all doubt that the human soul is completely incapable of a shape. Further, it is clearer than daylight that what is freed of all extension cannot be surrounded by a surface from which light rays could either shoot out immediately or reflect back off of (due to mathematical reasons). Consequently, the soul is necessarily invisible due to its nature. Q.E.D.

[...]

§13. *What imperishability is and that the soul is imperishable.* The order of all those properties that we had to mention in explaining the simple and immaterial nature of our soul due to its indissoluble connection to the soul is finally concluded with its imperishability, or with that property according to which it is not subject to perishing. We call **imperishable** whatever cannot be destroyed through a division of parts. But since it is already clear from what we have previously established in this treatise (§8) that our soul is immaterial and consequently exempt from all parts, no doubt remains that it should also be imperishable or incapable of all perishing. Q.E.D.

[...]

3

Alexander Baumgarten

Alexander Baumgarten was born in Berlin in 1714 and began his primary education there. After the death first of his mother (when he was three) and then of his father (when he was seven), he was raised by his grandmother for several years and taught by a private tutor (financed by a family friend). In 1727 he moved to Halle to attend the preparatory Latin school of Francke's so-called *Waisenhaus* (orphanage), where he proved to be an exceptionally gifted student in both artistic and academic subjects. At the university in Halle, he enrolled in theology and ancient philology, studying Wolffian philosophy privately as well since it was still forbidden to teach Wolffian philosophy at the university. After graduating with a master's degree in 1735, Baumgarten began teaching in Halle as a private lecturer. He was promoted to extraordinary professor there in 1737. In 1740, at least in part because of his financial situation, he accepted an ordinary professorship at Frankfurt an der Oder (which others had turned down), where he remained until his death in 1762.

Baumgarten published a wide range of philosophical works during his career: *Meditationes philosophicae de nonullis ad poema pertinentibus* (Philosophical Meditations on Poetry) in 1735, *Metaphysica* (Metaphysics) in 1739, *Ethica philosophica* (Philosophical Ethics) in 1740, Part One of *Aesthetica* (Aesthetics) in 1750, Part Two of *Aesthetica* in 1758, *Initia philosophiae practicae primae* (Introduction to First Practical Philosophy) in 1760, and *Acroasis logica in Christianum L. B. Wolff* (Lectures According to Christian Wolff's *Logic*) in 1761. Several of his other philosophical and theological writings, along with a German translation of the *Metaphysics* by one of his students, Georg Friedrich Meier, were published after his death. While Baumgarten's *Metaphysics* was an important metaphysics textbook, it was primarily his work in aesthetics, his *Aesthetics* in particular, that established Baumgarten's considerable reputation in eighteenth-century Germany and beyond.[1]

In the *Metaphysics* Baumgarten generally takes up a position that is closer to Leibniz's position than it is to Wolff's, though he does follow Wolff's division of metaphysics into ontology, cosmology, psychology, and natural theology. Baumgarten's Latin prose is extraordinarily terse (a style not easily duplicated in English), and the structure of his paragraphs amounts, by his own admission in the first edition preface, to nothing more than a "solid skeleton of metaphysics." Further, he does not explicitly indicate either what he might be arguing for in his own right or how his own position relates to that of his predecessors (other than to mention Leibniz, Wolff, Bilfinger, and Reusch as "distinguished reformers of metaphysics"). Still, there are many detailed points on which Baumgarten takes a distinctive line. For instance, Baumgarten stresses that accidents can appear to us as substances (§193), a view that has certain similarities to Kant's doctrine of phenomenal substances. Also, perhaps as a reflection of the changing times, Baumgarten openly embraces a full-fledged version of preestablished harmony, along with a distinction between real and ideal grounds, so that he ends up being much closer to Leibniz than Wolff on this point (though Baumgarten develops the distinction between real and ideal grounds differently from Leibniz). He also presents new, global arguments in favor of preestablished harmony, based on the perfection of the world.

Baumgarten's *Metaphysics* is particularly important to Kant, both because he based his metaphysics lectures on it for almost his entire career (except for the winter semester of 1756–1757 and possibly the summer semester of 1757, when he appears to have used Baumeister's *Institutiones metaphysicae,* which had been published in 1736) and because it was for Kant a prominent example of the rationalist position that would stand in need of "critical" scrutiny, an issue that is discussed in detail in both the Transcendental Dialectic and the Amphiboly. The transcripts from Kant's metaphysics lectures are especially illuminating insofar as they give us more detailed information about Kant's attitude toward myriad specific topics in "traditional" metaphysics throughout his life and thus provide a crucial bridge between Baumgarten's *Metaphysics* and the first *Critique,* where Kant's stance on these traditional topics is sometimes obscured by the requirements of his radically

[1] In particular, Baumgarten played a crucial role in the development of aesthetics by synthesizing Gottsched's classicist and more Wolffian views with Bodmer's and Breitinger's less *a prioristic,* English-based approach.

new architectonic system. As a result, the vast majority of paragraphs
from Baumgarten's *Metaphysics* that are cited in Karl Ameriks and Steve
Naragon's translation of these lectures are translated below.[2] In light
of the fact that Kant rarely cites specific works of Leibniz, Wolff, and
his other predecessors, Baumgarten's *Metaphysics* is also important in
the straightforward sense that it offers one concrete formulation of
the Leibnizian position we know that Kant was intimately familiar with
from the very beginning of his career. To render more transparent the
implicit references to Baumgarten's *Metaphysics* that Kant would have
had in mind in the Transcendental Dialectic, all paragraphs in this
work that are referred to in Paul Guyer and Allen Wood's translation of
the *Critique of Pure Reason* have been selected as well. In sum, almost a
quarter of Baumgarten's *Metaphysics* is translated below.

---

[2] See Immanuel Kant, *Lectures on Metaphysics*, ed. Karl Ameriks and Steve Naragon
(New York: Cambridge University Press, 1997). This volume is extraordinarily helpful
for understanding Kant's *Critique of Pure Reason* in its historical context.

---

[3] Only those headings containing selections that have been translated in this volume are included.

METAPHYSICS (1739)[4]

Prolegomena to Metaphysics [§§1–3]

§1. METAPHYSICS is the science of first principles in human cognition.

§2. Ontology, cosmology, psychology, and natural theology belong to metaphysics.

§3. NATURAL METAPHYSICS is the cognition of matters treated in metaphysics that are attained through the mere use of these matters. If artificial [metaphysics] explained in §1 is also added to it, then it is useful (1) for the development of its concepts, (2) for the determination and conception of its first principles, and (3) for the continuation and certainty of its proofs, etc.

PART ONE: ONTOLOGY [§§4–350]

Prolegomena [§§4–6]

§4. ONTOLOGY (ontosophy, metaphysics, cf. §1, universal metaphysics, architectonic, first philosophy) is the science of the general predicates of a thing.

§5. The predicates of a thing that are more general are the first principles of human cognition, thus ontology belongs (§2), with reason, to metaphysics (§1, 4).

§6. Ontology contains the predicates of a thing (§4), (I) [that are] internal, (1) universal, which are in each thing, (2) disjunctive, one of which is in each thing; (II) relative.

Chapter One: On the Internal General Predicates
of Things [§§7–100]
Section I: On the Possible[5] *[§§7–18]*

§7.[6] Negative *nothing* (cf. §54), the unrepresentable, the impossible, the repugnant (the absurd, cf. §13), what involves [or] implies a contradiction,

---

[4] Translated from Alexander Baumgarten, *Metaphysica* (Frankfurt, 1757, 4th ed., 1739 1st ed.), reprinted at 15:5–54 and 17:23–226 of Immanuel Kant's *Gesammelte Schriften* (Berlin: Königlich-Preussischen Akademie der Wissenschaften zu Berlin, 1902–).

[5] GW refers §§7–18 to A290/B346 (at the very end of the Amphiboly chapter).

[6] See *Negative Magnitudes* (2:171–172).

is A and non-A; or there is no subject with contradictory predicates; or nothing both is and is not. $0 = A + non-A$. *This principle* is called *the principle of contradiction,* and is the *absolutely first principle.*

§8. Whatever is not nothing is SOMETHING: whatever is representable, whatever does not involve a contradiction, whatever is not A and not-A, is POSSIBLE (§7).

§9. What is A and not-A is not something (§8), hence it is nothing and contradictory (§7), or a subject that implies [a contradiction] has no predicates, or whatever is and is not, is nothing. $A + not\text{-}A = 0$.

§10. Everything possible is either A or not-A or neither (§8). Now, neither is nothing, because it would have to be both (§9). Therefore *everything possible is A or not-A,* or, one of all contradictory predicates is to be attributed to every subject. *This proposition* is called *the principle of the excluded third, or middle, between two contradictories.*

§11. Every possible A is A; or, *whatever is, is what it is;* or every subject is predicated of itself. If you deny this, some possible A would be not-A (§10); hence, A and not-A, or nothing (§7), which is impossible (§9). *This proposition* is called *the principle of positing, or identity.*

§12. A CONTRADICTION ARISES by positing the impossible. What not only seems to be, but also is, is said to be TRUE; what only seems to be, but is not, is said to be [MERELY] APPARENT. Hence a contradiction that has arisen is either true or apparent.

§13. A contradiction arises by positing A and not-A (§9, 12). If A and B are posited, by the positing of which not-A is posited, the impossible is posited (§9), hence a contradiction arises (§12), which was first called OBVIOUS (direct, immediate, and explicit), and later LATENT (indirect, cryptic, mediate, and implicit). That in which a true contradiction is clear is ABSURD.

§14.[7] THE GROUND (cf. §640) (condition, hypothesis) is that from which it can be cognized why something is. Whatever has a ground, or of which something is the ground, is said to BE GROUNDED by it and DEPENDENT

---

[7] See *New Elucidation* (1:391–393).

on it. CONNECTION is a predicate due to which something is a ground or is grounded or is both.[8]

§15. Whatever is considered, but not in connection with others that are posited outside of it, is CONSIDERED IN ITSELF. What is not even considered representable in itself is IMPOSSIBLE IN ITSELF (intrinsically, simply, absolutely, per se). Whatever is considered possible in itself is POSSIBLE IN ITSELF (intrinsically, absolutely, per se, simply).

§16. Whatever is also possible in connection with others that are posited outside of it is HYPOTHETICALLY POSSIBLE (respectively, relatively, extrinsically, through and according to another).

§17. Whatever is not impossible, except in some other connection with others that are posited outside of it, is HYPOTHETICALLY IMPOSSIBLE (respectively, relatively, extrinsically, through and according to another).

§18. Nothing absolutely impossible is hypothetically possible (§15, 16). Therefore, nothing hypothetically possible is absolutely impossible. *Everything hypothetically impossible* and possible *is possible in itself* (§17, 15). Therefore, absolute impossibilities are neither hypothetical possibilities nor hypothetical impossibilities. Something that is an absolute possibility can be hypothetically impossible.

Section II: On Connection [§§19–33]

§19. The possible in connection, i.e., that in a connection to which connection is to be attributed, is the CONNECTED (the rational); the impossible in a connection is the IRRATIONAL (the unconnected, the incoherent). Hence, irrational things are either impossible in themselves or impossible hypothetically (§15, 17).

§20. Everything possible either has or does not have a ground (§10). If it has a ground, then something is the ground of it (§8). If it does not have a ground, nothing is the ground of it (§7). Therefore, the ground of everything possible is either nothing or something (§10). If nothing is to be the ground of something possible, then why something is could be cognized from nothing (§14). Hence, this very nothing would be representable and something (§8), and nothing something (§14, 8). Hence,

---

[8] See A769–A782/B797–B810 (Doctrine of Method).

this possible would be impossible (§7, 8, 9). Therefore, something is the ground of every possible thing, or every possible thing is grounded, or *nothing is without a ground,* or, if something is posited, then some ground of it is posited.[9] *This principle* is called *the principle of reason,* which you can also understand from §265, 279, in part through abstraction, in part by avoiding a circle.

§21. The ground of each thing in another is THE SUFFICIENT GROUND OF IT (complete, total), the ground of only some others in it is THE INSUFFICIENT GROUND OF IT (incomplete, partial).

§22. *Nothing is without a sufficient ground,* or, having posited something, some sufficient ground of it is posited. Each possible in every thing has a ground (§20); therefore, everything possible has a sufficient ground (§21). *This proposition* is called *the principle of sufficient reason* [or ground] (of attribution).

§23. Everything possible is a ground, or *nothing is without a consequence,* nothing is without its corollary and due, nothing is completely barren, otiose, and unfruitful, or if something is posited, then something of what it grounds is posited as well. For everything possible either has or does not have a consequence (§10). If it has one, something is grounded by it (§8), but if it does not have one, nothing is grounded by it (§7). Therefore, in everything possible either nothing or something would be grounded (§10). If nothing were grounded in something possible, it could be cognized from this (§14), hence would be something (§8), and therefore the possible would be impossible (§7, 8, 9). *This proposition* is called *the principle of the grounded.*[10]

§24. *Everything possible is a ground and a consequence* (§20, 23), hence is connected in a two-fold manner (§14); as connected with its ground (§19), it can be cognized *a priori,* as connected with its consequent it can be cognized *a posteriori. This proposition* is called *the principle of things connected on both sides* (from the prior part and from the later part).

§25. If A is the ground of B, it is also the ground of C, if C is grounded in B. From the ground of B it can be understood why C exists (§23), hence A is the ground of C (§14).

---

9 Kant criticizes this argument at *New Elucidation* (1:397–398).
10 See Kant's *New Elucidation* (1:408–409) for his objection to this argument.

§26. If C is a consequence of B, which is a consequence of A, then C is a consequence of A (§25, 14).

§27. If A is the ground of B, on which C depends, then A is the MEDIATE GROUND of this C (ultimate, remote); a ground that is not mediate is IMMEDIATE (proximate).

§28. A ground that has yet a further ground is called A GROUND IN SOME RESPECT (intermediate), a ground which does not is called A GROUND WITHOUT QUALIFICATION (ultimate). Grounds and consequences are considered either subordinate, if they are related to each other as ground and what is grounded, or coordinate, if they are not.

§29. If what is grounded has been posited, some ground of it (§20, 14), and a sufficient one (§22), must be posited, or [one can infer] *from what is grounded to the ground, and a sufficient one,* etc.

§30. If the ground, and a sufficient one (§21), has been posited, what is grounded is posited (§23), or [one can infer] *from the ground, and a sufficient one, to what is grounded.*

§31. *If a ground, and a sufficient one, is removed, something of what is grounded is removed,* because in positing the one, the other is posited (§29).

§32. *If what is grounded is removed, its ground, and a sufficient one, is removed,* because in positing the one, the other is posited (§30).

§33. *If A and B are connected to a third C, then on that account they are also connected among each other.* A is connected to C which is connected to B. Therefore, there is something in A due to which it can be cognized from B why it is, hence A and B are connected (§19).

Section III: On a Thing [§§34–71]

§34.[11] Something is DETERMINATE if it is posited that it is A or that it is not A, but if it is posited only that it is either A or not A, it is INDETERMINATE. Or, if nothing with respect to contradictory predicates is posited in the subject except that one or the other is attributed to it, that subject is indeterminate in respect of those predicates. However, it is determinate, if one of them is posited in the subject. Whatever can be determined

---

[11] See *The Only Possible Argument* (2:76).

is DETERMINABLE. Therefore, concerning this it can be posited that something is A or that something is not A, [hence] that something is determinable.

§35. The ground by which determining [is to occur] is a DETERMINING GROUND. Therefore, all grounds determine, sufficient grounds determine sufficiently, and insufficient grounds determine insufficiently (§34, 21). Hence, if determinations are posited, then what is determined is posited (§30, etc., §29). By removing what is determinate, the determining ground is also removed (§32, etc., §31).

§36. Those things that are posited in something in determining [it] (marks and predicates) are DETERMINATIONS; some are positive and affirmative (§34, 10), which if they exist in fact are REALITY, while others are negative, which if they exist in fact are NEGATION. Apparent negation is CRYPTIC REALITY, apparent reality is IDLE REALITY.

§37. DETERMINATIONS of possible things are either representable in themselves, even if they are not yet considered in connection [with others], [in which case they are] ABSOLUTE, or not [representable] unless they are considered in connection [with others] (§10), [in which case they are] RESPECTIVE (assumptive). Respective determinations of possible things are RESPECTS (conditions [*habitudines*], τα προς τι, recently called relations, whether external or internal). Respects of possible things in those representables not considered in themselves are RELATIONS (in the narrow sense, to what is external [*ad extra*]). Relations of possible things are their EXTERNAL DETERMINATIONS, while the remaining ones are their INTERNAL DETERMINATIONS.

§38. If those things that are in B are in A, A and B are THE SAME. Things that are not the same are DIVERSE (different).

§39. Internal DETERMINATIONS of possible things are either grounds of the remaining internal determinations in these things without qualification or they are not (§10). The former are FIRST (principles) or ESSENTIAL DETERMINATIONS.

§40. The sum of essential determinations in a possible thing, or its internal possibility, is its ESSENCE (being a thing, formal ground, nature, cf. §430, thisness, form, formal wholeness [*formale totius*], ουσια, τινοτις, substance, cf. §191, first concept of a thing).

§41. Internal determinations of possible things, according to what is grounded in their essences, are AFFECTIONS.

§50. Affections have their ground in the essence (§41), which may be either a sufficient ground or less than sufficient (§21, 10). In the former case, the affections are ATTRIBUTES; in the latter case, they are MODES (predicable accidents or adjuncts from a logical point of view cf. §191, secondary predicates).

§53.[12] Every possible thing is determinate with respect to its possibility (§34, 8). Hence it is possible in itself with respect to its internal possibility (§15). Now since internal possibility is the essence (§40), [it follows that] every possible [thing] has an essence, [and is therefore] determinate with respect to its essence. Therefore, nothing is altogether indeterminate.

§69. Internal differences can be represented in a being considered in itself (§67, 37); hence they can in some way be cognized or BE GIVEN. Either we are also able to conceive and understand what is given (without its co-presence) without assuming another thing, without a relation to another thing, that is, we are able TO COMPREHEND it distinctly, or we are not able to. In the first case, what is given are QUALITIES; in the second case, what is given are QUANTITIES (magnitudes).

Section IV: On Unity [§§72–77]
§72. The determinations of a thing are SEPARATED if certain ones can be removed from those that are posited simultaneously. Hence determinations are INSEPARABLE if none can be removed from those that are posited simultaneously.

§74. If A is one and B is one, etc., and if they are partly the same and partly different, then there are MANY. Whatever we might think, either there are or there are not many things. The former determination is MULTITUDE (plurality), the latter is CATEGORIAL UNITY.

§76.[13] The inseparability of determinations because of the impossibility of separation is either absolute or hypothetical (§15, 16). Hence, unity is either absolute or hypothetical (§73).

---

[12] GW refers §53 to A571–A572/B599–B600 (The Transcendental Ideal). See also *The Only Possible Argument* (2:76).
[13] GW refers §76 to A412/B439 (concerning the Antinomies in general) and to the First Antinomy.

Section V: On Order [§§78–88]

§79. Diversity in the conjunction of many is CONFUSION (disorder). The conjunction of inseparables is UNIFICATION [*unitio*].

§81. If B is removed when A is posited, A and B are OPPOSITES.

Section VII: On Perfection [§§94–100]

§98. The harmony among what is essential to a thing is (essential) TRANSCENDENTAL PERFECTION, that among its accidents is ACCIDENTAL PERFECTION, and that among both is INTERNAL PERFECTION. The harmony of relations is EXTERNAL PERFECTION.

§99. The essential determinations of everything harmonize into its essence (§63, 40) and its attributes (§50, 94). Therefore, *everything is perfect* transcendentally.

§100. Good is what is posited when perfection is posited. Therefore, *everything is good* transcendentally (§99).

Chapter Two: On the Internal Disjunctive Predicates of
Things [§§101–264]
Section I: On Necessity and Contingency [§§101–123]

§101. That thing is NECESSARY whose opposite is impossible, what is not necessary is CONTINGENT.

§108. The opposition of modes in a thing is absolutely possible (§65, 81), hence modes are contingent determinations of a thing in itself (§104). Therefore, they are not absolutely necessary (§105). The opposition of absolutely necessary determinations in a thing is absolutely impossible in that same thing (§102). Therefore, they are absolutely possible in a thing (§81), hence they are representable in the same thing considered in itself (§15). However, relations are not representable in a thing considered in itself (§37). Therefore, no relations of a thing are absolutely necessary, all are contingent (§101).

Section III: On the Real and the Negative [§§135–147]

§137. Every thing is real (§136) and either no negation inheres in it or a certain one inheres along with its realities (§10) and this [negation] is either absolutely necessary or contingent in itself (§102, 104). The former is NEGATION IN THE NARROW SENSE (a negative thing, in the narrow sense). The latter is PRIVATION or a privative thing. Negative essential determinations and attributes are negations in the narrow sense (§106, 107), negative modes are privations (§108).

§146. What is posited when imperfection is posited is BAD, hence negations are bad (§142), and they are either negation in the narrow sense, in which case they are METAPHYSICALLY BAD – when positing also means positing imperfection with absolute necessity – or privations, in which case they are CONTINGENTLY BAD (called, of late, natural evil) – when positing it posits imperfection contingently (§144).

Section IV: On the Singular and Universal [§§148–154]

§151.[14] Those determinations of an inferior thing that are indeterminate in its superior are its DIFFERENCE. The sum of those determinations that are determinate in its kind, but still indeterminate in its superior kind is its GENERIC DIFFERENCE. The sum of those determinations that are determinate in it, but are still indeterminate in its inferior kind is its SPECIFIC DIFFERENCE. The sum of those determinations that are determinate in an individual thing, but indeterminate in its kind is its NUMERICAL DIFFERENCE (haecceity, principle of individuation) (§148).

Section V: On Wholes and Parts [§§155–164]

§159.[15] A multitude of parts is (absolute, cf. §161) MAGNITUDE or continuous quantity (§75). A multitude of wholes is (absolute, cf. §161) NUMBER or discrete quantity (§75). If the wholes that constitute a number are in turn considered as parts, the NUMBER is a FRACTION (a fraction, a particle); if not, the NUMBER is an INTEGER.

§160. That whose part is equal to another whole is greater [than that whole], while that whose whole is equal to the part of another is less [than that whole].

§161.[16] A MINIMUM is only what is greater than nothing, or that with respect to which a smaller is impossible; a MAXIMUM is only what is less than nothing, or that with respect to which a greater is impossible. A greater multitude is a COMPARATIVE MULTITUDE (cf. §74), a

---

[14] GW refers §151 to A571–A572/B599–B600 (The Transcendental Ideal).

[15] GW refers §159 to A526/B554 (Resolution of 2nd Antinomy). See also *Metaphysics Volck-mann* (28:423): "We can also consider a continuum as discrete, if we view it first as unity and then also as multitude, e.g., I can consider minutes as units of the hour, but also again as a multitude itself containing units, namely, sixty seconds."

[16] GW refers §161 to A430/B458 (First Antinomy).

lesser multitude is a PAUCITY. A greater magnitude is A COMPARATIVE MAGNITUDE (cf. §159), a lesser magnitude is SMALLNESS. A greater number is a COMPARATIVE NUMBER (cf. §159), a lesser number is a RARITY.

Section VII: On Substance and Accidents [§§191–204][17]

§191. A thing either cannot exist except as the determination of another (in another), or it can [exist otherwise] (§10). If the former, then it is AN ACCIDENT (predicamental or natural, cf. §50, whose being is in the being of another, συμβεβηκος), if the latter, then it is A SUBSTANCE (being subsisting per se, form, εντελεχεια, ουσια, υποστασις, ενεργεια) which can exist, even if it does not exist in another, [that is] even if it is not a determination in another.

§192. The existence of accidents, as such, is INHERENCE, the existence of substance, as such, is SUBSISTENCE.

§193. Accidents that seem to subsist through themselves are SUBSTANTI-ATED PHENOMENA [WHAT APPEAR TO SUBSIST].

§194. *Accidents* can exist only in other things. Now, [those other things] are not different from accidents, unless they are substances (§191). Therefore, accidents cannot exist except in substances, i.e., *they do not exist outside their substances* (§58).

§195. Essential determinations, attributes, modes, and relational acci-dents (§191, 52) can exist only in substances (§194).

§196. What accidents are able to inhere in within a substance, or a sub-stance insofar as it is a subject (cf. §344) in which accidents are able to inhere, is called THE SUBSTANTIAL, and accidents do not exist outside of the substantial (§194).

§197. If accidents inhere in a substance, then there must be a ground of this inherence (§20) or a POWER IN THE BROAD SENSE (efficacy, energy [*energia*], activity, cf. §216) and [the ground must be] sufficient (§22). This is POWER (IN THE NARROW SENSE), and is sometimes simply called cause for brevity's sake.

---

[17] This whole section is relevant to Kant's First Analogy of Experience (A182–A189/ B224–B232).

§198. Power in the narrow sense is either a substance or an accident (§191). Now it is not an accident because it is the sufficient ground of all of them (§197). Therefore, it is a substance and insofar as accidents can inhere in it as a subject, it is substantial (§196).

§199.[18] Every substance has something substantial (§191, 196), and hence has a power (§198), [or rather every substance] is what is called substantial and hence [has] power in the broad and narrow sense (§198, 197).

§200. If substances appear to be accidents or PREDICATES OF SUBSTANCES, then they are individual SELF-SUBSISTING things.

§201. Powers are attributed to what appear to subsist through themselves [substantiated phenomena] (§199, 193), and they are also called powers in the broad sense, or are endowed with powers in the broad sense (§197, 23). But if powers in the narrow sense are attributed to accidents, they appear to subsist through themselves [i.e., are substantiated phenomena] (§198, 193).

§202. Every substance has essential determinations and attributes with absolute necessity (§107), hence every substance has accidents (§191, 195). But it either has or does not have modes (§10). What has modes is a contingent thing; what does not is a necessary being (§111). Therefore, substance is either necessary or contingent. The subsistence of a contingent substance is a mode (§134, 192).

Section VIII: On State [§§205–223]

§210. Changes of state are accidents (§191), and hence cannot exist except in substances (§194), and in fact by positing a power, even in the narrow sense (§197, 22). This power, which is the sufficient ground (§197) of change or, in general, of the inherence of accidents, is either the substantial that changes, i.e. that in which the accidents in general inhere, or a power different from it (§10, 38). If the former, the substance whose state is changed or that in which accidents in general inhere, ACTS. If the latter, the substance whose state is changed, or that in which accidents in general inhere, SUFFERS. For this reason, ACTION (act, operation) is a change of state, or, in general, the actuation of accidents in the substance, through its own power; PASSION is a change of state, or the actuation of accidents in the substance in general, through a power not its own.

[18] See A204/B249–B250 (Second Analogy).

§211. A substance acting on a substance outside of itself INFLUENCES it. Therefore, INFLUENCE (transeunt action) is the action of a substance on a substance outside of itself. ACTION that does not influence [another] is IMMANENT.

§212. If the passivity of a substance that another influences is at the same time an action of the one being acted upon [i.e., of the patient], then the PASSIVITY and INFLUENCE are said to be IDEAL. If, however, the passivity is not an action of the patient, then the PASSIVITY and INFLU-ENCE are said to be REAL.

§213. The activity of the patient on the agent is reaction and the mutual action and reaction of substances is CONFLICT.

§221. A HINDRANCE (an obstacle) is what is opposed to the inherence of an accident; hence a hindrance is also what is opposed to changes (§210).

§222. RESISTANCE is the hindrance of an action. Because what is opposed to the inherence of accidents and change is an accident (§191, 81), hindrance and resistance have a sufficient ground in power (§197, 27). When a hindrance has been posited, a hindering power is posited; when resistance has been posited, a resisting power is posited (§22).

Section IX: On Simples and Composites [§§224–229]
§224. A COMPOSITE THING (in the narrow sense or *simpliciter*) is a whole of parts outside of parts, a SIMPLE THING (*simpliciter* or precisely speak-ing) is not composite. A COMPOSITE THING IN THE BROAD SENSE is what-ever has parts, and whatever has fewer parts is COMPARATIVELY SIMPLE.

§225. The parts of composite things are either accidents, individually and taken together, or some of its parts are substances (§10, 191). If the former is the case, the composite thing is an accident (§224, 155). If the latter is the case, it is A COMPOSITE THING IN THE NARROW SENSE.

§227. GENERATION is a change from non-existing into existing. The change from existing into non-existing is DEATH. Hence the generation and death of a necessary thing and a necessary substance is absolutely impossible (§132, 202).

§228. GENERATION OUT OF NOTHING is the origination of that of which no part exists before itself, and ANNIHILATION is the death of that of which no part remains in existence. The origination from nothing and annihilation of a necessary being and substance is absolutely impossible (§227).

Section X: On Monads [§§230–245]

§230.[19] A substance is either simple or composite (§224). The former is called a MONAD (atom, perfect unity).

§231. Every part of a composite substance is either something substantial or something accidental. Accidents cannot exist outside of what is substantial (§196). Therefore, substantial parts of a composite substance are posited outside of each other (§224).

§232. A composite substance has powers, hence has substances posited outside of itself for its parts (§231, 198), hence is a composite thing in the narrow sense (§225).

§233. A composite substance cannot exist except as a sum of other substances posited outside of each other mutually (§232, 155), and with a certain mode of composition (§226). Therefore, it cannot exist except as a determination of others (§36, 38). Therefore, it is an accident (§191), and if it seems to subsist as such and have attributed to it a power, it is a substantiated phenomenon (§193, 201).

§234. Every substance is a monad (§233, 230). A composite thing in the narrow sense is not a monad (§225). Therefore, it is what appears to subsist through itself [i.e., is a substantiated phenomenon] (§193, 201).

§235. A composite in the narrow sense is composed of monads (§225, 234).

§236. Monads can arise only out of nothing. For its parts are what is substantial and the accidents that inhere therein (§196). The substantial does not exist prior to the substance. For as soon as it exists, power exists and hence substance exists (§198). No accident exists prior to its substance (§194). Therefore, no part exists prior to the arising of monads, hence monads can arise only out of nothing (§228).

---

[19] GW refers §§230–245 to A439/B467; obviously, these passages are also relevant to the Second Antinomy in general.

§237. What is substantial survives as long as the substance has not yet perished (§198); no accident survives apart from its substance (§194). Therefore, a monad can perish only through annihilation (§228, 196).

§238.[20] Connected things posited next to each other are SIMULTANE-OUS, those posited after each other are SUCCESSIVE. A whole of simultaneous things is A SIMULTANEOUS THING, a whole of successive things is A SUCCESSIVE THING.

§239.[21] The order of simultaneous things mutually posited outside of each other is SPACE, the order of such successive things is TIME.

§240. If simultaneous things are posited outside each other, space is posited. If spatial things are posited outside each other, simultaneous things are posited. If successive things are posited, time is posited, and if temporal things are posited, different (§74) and successive things are posited (§239, 78).

§241. What is in space, is said to be EXTENDED, and fill space or a place (being in space, or a place, that is, filling). Now, in every composite thing in the narrow sense there is space (§240, 224). Therefore, every composite thing in the narrow sense is extended and fills space. Everything extended has parts outside simultaneous parts (§240), hence is composite (§224).

§242.[22] A monad is not extended, and does not fill space (§243, 230). But a whole of monads (§235) is extended (§241).

§243. Everything composite has a magnitude (§159, 224). The MAGNI-TUDE of a composite in the proper and narrow sense is QUANTITATIVE. Hence monads do not have quantitative magnitude (§230).

§244. PHYSICAL DIVISION is the decrease of an extended magnitude. Just as the logical division of a single thing is impossible (§148), so too what it is impossible to divide physically is indivisible. Therefore, indivisibility is either absolute or hypothetical (§15, 17). Nothing absolutely indivisible is hypothetically divisible. Some absolutely divisible things are hypothetically indivisible (§18). Hence a monad is indivisible (§243), and indeed per se (§15).

---

[20] GW refers §238 to A412/B439 (The Antinomy in general) and to the First Antinomy.
[21] §§239–241 are relevant to the Transcendental Aesthetic (A19–A49/B33–B73).
[22] See *Physical Monadology* (1:480ff).

§245. A composite cannot exist, except as the determinations of others (§§225, 233). Now, apart from composites, there are only simples (§§224, 38). Therefore, if composites exist, monads exist (§§230, 233).

Section XI: On the Finite and Infinite [§§246–264]

§246.[23] The quantity of a quality is its DEGREE (the quantity of strength). Hence we are unable to understand one degree unless another has been assumed.

§248.[24] To be a real thing is a quality (§69) belonging to all things (§138). Now since a certain number of realities are found in every thing (§§136, 159), all things have a certain degree of reality (§§246, 159). Hence, this degree is either the greatest or it is not (§§10, 247). And because a degree of reality than which a greater is possible is not the greatest (§247), it is called a BOUNDARY (limit, cf. §350, end, cf. §341). What has boundaries is FINITE (cf. §341, limited), what has no boundary is infinite (real, unlimited). Therefore, the thing having the greatest degree of reality or most real being (§190) is infinite; all the remaining things are finite. A finite thing whose boundaries we cannot determine or resolve is INDEFINITE (which is mathematically infinite or in imaginary things).

Chapter Three: On the Relative Predicates of Things [§§265–350]
Section IV: On Cause and What Is Caused [§§307–318]

§307. Whatever contains the ground of another is its PRINCIPLE. What depends on a principle is DERIVATIVE [*principiatum*]. The principle of existence is a CAUSE, what is derivative on a cause is CAUSED. Whatever cannot exist except as what is caused by another posited outside of itself is a THING DERIVED FROM ANOTHER (dependent), but whatever can exist even if it is not caused by another posited outside of itself is a SELF-SUFFICIENT THING [*ens a se*] (independent).

§308.[25] The existence of a contingent and hence finite thing is a mode (§§134, 257). Hence it is not sufficiently determined by the essence of a contingent and finite thing (§65), nor, therefore, by its attribute (§§64, 25). Therefore, there is no sufficient ground of its existence in the internal

---

[23] This paragraph is relevant to Proposition 1 in the Mechanics of the *Metaphysical Foundations* (4:537–541).

[24] GW refers §248 to A511/B539 (Antinomies, Regulative Ideas). See also *Optimism* (2:31–33), where the pre-Critical Kant employs a similar line of reasoning.

[25] GW refers §§308–310 to A604/B632 (which contains a presentation of the cosmological argument). See also *The Only Possible Argument* (2:157–158).

determinations of a contingent and finite being (§52). But a sufficient ground is still necessary for the existence of a contingent and finite being (§22, 101). Therefore, it is necessary that because those things that are its cause (§307) contain the sufficient ground of its existence outside the contingent and finite thing, a finite and contingent thing cannot exist, except as caused by what is posited outside of it, i.e., it is a dependent being (§307).

§309. A self-sufficient thing is neither contingent nor finite (§308, 307), hence is necessary (§109) and infinite (§258).

§310. A necessary and infinite thing (§258) can exist even if it is not caused by another posited external to it (§109, 102); therefore it is a self-sufficient thing and independent (§307).

PART TWO: COSMOLOGY [§§351–500]

Prolegomena [§§351–353]

§351. General cosmology is the science of the general predicates of the world, and is either empirical, if derived from experience proper, or rational, if derived from the concept of the world.

§352. Cosmology, which contains the first principles of psychology, theology, physics, teleology, and practical philosophy, belongs (§2), with reason, to metaphysics (§1).

§353. Cosmology teaches of the (1) concept, (2) parts, and (3) perfection of the world.

Chapter One: On the Concept of the World [§§354–391]
Section I: On the Positive Concept [§§354–379]

§354.[26] The world (cf. §91, 403, 434, the universe) is a series (multitude, whole) of actual finite things that is not part of any another [series or whole].

§355. This world exists. Therefore, this world is possible in itself (§57, 18).

§356. Actual things are posited outside of each other in this world. Hence there is a universal, actual connection [in this world] (§279, 306).

---

[26] GW refers §354 to A408/B434 (the introduction to the Antinomy of Pure Reason). See also the *Inaugural Dissertation* (2:387ff).

§357.[27] In every world there are actual parts (§354, 155), each of which is connected with a whole (§14, 157) and hence each one is connected with every other or in every world there is a universal harmony among its parts (§48), i.e., *there is nothing isolated in the world.* Put otherwise: the parts of the world are either actual [things] outside each other, in which case each one is connected to the others (§279, 306) or they are posited as internal determinations, not outside each other (§10, 37), in which case, too, each one is connected to each other (§49).

§358.[28] An effective connection (the rule of power) (§335) exists in this world, a connection of usefulness (§338), a connection of uses (§339), a final connection (the rule of wisdom) (§343), a subjective and formal connection (§345), an exemplary connection (§346), and a signifying connection (§347). Hence, connections of this sort are possible in the world (§57).

§361.[29] All individual parts of the world are contingent things (§354, 257). Hence, their existence is a mode (§134). Now, the existence of the world is the existence of each individual part taken together (§155). Therefore, the existence of the world is a mode and every world is a contingent thing (§111). Put differently: Suppose that some world were a necessary being. All of its internal determinations would exist with absolute necessity and none of the parts of the world would have modes (§108, 157). Each part of this world would not be a contingent thing (§134), but rather a necessary being (§109) and, therefore, infinite (§258, cf. §354).

§362.[30] Every world is one (§359), yet has modes (§361, 112), hence has determinations that are separable from each other (§72, 65), hence has a hypothetical (§76) and intrinsically contingent unity (§115).

§363. No conjunction of the parts of the world is absolutely necessary (§362, 102), yet it is coordinated (§78). Therefore, in every world order (§117), and hence truth (§119), is intrinsically contingent.

---

[27] GW refers §357 to A408/B434 (the introduction to the Antinomy of Pure Reason). See also *Inaugural Dissertation* (2:390).

[28] GW refers §358 to A414/B442 (concerning the Antinomies in general) and to the Third Antinomy.

[29] GW refers §§361–364 to A415/B442 (concerning the Antinomies in general) and to the Fourth Antinomy. See also *Inaugural Dissertation* (2:408).

[30] GW refers §362 to A412/B439 (concerning the Antinomies in general) and to the First Antinomy.

§364. All parts of the world are real (§136), because they agree with the degree of reality to be attributed to the parts of the world (§248, 140), yet in such a way that they can also not agree or rather not agree inasmuch as [they are] contingent things (§354, 257): in every world, perfection is contingent in itself (§122).

§374.[31] Because the parts of the world are either simultaneous or successive (§238, 354), if they are mutually posited outside each other, they are connected in the world either by time or by space or by both (§239, 306).

§375. Every world is a thing derived from another (§361), or a dependent thing (§308), and this world has an efficient cause posited outside itself, and is its effect (§334), testifying to a cause (§333).

§376. Every part of the world is actual (§354), hence each one has truth and certainty in its world, and therefore the parts of the world that are determined (§54) as its internal determinations (§37, 93) have truth (§90) and certainty (§93) in that world.

§377. Finite things that are not merely absolutely possible and not just hypothetically possible in some connection, but rather in a universal connection of ANY WORLD, are called the POSSIBLES of a world. Hence, there are possibles of this world that, when considered in its universal connection, are still hypothetically possible, and hence have a greater degree of possibility (§165, 246).

§378. If a single part of this world were other than it is, this world would not be totally the same as it is (§155, 267). Now, all parts of this universe can be other than they are (§354, 260). Therefore, possibles are in part different from this world (§38), and in part the same with it (§265), i.e., many worlds are possible (§74).

§379. This world alone is actual (§77). For if we suppose that many were to exist, then they would thereby constitute a series or multitude (§74). Hence, it [this world] would not be a world (§354), or all of these worlds would be merely parts of this world, which would then be the only actual world (§354, 77).

---

[31] GW refers §§374–379 to A412/B439 (concerning the Antinomies in general) and to the First Antinomy. See also Inaugural Dissertation (2:406–407).

Section II: On the Negative Concept of the World [§§380–391]

§380.[32] PROGRESSION (regress) TO INFINITY would be a series of contingent things posited mutually outside each other, of which one is the proximate cause of the other, but without there being a cause *simpliciter* as such. If a progression is assumed in which a contingent thing is itself its cause, one has a CIRCULAR progression to infinity, whereas if this is not assumed, it is a LINEAR progression to infinity.

§381. A progression to infinity may be assumed to be as large as one likes, nonetheless it is still a contingent thing (§380, 155), and hence has an efficient cause posited outside itself (§334). This [cause] cannot be a contingent thing, for in that case it would be a thing that depended in turn on another (§308), would have a cause outside of itself and consequently would be only an intermediate cause in the progression (§28). Therefore it would not be posited outside of this progression, but rather as its part (§155, 380). Therefore, an efficient cause in a progression to infinity ought to be a necessary being (§109), and independent (§310). It exists in whatever way it can exist (§259). Now it can exist without having a cause outside of itself (§310). Therefore, there is also no cause outside of it; rather, it is the first cause of its effects (§28). Hence a progression to infinity that is supposed to be without a cause *simpliciter* as such (§380) must still have one, which is impossible (§7), and thus is to be assumed neither in this nor in any other world (§354, 58).

§382.[33] FATE is the necessity of events in the world. FATE from the absolute necessity of the world is SPINOZISTIC and is not something (§361, 105) to be assumed either in this or in any other world (§354, 58).

§383. An event in the world of which the sufficient ground is unknown is CHANCE. PURE CHANCE, for which there is no sufficient ground, is impossible (§22), and is to be assumed neither in this nor in any other world (§354, 58).

§384. An ORDINARY event is one whose existence is determined according to some certain ordered rule, an EXTRAORDINARY event is an event that is not ordinary. An ABSOLUTELY EXTRAORDINARY event is one whose existence is determined by no such ordered rule. A RELATIVELY extraordinary

---

[32] GW refers §§380–381 to A414/B442 (concerning the Antinomies in general) and to the Third Antinomy.

[33] See A227–A230/ B280–B282 for Kant's discussion of the principles of no fate (§382), no chance (§383), and no leaps (§386).

event is one that it is not in accord with an ordered rule that is given. An extraordinary event is called DISORDERED on account of confusion.

§385. An absolutely extraordinary event is not true (§384, 89), is hence impossible (§90, 62), and is to be assumed in neither this nor any other world (§354, 58).

§386. An event without any proximate sufficient ground is an ABSOLUTE LEAP. An event without an ordinary proximate sufficient ground is a RELATIVE LEAP.

§387. What exists without any proximate sufficient ground (§27), exists through pure chance (§22, 383), [but] such an absolute leap is impossible (§386, 284), and is to be assumed in neither this nor any other world (§354, 58). A relative leap is certainly possible if something is not disordered, but rather simply extraordinary (§384).

§388.[34] The world is neither an infinite substance (§372, 248) nor one of its internal determinations (§365, 252), hence it is neither the essence (§40), nor an attribute, nor a mode (§50), nor a modification (§209) of an infinite thing. Hence every world must be posited outside the infinite substance, and so this world also exists outside the infinite being, which is therefore called THE EXTRAMUNDANE BEING, an actual being outside this world.

§389. Every world, and hence this one as well, is either a substance or an accident (§191). If this world were a substance, it would subsist outside an infinite substance (§388) so that therefore an infinite substance would not be the only substance (§77).

§390. If this world were an accident, it still could not be an accident of an infinite substance, since it could not exist outside of what is substantial (§196, 388), and cannot exist except in substance or substances (§194). Therefore, if this world were an accident, then the infinite substance is not the only substance (§77, 389). Now, one or the other case is necessary (§191, 10). Therefore, an infinite substance is not the only substance.

[34] GW refers §§388–390 to A414/B441 (concerning the Antinomies in general) and to the Third Antinomy.

§391. Infinite power is not the only power (§390, 198), in every world and [hence] this one, there are finite powers (§390, 388).

Chapter Two: On the Parts of the
World [§§392–435]
Section I: On the Simple Parts of the World [§§392–405]

§392.[35] Every world is either a simple or a composite thing (§224), this world is a composite thing. Whoever takes this world to be a simple thing and [identical to] himself is AN EGOIST.

§393. The parts of the composite world taken individually and together cannot be accidents. For such a world cannot exist except in substances (§155, 191), and it can inhere neither in an infinite substance (§388), nor in a single finite substance (§224, 194). So it would require several finite substances in which to inhere (§77). But those finite substances would constitute a series of finite actuals. If that series were not a part of the world composed of mere accidents, then in conjunction with that world it would constitute a series of finite actuals greater than that world and hence would not be a world (§354). If the series constituted by the finite substances were a part of the world, then that world would not be composed of mere accidents (§155). Hence, a world composed of mere accidents is impossible (§61, 62). Every composite world is composite in the narrow sense (§225). Every world is either a substance (§389, 392) or a composite in the narrow sense.

§394. The parts of a composite world are either substantial or acciden-tal (§393), and the former are monads (§235). Hence every composite world, and this one as well, is composed of monads (§392). From which it is once more clear that a world can arise only from nothing (§236) and can perish only through annihilation (§237, 393).

§395. This world is a composite thing in the narrow sense (§393), con-sists of monads, and there is nothing substantial in it besides monads (§394). Whoever denies the existence of monads is A UNIVERSAL MATE-RIALIST. Whoever denies the existence of the monads of the universe, e.g., its parts, is A COSMOLOGICAL MATERIALIST (cf. §757).

---

[35] GW refers §§392–405 to A413/B440 (concerning the Antinomies in general) and to the Second Antinomy.

§396.[36] All monads of this and any composite world are possible (§8), connected [*rationalia*] (§24), things (§63), one (§73), true (§90), objectively certain (§93), perfect (§99), good (§100), contingent things (§257), mutable (§133), real (§136), universally connected [*connexa*] (§357), are endowed with power, even powers in the narrow sense (§199), have an inner (§206) and outer state (§207), are capable of being modified (§209), are not extended and do not individually fill space, but rather as aggregates (§242), do not have quantitative magnitude (§243), are indivisible (§244), finite (§354), hence have a certain limit to their power (§249), are metaphysically bad (§250), are partially similar to each other (§265, 268), and are also partially more dissimilar the more unequal they are (§273), individually they do not admit of figure, nevertheless they are such that the whole of them does (§280).

§397. All monads of any composite world and hence this one as well, because actual things are mutually posited outside each other (§354, 224), are either simultaneous things or successive things, or both (§238). Hence each one has either a position in the place (§148) of simultaneous things or a position in the lifetime of successive things, or both (§281), although individually each one does not fill a space (§396).

§398.[37] Each finite monad of this and any universe (§354), because it exists outside of all the rest that constitute the world with it (§192), cannot exist in the same total place along with any other (§282). *A substance whose place no other substance posited outside of it can occupy is impenetrable* (solid). Therefore, all substances, hence also all monads, of this and of every composite world are impenetrable (§230).

§399. The monads of this and any composite, and hence extended, world (§241, 393) are POINTS (§286), but not MATHEMATICAL points, in which nothing other than the absence of extension is posited (§396–398). Nor, if placed next to each other, do they meet together or coincide (§70, 396). Rather, if a plurality of them have been posited as coexisting, since any given one of them is impenetrable, they are placed simultaneously outside each other in a certain ordering (§396, 78). Hence, in the aggregation of them is space. Therefore, every aggregate of monads of this and

[36] GW refers §§396–405 to A439/B467 (The Second Antinomy).
[37] See *Physical Monadology* (1:482). See also the discussion on Knutzen in Chapter 2.

every composite world is an extended thing (§241). If a mathematical point, which is an abstract possibility, is imagined to exist, it is a ZENONI-CAL POINT, which is a fiction. If by a PHYSICAL POINT you mean an actual thing that is completely determined beyond its simplicity, then certain monads of this universe, namely, those the aggregation of which is an extended thing, are physical points.

§400. All monads of this and any composite world are universally connected (§357), hence each one is either the ground of, or is grounded in, another, or both (§14, 48). A ground can be cognized from what is grounded (§29). Therefore, from any individual monad of this or any other world the parts of the world to which it pertains can be cognized (§14), i.e., every single *monad* of this or any composite *world* has the power (§199) of representing *its universe* (*they are active mirrors* of it (§210), *indivisible* (§244), *microcosms, worlds in miniature, condensations of their own worlds,* or have powers or are endowed with the power of representing the universe).

§401. Monads that represent the world (§400) represent it by means of its perceptions which they are [either] at least in part conscious of or not (§10). And hence monads of this universe represent the world either only obscurely or, at least in part, clearly. The former are NAKED MONADS (sound asleep).

§402.[38] Monads that represent the world clearly represent it either distinctly, at least in part, or not at all (§10). The former UNDERSTAND (§69). Therefore, they have the faculty of cognizing distinctly (§216), i.e., have an intellect (in the narrow sense, cf. §519). An INTELLECTUAL substance, i.e., one endowed with an intellect, is a spirit (intelligence, person). Therefore, intellectual monads of this universe are spirits (§230). Whoever admits only spirits in this world is an IDEALIST.

§403. The connection of spirits in a world among each other is PNEU-MATICS. Now, in this and every world that spirits inhabit, each one is connected to every other one. Therefore, in this and every world that spirits inhabit there is a universal pneumatic connection (§357) (world, cf. §354, pneumatics, intellectual, moral, cf. §723, the rule of grace).

---

[38] GW refers §402 to A367 and A377 (The Fourth Paralogism) and §§402–405 to A348 (The First Paralogism).

§404. Every substance is a monad (§234). Every spirit is a substance (§402). Therefore, every monad is also a simple thing (§230).

§405. All spirits of this and any world that they inhabit are monads (§404), [and] have powers of representing the world at least in part distinctly (§402). They are not extended, do not individually fill space, and do not have quantitative magnitude. They are indivisible, finite, endowed with a certain degree of power, and are subject to metaphysical badness. They are partially similar to each other, but also partially dissimilar and unequal, have no known figure individually (§396), and one is the most perfect of all (§77, 185).

Section II: On the First Genesis of Bodies [§§406–429]
§408. The monads of this world that exist at the same time mutually determine each other's place, and those that follow each other determine their age (§281, 85), hence they mutually influence each other (§211) and are posited in conflict (§213). Therefore, universal influence and universal conflict exist in this world (§48, 306) (*the war of all against all, discordant harmony, harmonious discord* §364).

§414. Things *cohere* when they touch each other in such a way that they can be separated only by some third force. Therefore, the monads of a world that touch each other mutually cohere with each other (§413). *There is no contact without cohesion.* Therefore, certain monads of this world cohere (§409), constitute a single thing (§413), and are extended (§407).

§415. No alteration occurs in a composite world without motion. For, suppose A is to be altered from B to non-B. It had coexisted with simultaneous things posited outside of it, as B. Now it coexists with them as non-B. Hence, it acquires a different relation to them (§37, 38), a different position (§85), and a different location (§281), and motion will occur (§283, 125). Whenever such alteration, such motion, happens in a composite world, the state of the altered thing, and the state of the universe of which the thing is a part, is partly the same as the preceding states (§265) and partly different (§125). Hence, there was some certain motion, in as much as the new state differs from the original state; so, in as much as the state remained the same, this duration of state in a composite world is at the same time a duration of location (§299), an absence of a certain motion, rest (§283), and it was an obstacle for (§221), and a resistance to (§222), a certain motion.

§416. Monads that constitute an extended thing in the universe (§414) always act (§216, 285) by their own power (§400), representing each of the states of their universe, and even their own future states (§298). And insofar as this power is not able to alter its state completely by its action so that it can persist with its antecedent states, to this extent it hinders or resists a certain motion (§415, 210). However, insofar as this state is in fact altered, to this extent it effects a motion (§415, 210). Hence certain monads of this universe constitute an extended thing to which the force of inertia is attributed (§294), hence [they constitute] matter (§295). Neither in this universe nor in any other can matter be totally homogeneous (§407).

§420. Bodies have parts outside of parts (§296, 224). The actual parts of bodies outside of each other are called first ELEMENTS.

§421. Elements are either the absolutely first parts of bodies, i.e., they do not themselves have further parts outside of parts, or they are [only] relatively first, beyond which one does not care to advance in the investigation of composition (§420). The former are called simples or monads (§419, 224).

§422. What is not matter is called IMMATERIAL, whereas what is matter is called MATERIAL. The absolutely elementary parts of bodies are immaterial (§421, 295). What is not a body is INCORPOREAL, whereas what is a body is CORPOREAL. Further, everything corporeal is material (§296). Therefore, the absolutely elementary parts of bodies are incorporeal, hence individually they are not bodies (§296).

§424. A thing indivisible in itself is said to be AN ATOM. Every monad is indivisible in itself (§244). Hence, every monad is an atom. Therefore, the elements are atoms (§423); hence they are called atoms of nature.

Section III: On the Nature of Bodies [§§430–435]

§430. The NATURE (cf. §431, 466) of a thing is the sum of those of its internal determinations that are the principles of its alterations or of the accidents that inhere in it in general. Hence, to the nature of a thing belong its (1) essential determinations (§39), (2) essence (§40), (3) faculties, (4) receptivities (§216), (5) all powers it is provided with (§197). The beginning of a nature is its BIRTH, its duration LIFE, its end DEATH.

§433. A MACHINE is a composite thing in the narrow sense that is movable according to the laws of motion. Therefore, *every body* in the world *is a machine* (§419, 432). Every machine given in the world is contingent (§361). The nature of a machine that is determined by the laws of motion is MECHANISM. And whatever is not a composite thing is not a machine. Hence no monad is a machine (§230).

Chapter Three: On the Perfection of the Universe [§§436–500]
Section I: On the Best World [§§436–447]
§436. The most perfect world is that in which the most and the greatest parts compossible in a world agree to the extent that is possible in a world. Hence, the most perfect world has the greatest composite perfection, and if the only perfection that belongs to the world is simple perfection, then it is not the most perfect (§185).

§437. By positing the most perfect world, the greatest perfection that is possible in the world is posited (§436). For this reason *the most perfect world is* also *the best* of all possible worlds (§187). Now, the actual parts of the world (§354) are either simultaneous or successive (§306). Therefore, the most perfect world comprises as many simultaneous things, as many successive things, and as much as is compossible in the best world, i.e., the *best* of worlds *is greatest* (1) *extensively*, (2) *protensively*, (3) *intensively*.

§438.[39] If only two contingent things posited outside of each other are compossible in a world, whether as simultaneous or successive, one of whose perfections diminishes the perfection of the other either not at all or to such an extent that it adds to the perfection of the whole, then the egoistical world, such as is now posited by egoists, is not the most perfect.[40] If one non-intellectual monad is possible in itself and is compossible with spirits in the world and its perfection diminishes the perfection of spirits not at all or to such an extent that it adds to the perfection of the whole, then an idealistic world, such as is now posited by idealists, is not the most perfect (§437).

§439. A materialist denies that monads are given in the world (§395), hence imagines a world that is impossible (§394). Therefore, the MATERIALISTIC WORLD such as the materialist supposes it to exist is neither any world at all nor the most perfect one (§436).

[39] GW refers §438 to A367 and A377 (The Fourth Paralogism).
[40] See *Inaugural Dissertation* (2:389).

PART THREE: PSYCHOLOGY [§§501–799]

Prolegomena [§§501–503]

§501. Psychology is the science of the general predicates of the soul.

§502. Psychology, which contains the first principles of theology, aesthetics, logical, and practical sciences, belongs (§2), with reason (§501), to metaphysics (§1).

§503. Psychology asserts its claims (1) from experience proper [in which case it is empirical psychology], (2) from the concept of the soul deduced from a rather long line of reasoning [in which case it is rational psychology].

Chapter One: Empirical Psychology [§§504–739]
Section I: On the Existence of the Soul [§§504–518]

§504.[41] If there is anything in a being that can be conscious of something, it is a SOUL. There exists in me (§55) what can be conscious of something (§57). Therefore, a soul exists in me (I exist as a soul).

§505. I think; my soul is [thereby] changed (§125, 504). Therefore, thoughts are accidents of my soul (§210), some of which, at least, have their sufficient ground in my soul (§21). Therefore, my soul is a power (§197).

§506. Thoughts are representations. Thus, my soul is a power of representation (§505).

§507. My soul thinks at least certain parts of the universe (§354). Therefore, my soul is a power of representing the universe at least in part (§155).

§508. I think of certain bodies in this universe and of their changes. I think of few changes in some, more in others, and most in one, and that is a part of me (§155). Hence MY BODY is the body whose changes I think of more than any other.

§509. My body has a determinate position (§85), place, lifetime (§281), situation (§284) in this world.

---

[41] GW refers §§504–518 to B422–B423 (Second Edition Paralogisms).

§510.[42] Certain things I think distinctly, certain things confusedly. Whoever thinks something confusedly does not distinguish its marks, yet he [still] represents or perceives them. For if one were to distinguish marks that were represented confusedly, one would think distinctly. If one did not perceive such marks at all, one could not thereby distinguish confused perception from others. Therefore, whoever is thinking something confusedly represents certain things obscurely.

§511. There are obscure perceptions in the soul (§510). The sum of these is called the FOUNDATION OF THE SOUL.

§512. From positing my body in this universe one can cognize why I perceive some things obscurely, others clearly, and yet others distinctly (§306, 509), i.e., I REPRESENT ACCORDING TO THE POSITION OF MY BODY in the universe.

§513. My soul is a power (§505), of representing (§506), the universe (§507), according to the position of my body (§512).

§514. A whole of representations in the soul is a TOTAL PERCEPTION, and its parts are PARTIAL PERCEPTIONS, and the sum of those that are obscure is the FIELD OF OBSCURITY (of darkness) which is the foundation of the soul (§511), whereas the sum of those that are clear is the FIELD OF CLARITY (of light), comprehending the FIELDS OF CONFUSION, DISTINCTNESS, ADEQUACY, etc.

§515. True cognition is reality (§12, 36), the opposite of which is a negation (§81, 36), whether it be no cognition, i.e., a defect in cognition, IGNORANCE, or illusory cognition, i.e., ERROR. The minimal cognition is the minimally true [cognition] of a single minimal [cognizable unit] (§161). Therefore, the more numerous [the things cognized], the greater [the things cognized], and the truer [the cognition], the greater [the cognition] (§160), so that the greatest possible [cognition] is the truest possible cognition of the most numerous, greatest possible things. The degree of cognition by which it knows many is its RICHNESS (abundance, extensiveness, wealth, vastness), that by which it knows few, SCARCITY, that by which it knows greater [things] is DIGNITY (nobility, magnitude, weightiness, majesty), that by which it knows lesser [things] is WORTHLESSNESS (meagreness, shallowness). The more correct and the more orderly a cognition

---

[42] See *False Subtlety* (2:58–59).

represents, the more correct it is (§184) and hence the greater it is as well. An EXACT COGNITION represents more correct [things], and a CRASS cognition displays less true [things]. A greater order or method in a cognition is the METHOD OF COGNITION (discipline), while a lesser order is TURBULENT. Cognition and its representations in my soul are either smaller or greater (§214) and insofar as they are also grounds, they are ARGUMENTS IN THE NARROW SENSE and efficient power is attributed to them (§197). No cognition is completely sterile (§23), still cognition of greater efficacy, i.e., strength, is STRONGER, while cognition of lesser efficacy, that is, FEEBLE, IS WEAKER (soft, inert). When weaker representations arise, they change the state of the soul less, whereas when stronger representations arise, they change the state of the soul more (§208, 214).

§516. PERCEPTIONS that are with other parts of a total perception are called ASSOCIATED, and the strongest of the associated perceptions REIGNS (is dominant in the soul).

§517. The more marks a perception contains, the stronger it is (§23, 515). Hence, an obscure perception comprehending more marks than a clear one is stronger than it, while a confused perception comprehending more marks than a distinct one is stronger than it. PERCEPTIONS that contain more in themselves are called PREGNANT. Therefore, pregnant perceptions are stronger. Hence, ideas have great strength (§148). Terms that have a pregnant meaning are EMPHATIC. The science of these is emphaseology. Proper names have no small power.

§518. The state of the soul in which dominant perceptions are obscure is the REALM OF DARKNESS, and that in which clear perceptions reign is the REALM OF LIGHT.

Section III: On the Senses [§§534–556]

§535. I have the faculty of sensing (§534, 216), i.e., SENSES. INNER SENSE represents the state of my soul, while OUTER SENSE represents the state of my body (§508). Hence, INNER SENSATION is by inner sense (consciousness in the narrow sense) while OUTER SENSATION is made actual by outer sense (§534).

Section XII: On the Intellect [§§624–639]

§624. My soul cognizes certain things distinctly (§522), [thus it has] the faculty of cognizing something distinctly, which is the HIGHER COGNITIVE FACULTY (mind) or, as is suitable to me (§216), the intellect (§402).

§625. Because I have the faculty of paying attention, ATTENTION, and the faculty of abstracting, ABSTRACTION, (§529) and [the faculty] of pre-scinding or abstracting a part from the whole (§589), and they [i.e., these faculties] reveal themselves in sensations, imaginations, what is foreseen, etc., as their objects are related to my body (§538, 600), they are actualized according to the power of the soul for representing the world according to the position of the body (§513).

§626. Attention that is successively directed to successive parts of a whole perception is REFLECTION. Attention to the whole perception after reflection is COMPARISON. I reflect. I compare. Therefore, I have the faculty of reflecting and comparing (§216), of making actual accord-ing to the power of representing the universe according to the position of the body (§625).

§627. The law of attention is: I perceive more clearly than other things those things of which I perceive more marks and fewer obscure marks than of the others. This is the rule of reflection: Prior to the remain-ing ones I attend to the marks of that part of the whole that I perceive and perceive as less obscure, (§626) and this is the rule of compari-son: By perceiving, through reflection on the parts of the whole percep-tion, more and clearer marks of it, I pay more attention to it afterwards (§529).

Section XIII: On Reason [§§640–650]
§641.[43] The faculty of seeing distinctly the identity and diversity of things (§572, 579), hence intellectual talent and skill (§575), intellectual memory, or PERSONALITY (§579, 306), the faculty of distinct judgment (§606, 94) to which intellectual judgment belongs (§607), intellectual presentiment, or PROVIDENCE (foresight) (§610), the faculty of intellec-tual characteristics (§619), is reason (§640).

Section XVI: On the Appetitive Faculty [§§663–675]
§663. If I attempt or try to produce some perception, i.e., if I determine the power of my soul or myself to produce a certain idea, I DESIRE. I SHUN [AM AVERSE TO] that thing whose opposite I desire. Therefore, I have the faculty of desiring and shunning (§216), an APPETITIVE FAC-ULTY, (called a volitional faculty in the broad sense, cf. §690). These

---

[43] GW refers §641 to A361 (the Third Paralogism).

same attempts, or strivings, or the determinations of my powers, are appetites for what is desired and aversions to what is shunned.

Section XVII: On the Lower Appetitive Faculty [§§676–688]

§679. Since affections, which are stronger desires, arise from a stronger sensory pleasure (§678, 665), they will increase the associated pleasure (§162), whence affections of this sort are called PLEASANT (§658); and insofar as the pleasure from which they arise hides the associated displeasure (§529), they are called GRATIFYING (§658). [...]

Section XVIII: On the Higher Appetitive Faculty [§§689–699]

§690. Rational desire is volition. I will. Therefore, I have the faculty of willing, or VOLITION (§216). Rational aversion is nonvolition. I am unwilling. Therefore, I have the faculty of unwilling, or nonvolition (§216). The higher appetitive faculty is either willing or unwilling (§689). Representations [which are] impelling causes of willing and unwilling are MOTIVES. The incentives of the soul (§669) are either stimuli or motives (§677, 521).

Section XIX: Spontaneity [§§700–707]

§700. I am changed (§505–699) internally (§126). Therefore, I am a finite (§254) and contingent thing (§257). Therefore, my existence is a mode (§134), and so all my states are contingent in themselves (§205, 108). Therefore, all of its changes are as well (§124, 125). Therefore, all my actions and passions are contingent in themselves (§210). Hence, all my future actions are too (§298). Hence none of my actions and passions is absolutely or intrinsically necessary (§105).

§701. NECESSITATION (compulsion) is the change of some thing from a contingency into a necessity; hence it is either ACTIVE NECESSITATION, if it is of the thing that necessitates, which is not proper except in substances (§198), or PASSIVE NECESSITATION, if it is of the thing that is necessitated, which is attributed partly to accidents – whether they be actions or passions – that are changed from being a contingency to a necessity, and partly to the substance in which its necessary accidents inhere.

§704.[44] An ACTION that depends on a sufficient principle internal to an agent is SPONTANEOUS. Accordingly, spontaneity is attributed (1) to an

---

[44] See *New Elucidation* (1:402) for a similar discussion of spontaneity.

action that depends on the sufficient principle internal to the agent, (2) to the substance that brings about such actions. Now, every such proper action depends on a principle that is internal to the agent (§210, 37). Therefore, every such proper action is spontaneous. Still, because changes composed of actions and passions are sometimes called actions due to their more important part, to the extent that they are passions they are understood as not spontaneous (§210).

§705. Many of my actions, or rather all of them properly so called, and hence the actions of my soul as well, are spontaneous, and so are to be attributed to it as much as spontaneity is to be attributed to my soul (§704). If something changing itself is called an AUTOMATON, then the soul would be an automaton.

§706. If the intrinsic principle of the agent barely suffices for one smallest action (§704, 161), spontaneity is smallest. Therefore, if the intrinsic principle of the agent suffices for greater actions, its spontaneity is greater, and finally, the greatest spontaneity is in that agent in which it suffices for the most greatest actions. Great spontaneity is to be fully attributed to our soul (§705).

§707. EXTERNAL NECESSITATION (coercion from without) depends on a force existing outside of the necessitated substance, and is either ideal or real (§701, 212). An action that is really necessitated externally is neither spontaneous nor properly action (§704), but is rather a passion of the real (§210). External necessitation of the real is EXTERNAL NECESSITATION SIMPLICITER (coercion). Therefore, actions that are coerced by external necessitation *simpliciter* are real passions. SUBSTANCE and ACTIONS that are not necessitated absolutely are FREE (§719) FROM ABSOLUTE COERCION. SUBSTANCE and ACTIONS that are not necessitated by such external coercion *simpliciter* are FREE (§719) FROM EXTERNAL COERCION *simpliciter*. Therefore, all my changes are free from absolute coercion (§702), all my actions, all spontaneous actions of my soul, i.e., all actions properly so called (§704), and my soul insofar as it acts spontaneously, are free from external coercion *simpliciter*.

Section XX: On Choice [§§708–718]
§712.[45] WHAT PLEASES ONE [*lubitus*] is the cognition of a substance from which one can cognize according to the laws of desires and aversions

[45] GW refers §§712–719 to A534/B561 (Resolution of the Third Antinomy).

why it determines itself in this way and not otherwise concerning those actions that are performed freely. But this can be cognized from foresight, foreknowledge, pleasure or displeasure (§665), stimuli, and motives (§677, 690). Therefore, foresight, foreknowledge, pleasure or displeasure (§665), stimuli, and motives that can be cognized by a certain substance constitute what pleases it. If a substance determines its power concerning actions performed freely so that they can be cognized from what pleases it, IT DESIRES AND IS AVERSE ACCORDING TO WHAT PLEASES IT. Therefore, whoever desires either those future things that are not foreseen, or that are not foreknown by any of its strivings, or does not please or displease, without any stimuli or without any motives, does not desire and is not averse according to what pleases him. I desire much and am averse to much, according to what pleases me. Therefore, I have the faculty of desiring and of being averse as I please, that is, [I have] the POWER OF CHOICE [*arbitrium*]. Those very actions that are determined by what is arbitrarily posited in the capacities of some substance are ABITRARY [*arbitrariae*].⁴⁶ Many of my actions are arbitrary.

§713. I GLADLY DESIRE AND AM AVERSE (1) to whatever I desire and am averse to according to what pleases me, and I UNWILLINGLY desire and am averse to nothing (§712, 665), (2) if what pleases me consists either in displeasure or in a pure pleasure, or if it contains a great preponderance. Accordingly, I act unwillingly if there is no great preponderance in what pleases me or if I have many strong incentives for the opposite of what I desire and am averse to. According to this last explanation, I still desire and am averse to what I unwillingly desire and am averse to according to what pleases me, and an action that I unwillingly do or refrain from doing is nonetheless arbitrary (§712).

§714. Because COERCION IN THE NARROW SENSE (cf. §701) is the production of an action that occurs unwillingly, AN ACTION THAT WAS EXTERNALLY COERCED *simpliciter* would be one that was not produced according to what pleases or against what pleases, [but rather] by an external necessitation *simpliciter*. However, that would not be an action in the proper sense (§707). If I unwillingly do something according to what pleases me, according to the explanation of §713, its preponderance goes to what I desire or am averse to viewed either as brought about by myself, and then one says that I COERCED MYSELF, or as brought about

---

⁴⁶ Arbitrary thus has a precise technical meaning for Baumgarten and is used in this sense in several of the next paragraphs.

by something other than me (§22), and then it is said that the action is in a sense externally coerced.

§715. Actions that are done unwillingly by myself or in a sense by something external occur (§714) according to what pleases me and hence are arbitrary (§712) and are called necessitated insofar as they are understood as less necessary if either I myself or other things had not brought about the preponderance through which it was produced (§701, 188).

§716. ACTIONS THAT ARE DONE UNWILLINGLY DUE TO IGNORANCE OR ERROR are those that I would not have done according to what pleases me except that I did not know or was in error about something. Because they nonetheless occur according to what pleases me, they are still arbitrary actions (§712).

§717. A smallest choice would be determining a single action by what pleases the least (§161). Therefore, the greater something pleases, the more and greater actions it determines, the greater it [i.e., the choice] is (§160), while the greatest [choice] would be determining the most, greatest actions by what pleases the most (§161, 712).

§718. Because choice is the faculty of desire and aversion according to what pleases one (§712), a substance endowed with choice will have either a sensitive faculty of desire and aversion, or a faculty of volition and non-volition according to what pleases, or a faculty of volition and non-volition and of sensitive desire and aversion according to what pleases (§676, 689).

Section XXI: Freedom [§§719–732]

§719. The faculty of desire and aversion according to what is pleasing to the senses is SENSITIVE CHOICE, while the faculty of willing and not-willing according to what pleases itself is (free choice) FREEDOM (CF. §707, 708, 710, moral, so-called *simpliciter*). Freedom purely to desire and not-will is PURE FREEDOM. Therefore, a substance endowed with choice has either such a sensitive choice, or only pure freedom, or freedom mixed with sensitive choice (§718). ACTIONS in which it is supposed to be in the power of some substance to determine itself through freedom are FREE, and the SUBSTANCE itself, insofar as it is able to perform free actions, is FREE.

Chapter Two: Rational Psychology [§§740–799]
Section I: On the Nature of the Human Soul [§§740–760]

§740. THE HUMAN SOUL is a soul that is in closest interaction with a human body. And because an ANIMAL is constituted by a soul along with the body with which it is in closest interaction, the human animal, with which the human soul is in closest interaction, constitutes an animal that we call MAN.

§742.[47] Thinking requires (1) perception of a thing, (2) of marks sufficient to distinguish it (§524), [and] (3) the distinction itself (§67). However, thinking is an accident (§191). Therefore, it cannot exist except in a substance or in an aggregate of substances (§194). An aggregate of substances the parts of which are gathered together from changes and accidents, none of which is yet a thought, which nevertheless results, as a whole, in a thought, would be THINKING MATTER. There is an aggregate of finite substances (§354) in this world, of which one contributes more to thinking than the remaining ones (§272) that aid it (§210, 321). But it is passive, unless it is ideal (§451, 463). Therefore, if there were thinking matter in the world, then there would be one substance in which the finite things that satisfy all of the conditions for thinking by a single force have a sufficient ground, and still (1) the dominant substance given with the aggregate never thinks per se, which is against (§30, 220), (2) the finite things that satisfy all the conditions for thinking have a sufficient ground in the dominant substance given, as demonstrated, at the same time, unless they are in fact made actual through the aggregate of substances, i.e., unless they have a sufficient ground in the power of a plurality of finite substances (§210, cf. §7). Thinking matter is impossible in the world. Whatever can think is either a substance, a monad (§234), or a whole of which a substance that can think is a part. Therefore, every soul is a substance, a monad (§504). Whatever can understand, can think (§69). Therefore, whatever can understand, is either a substance, monad, or spirit (§402), or a whole of which a spirit is a part. A whole of spirits is (a moral person) a MYSTICAL BODY. An intellectual soul is a spirit (§504, cf. §402, 296). A human soul is a substance (§740). Therefore, it is a monad, a spirit (§741).

§743. The human soul subsists through itself (§742, 192). Therefore, it is not a substantiated phenomenon (§193). Still, because it represents

---

[47] GW refers §742 to A348 (the First Paralogism).

according to the position of the human body in the world, which is in perpetual motion (§417, 296) and hence always changing its position (§283, 281), its representations are always changing (§512). Because those determinations of the human soul are internal (§37, 741), the human soul is a substance with internal changes, and hence is contingent (§202) and finite (§255). Accordingly, it is also clear that every finite human soul is also a contingent substance: the human soul represents according to the position of its body (§741). Therefore, it perceives certain things distinctly and certain things less distinctly (§512). Now, whatever it in fact conceives distinctly is reality (§515, 531). Therefore, the human soul does not have the greatest degree of reality (§161), hence it is limited (§248). Therefore, it is a finite and contingent (§257) substance (§742).

§744. The human soul cognizes, desires, and has aversions (§741). These are actions that are partially diverse (§267). Therefore, the human soul has partially diverse faculties (§216) that are not called powers in the narrow sense (§197, 59). Rather, they are understood through a single human power of representation in the narrow sense (§§521–720) and they are not posited outside of each other given that accidents (§191) are not outside of their substance (§194).[48] It is not accurate to say that they act on or influence each other (§211), because action proper can occur only in substances (§210).

§745.[49] The human soul is a monad (§742), contingent (§743), can arise only from nothing (§236), can perish only through annihilation (§237), is not extended, does not fill space (§241), i.e., is not space-filling (§241). Still, coexisting with simultaneous things posited outside of it, it is in space (§239), in a place (§281) such that some others posited outside of it are closer to it, while some others are more remote (§288, 282). The sum of simultaneous things that are closer to the human soul is called its SEAT: the human body, which is prior to other bodies, and [in particular] those of its parts that are prior to its other members, is the seat of the soul (§409).

§746.[50] The human soul does not have a quantitative magnitude (§744, 243), and is indivisible (§244). Perishing by division is PHYSICAL

---

[48] See A648–A650/B676–B678 (Appendix to the Transcendental Dialectic).
[49] GW refers §§745–747 to A351 (the Second Paralogism). §§745–747 and 750 are also relevant to *Dreams of a Spirit-Seer* (2:319ff.).
[50] See Refutation of Mendelssohn's Proof of the Persistence of the Soul (B413ff.).

CORRUPTION. Therefore, physical corruption is impossible in itself for the human soul (§15, 745), i.e., the human soul is absolutely PHYSICALLY INCORRUPTIBLE.

§747. The human soul does not in fact admit three-dimensional extension (§290, 745), yet philosophical and mathematical cognition of it, like that of a human body, is possible (§743, 249). A human consists of a soul and of a finite body (§741, 743), hence is internally mutable (§740) and a finite and contingent thing (§202, 257). Therefore, philosophical and mathematical cognition of man, i.e., philosophical and mathematical anthropology, or anthropometry, as of empirical [objects] through experience, is possible (§249). The set of rules [that are to be followed] in cognizing what is to be observed about man is ANTHROPOGNOSIA.

§750. The human soul moves its own body (§740, 734). Therefore, it has THE FACULTY of moving something posited outside of itself, i.e. [a] LOCOMOTIVE [faculty], that is activated, as are the remaining faculties of the soul (§744), by its power of representing the universe according to the position of its body (§741, 417).

§755.[51] Every spirit is a substance (§402), therefore, a power (§199), hence the sufficient ground of the inherence of its accidents (§197), and thus acting (§210). Because it is an intellectual substance (§402), it has a faculty for making actual certain distinct representations (§216). Therefore, [it has a faculty] for determining its power with respect to them (§210), and desiring (§663). Whatever desires [something] is averse to its opposite; hence spirit has the faculty of aversion (§663). The desires and aversions of a spirit are its internal determinations (§37). Therefore, they are in universal connection with its remaining internal determinations (§49) and they are, therefore, also in universal connection with its cognition, since cognition is an internal determination (§37), and so come to be according to what pleases the spirit. Therefore, spirit has choice (§712), and when what pleases it can be distinct (§402), it is free or has freedom (§719).

§756.[52] The human soul is a spirit (§754). Therefore, it has freedom (§755). And because spiritual, intellect, personality (§641, 754),

---

[51] GW refers §755 to A348 (the First Paralogism).
[52] GW refers §§756–757 to A351 (the Second Paralogism) and §756 to A361 (the Third Paralogism).

freedom, absolute simplicity (§744), and incorruptibility are attributed to it with absolute necessity (§746), they are not its modes (§108). Because they are internal determinations (§37, 52), they are either its essential determinations or its attributes. By removing one of them, the human soul is removed (§63). Hence, if a human soul were unable to conceive something distinctly at all, [were unable] to determine [itself] according to what distinctly pleases it, [that is] if such a soul had lost all its personality and freedom, were constituted by many powers that were posited outside each other as parts, and were physically corruptible, it would be a chimera (§590).

§757. The human soul is immaterial and incorporeal (§744, 422). Whoever denies that the human soul is an immaterial substance is a MATERIALIST IN THE PSYCHOLOGICAL SENSE (cf. §395), and is deceived, whether it be held to be a mere accident of a body (§742), or a material atom (§429), or some most subtle corpuscle (§426). A universal materialist is also such a materialist in the psychological sense (§395), but by not positing that every material substance is a human soul, a psychological materialist is not necessarily a universal materialist (§395).

Section II: On Psychological Systems [§§761–769]

§761. PSYCHOLOGICAL SYSTEMS are views which seem fit to explain the interaction of the soul and body in man. Therefore, psychological systems are particular systems (§462), whether simple or composite (§457). None of them is possible except the systems of pre-established harmony, physical influx, and occasional, perhaps psychological, causes (§458).

§762. If one of the simple general systems is posited, then one of the psychological simple systems is also posited (§761, 457). Therefore, if universal pre-established harmony has been demonstrated (§463), then psychological pre-established harmony has been demonstrated at the same time. However, if one of the simple psychological systems is posited, one of the general systems is not necessarily posited as well (§761, 457). If the soul and the human body can be in closest interaction in pre-established harmony, then they are also connected by pre-established harmony in the best world (§461). Therefore, neither physical influx nor the system of occasional causes is to be accepted unless interaction according to pre-established harmony is impossible (§462).

§763.[53] The psychological system of physical influx, because it is simple, posits that all harmonious changes of all souls and human bodies occur through physical influx (§457). Therefore, if one single harmonious change either of one soul or of one human body can be proved possible according to the pre-established harmony in the best world, the system of physical influx cannot be defended any longer as having a place in the best world (§762). The psychological system of pre-established harmony, because it is simple, posits that all harmonious changes of all souls and human bodies occur through pre-established harmony, and on account of a certain ground the psychological system of occasionalism posits that they occur solely through an infinite power (§457). Therefore, if one single harmonious change either of one soul or of one human body is impossible in the best world according to the pre-established harmony, this system cannot be defended any longer as having a place in the best world. If one single harmonious change either of one soul or of one human body can be proved possible according to pre-established harmony or physical influx in the best world, the system of occasionalism cannot be defended any longer as having a place in the best world (§762, 460). The psychological system of physical influx is no more obvious from experience than are the systems of pre-established harmony and occasional causes (§737, 738).

§764. The psychological system of physical influx posits that the human soul really influences its body and the human body influences its soul in harmonious changes (§761, 450). Hence according to the psychological system of physical influx (1) in no harmonious changes that occur in the human body does the body act by its own power (§212). Now, even all changes of the human body, as parts of the world that the soul represents, can be cognized sufficiently by the soul's power (§354, 751). Therefore, all changes are harmonious (§448) and the body does not act by its own power in any of its changes, according to the psychological system of physical influx, and is really acted upon by the soul in everything. If the body never acts, it does not react (§213). Therefore, according to the system of physical influx the soul's action on the human body in the world occurs without reaction as often as the soul acts on its body, which at once goes against §410.

---

[53] GW refers §§763–768 to A390 (Observation on the Paralogisms).

§765. The system of physical influx posits (2) that the human body really influences its soul as often as change that can be cognized sufficiently from the power of the body occurs in the human soul (§764, 448). Thus, according to the psychological system of physical influx, in harmonious changes encountered in the soul the body, which is to be posited as acting in none of its changes at any time according to that system (§764), really has influence. According to the view of the system of physical influx, the soul is not acting at all (§212) when it nonetheless represents the present state of the world by its own power (§751).

§766. The human body consist of elements (§420), monads, [containing] representations of its world from which each of its parts, hence also each of the changes of each soul, [i.e.] the parts of the world (§354) can be cognized (§400). Therefore, every action of the soul is a harmonious change (§448, 22). Further, every volition and nonvolition of the soul is one of its actions (§210, 690). Therefore, every volition and nonvolition of the human soul is one of its harmonious changes. Now, according to the psychological system of physical influx the human soul acts by its own power in none of its harmonious changes, but rather is acted on by the body. Therefore, according to the system of physical influx, in all of its volitions and nonvolitions the soul acts on nothing whatsoever, yet is acted upon by the body, which is contrary to freedom (§755).

§767. According to the psychological system of occasional causes (1) the human body does not act in any of its harmonious changes, but rather an infinite thing [acts] (§761, 452), from which it is clear in the same way as is shown in §764 that according to the system of assistance the body acts in none of its changes, but rather only an infinite thing [acts]. (2) According to the same system, the human soul does not act in its harmonious changes, but rather only an infinite thing [acts] (§761, 452), from which it is clear in the same way as is shown in §766 that according to the psychological system of assistance the human soul acts in none of its volitions and nonvolitions whatsoever, and to such an extent is really acted on in them by an infinite thing, which is in the same way contrary to freedom (§755).

§768. According to the psychological system of pre-established harmony, each part interacting with another brings about, by its own power, the harmonious changes that occur, and is acted on ideally by the other part (§761, 448). Hence, the psychological system of pre-established harmony posits that (1) the arbitrary motions of the human body are sufficiently determined by its mechanisms and the other bodies that surround it no less than merely natural or vital bodies, (2) the soul's sensations are sufficiently determined through its representational power no less than its freest thoughts (§758, 433).

Section V: State after Death [§§782–791]

§784. The state of the human soul after death can be considered (1) by assuming man's absolute death, in which case the human soul would lack any body at all after death, or there would be no body with which it would then come into closest interaction (§742, 740); (2) by assuming the death of man to the extent that it is, in turn, placed in interaction with a new body (§778). The beginning of the soul's new closest interaction with a new body is called PALINGENESIS [the exchange of its body for another] (regeneration, metensomatosis, and metempsychosis in the broad sense). Whoever maintains this either defends the cup of forgetfulness and assumes that the new body would be one such that we are familiar with it on earth or neither of them is assumed with it. The former defends CRASS METEMPSYCHOSIS in the strict sense and it is improbable (§783).

Section VI: On the Souls of Brutes [§§792–795]

§792.[54] Because every soul is that in a thing which can be conscious of something (§504), it has the faculty of cognizing (§519), and either an inferior or a superior faculty (§520, 524). The former would be a MERELY SENSITIVE SOUL. An animal that has a merely sensitive soul is a BRUTE; an animal of which the soul is a spirit is a RATIONAL ANIMAL. Therefore, man is a rational animal (§754, 740).

§793. The souls of brutes are in closest interaction with animal bodies (§740), hence they represent their bodies clearly and obscurely (§792, 736). Therefore, they are powers of representing the universe according to the position of the bodies of the brutes therein (§741), and are hence substances (§198), monads (§234), simple things (§230), they do not have parts outside of parts (§224), they are finite (§202, 792), indivisible (§244), and are hence physically incorruptible (§746), immaterial and incorporeal (§422), are endowed with the faculties of bringing about

---

[54] GW refers §§792–793 to A534/B561 (Resolution of the Third Antinomy).

sensation, imagination, foresight and the rest without distinct cognition by the power of representing the universe according to the position of its body (§792). Therefore, they are impelled by sensitive desires and aversions (§667), choice (§718), instincts, flights, and stimuli (§677), and also affects (§678).

PART FOUR: NATURAL THEOLOGY [§§800–1000]

Prolegomena [§§800–802]

§800. NATURAL THEOLOGY is the science of God to the extent that he can be cognized without faith.

§801. Natural theology contains the first principles of practical philosophy, teleology, and revealed theology. Therefore, it belongs (§2), with reason, to metaphysics (§1).

§802. Natural theology considers (1) the concept of God, (2) his operations.

Chapter One: The Concept of God [§§803–925]
Section I: The Existence of God [§§803–862]

§803. A MOST PERFECT THING is that to which the greatest perfection in things is to be attributed, i.e., in which as much and as great [perfections] are combined in as many and great [a thing] as can be combined in any being (§185). Therefore, a certain plurality in the most perfect thing is absolutely necessary (§74).

§804. The predicates of a most perfect thing are called its perfections. In a most perfect thing there are as many perfections consistent in the highest degree as can exist at the same time in one thing as are compossible (§803).

§805. There is as much perfection in every perfect thing as can be in any thing (§803, 804).

§806. A most perfect thing is a real thing (§803, 135). Therefore, reality agrees with it as much as can be in a thing. A most perfect thing is a most real thing (§805, 804), in which the greatest amount of reality [can be found]. It is metaphysically the greatest good, and the best (§190).

§807. All realities are indeed positive, and no negation is a reality (§36). Therefore, if everything in a thing is conjoined maximally, a contradiction can never arise between them (§13). Therefore, all realities are compossible in a thing. Now, a most perfect thing is a most real thing (§806). Therefore, it has all realities and the maximum of what can be in any thing (§805, 190).

§808. If a reality is posited, a negation is removed (§36). Now all realities are to be posited in a most perfect thing (§807). Therefore, all negations are to be removed.

§809. In everything impossible, something is to be posited and removed at the same time (§7). It is either a negation or a reality (§36, 9). No reality is to be removed from a most perfect thing (§807). No negation is to be posited in a most perfect thing (§808). Therefore, nothing in a most perfect thing is to be posited and removed at the same time. A perfect being is possible (§8).

§810. Existence is a reality that is compossible with the essence and the remaining realities (§66, 807). Therefore, a perfect thing has existence (§807).

§811. GOD is a most perfect thing. Therefore, God is actual (§810, 55).[55]

---

[55] For translations of some of the sections from Baumgarten's *Metaphysics* that follow, see Immanuel Kant, *Religion and Rational Theology*, ed. Allen Wood and George di Giovanni (New York: Cambridge University Press, 1996), pp. 476ff.

4

Christian August Crusius

Christian August Crusius was born in 1715 in Leipzig, where he was educated first at a grammar school and then at the university; there he became a follower of Adolf Friedrich Hoffmann, a Pietist highly critical of Wolff. Shortly after graduation Crusius accepted the extraordinary professorship of philosophy in 1744 and then the more prestigious (and remunerative) ordinary professorship in theology in 1750. Until his death, in 1775, he then devoted his intellectual energies to a wide variety of primarily orthodox theological issues (often in opposition to those of his more reform-minded colleague, Johann August Ernesti).

Crusius's publications in philosophy span a mere seven years, from 1743 to 1749. His dissertation, in 1743, *Dissertatio de usu et limitibus principii rationis determinantis vulgo sufficientis* (Dissertation on the Use and Limits of the Principle of Determining Reason, Commonly Called Sufficient Reason), contains a criticism of Wolff's principle of sufficient reason. His *Entwurf der Notwendigen Vernunft-Wahrheiten* (Sketch of the Necessary Truths of Reason, 1745) presents his distinctive metaphysical view, while his *Weg zur Gewißheit und Zuverläßigkeit der menschlichen Erkenntnis* (Path to the Certainty and Reliability of Human Cognition, 1747) lays out his position on logical and epistemological issues. His *Anweisung, vernünftig zu leben* (Directions for Living Rationally, 1744) and *Anleitung über natürliche Begebenheiten ordentlich und vorsichtig nachzudenken* (Introduction to Proper and Cautious Reflections on Natural Events, 1749) treat ethics and natural philosophy respectively, so that he had covered a fairly comprehensive gamut of traditional philosophical topics by the time he turned to theology. Like well-known Pietists before him, such as Franz Budde, Andreas Rüdiger, and Hoffmann, Crusius rejected many of Wolff's fundamental principles, but his criticisms were motivated by a positive philosophical position that is articulated with much greater philosophical sophistication, insight, and systematicity. Crusius thus represents an important bridge from the Pietists in the first part of the eighteenth century to thinkers later in the century, such as Johann Georg Hamann, Friedrich Heinrich Jacobi, and Thomas Wizenmann, who drew heavily on Pietist themes in their criticisms of Kant's position.

Crusius's position in the *Sketch of the Necessary Truths of Reason* represents an interesting synthesis of a variety of different elements, which resulted in an independent voice. While he is clearly sympathetic to empiricism insofar as he holds that everything must ultimately be grounded in actual objects of sensation (e.g., he defines power in terms of what makes something else actual), he also thinks that metaphysics aims to establish necessary truths that are based on the essences of things, essences that involve simple concepts arrived at through abstraction from actual objects. He is clearly critical of Leibniz and Wolff as his main opponents by accepting a voluntaristic view of God, libertarian freedom for both God and finite rational creatures, causal interaction between mind and body, and substantive principles that cannot be derived from the principle of contradiction alone or even this principle plus the principle of sufficient reason. However, after distinguishing essence and existence as the two main components of every complete thing, he argues for "metaphysical essences," "fundamental powers" (i.e., primitive causal powers), and "fundamental activities" in ways reminiscent of his rationalist predecessors. The net result of this mixture is both original and interesting. Space and time are necessary as the two simple concepts that constitute existence since, so Crusius wants to argue, we cannot even think of a complete thing without thinking of it as existing somewhere and at some time, while power, space, and time are structurally necessary components of the complete possibility of a thing (which pertains to its essence). The concept of power, in particular, is subjected to detailed analysis, resulting in distinctions between real and ideal as well as active and inefficacious, or existential, grounds.

Crusius's importance for Kant's *Critique of Pure Reason* can hardly be exaggerated. As Guyer and Wood rightly note in their introduction to the first *Critique:* "To the extent that Kant was a critic of the Leibnizian-Wolffian philosophy, his criticisms came not only from Hume but even more from Wolff's Pietist critic Christian August Crusius."[1] If Wolff is

---

[1] Immanuel Kant, *Critique of Pure Reason,* ed. Paul Guyer and Allen Wood (New York: Cambridge University Press, 1998), p. 24.

important for laying out the general structure of traditional metaphysics along with many of the rationalist doctrines that Kant would be attacking in the *Critique of Pure Reason,* Crusius is significant not only because he (1) develops various criticisms (especially of the rationalist position) that Kant ends up being quite sympathetic to and (2) adopts a position different in fundamental ways from Leibniz's and Wolff's, but also because he (3) transforms the very framework in which rationalist questions are posed.

(1) For instance, Crusius's treatment of space and time is of special relevance to Kant's discussion in the Transcendental Aesthetic. For Crusius criticizes the Leibnizian-Wolffian position that space and time are relations by raising the possibility (§49) that we could imagine a world consisting of a single substance that was nonetheless still spatial, a view that does not seem to be possible for a relationalist account of space and time. Crusius also raises objections against the Newtonian position that space and time might be independent things, that is, substances, given that it seems inconsistent to him to hold that there be necessary substances other than God (§51). As a result, the structure of Crusius's critique of standard positions concerning space and time clearly anticipates Kant's own in the Transcendental Aesthetic. Moreover, Crusius's positive explanation of space and time (given that they can be neither substances nor relations between them) invites interesting comparisons with Kant's own view. As we saw above, he suggests that space and time are necessary conditions for both actual things – a view Kant endorses for phenomenal entities – and merely possible things – a view Kant rejects. Further, Crusius thinks that space and time themselves are simply abstractions from reality that are brought about by the essence of our understanding, which contrasts with Kant's Critical view, which invokes an intuitive, and nonintellectual, or sensible, faculty.

(2) With regard to his doctrinal differences with Leibniz and Wolff, Crusius's libertarian account of freedom is especially fundamental. While the historical and systematic significance of the issue of freedom is already clear, quite a bit of Crusius's positive account of metaphysics ends up being structured the way it is so as to allow for libertarian freedom. Thus, in addition to attributing powers and first free actions to substances, Crusius revises his basic ontological principles (§§81–82) in order to make sense of how a first cause, that is, an agent, could act in such a way that it could have done otherwise. Specifically, this requires that Crusius distinguish between the principle of determining ground and the principle of sufficient reason in such a way that an agent is

sufficient to cause himself to act in one way, while still allowing that he could have caused himself to act a different way under precisely the same circumstances (§§83–84). This line on freedom goes hand in hand with the other systematically deep feature of Crusius's metaphysics, namely, his voluntaristic conception of God, which significantly limits the scope of what we can cognize.

(3) Perhaps more important, however, than any particular criticism or positive doctrine that Crusius might have provided is the way in which his work, taken as a whole, attempts to redraw the philosophical landscape in fundamental ways. For example, Crusius seems to recognize, even if only implicitly and for reasons different from Kant's, that not all truths can be analytic truths reducible to the principle of contradiction. While Crusius's positive account of the source of truths that go beyond the principle of contradiction is not articulated in great detail, resting, as it does, on remarks about the "essence of our understanding," his reflections on such epistemological questions are clearly quite provocative and fecund for the development of Kant's position. (Certainly in retrospect one can surmise that Kant would have seen the need to investigate exactly what the "essence of our understanding" is and, ultimately, demarcate it from sensibility.) Crusius also formulates *in nuce* the idea that the necessary truths of metaphysics might be justifiable only as *a priori* conditions, an idea Kant finds fruitful in a systematic way in the *Critique of Pure Reason*.

Sketch of the Necessary Truths
of Reason (1745)[2]

Preface

[...] Metaphysics in this work will hopefully be what one seeks in it, namely, a universal fundamental science [*Grundwissenschaft*] from which all other human cognition that is to be established *a priori* can obtain its grounds and which also contains in itself the grounds for mathematical and practical sciences, although the determinate constitution of the necessary truths that they contain in themselves cannot be justly incorporated into metaphysics. Accordingly, all other sciences contain further determinations of those things that arise in metaphysics. One learns of their actuality mostly *a posteriori*, but metaphysics reveals the grounds of possibility or necessity *a priori*, through which cognition thereof becomes more distinct and complete.[3] [...] According to the example set by other scholars, our current metaphysics has been divided into four sciences, namely, ontology, theoretical natural theology, cosmology, and pneumatology. However, a change has been made. [...] Natural theology comes before cosmology and pneumatology, because in the latter two the most noble and important theorems can be established only by referring to a consideration of the divine attributes, although they can be proved with irrefutable certainty after the divine attributes have been presupposed.[4] [...]

[PART ONE] ONTOLOGY, OR THE DOCTRINE
OF THE ESSENCE AND MOST UNIVERSAL DISTINCTIONS
OF THINGS IN GENERAL

Chapter One: On Metaphysics in General and Ontology in
Particular [§§1–10]

§1.[5] *What the object of metaphysics in general consists in.* [...] [While various scholars have proposed concepts of metaphysics that seem to differ from each other,] its universal concept is the following. There are **two kinds of truths**. Some are **contingent**, that is, they are concerned only with matters that belong to the contingent configuration of things in

---

[2] Translated from *Entwurf der nothwendigen Vernunft-Wahrheiten* (Leipzig, 1745).
[3] See B20–21 (B-Introduction), where Kant makes similar claims about the nature of metaphysics.
[4] See Wolff's and Baumgarten's divisions of metaphysics in Chapters 1 and 3.
[5] See B3–5 (B-Introduction).

the world. However, others are **necessary**, namely, they concern either what is necessary *simpliciter* and cannot possibly not be or at least what is unavoidable when a world is posited and thus must occur in each and every world just as much as it must occur in the present one. Now, metaphysics ought to treat of necessary truths. [...]

§3.[6] *To what extent the universal object of metaphysics is to be limited.* Despite the fact that the object of metaphysics in general has been determined in this way, the limits of metaphysics have not yet been determined thereby precisely enough. [...]

§4.[7] *What metaphysics is.* [...] In short, **metaphysics** is the science of those necessary truths of reason that are something different from the determination of extended magnitudes.

§7.[8] *How simple concepts are to be rendered distinct in ontology.* Because ontology is supposed to treat the universal essence of things (§5), we must arrive at the **simplest concepts of all**, which do not contain yet further properties that they might consist in. Now, although one can represent the way in which the concepts of things that are more composite, once they are attained, arise from their composition according to the synthetic way of thinking, one must nonetheless notice that the simplest concepts themselves can be rendered distinct only through the analytic mode of reflection. With such concepts one can do nothing further, and one may not request any more, than that one explain the way in which one attains the simple concepts, that is, how one who pays careful attention to everything ultimately ends up with simple concepts after the repeated dissection of the composite things that affect our senses. This distinguishes ontology from all other sciences. [...]

§8. *Explanation based on kinds of distinctness in general.* I am presupposing here as familiar from logic that there are **three kinds of distinctness** of which human concepts are capable. Yet I call **distinctness** that perfection of thoughts in which they can be distinguished from all others. Thus, first, our concepts can have **common distinctness** if they can be distinguished from all others, even though they have not yet been

---

[6] See Bxxx (Preface).
[7] See A162/B203 (Axioms of Intuition).
[8] See A64/B89 (First Division of Transcendental Logic) and *Inquiry* (2:280–283).

dissected through analysis. Color concepts, e.g., have such distinctness. The second kind of distinctness is given by the dissected representation of the content of a concept, since one becomes aware of the parts and properties contained therein, and thereby distinguishes it from others. One calls it **distinctness of essential content**. One attains this kind of distinctness according to the kind of definition that is common in nearly all sciences other than certain matters of ontology. The third kind of distinctness arises during the dissection of those composite concepts that come from the senses, by paying attention to how simpler concepts arise out of more composite ones while taking away what does not belong to them in such fashion that nothing remains in thought other than what belongs to them. One can call this distinctness **logical distinctness** in the narrow sense. Now, since the simplest concepts, precisely because they are simple, are incapable of any kind of distinctness other than logical distinctness, one ought not to demand any other [kind of distinctness] in them.[9]

Distinct cognition of the human understanding necessarily terminates with common distinctness below and logical distinctness above.[10] For our cognition must start with the senses.[11] [...]

§9. *Outline of ontology*. Thus, whoever is attentive and acute enough can abstract the entirety of ontology from any actually present object that comes before our senses, or at least repeat the entire science by observing what can be noticed and distinguished in that case. And precisely so that this can occur all the more easily, I want to provide a preview of the **outline of ontology** by means of which it will become easier to have insight into how one must be able to recognize the entire science from any example. First, I shall dissect the manifold that can be distinguished in the **essence** and **existence** of any actually present thing. Thereafter I have to explain those **possible differences** of things that can be surveyed *a priori* from the necessary essence of any actual thing due to which it must be **simple** or **composite**, **necessary** or **contingent**, **finite** or **infinite**.[12] Then the **universal properties** of things that must be abstracted not from the individual circumstances of an essence or

[9] See A64–A65/B89–B90 (Introduction to Transcendental Analytic) and A65–A66/B90–B91 (Introduction to Analytic of Concepts).
[10] See A411/B438 (First Section of the Antinomy of Pure Reason).
[11] See B1 (Introduction).
[12] See A415/B443 (First Section of the Antinomy of Pure Reason).

existence, but rather from the entire thing, remain to be discovered, namely, the **unity**, **size**, **perfection**, and **goodness** of things. [...]

Chapter Two: On the Concept of a Thing in General [§§11–18]
§12.[13] *What the distinguishing feature of things and non-things are.* [...] Now, first, concerning the **distinguishing feature of a possible thing**, it consists in **whether something can be thought** by means of a concept. [...]

§13.[14] *How the principle of contradiction is comprehended under this distinguishing feature.* [...] Hence, the first and most universal principle of the *distinguishing feature* of possible things is the principle of contradiction, namely, that nothing can be and also not be at one time in exactly one sense. [...]

§14. *How one ought to view what cannot be thought, although no contradiction arises.* [...] And we should consider that, even if we cannot think something, that is, cannot distinctly and completely combine several individual concepts into one concept, still an understanding can be thought that can perhaps combine them, and thus think a thing that we are incapable of thinking. [...]

§15.[15] *The three highest principles of reason concerning the distinguishing features of things and non-things.* Accordingly, all of the distinguishing features of possible and actual things are contained in three highest principles. They are (1) the **principle of contradiction**: Nothing can be and not be at the same time; (2) the **principle of the inseparable**: What cannot be thought apart from each other also cannot exist apart from each other; (3) the **principle of the uncombinable**: what cannot be thought with and next to each other also cannot exist with and next to each other. [...] **But the very highest distinguishing feature of possible and actual things is the essence of the understanding, namely, that what cannot be thought as such is not possible or actual, and that, by contrast, what can be thought is possible, but that by whose denial one would have to admit something, either mediately or immediately, which cannot be thought to be true or in accordance with the perfection of rational**

---

[13] §§12–16 are relevant to the Postulates of Empirical Thought (A218–A235/B265–B287).
[14] See A150–A154/B189–B193 (Supreme Principle of All Analytic Judgments).
[15] See *Inquiry* (2:293ff.) for an evaluation of some of these principles.

deeds, is even actual. The three previous principles are themselves only parts of this highest distinguishing feature of the truth. [...]

§16.[16] *More precise determination of the distinguishing feature of actual things.* [...] *It is ultimately always sensation.* This makes clear that and why **the distinguishing feature of actuality is ultimately always sensation in our understanding**. For **sensation** is precisely that state of our understanding in which we are forced to think something immediately as existing, without first needing to cognize it through inferences and without it being the case that another state follows it from whose comparison with the former we perceive that we would have merely imagined something, which happens, e.g., in dreams. [...]

§17. *What the metaphysical essence is.* For any thing whatsoever [...] one must think something that distinguishes it from other things. What one thinks for such a thing and what distinguishes it from others I shall call the **metaphysical essence** of a thing. [...] *What a property is.* If one views a part of the metaphysical essence in particular and to the extent that it allows one to distinguish it from certain others, then it is called a **property** (quality).

Chapter Three: On the Essence of Things
and the Concepts That Lie Therein [§§19–44]

§19. *Explanation of intent.* In an actual thing **existence** and **essence** are to be distinguished. And in this broad sense, since we have opposed essence and existence, we consider a part of the essence everything that we think of with respect to a thing and by means of which we distinguish it from others. I called this the **metaphysical essence** (§17). In the present chapter, we intend to investigate this further and see what needs to be distinguished in it.

§20.[17] *What a subject* [subjectum] *and predicamental accident* [accidens praedicamentale] *are.* In every complete thing there arises something that we represent as subsisting in another and something that we represent as that in which other things subsist, but which does not itself in turn subsist in another, at least not in precisely the same way as certain other incomplete things subsist in it. That in which we think nothing

---

[16] See A225/B272 (Postulates of Empirical Thought).
[17] See the First Analogy of Experience (A182–A189/B224–B232).

further than something that, when it exists, must necessarily subsist in another is called a predicamental accident [*accidens praedicamentale*]. In German one can call it a **metaphysical property**, or a **property in the narrow sense**. That, however, in which we think that the properties subsist and which does not at all subsist in another, or at least not in precisely the same way as properties do in it, is called a **metaphysical subject**. The subject as well as its properties are incomplete things, neither of which can exist without the other. However, they are not identical, but rather must be distinguished in each complete thing. A complete thing insofar as it is viewed as consisting of a subject and properties is called a **substance**. **The concept of subsistence** is simple and cannot be analyzed further, but rather can be abstracted only from examples. E.g., we represent a book and distinguish its matter and shape. We say that the shape subsists in the matter. Now if we subtract from our thoughts whatever belongs to the essence of shape in general and this shape in particular, and pay attention only to the kind of combination that we are thinking of between the shape and the matter due to which the shape would be nothing if the matter that it was in did not exist, then the concept of subsistence remains and shape is thus a predicamental accident. Now we say further that the matter that the book consists in occupies a space and could not exist without any space. However, everyone will notice that we do not mean the same kind of "being in" when we say that the shape **subsists** in the matter and that the book **exists** in space. For that reason the matter of the book is not in another in precisely the same way as shape is in it. Therefore, it is a metaphysical subject insofar as we distinguish it from its properties. Now if we view the book as something in which a subject as well as its properties exist, one calls it a substance.

§29.[18] *What a power is.* The existence of a thing cannot be viewed as equal to its non-existence. Accordingly, through every thing something else must become possible or actual, whether it be made possible or actual through itself alone or by adding several things. The possibility of one thing, B, which is connected to another thing, A, is called a **power** in the broadest sense in thing A. Consequently, every thing has several powers, but at least one power. For that reason every positive property, if one takes it in a different respect, is a power. [...]

---

[18] Compare and contrast this definition with Wolff's and especially Baumgarten's definitions of power in Chapters 1 and 3.

§30. *What a logical essence and contingent properties are.* What is constantly attributed to a thing, taken together, is its **logical essence**. [...] What is not constantly attributed to a thing constitutes its **contingent properties** or accidental predicables. [...]

§31.[19] *What efficacious causes and effects are, besides the principle of sufficient cause.* Each thing that exists now and did not exist previously has its origin in the efficacious power of another thing, which is called its efficacious cause. And when the latter applies the power it has and no hindrance is otherwise present, that thing arises and is accordingly called an effect. [...] One can call [this principle] the principle of sufficient cause. Those who do not have an overview of all signs of truth together and therefore hold that one would have to establish everything from the principle of contradiction have also attempted to derive this principle from the principle of contradiction. It is, however, not possible, because a cause and its effects do not exist at one and the same point in time, but rather are supposed to follow one another, whereas, by contrast, the principle of contradiction is a completely empty proposition and says merely that nothing can be and also not be at the same time in the same sense, by which it says nothing more than what is, is, and what is not, is not. [...]

§32. *That the concept of causality is simple.* The concept of **causality**, or of what underlies words such as **make**, **bring about**, **produce**, etc., is simple and in light of this one can thus do nothing more than reflect in a comfortable way on simplifying the path to inner sensation so that one perceives how this concept can be abstracted from examples. [...]

§33. *The principle of contingency.* Further, it is in accordance with the essence of our understanding to think that **that whose non-existence can be thought also did not exist at one time**, which one can call the **principle of contingency.** [...] **Everything whose non-existence can be thought has its sufficient cause, which gives it actuality through the application of its power.**

§34.[20] *What a ground or cause is in the broad sense.* Everything that brings about something else either in part or in whole and insofar as it is viewed

---

[19] See A150/B189ff. (On the Supreme Principle of All Analytic Judgments). Note also the similarity of these remarks to Kant's criticism of (Wolff's formulation of) the principle of contradiction in the *New Elucidation* (1:388–389).

[20] See *New Elucidation* (1:391–392); see also *Negative Magnitudes* (1:202–204).

as such is called a **ground** or **cause in the broad sense** (*principium, ratio*).
For that reason efficacious causes are one kind of ground, whose necessity is clear from the preceding (§15, 29). But they are not the only
kind. For that reason we must also consider here the remaining kinds
of grounds. Namely, what one calls grounded and whose production
one attributes to another is either cognition in the understanding or it
is the thing itself, outside of our thoughts. For that reason a ground is
either a ground of cognition, which can also be called an ideal ground
(*principium cognoscendi*), or a real ground (*principium essendi vel fiendi*). A
ground of cognition is one that brings about cognition of a matter with
conviction and is viewed as such. A real ground is one that brings about
or makes possible, either in part or in whole, the thing itself, outside of
our thoughts.

§36.[21] *Further division of real grounds into efficacious causes and inefficacious
real grounds or existential grounds.* When a **real ground** brings about or
makes possible a thing outside of thought, it does so either by means
of an efficacious power and, in that case, is called an **efficacious cause**.
Or the laws of truth in general do not allow anything else other than
that after certain things or certain of its properties have already been
posited, something else is now possible or impossible, or must be possible in this way and not otherwise. This kind of ground I wish to call
an **inefficacious real ground** or also an **existential ground** (*principium
existentialiter determinans*). Accordingly, an **existential ground** is one that
makes something else possible or necessary through its mere existence
due to the laws of truth. E.g., the three sides of a triangle and their relations to each other constitute a real ground of the size of its angle, but
only an inefficacious or existential ground. By contrast, fire is an efficacious cause of warmth.

§38. *Why it is preferable to take the word* "ground" *in the broader rather than
narrower sense.* Some take the word **ground** in a narrower sense and
understand by it something from which one can comprehend why something else exists and why it is such and not otherwise.[22] Now when we pay
attention to what we think with the word **why**, it is clear in that case that
only **both senses of real grounds** [i.e., *a priori* and *a posteriori*] along with
ideal grounds *a priori* are to be counted as falling under the concept of

---

[21] §36 and 38 are relevant to *Negative Magnitudes* (1:202–204).
[22] See Wolff's *Rational Thoughts* (§30) and Kant's *New Elucidation* (1:393).

ground. By contrast, when we attend to ideal grounds *a posteriori*, we find that we do not thereby cognize **why something exists**, but rather only **why we must let it be considered to be true**. [...]

§39. *How one arrives at the concept of a fundamental essence or of an essence in the narrowest sense.* Thus, whatever is mutable in a thing ultimately has its origin either in what is constant in the thing, or it can even be grounded in something external to that thing, whether in whole or in part (§31). Further, a logically essential property of a thing can also be found to be grounded in another, whether it be grounded in it as an effect or as a consequence drawn *a priori*. But this series cannot proceed infinitely. Rather, one must ultimately arrive at one or several essential properties that are not in turn grounded in other properties of that very thing. And they are called **the fundamental essence, or the essence of a thing in the narrowest sense**. [...]

Chapter Four: On the Existence of Things and the Concepts That Are Connected to It [§§45–61]

§45. *How one attains a distinct concept of existence.* Our first thoughts are sensations, and they are thoughts of existing things. Accordingly, in ontology we need to show only how we abstract the concepts of existence and essence from them and what remains for existence after what belongs to their essence has been separated off.

§46.[23] *What existence is.* If we represent something as existing, then the essence of our understanding requires us, apart from that through which we think it and distinguish it from others, to think also this in addition, that it exists somewhere and at some time, and thus we must also add in thought, beyond the metaphysical essence of the thing, a where and when [*ubi & quando*] that is attributed to it. For that reason **existence** is the predicate of a thing due to which it can also be found outside of thought somewhere and at some time. [...] That this is the true concept of existence can easily be comprehended thus. One posits what exists in opposition to what is merely thought or, which is the same, one distinguishes the actual being [*das wirkliche Dasein*] of a thing from its mere being [*Sein*] in thought. [...] Now when we pay attention to what the positive is that is added to the possible when it exists, it is impossible for

---

[23] See *The Only Possible Argument* (2:76–77) and the Transcendental Ideal of Pure Reason.

us to think something other than this, [namely] that a where [*ubi*] and when [*quando*] can be affirmed outside of thought as well. As soon as we add this in thought in such fashion that we actually posit it, we think of something as existing. Accordingly, existence consists in a [thing that is thought] being somewhere and at some time.

§47. *Explanation that the definition here is not circular.* It could appear as if I were providing a circular definition when I use the word **exists** in my definition of existence. However, one need only notice that the concepts *inesse, subsistere,* and *existere* do not mean the same thing. *Inesse* is the genus. Subsist or *subjecto inesse* is a species of it. And what constitutes the specific difference is a completely simple concept, as §20 shows. Two other noteworthy species of this genus are *inesse spatio* or *ubi* and *esse in tempore* or *quando* or, which is the same, *alicubi* and *aliquando esse*. The specific differences thereof, namely, the idea that underlies the word **somewhere** and the idea of succession, are likewise simple, as shall soon be even clearer. [...]

§48.[24] *Space and time are the two main concepts in the concept of existence.* Thus, the two main concepts that lie in the concept of existence and which we are now to explain are the *ubi* and *quando*, i.e., the concept of **space** and **time in the broadest sense.** *The two main axioms of existence.* And the two main axioms [that follow] from the concept of existence are these, that **everything that exists, must be somewhere, or found either mediately or immediately in some space**, and, further, that **everything that exists is sometime or at some time.**[25] *What space is.* **Space**, according to its primary concept, is nothing other than that in which we think that substances exist and which remains in thought when we abstract from them what relates uniformly to all substances that are in it. [...]

§49. *That the concept of space just given is in accord with linguistic usage.* I establish that the concept of space just given is in accord with linguistic usage as follows. First, space, due to the concrete idea that we have of it, cannot be a **substance**. Rather, the substances are supposed to be in space and, in fact, immediately so. Further, it also cannot be an **inhering property**. For space is not in the subject. Rather, the subject is in it, yet not in precisely the same way in which qualities are in the subject. Inhering

---

[24] §§48–49, 51, and 54 are relevant to the Transcendental Aesthetic (A19/B33ff.).
[25] See *Inaugural Dissertation* (2:413–415) for criticism of these axioms.

properties ought to be not in space, but rather in the subject, and the subject should be in space in the first place. Finally, **space** should **not** be a **mere relation**. For those who turn space into a relation do nothing other than change the state of the controversy. If one says that space is the order or manner in which several things exist next to each other at the same time, one certainly defines a possible thing, but not what we call space or *ubi* according to the nature of the thing itself. And if one did not have a different concept of space due to nature, nothing could be thought along with these words. For the true concept of space already lies in the word "next to each other"; similarly, it also already lies in the fact that among the things whose order or whose mode of coexistence is supposed to constitute space one can have in mind nothing other than substances if one does not want to be ridiculous. For music or meditation or a definition would otherwise be a space, because many things are next to each other in them. Pre-established harmony would likewise be a space, because it is the mode of coexistence between the body and the soul. By contrast, if one also wanted to seek space only in the order of the coexistence of substances, that one is not defining space in its typical meaning is already clear from the fact that according to its usual concept one can also still attribute a *ubi* or a space to a simple substance, even if one represents it all by itself and cannot represent it in any other way. [...]

§50. *That the given concept of space is more to you and does not stem from the imagination.* However, even our opponents could easily agree with us that according to the concepts assumed in common linguistic usage one represents space as something in which substances exist. However, they will view this as a mere figment of the imagination, which a scholar would have to reject and depart in this regard from the use of the word. However, one cannot take something for a figment of the imagination simply because such men say so; otherwise they would hold everything that does not agree with their doctrines to be such a figment. For one, it is certain that we represent all substances, even simple ones, as **somewhere**. Therefore, one must provide a criterion through which one can distinguish in our representations what belongs to the imagination and what to the essence of the understanding. For except for certain cases of disagreement cited in §14, the essence of our understanding is the criterion of truth. Yet we can ascribe to the imagination only that other things occur to us with a concept, for which reason we also let ourselves be led astray for a while to combine different concepts together into a single one without sufficient investigation in such a way as they arose in us one after another and how they occurred to us one after another. Accordingly, the rule by means of which one can distinguish figments of the imagination from what the understanding teaches, must be the following: Whatever only the imagination has combined must be capable of being separated by the understanding in turn such that the concept of the one does not disappear, even if the other is left out and rejected. By contrast, if, when we attempt to separate two concepts, the one disappears or becomes impossible to think when one rejects the other, these concepts are not combined by the imagination, but rather through the essence of the understanding. And for that reason they belong to each other, according to the truth. [...] Now inner experience teaches anyone that it is impossible to think something as **existing** and yet as not **somewhere**, to say that it **is** and yet that it is **nowhere**. [...]

§51.[26] *Explanation of and responses to several objections.* [...] *Space is neither a substance nor an inhering accident, but rather an abstraction of existence.* First, one might think that if space is supposed to be something other than a mere relation, **then it would have to be either a substance or an inhering accident**, which, however, we do not assert ourselves. I answer that in addition to these two options there is also yet a third toward which the previous proofs lead us. Subject and inhering accident are abstracted from the metaphysical essence of things, which is contrasted with the existence of things. Thus, space can of course be an abstraction **of existence**, as it actually is. Space is not a complete thing. One can object further that if space is an absolute thing, **then there would be in addition to God another eternal and necessary thing, namely, space**.[27] The following serves as an answer, that I maintain that space is not a complete thing, but rather a circumstance that is to be abstracted from the existence of complete things. [...] The necessary and infinite space is not a separate thing, it is also not God. Rather, it is an abstraction from the existence of God that is to be distinguished merely by the understanding. **There is also no completely empty space.** For abstracting a completely empty space means nothing other than to confuse an incomplete thing with complete things. [...]

§52. *Explanation of those concepts that are connected with space.* Now that the concept of space has been explained, the concepts of **place, spatial**

---

[26] See A26/B42 (Transcendental Aesthetic).
[27] See B71–B72 (§8 of Transcendental Aesthetic).

direction, position, and **figure** that are connected with it can easily be defined. *Two meanings of place.* The word **place** is taken in two different meanings. *What absolute place is.* Either one understands by it something **absolute**, and then **place** is nothing other than a certain part of space in which something one is talking about exists. *What relative place is.* Or one understands by it something **relative**, and then **place** is a relation in which several things that occupy a space are found with respect to each other in light of it. *Consequences from place.* For that reason as many relative places arise as one compares simultaneously existing substances with each other. If there were no absolute place, then there would be no relative place either. A thing can change its relative place even if it does not move from its position to the extent that only one other that one compares it with changes its absolute place. Even if two things, or a whole system, change their absolute place, it can still be the case that the relative places all remain unchanged. [...] A finite understanding cannot distinguish any part of absolute place from any other through itself alone. We must first perceive all changes of absolute place through the comparison of things to each other. For that reason we frequently confuse the changes of absolute and relative places. [...]

§53. *What spatial direction is.* **Spatial direction** (*directio localis*) is the determination of place against which a line proceeds. For that reason we measure it through the determination of the region of the world against which a line is drawn. *What position is.* **Position** (*situs*) is the determination of places between two things that are found in places that have some constancy. I include the last addition so that place is not in general the same as direction. [...] *What figure is.* **Figure** is the determination of the limits of the place that a substance occupies. [...] One must only take care that one does not for that reason immediately hold that everything that needs a place for its existence is extended. For it will be shown in its place that the composition of a thing out of several substances is required for extension, and that the parts that one distinguishes in space, to the extent that one abstracts it from the substance that is found therein, are not truly parts but rather parts only in thought, or divisions of an incomplete thing into other incomplete things.

§54. *What time is.* The *quando* or time, taken in the broadest sense, is that in which we think the succession of things that follow each other, whether we are representing the succession of actual or [merely] possible things one after another. Such an *abstractum* of existence forces us to add in thought the essence of our understanding as well as space to all actually existing things. The thing may itself consist of successive states or not. It is, however, essential to the understanding to think it with such a *quando* or time. [...] *Difference between real and merely ideal or possible time.* If the things of which we think that they succeed each other are actually distinct from each other, then we call the time in which they succeed each other **real time** or **time in the narrow sense**. But if what we think of as successive is nothing other than parts of a time or of a *quando* in general, namely, the parts of that in which we think that the successive things, if they were there, could or would have to succeed each other, this is called **merely ideal**, or **possible time**, or that *quando* that is opposed to time in the narrow sense. However, a finite understanding cannot distinguish the moments of possible time through anything. Rather, in general it is forced to think only that some [moments] are there and succeed one another.[28] *The concept of succession is simple.* **The concept of succession** itself, however, is simple. [...] It is, namely, easy to see that our concept is in accord with linguistic usage. For it is apparent that in light of our usage one does not call the succession of things one after another itself time. For one means by time something which relates uniformly to all things that actually or possibly occur in it. And time, which we represent according to a convenient sensible measure in which sensible things succeed each other – since we cannot distinguish its intrinsic moments by anything else – remains the same, regardless of what may occur in it. We thus understand time not as the actual sequence of things one after another, but rather only something in which they do and can follow one another. That this concept, too, does not stem from the imagination but rather from the essence of the understanding is clear because it is impossible for us to think of something as existing **that does not exist at some time or other**. [...]

§57.[29] *The concept of the actual is prior to the concept of the possible.* [...] But it deserves to be noted that, although there is less in the concept of the possible than in the concept of the actual, **the concept of the actual is still prior to the concept of the possible both according to nature and according to our cognition.** First, I say that it is prior **according to nature**. For if nothing were actual, then nothing would be possible, because all possibility of a thing that does not yet exist is a causal connection between

---

[28] See esp. B232–B233 (Second Analogy of Experience).
[29] §§57–59 are relevant to the Postulates of Empirical Thought (A218–A235/B265–B287); they are also relevant to *The Only Possible Argument*, Section 1, Second Reflection (2:76–82ff.).

an existing thing and a thing that does not yet exist. Further, the concept of the actual is also prior to the concept of the possible **according to our knowledge**. For our first concepts are [of] existing things, namely, sensations, by which we can attain a concept of the possible only afterwards. In fact, even if one also wanted immediately to meditate *a priori* most precisely, then the concept of existence is certainly prior to the concept of possibility. For all I need for the concept of existence are the simple concepts of **subsistence, coexistence** [*Nebeneinander*], and **succession**. By contrast, for the concept of possibility I require the concept of **causality, subsistence**, and **existence**. [...]

§58. *What is impossible.* If one understands what the essence of the possible consists in, then it should also be easy now to determine what is called **impossible**. Namely, something is **impossible** if no cause is or will be present that can bring about what one is thinking or trying to think. [...] Thus one thinks that it is **impossible** either *simpliciter* [*schlechterdings*] or **by positing certain circumstances**. Only what contradicts either itself or the properties of the universally necessary cause of all things is impossible *simpliciter*. Everything else is only impossible by positing certain conditions. At the same time the following rule is evident, that something can occur in our understanding as possible that is in fact impossible. This case occurs in two ways. First, if we view something in this world in general or in a particular case as possible because we see no contradiction in it, although no causes for it are present in this world, and second, if we view something as possible if we find no contradiction, although causes for it also cannot be present in any world, which we merely happen not to know, but rather would have insight into only if we were to understand completely the essence of all things and, in particular, the inner essence of the first necessary cause of all things. If one had these *a priori* and easily understood propositions in mind, one would not be overly hasty so often in the mysteries of religion, and view certain things immediately as impossible because we cannot think them determinately or because we do not have any insight into the ground for them from the nature of things. One would understand rather that in that case it would depend merely on *a posteriori* proofs. [...]

§59. *Power, space, and time, together, constitute the complete possibility of a thing.* It has been shown previously that the possible is what does not yet exist, or is viewed as not yet existing, but which does not contain in itself anything contradictory to existence, and for which, if it does not yet

exist, a sufficient cause must be present or lie in the future to the extent
that something real ought to be in the possibility. Hence arise numerous
concepts that can be drawn from the concept of complete possibility by
analysis. If a substance is to exist, it must exist immediately somewhere
and at a time. Thus, if the possibility of a substance is not to contain anything contradictory to existence, space and time in the broadest sense
are already presupposed and taken to be familiar and they are a part
of what is required for the possibility of a substance. Further, if a thing
that does not yet exist is to be truly possible, then something is already
presupposed in another existing thing by which it can give it actuality by
means of causality, and which is simply called the power for it. For this
reason, **power**, **space**, and **time** are parts that belong to the complete
possibility of a thing that is thought. For this reason we can also define
all three so that we turn possibility into a genus. For **power**, which is connected to a substance, is the **possibility** of a thing that is thought. Thus,
it is an efficacious possibility. **Space** and **time**, by contrast, are **inefficacious possibilities**, whose definition is hereby elevated and made more
complete. For **space** is the possibility of the coexistence of substances
next to each other that is distinct from the power of their efficacious
causes. [...] But time is the possibility of the **succession** of things, or the
sequence of them **one after the other**, that is distinct from the power of
their efficacious causes. This possibility existed even before things actually followed each other. For this reason time in the broad sense is once
again defined by this concept as well. [...]

Chapter Five:[30] On Efficacious Causes [§§62–89]

§62. *Explanation of intentions.* Through every thing something else
becomes possible (§29) in which respect it is called a cause (§31). Now
if it is not a complete thing, then it must be found in or with a complete
thing, and must be only a circumstance of the causality of a complete
thing that has been abstracted in thought. Now we intend to investigate
further those circumstances of causality and its differences that can be
noticed in those causes that are complete things. [...]

§63.[31] *What power is in the broad sense.* The first thing that needs to be
distinguished in an efficacious and complete cause is power. **Power in**

---

[30] The selections from this chapter are relevant to the Second Analogy of Experience
(A189/B232ff.).
[31] See A204–A205/B249–B250 (Second Analogy of Experience).

the broad sense is the possibility of one thing attached to another thing (§29). Ultimately, it must always be connected to a substance. For this reason one can also say that **power** is the possibility of a certain thing B attached to a substance A, due to which something subsists in A by which B has or receives its actuality. Thus the concepts of **causality** and **subsistence** belong to the concept of power, if it is to be thought distinctly. For that causality due to which A contributes something to B is a property subsisting in the subject A, which is also connected to the subject in case nothing is brought about. This property in subject A is now called a power. E.g., if we represent any positive thing whose non-being or being-otherwise can be thought, then we shall feel compelled to admit another thing from which it comes. If we leave off the determinate essence of the thing and retain only the relation thought between them, then the concept of causality becomes distinct. [...]

§70. *How one is led from the concept of power in the broad sense to the concept of power in the narrower sense,* i.e., fundamental power [*Grundkraft*]. Previously we took the word **power** in its broadest sense. But it should be noted that in this fashion one can arbitrarily abstract many powers from a thing that are not distinguished by nature as we distinguish them and that are not appropriate to a distinct causal explanation of those effects about which one wants to know from what causes they arise, and how. For one can, in that case, combine every thing, effect, or property, or capacity of a thing with the idea of a power in general, and the concept of a power arises from it. E.g., I say that man has the power to write, to compose poetry. The stomach has the power to digest. Magnets have the power to attract iron, etc. With all of this, however, nothing yet has been explained. Many believe that if they can easily subsume [under a cause] the effects that are to be explained, or view them as determinations of what they suppose to be in them, then, accordingly, they immediately imagine that they would have thereby explained the matter from its causes. [...] However, it could certainly be that the effect that one abstracts and due to which one names the assumed power is only an effect that derives from many causes taken together. It could also be that it is only a part or a circumstance abstracted from the action or effect of a single true power. And it should be noted further that if one intends to explain the causes of things, then one must have insight into an actual causal connection between [the cause] and its effects, and that subsuming and other existential connections are not sufficient here. Everything that is attributed to things is grounded in their own

fundamental essence or in the fundamental essence of other things
(§39). Thus we must search out, as much as possible, those powers that
constitute its fundamental essence and – whether one views them individually, compares them against each other, or takes them together
with the powers of other things – on the basis of which one must seek
to explain, as much as possible, what is attributed to a thing. In this
way we are led to the concept of a power in the narrow sense that is
opposed to a mere capacity and those general powers that have been
abstracted arbitrarily. [. . .] One can call this a **fundamental power**. Now
it is not to be denied that one cannot advance to cognition of this true
and fundamental power everywhere. Rather, one must often rest content if one simply knows at all what kind of effects a thing is capable
of, and in what substance one should look for the ground of certain
effects. But so that we should go as far as we can and, in explaining what
we perceive of things, not merely list the properties and states of those
things, but rather either discover their true fundamental powers or at
least approach them as much as possible, I intend to determine the distinguishing features of truly fundamental powers in several rules.

§72. *Second distinguishing feature* [of a fundamental power]. *As long as one
cannot intelligibly derive an effect from an assumed power, either one has not
yet attained a fundamental power or one does not yet understand it completely
distinctly.* **As long as we cannot yet provide a causal explanation for
what we attribute to an assumed power, but rather either accept the
causal connection due to other inferences or even abstract the effect
to be explained simply as a species or part thereof, we either do not yet
have a truly fundamental power or at least do not yet understand the
true constitution of the power with complete distinctness. For the universal rule, according to which the causal connections of things that
come to be must be judged is this: If two changes regularly follow each
other and it does not contradict the essence of the one if it is held to
be the cause of the other and, further, it can be proved or at least postulated that no more distinct or correct cause can be given, finally, no
proof to the contrary can be based on the highest principles of reason
(§15) and their limitations (§14–57), then the one is also to be held to
be the actual cause of the other.**

§73. *Third distinguishing feature. A finite fundamental power constantly has
one and the same proximate effect, and more remote effects must be comprehended
through it.* [. . .] I say, first, that a finite fundamental power must constantly

produce one kind of action and cause one proximate effect as often as it acts. For if one were permitted to attribute several proximate actions and effects to a single finite power, the assumed power could not be anything other than a general concept under which one would only have gathered together several other concepts. For since none of the actions cited could be comprehended from the power by means of the others, one is not thinking of any persisting thing from which one could comprehend what one attributes to it. And so one thinks either only one causal connection in general between certain consequences and the essence of certain substances, but [then] one does not at all know the fundamental powers of that essence, or one must admit a special power for each proximate consequence and effect, and then we have what we want. One can also convince oneself of this in another way. If one were permitted to ascribe more than one proximate action and effect to a finite power, then the doctrine of nature, in fact all of our causal investigations, would lose all of their boundaries and certainty. Anyone could simply make up a convenient concept in which he brings together what he is supposed to explain, and in turn derive it from there. And assuming that there were things, as there really are, that had more than a single fundamental power, which, as this is possible, one would not want to deny at the outset, then from the beginning one would immediately exclude in this way, without any reason, the path of ever attaining cognition thereof. [...] Further, I have said that one must judge differently with respect to the infinite power, and not attribute only a single proximate action [to it]. For the grounds that have been developed previously are not suited to it, and its concept rather forces one to say the opposite. [...] It [i.e., the infinite power] must be a power that is suited to the execution of all actions that are jointly and intrinsically possible and the production of all effects that are jointly and intrinsically possible. And, by contrast, our own finitude convinces us that we are incapable of thinking its inner constitution. Now, since we shall establish the actuality of an infinite power in God in its proper place,[32] we will thereby be assured that there is a true and single fundamental power of which, however, we have not intuitive, but rather only symbolic cognition.[33] For that reason, if a finite thing is supposed to be capable of more than one kind of action, then its fundamental essence must consist in more than one power, [in] which [case these powers] are combined according to

---

[32] See §213 and §221 for two of Crusius's arguments for God's existence.
[33] See Kant's *Inaugural Dissertation* (2:396) for a similar remark about how our cognition of God would be symbolic and not intuitive.

certain laws of action among each other. There is also nothing absurd in combining several fundamental powers into a single one, even in a simple subject, as long as one does not represent the powers as something corporeal, but rather notices that uncountably many of them can be combined in a single subject, which do not subsist in different spaces, but rather in a completely identical point of the subject, and which completely penetrate it if it is simple.

§74. *Fourth distinguishing feature. The conditions by which the action of a fundamental power is to be restricted must lie in the very same subject.* If the action of a power that one attributes to a subject is to be restricted by certain conditions under which it can occur in the first place, then those very conditions must lie in the very same subject, if the given power is to be a truly fundamental power. For assume that they lie in another subject. Then the effect through which one thinks the power could either not at all be understood on its basis, in which case, however, one would not have discovered a truly fundamental power (§72, 73). Or it would have to be understood on the basis of its own power and action, along with the other subject at the same time, in which case, however, it would be a composite and not a proximate effect, and thus one would once again still not know the fundamental power (§70). For this reason, e.g., the concept of an attractive power, which substances at a distance are supposed to exercise against each other, and which they are supposed to exercise against each other all the more, the closer they get to each other, is not an explanation of a fundamental power. For the conditions under which each one of these substances is supposed to move in a certain way are external to both of them.

§78. *Eighth distinguishing feature.* […] **Nothing can occur in the effect for which a power cannot be found in what one posits as its sufficient cause.** […] In this way one cognizes, e.g., that in the human soul the will is a special power [beyond the mere power of representation], or rather a sum of special powers. For although desire already presupposes certain representations, it still does not yet let itself be comprehended on the basis of these representations, but rather something else lies in it that representations alone do not have the power to cause, whatever they may be like. Therefore, a special power is necessary for it.

§79. *Division of power in general into the inefficacious capacity of an existential ground and an active power.* Whatever a cause contributes to the production of an effect, it accomplishes either (1) **through its mere existence because**

through it the existence, or a certain manner of existing, of another thing is made possible, impossible, or necessary. For this reason, in that case, its power is also nothing other than the possibility, impossibility, or determination of another thing that is connected to the mere existence of a thing by means of the laws of truth. Above, we called such causes **existential grounds** (§36). The power thereof can be called the **inefficacious capacity of an existential ground** (*facultas existentialis*). E.g., a wedge or a lever has the power to create some easing by overcoming a resistance. But this occurs by means of the mere existence of their shape and structure. For this reason they are merely existential grounds, and their power consists in an inefficacious capacity. This is how it is with all mechanical causes, that is, with all those substances that, and to the extent to which, they have an influence on the determination of their effect by the shape and position of the parts of a composite thing. Or (2) **the cause acts due to an inner property of its essence, which is now directed toward the production of this effect.** One thus attributes an **activity** or **self-activity** to it. It is called an **active cause** and its power an **active power** (*Facultas actiua*). Thus, an **active power** is a property connected to a substance belonging to its inner essence due to which something else is actual through it or comes to be, without it being merely a conclusion that one would immediately have to concede according to the principle of contradiction after positing existential circumstances. Of such a sort are the active powers of the elements, thinking, and desiring. **Both of these can even coincide in a single cause.** E.g., when a body acts, an inefficacious capacity by which its effect is to a certain extent determined lies in its shape and in the position of its parts. However, one should not forget the active power of the elements or the active power of other things external to it that move it, without which the effect could not occur. E.g., the axe splits the wood according to the laws of the wedge. To that extent, it is an existential ground. But the active power is to be sought in the elements it consists in, in the combination of the bodies among each other in the world, and in what guides them.

§80. *What reaction or resistance is.* The difficulty found in an object for accepting the action of a cause is called **reaction** or **resistance**. [...]

§81.[34] *What a fundamental activity or first action is.* Among active substances one activity can depend in turn on another of which it is an effect. But

---

[34] §§81–84 are relevant to the Third Antinomy and A532–A559/B560–B587 (Resolution of the Third Antinomy); they are also relevant to *New Elucidation* (1:398–405).

this series cannot proceed infinitely, but rather one must ultimately come to first actions that arise from the power of subjects not through another action, but rather immediately, and are nothing other than an application of the first fundamental powers themselves. I intend to call them **fundamental activities** (*actiones primas*). *Division of fundamental activities.* **Two types** of these are conceivable. *Some persist due to the essence of the substances.* First, such fundamental activities **that persist due to the essence of the substance** and that simply constitute the inner essence of active substances. If the substance is necessary, then they need no further cause. Such are, e.g., the actions of the divine understanding. If the substance is contingent, then they need no further cause than that the fundamental essence of the substance is conserved. Such are, e.g., the active powers of the elements. *Some do not persist.* Further, there is such a type of fundamental activities **that do not occur constantly**. Those are, e.g., the actions of the human understanding and will.

§82. *Further division of fundamental activities that do not occur constantly.* Of those fundamental activities, or primary actions, **that do not occur constantly**, two further kinds can, in turn, be thought. Namely, **first there are those that must occur under certain circumstances, to which they are connected as conditions, in such fashion that they cannot fail to occur after the circumstances have been posited**. Of such kind are, e.g., sensations, particularly the first stirrings of desires. Further, **there are those that are not made more than perfectly possible by the requisite conditions, and for that reason do occur when the latter are posited, but can also fail to occur or occur otherwise**. In that case the active power determines itself to one among several ways of acting, which are all perfectly possible after certain circumstances have been posited, i.e., it is active in such a way that the activity through which it undertakes one of the possible acts does not in turn presuppose something else by which it is determined to act now and in this very way and not otherwise. [...]

§83. *That such fundamental activities that can occur or fail to occur under one and the same circumstances are possible.* The possibility of the latter kind of activities, which can occur or fail to occur or can occur otherwise under one and the same circumstances, are denied or called into doubt by some without cause. For no contradiction can be uncovered in its concept, and thus they are possible. In our causal investigations of things in which they [i.e., these kinds of activity] do not occur and that constitute the largest part of our science, namely, in our investigation of the effects of bodies, the understanding, the souls of animals, and even certain effects of the human will, we are simply used to searching everywhere for [the kind of] causes that are determined to be efficacious only in one and the same way under certain circumstances. But this need not keep a rational person from also considering the possibility of the other kind of activities and from paying attention to where they occur. One main objection that is made against it is that one imagines that blind chance is introduced [into our free actions]. This is not yet the place to provide all of the grounds for refuting this objection. However, after the existence of a necessary and most perfect substance has been established, from which the other substances derive and which must create the world, if it should want to create it, in such fashion that it is not in vain, it will be clear that such an activity is not only in it itself, namely, in God, but also that it must be in the created rational spirits so that they are capable of moral culpability for their actions and virtue, as one finds *a posteriori*. [...] Precisely because this kind of fundamental activity occurs only in rational spirits, for whom it constitutes freedom in the telematological sense, we would like to call them the **fundamental activities of freedom** (first actions of freedom), from which it is sufficiently clear that there is no cause for concern that blind chance would thereby be introduced [into our free actions]. For in the efficacious subject they always have a truly sufficient cause and also always occur according to ideas, and, in fact, according to the ideas of a rational spirit. [...] Nothing more belongs to ontology than to show its possibility and to provide instructions as to how one is led in the natural order of *a priori* abstraction to this kind of fundamental activity. Its actuality, however, must be established in its proper place in part from our own inner consciousness,[35] in part from the creation of the world, which must have occurred freely at some point in time, in part from the ultimate purpose of the world, which is something that is advanced by free acts, and in part from the actuality of truly moral divine laws.[36] [...]

§83.[37] *The distinguishing features of fundamental activities.* Now we should like to investigate a bit more precisely the **distinguishing features of fundamental activities** from the concepts given [above], which will pave

---

[35] See A546/B574 (Resolution of the Third Antinomy).

[36] Crusius refers to §42 and §211 of his *Anweisung, vernünftig zu leben* for these arguments.

[37] Crusius made a mistake in numbering these sections, as both this and the previous section are labeled 83. Rather than renumber all of the following sections through §88 (§89 is omitted), this edition reproduces Crusius's mistake.

the way for us to determine even better how far one should go in the investigation of the grounds of things and what sorts occur in different kinds of things. The distinguishing features of fundamental activities are the following: (1) **a fundamental activity must be something in the efficacious subject itself. However, that which the efficacious cause brings about in an object is no fundamental activity.** [...] (2) **If something is immediately found in the efficacious subject, but it is brought about by a sufficient cause preceding it, insofar as it has thus been brought about, it, too, is not to be held a fundamental activity.** [...] (3) **If a substance changes its outer state through motion, it is not a primary action.** [...] (4) **If the efficacious substance is active in such a way that the activity cannot fail to be either at all or under the current circumstances, then the action can be fundamental, but, to the extent that it cannot fail to be, it cannot be a first free action, or a fundamental activity of freedom** (§83). [...]

§84. *Definition of the principle of determining ground*. By a **ground** we have understood anything through which something else is made either actual or possible and insofar as it is viewed in this respect (§34). For that reason a **determining ground** is one through which what is grounded in it is made actual or possible in such a way that it cannot be otherwise under these circumstances (§23). It was established further that everything that arises presupposes a sufficient cause, that is, a cause in which nothing is lacking that is necessary for causality, and that it must receive its actuality through the power of the cause (§31), and the distinguishing feature of whether something is contingent, and thus arose at one time, consists in whether its non-being can be thought (§33). *The fundamental activities of freedom need a merely sufficient cause.* **Now if the arising thing about whose ground one is inquiring is a fundamental activity of freedom, due to its definition (§82, 83) one cannot ask for more than a merely sufficient cause of action.** *By contrast, all effects of the fundamental activities have a determining cause.* In all other cases one can proceed even further. For if something is first brought about by a first action as an effect (§68), then, after its sufficient cause is posited, it could neither not take place nor occur otherwise. One would contradict oneself if one were to say that it could have not occurred and yet that one posited an unhindered activity in the sufficient cause to which the occurrence of the effect is essentially connected. By contrast, if one were to say that it could have happened otherwise, since the ground for the present state and not for another state as well is to be found in the cause, the changed state, insofar as it should occur, would have to arise without a sufficient reason, which is, however, absurd. **Thus, all effects (§68) have not only a sufficient, but also a determining cause**. Similarly, it is understood that even **all fundamental activities that are not fundamental activities of freedom** can neither be nor arise otherwise than they are or arise, due to the inner essence of things or due to the truths and conditions that are simultaneously posited outside of them. **All of these conditions, taken together, constitute in every case its determining ground, and [this is true], even if they should constitute either entirely or only in part an existential ground** (§36, 79). From these two principles, we can define the true **principle of determining ground**, which must be as follows: **Everything that is not a fundamental activity of freedom has, when it arises, a determining ground, that is, a ground according to which, after it is posited, what it posits cannot be or occur otherwise**. [...]

Chapter Six: On What One, Identical, and Distinct Are [§§90–102]

§94.[38] [...] *Every real connection of contingent things is based on a causal connection*. Any connection of finite things that is to be a real *unio existentialis* outside thought must rest on a causal connection of things due to which at least one must act on the other, but also both can act on each other reciprocally as well as be passive with respect to each other. For there is otherwise nothing else outside thought that can provide a ground of connection between complete things. But as soon as one takes this away, then one must connect them only in a concept in the understanding, i.e., the things thus have either no or a merely ideal connection. Consequently, I cannot, e.g., admit that those who believe in pre-established harmony leave a real connection between body and soul. [...] Their connection is only ideal even with respect to God. One cannot even say that they are connected by the intervention of God. For then at least the arrangement [*Einrichtung*] of the essences of the body and soul would have to be attributed to God. But the defenders of pre-established harmony can never say this in the Leibnizian sense because they do not leave God any honor beyond bringing the essences of substances into existence, rather than arranging them, because all beings are to be eternal. Thus, a mere correspondence rather than a real connection remains. [...]

---

[38] See the Third Analogy (A211–A215/B256–B262). See also *New Elucidation* (1:413–416).

§102.³⁹ *Remark on simple concepts.* In my discussion during the previous chapters of what is to be distinguished in a complete thing, we came, little by little, to those concepts that I believe are the simplest. So that one can now retain them all the easier, it will be useful to present them again here in a remark, and add what is to be remembered about them. Those concepts that we can view as the **simplest** are the following. (1) The concept of **subsistence** (§20). (2) The concept of the **somewhere** and **external to each other** insofar, namely, as one intends spatial externality (§46, 47). (3) The concept of **succession**, which constitutes part of the meaning that we think of under the phrase "after each other" (§54). (4) The concept of **causality**, or of what we typically signify with the words "make," "bring about," and "produce." (5) The concept of **external to each other** insofar as it does not thereby indicate a spatial externality, but rather only a distinction according to which the one is not a part, property, or determination of the other (§83). E.g., if I say that memory and the power of judgment are actually distinct from each other even outside of thought. (6) The concept of **unity** (§91). (7) The concept of **negation** in the broadest sense (§95). Beyond this we also have (8) that concept of being within, according to which one means something other than subsistence or something other than enclosing a substance spatially within other substances. E.g., when I say that substance is in space. I cannot actually guarantee [*Ich kan nicht eben gut davor seyn*] that further simple concepts could not be discovered. However, through repeated dissections of many examples I have at all times been led to these ones. One should not confuse simple concepts, or those that have been completely dissected, with those that are merely indissoluble [*unauflöslich*], and thus that appear to our senses as simple. Similarly, [one should not confuse simple concepts with] those concepts that we cannot at all think in their true constitution, but [for which we] must rather rest satisfied with symbolic cognition. In the latter case, namely, the absolute that we attribute to them is only something indeterminate, but we do not know the true constitution of its determination and, for that reason, represent it as merely relative and negative. [...] In that case, we have a true and usable cognition of the object, yet not an intuitive, but rather merely a symbolic cognition. Its concept can thus be distinct to the extent that it can be distinguished from all others. However, it is only not yet complete, namely, insofar as we are not familiar with everything attributed to it that

---

³⁹ See A80/B106 (Metaphysical Deduction) and A235/B294ff. (On the Ground of the Distinction of All Objects in General into Phenomena and Noumena).

is positive. E.g., the inner constitution of both the elementary and mental fundamental powers are unknown to us. In similar fashion, we have no intuitive cognition of the inner constitution of the divine essence. [...] Two things follow from this limitation of our understanding. First, that we cannot deny the existence or possibility of certain things or several of their modes, despite the fact that we cannot comprehend them.[40] [...]

Chapter Nine: On the Finite and Infinite [§§133–156]

§134.[41] *The infinity of a substance is three-fold, the infinity of power, of immeasurability, and eternity.* If a substance is to be infinite, infinity must be attributed to it with respect to those circumstances that are required for a substance. Those are its essence and existence. With respect to essence, it is ultimately determined by its fundamental essence (§39), which must consist in one or several fundamental powers in a substance. The abstract circumstances of existence are space, which its subject fills, and time or duration (Chapter Four). Accordingly, three kinds of infinity can be thought that can be attributed to a substance. (1) The infinity of essence or power, due to which all possible actions occur and all possible effects are brought about. (2) Immeasurability, due to which substance fills all possible space. (3) Eternity, or infinite duration, due to which a substance neither has nor even can have either a beginning or an end.

§135.[42] *Distinction between true infinity and progressive infinity.* With all of these kinds of **infinity**, since one has already asserted that they are to be attributed to a thing, one should not get confused about the meaning of the word **infinity**, since one uses this name for such a series of successive things that are constantly increasing. One can call this a *progressive infinity (Infinitatem progressivam)*. In fact, such a series is and remains finite at all times. I maintain that the sum of what exists at one time is finite at all times, only that more can be added to it at each time. The duration of a created thing that does not ever perish, and thus that has a beginning but no end, is of such a kind. One calls such a duration *aevum*. One can also represent such a progressive infinity if one considers past time. You can think as far back in the past and as many years as you like, whatever it is that you are thinking positively is at all times a finite time, but one to which yet more can always be added. [...]

---

[40] This consequence represents an important limitation to the three highest principles Crusius asserts in §15.

[41] §§134–135 are relevant to the Antinomies, esp. the First and Second Antinomies.

[42] See esp. A430/B458, A518/B546, and A523/B551.

§149. *A series of causes and effects and thus also the number by which one represents them is necessarily finite.* We come now to the other main point that was stated in §146. Namely, if one takes a number to be a unity of what brings about another, which, in turn, brings about yet another, and so on, in short, **if one speaks of a series of effects and causes, one can immediately establish through the principle of contradiction that every such series or number is necessarily finite.** I infer as follows. If a series of causes and effects exists, then either all members of this series are brought about, or they are not all brought about. If they are not all brought about, then one cause must be the first, with which the series begins, and thus the series is not infinite. However, if one posits that all members of the series are brought about, then they all did not exist at some time and thus the entire series did not exist at one time. Consequently, it has a beginning and is thus once again not infinite. And since each thing that is posited now as existing, and yet did not exist at one time, needs a sufficient cause (§31), in every case one arrives at a first cause from which the series begins and is thus finite.[43] [...]

Chapter Ten: On Quantity [§§157–179]

§157.[44] *What quantity is.* If we think a single essence several times in a whole, we attribute a quantity to it. Thus, **quantity** is that property of things due to which a certain considered thing is posited more than once. Now, since we cannot sense what is simple, and even if we could cognize it ever so intuitively that degrees and arbitrary parts could be assumed in it, we must at least attribute a quantity to all complete things, but [one] which is not, for that reason, always grounded in a real composition in them. [...] E.g., all powers and capacities, similarly all extensions must have a quantity, for they can be posited more than once in a thing and can be attributed to it. [...]

Chapter Eleven: On Goodness and the Perfection of
Things [§§180–203]

§180.[45] [...] *What the perfection of a thing is.* Accordingly, perfection is the relation of a thing to the sum of effects that become actual or possible

---

[43] In §§150–151 Crusius notes that this argument rests on an inference from the parts of a whole being brought about to the whole being brought about, and then defends it at length. At §156 Crusius attempts to show that the argument establishing the impossibility of an infinite series of causes does not apply to space and time as well.

[44] This chapter is relevant to the Axioms of Intuition and Anticipations of Perception.

[45] See *Optimism* (2:31).

by it or, which is the same, **perfection** is the sum of positive reality that one attributes to a thing. [...]

§195. *What is called good and bad.* If one compares a thing with the ultimate purpose [*Endzweck*] of a spirit with desires, one calls it in this respect, if, and to the extent to which, it harmonizes with that purpose, **good**, whereas if, and to the extent to which it conflicts with that purpose, [it is called] **bad**. [...]

[PART II] THEORETICAL NATURAL THEOLOGY, OR THE DOCTRINE OF THE ACTUALITY, THE PROPERTIES, AND THE WORKS OF GOD

Chapter One: On the Concept and Actuality of God [§§204–236]

§204.[46] *Why God is treated in metaphysics.* After the concepts that either lie in the concept of a complete thing (§18) or can be understood *a priori* from the universal essence of things as properties or distinguishing features have been analyzed in ontology, the next thing that we now need to do is to investigate the existence, properties, and effects of the first and universal cause, in which all those things with whose existence we are acquainted *a posteriori* have their origin. For, since the very first cause of things is a perfectly necessary being (§128), it belongs primarily to the objects of metaphysics that it be treated therein. This first cause is called **God**, for which reason we now come to **natural theology**. [...]

§208.[47] [...] *Division [of proofs of the existence of God] according to kinds of inference.* But in light of the [different] kinds of inference that occur in the proofs of the existence of God, they can be divided into **three kinds**. First, one can follow what is properly called the **path of demonstration**. Further, following this there is the **path of probability that is of infinite magnitude**, and, for that reason, is just as valid as a demonstration (§207). Finally, one can also choose **the path of common probability**. But all of these kinds of proofs are useful and necessary. And because the entirety of philosophy is of no use without a proof that God exists, it is prudent that more than one proof of the actuality of God is given in natural theology. [...]

---

[46] This chapter is relevant to The Ideal of Pure Reason, Sections 4–7 (A592–A642/B620–B670).

[47] See A590/B618.

§213.[48] *Proof of the actuality of God from the changes of which the world consists.* A second proof of the actuality of God can be [developed] as follows. We find a series of changes in the world that occur with a certain similarity, for which reason certain laws can be abstracted from it. And these changes, taken together, along with the substances they are found in, constitute the present world. Now since these changes are things that are really distinct from each other, and thus the series in which they follow each other cannot be infinite (§148, 149), yet at the same time its first beginning must have a first cause, one must eventually come to a cause of it that is necessary and eternal. Now, if one were immediately to assume a power as the next cause, it would still have to be in a substance. Accordingly, the first cause of the series of changes that we find in the world and that constitute the world would have to be found in one or several substances. Because this first cause is eternal and necessary, it must have already been there an infinitely long time before it brought about the effect from which the present world arose. This is possible in no more than two ways. Either the first causes of the world have an essence that can begin to exercise a first free activity that they did not have previously, or they have been eternally active in one and the same way, but a world did not arise from it until a certain point in time, which must be due to the fact that it had not come into its necessary connection until that point in time. The latter was Epicurus's opinion, who suggested that the smallest parts of matter were in eternal motion until the present world finally arose out of uncountably many connections. But such a suggestion is very absurd. For in this case (1) very many finite things are posited as eternal, though every finite thing is contingent (§33). Further (2) with and in them an infinite series of actual changes would have preceded, although this contradicts an infinite series (§148, 149). (3) The order that we find in the world would thereby be impossible, which is to be explained further below. Consequently, the first cause of the world must be one that can begin first free fundamental activities. However, the elements of bodies in which we do not find a trace of such a capacity are not of this kind insofar as they act at all times such that their action cannot fail to occur or occur otherwise under the very

---

[48] Crusius develops five distinct demonstrative proofs of the existence of God. However, all are versions of the cosmological argument, and most depend explicitly on the impossibility of a finite thing (or series) being eternal, which Crusius argues for in §§148–149. For Kant's discussion of the cosmological argument, see A603–A620/B631–B648.

same circumstances. That our souls are not the cause of the world, although they can begin free fundamental activities, was already clear and no one would say it anyway. Consequently, no possibility remains other than that the first cause of all changes occurring in the world is an eternal substance that is distinct from the world, but that must also be intelligible, because order is found in those changes in the world (§185, 222). Consequently, God exists, from whose essence it is immediately clear that he must be a free spirit.

§221.[49] *Proof of the actuality of God from the regularity of the world.* Now we would also like to take a proof of the truth that God exists from the regularity of the world, viewed in its specifics. We find in the world an orderly and regular connection and sequence of things that apparently lead us [to the idea] that it was formed according to ideas and has an intelligible cause. It is beyond dispute that we are not the governing cause of this connection. Matter, since it is incapable of ideas, cannot act orderly according to ideas without being governed by an intelligible cause. Consequently, this order and regularity reveals either that the world was formed by an intelligible cause distinct from it or that one must admit that the order and regularity are merely apparent and are something that arose through chance. Now the latter is an infinitely great improbability. For that reason, to accept it nonetheless would be an infinitely great foolishness. Thus the former is to be viewed as demonstratively valid (§207), namely, that the order and regularity in the world is to be attributed to an intelligible cause that is distinct from the world, and that, consequently, God exists. [...]

§234. *Whether the proofs of the actuality of God are to be viewed as similar to geometrical proofs.* The question is often posed whether the proofs of the truth that God exists are to be viewed as equal in their acuity to geometrical demonstrations. I answer that they are to be viewed as completely equal with regard to their conclusiveness and validity. However, in light of the principles that form the basis of the demonstrations, the nature of the matter does involve a dissimilarity. Namely, in geometry one can establish everything according to the principle of contradiction,

---

[49] This is Crusius's sole proof for the existence of God that takes the path of probability that is of infinite magnitude. Crusius develops three arguments that are based on "regular" kinds of probability. The first is based on history (§229), the second, on the universality of religious belief (§230), and the third, on conscience (§232). §221 is relevant to On the Impossibility of a Physico-Theological Proof (A620–A630/B648–B658).

because one has in view either only existential propositions or, where one is speaking of grounds, still only existential grounds (§36, 79). By contrast, in the proof that God exists one must at least assume the principle of sufficient cause (§31), because the inquiry concerns the efficacious cause of the world. And because the principle of sufficient cause cannot be derived from the principle of contradiction by means of the concept of an efficacious cause, but rather must be established on the basis of another highest principle (§15), namely, that two positive things that cannot be thought without each other also cannot exist without each other. [...]

§235.[50] *Whether the existence of God can be established from the concept of the most perfect being.* However, several famous scholars, in order to be as satisfying in this purpose as possible, have attempted to see whether the existence of God could be established completely according to the geometric method, namely, from the mere principle of contradiction. Yet from the preceding one can see *a priori* that such a proof cannot be right and that the actuality of God can be cognized in no way other than from his works. At issue is the Cartesian proof, according to which one attempts to establish the existence of God on the basis of the concept of the most perfect being, namely, a concept that includes existence within itself. According to this proof, it is maintained that one need only establish the possibility of a most perfect essence, and then its existence is clear from the principle of contradiction. The inference thus must read: whatever essence has every possible perfection has existence as well. But now God is an essence that has all possible perfections. Accordingly, he also has existence and thus God exists. This inference can be deceptive because the first premise is an axiom, while the second is a definition. However, its form is not correct, as it is a syllogism with four terms. For the term of having existence means something different in the conclusion from what it means in the premise. For it means existence in the understanding in the premise, since, namely, a concept in the understanding contains existence in itself in such fashion that when it is thought or posited, existence must also be thought or posited as a part of it. But in the conclusion it means real existence outside of thought. The premises are both ideal propositions, whereas the conclusion is supposed to be a real proposition. For

---

[50] See On the Impossibility of an Ontological Proof of God's Existence (A592–602/ B620–630). See also *The Only Possible Argument* (2:70–77).

this reason it is indisputable that there is more in the conclusion than in the premises. [...]

Chapter Two: On the Essence and Properties of God [§§237–325]
§237. Now that the actuality of God has been established, it is necessary that we attempt to determine more precisely and in greater detail the constitution of the divine essence, insofar as this is possible, from his fundamental concept (§205), and try to cognize his fundamental essence (§39) and the attributes that follow from it (§40) as much as possible. On account of his fundamental definition God is the first cause of the world. From this follows the **first principle, that so much perfection must lie in his essence that the origin, the fundamental essence, the connection and conservation of all creatures in the world are possible.** Further, on account of his fundamental definition, God is an absolutely necessary and eternal substance. From this follows the **second principle, that an essence must be attributed to him due to which he can and must be eternal and necessary** in such fashion that our reason, as soon as it attributes existence to him, can no longer pose inquiries into a higher real ground for his eternal existence. He must have an essence from which eternity and necessity can be understood such that our desire for truth can and must be completely satisfied with it according to the essence of our reason. That such an essence is to be attributed to him is accordingly as certain as it is that the signs of truth must lie in the fundamental essence of our reason. [...]

§249.[51] Several of God's specific properties follow from the infinity of his existence, while others follow from the infinity of his essence. Because God is infinite, infinity must be attributed to him both with respect to existence and with respect to essence (§138). For both the abstract properties of his existence and those of his essence must have every perfection that is even possible. Therefore, we now need to determine more precisely what follows from a consideration of each of the two divine properties.

---

[51] Crusius discusses God's properties according to the principles that he laid out in his ontology for any complete being (esp. §19, 48, and 59), that is, according to its existence, as structured by space and time (§§250–253), and its essence, as structured by his powers, §§257–266, his understanding, §§267–274, and his will, §§275–318 (in which case, the will breaks down into considerations pertaining to his perfection [§§275–289] and those pertaining to his goodness [§§290–318]). Chapter Three (§§326–346) discusses God's creation and governing of the world as his primary effects.

[Part Three] Cosmology, or the Doctrine of the
Necessary Essence of a World and of What Can Be
Understood from It *a priori*

Chapter One: On the Essence of a World in General [§§347–389]

§350.⁵² *What a world in general is.* The concept of a world in general must thus be this one: a **world** is a real connection of finite things that are not in turn themselves a part of another to which they belong by means of a real connection. Or: **a world** is a system of finite and really connected things that is not in turn itself contained in another system. [...]

§351. *Every world is created by God and did not exist at some time.* From this we can immediately understand the following necessary properties of a world. Because everything that is outside of God is contingent (§128) and is created by him (§144, 145), of which the first and third chapters of natural theology serve as proof, **every world is created by God and did not exist at some time**. [...]

§354. *Every world is created for the sake of an ultimate purpose.* Because the world was created by God (§351), yet God does everything for the sake of an ultimate purpose according to the rules of wisdom (§281, 289), **the world was created for the sake of an ultimate purpose**. And in every world a lot rests on finding out what it is, because only on its basis can one reasonably judge the perfection of the world (§183). [...]

§356. *There is an actual space in every world.* Since many things are connected to each other in a world, among which each complete thing (§18) must occupy its place (§§48–50), there is **an actual space** in each world (§51), which has as many smallest real parts as such substances can exist next to each other, which are the smallest ones in the posited world (§167). However, the entire world exists at the same time as God. Therefore, God allows and makes it the case that it exists somewhere at the same time, where he, in virtue of his immeasurability, exists as well. Yet God is not restricted to the world, but rather he can, if he wants, create even more substances and *systemata* of creatures such that they exist outside the posited world. If he so desires, he can also place several creatures that belonged to a world outside of it, or even, in turn, into a prior world. Thus possible space is not exhausted by the world just as little as

---

⁵² This chapter relates in a general way to both the Analytic of Principles as a whole and to the Antinomies. See also *Inaugural Dissertation*.

God himself is, of whose reality the same is an abstraction without God himself being divided or composed thereby in the least (§51, 253). This is the true concept of extra-mundane space that will strike no one as absurd who merely does not undertake in vain to want to think something that is still material and sensible where there is nothing other than the completely simple, immaterial and incomprehensible God. Because space is an incomplete thing, it cannot be thought completely distinctly until we have a concept of substances that fill it and until we therefore have an intuitive concept of the essence of God and of spirits, or meet up with material things in it. The former is not yet possible for us, at least not presently. However, the latter takes place no further than to the extent to which the world extends and we can think it. For that reason we should not deny that extramundane things can exist as well. Yet if we have raised ourselves up in our thoughts to the boundaries of the world, a dizziness [*Schwindel*] as it were appears to us due to our finitude. According to this nothing remains for us other than that we take up a reverential admiration for the immeasurability of God (§252).

§357. *There is an actual time in every world.* Further, because changes occur due to the connection of many things in the world, there is also an **actual time** in it (§54). One must only not take the sequence of changes to be time, or the *quando* in general, and in the broadest sense (§54). If we go out beyond the beginning of the world, we experience it just as we do with space and we must put ourselves at ease in the eternity of the infinite God if we do not want to lapse into contradictions (§156, 255).

§358. [...] *Rule for judging the identity of the world.* Accordingly, the **rule for judging the identity of the world** is the following: **A world remains the same just as long as its main purposes remain and no change occurs in its kinds of things, in the laws of its connection, [or] in its individuals and essential actions by which the main purposes that are posited in it and the constitution of the means that are to be inextricably connected to it according to its constitution would be changed.** One thus ought not confuse what would imply that the world would cease to be the same with the mere change of its state. [...]

§359.[53] *Things in the world must be able to act on each other.* Because the world is a system of things whose parts have a real connection even outside of

---

[53] See the Third Analogy of Experience (A211–A215/B256–B262). See also *New Elucidation* (1:413–416).

thought (§350), **things in the world must be able to act on each other**
so that the one, as an efficacious cause (§36), can change the state of
the other (§94). Now this relation can be mutual or not. For this reason
two kinds of things are possible in the world: First, **active things**, which
can act on others just as others can act on them, and **merely passive**
things, which do not have an active power, but rather make something
else possible, impossible, or necessary by means of their very existence
(§36). Now because the possibility of causing something else is called
a power, two different kinds of powers are also possible in the world,
namely, active powers and those that are only inefficacious capacities of
an existential ground (§79). [...]

§361.[54] *What nature is.* The sum of all substances that belong to the world
in addition to the essential laws of their connection is called **nature**
(§227). [...]

§362. *Finite things in the world can act on each other only through motion.*
No finite thing can act on another except through motion (§145). [...]
Either they thereby only move each other, or inner active powers are awakened. But
**when one substance acts on another through motion, either it moves
the other from its space either only due to the impenetrability of both,
or the motion caused in the one, or its effort to move, becomes, according to a rule, a condition under which a certain active power acts on the
other substance or is awakened** (§74). By contrast, not all inner activity
of substances is motion, but rather it can also be a thinking or desiring.
Accordingly, we find here a reason for distinguishing **two highest main
classes** of substances in a world. Either they have no power other than
the capacity to move, and then we want to call it **matter**. Or they have
another power that is different from the capacity to move, whether it
has, in addition, the capacity to move or not, in which case we want to
call them **spirits in the broadest sense**. [...]

§363.[55] *Spirits and matter must be able to act on each other in every world.* **As
soon as one posits matter in a world, one must also admit that it can act
on spirits and spirits can act on it**. For, according to its essence, matter
is not God's ultimate purpose, but rather a means (§354). Consequently,
it must be created for the sake of a real connection that it has either

---

[54] See A418/B446 (First Section of the Antinomy of Pure Reason).
[55] §§363–364 are relevant to A381–396 (Observations on the Paralogisms).

mediately or immediately with those creatures that are God's ultimate purpose, namely, rational and free spirits. But it could not have this if spirits and matter could not act on each other. [...]

§364. [...] *The capacity to move can be understood from the essence of a finite spirit.* Further, one asserts without reason that the capacity to move cannot be understood from the essence of a spirit. It can in fact be understood from the essence of a spirit, not from the differential essence, but rather from the general essence of a finite spirit, which belongs to it just as much. For no substance can be understood otherwise than as impenetrable. On the basis of counter-arguments we have already established (§51, 58, 250) that this proposition is subject to an exception in the case of the infinite substance of God and that all creatures are penetrated by him, and that he is with them at the same time in the same place that they are. [...] Now since finite spirits are thus also impenetrable, just as matter is, matter must yield when there is a sufficiently strong effort in spirits to occupy the place of matter. Similarly, spirits must yield and thus be moved if a sufficiently strong effort is present in matter to move to the place at which they are currently found. Consequently, the capacity to move is comprehensible from the essence of every finite substance. [...]

Chapter Two: On Motion [§§390–423]

§390. *Why motion is treated here and what is to be discussed.* Because the creatures in every world must act on each other through motion and thereby be in a real connection (§359), it belongs to cosmology that motion in particular be treated now. Three things are relevant here, namely, the nature of motion in general, the laws of motion, and the method by which it is measured. [...] *There are two kinds of laws of motion, metaphysical and physical.* As far as the laws of motion are concerned, there are two kinds. Some can be understood from the essence of motion *a priori* to be necessary. Others can be learned only *a posteriori* when we abstract them from all or certain kinds of bodies that we find in the world. [...] It is easily seen that only the first kind of laws of motion belong to metaphysics, for which reason one calls them **metaphysical**, whereas the others can be called **physical laws of motion**.[56] [...]

---

[56] See B164–B166 (Transcendental Deduction), where Kant similarly distinguishes between *a priori* and a posteriori laws of nature.

§391. *What motion and rest are.* Motion is that state of a substance in which it changes its place. It is thus a change of state in a subject that concerns an abstraction of existence (§48). As soon as one has formed a first distinct concept of the abstractions of existence from Chapter Four on ontology, one will find no difficulties in the possibility and essence of motion, which, by contrast, one finds if one is accustomed to considering only the abstractions of essence that are discussed in Chapter Three of the ontology and neglects the abstractions of existence or at least cannot come to terms with them. [...]

§410.[57] *Motion is at all times continuous and does not occur through a leap.* Every motion must occur such that the moved substance always proceeds from one point to the next one, and cannot come to a more distant point other than through some line that continues from one point to the next. Or, as it is often expressed, motion never occurs through leaps. Rather, every motion is continuous. For assume that a motion were to occur from one point to a third, without the moved substance going through the intermediate point, one would need either only two moments so that the substance would be in the first point in the first moment and in the third point in the second moment, which cannot, however, be thought. Or one needs three moments so that the substance would be in the first point at the first moment, yet in the third point only in the third moment, in which case it would be in no space in the other moment, which is absurd. Now because two contiguous [*nächste*] points constitute a straight line, since a straight line is nothing other than one that takes the shortest path from one point to another, all smallest parts of motion occur in a straight line. [...]

[PART FOUR] PNEUMATOLOGY, OR DOCTRINE OF THE
NECESSARY ESSENCE OF SPIRITS

Chapter One: On the Concept of a Spirit and Its Actuality
[§§424–440]

§424.[58] *What metaphysical pneumatology is.* [...] I thus understand by **metaphysical pneumatology** the science of the necessary essence of a spirit and of those distinguishing features and properties that can be understood from it *a priori.*

---

[57] See A207–A209/B252–B255 (Second Analogy) and A228–A229/B281–B282 (Postulates of Empirical Thought).
[58] This chapter is relevant to the Paralogisms (A338–A405/B396–B432).

§426. *We are conscious that we are thinking.* We perceive **thoughts in our-selves**. In several of them we are necessitated, if we are awake, to represent things immediately as actual and present, and this state is called **sensation** (§16). [...]

§427. *We are conscious that we will and that several consequences and the faculty of the will are in us.* We perceive further that we desire and are averse, that we can decide something and also start it. If we attain what we desire, then we get **pleasure**. [...]

§428. *We are conscious that we and other things are moved.* When we pay attention to things external to ourselves, we attain the concept of motion. We are thus forced to think of the bodies that we see around ourselves as existing in space. [...]

§429. *We are conscious that motion is not the same as thinking and willing, even that the latter two cannot be understood as possible on the basis of the former.* However, if we compare the concept that we have of motion with what we are conscious of and call thinking and willing, if we compare motion with what we in that case call a representation, and if we compare the activity that we attribute to bodies when we observe their motions with what we desire and are averse to in ourselves and what we call, for short, willing, anyone who is not intent on deceiving himself will see with complete certainty that motion, thinking, and willing are not the same, that thinking and willing are not something that could be understood to be possible from motion as a sufficient cause. [...]

§432. *Many substances, among which we also count our own body, have only a capacity for motion and are thus mere matter.* [...] We thus consist of two main parts, namely, of one material body and of one substance that can think and will. Anyone can perceive this about himself, and that he must similarly attribute it to other human beings is to be judged in part on the basis of the similarity between his own substance and theirs, e.g., with small children, and in part on the basis of its effects, namely, purposefully designed actions and especially rational speech.

§435. *Appendix on an evaluation of the materialist error.* Because the correct definition of spirits is opposed to nothing as much as to the errors of materialists, I shall now turn to a better refutation of materialism and add a few remarks about the proofs I have adduced up to now. [...]

The refutation of materialism stems mainly from a postulate of inner sensation, namely, that with sufficient attention it is impossible to think that thinking and willing would be identical to motion, or that it could be comprehended as possible by motion (§429). [...]

§440. *Whether those who say that the soul fills a space are materialists.* By contrast it is ungrounded if one asserts that those would turn souls into matter or would partake of materialistic errors by saying that the soul occupies a space, moves and is touched, and can also touch other things, and that it should not exist as in a mathematical point (§115). This accusation is based on the fact that one seeks the essence of matter in extension, moreover, not philosophical, but rather mathematical extension (§108, 114), which is a mere concept and not a real thing. Both of these are incorrect, namely, that one seeks the essence of matter in extension and that one confuses the sense of the word "extension" in its philosophical meaning with that in its mathematical meaning. And if one reflects on the differential essence of spirits, one thereby forgets to pay attention to the general essence that all finite substances must have in common. [...]

Chapter Two: On the Properties of a Spirit
in General [§§441–475]
§441. *What understanding and reason are.* A spirit is a substance that can think and will (§434, 362). The entire power of thinking in a spirit, taken together, is called its **understanding**. The degrees of perfection of the understanding can be very diverse. An understanding that has so much ability that it can cognize the truth with consciousness is called **reason**. [...]

§443. *Every idea is an activity.* **Every idea is an activity.** For if it were a passivity, then it would be either an effect of an activity from without or from within. If it were an effect of an activity from another creature, it would have to be either a motion or an adequate effect of a motion, since no creature can act on another other than through motion (§362). But both are impossible (§429). If it were a passivity that came from the action of an inner power of the spirit, that power would be either a power of motion or another mental power. If it were a power of motion, it would revert to the previous case. Yet it cannot be another mental power because all activities of a spirit that are not themselves ideas already presuppose ideas. Consequently, every idea is itself a mental activity. [...]

§445. *What the will is in the broad sense.* The **power** of a spirit of acting according to its ideas is called the **will**. It would be premature to say immediately in the initial definition of the will that it is the power of desiring the good and avoiding what is evil. For desiring and being averse still stand in need of clarification. [...]

§449.[59] *The will of rational spirits must also be free.* The activities of the fundamental powers of the understanding as well as of fundamental desires are in fact fundamental activities, but they are of such a kind that they occur either constantly or such that they cannot fail to occur under those circumstances (§81, 82). But a higher kind of activity is possible, namely, one due to which the subject can act or refrain from acting or can act otherwise under one and the same set of circumstances (§82, 83). Thus, God can also connect this kind of activity with fundamental desires in a will, and in that case it is called freedom. But this power would be without purpose and would remove all regularity from the world if it were bestowed upon a subject other than those spirits that are God's ultimate purposes in the world. By contrast, after God has created a world, then he must also attribute such a power to them necessarily, because the rational and free acts of creatures belong to God's ultimate formal purpose (§281, 283, 284). Accordingly, the will of rational spirits must be free. However, because of divine perfection neither freedom without reason nor a rational subject without freedom is possible.

§471.[60] *Every spirit is immaterial.* **Every spirit is immaterial**, that is, it is impossible that a spirit could be matter or that matter could be a spirit. [...]

§473. *Every spirit is a simple substance.* **Every spirit is a simple substance**. For assume that it were composite. Then either thinking and willing would be something that was possible through composition, or the fundamental powers would have to lie in every particular part of the composite whole. If the former were the case, then thinking and willing would have to be a motion or an effect of it, which is contradictory (§429, 430). If the latter were the case, then the whole that one represented would not be a single spirit, but rather a number of spirits insofar as each one

---

[59] See the Third Antinomy.
[60] §471 and 473–474 are relevant to the First and Second Paralogisms.

would have the essence of a spirit individually and without the help of the others. Consequently, a spirit must be a simple substance.

§474. *Every spirit is imperishable.* **Every spirit is imperishable.** [...]

Chapter Three: On Those Properties of Rational Spirits in Particular That Have Their Ground in the Moral Properties of God [§§476–487]

§476.[61] *Explanation of intent.* Our ultimate goal in the present chapter is to investigate those main properties of rational and free spirits that are attributed to them due to their moral nature so that they have their ground in the infinite perfection of the divine will. We are thus talking not about something that is determined by the physical essence of its fundamental powers as a physical effect, but rather about something that rests on moral relations that have their ground in the properties of God. Its proof must thus be derived from natural theology, namely, from the concept of divine holiness, goodness, and justice. [...]

§477. *God necessarily wills the virtue of his rational creatures.* Due to his essential desire for perfection God wills that the state of the world and all actions in it should be structured according to the rules of the essential perfection of things (§282). Now insofar as no free activities of creatures interrupt the series of events in the world, everything occurs according to the rules of the essential perfection of things and the world is metaphysically good (§301, 355). [...] The correspondence of the moral state of a rational spirit with the rules of the essential perfection of things is called **virtue**. Consequently, **with respect to all rational and freely acting creatures there is in God a moral willing of virtue. Due to this, God wills that all of their actions and omissions are in accordance with virtue and nothing is contained in their states through which the virtue required of them would be made impossible.**

§478. *He also wills the happiness of his rational creatures.* Similarly, since God is good (§290), it is also certain **that he will that all morally efficacious spirits be happy.** [...]

---

[61] §§476–480 are relevant to the Canon of Pure Reason (A804/B832ff., but esp. A810/ B838).

§479. *God wills the happiness of his morally efficacious creatures under the condition of virtue.* [...]

§480. *Consequently, all rational creatures necessary stand under a divine law.* Because rational creatures, like all others, depend on God for everything, the divine moral will of virtue is a law for them, and they have an immutable obligation to orient themselves toward it. Consequently, **it is a necessary property in the essence of all rational creatures that they stand under a divine law.**

§482. *The immortality of rational spirits follows from the perfection of God.* [...]

5

Leonhard Euler

Leonhard Euler was born in Basel, Switzerland, in 1707, the son of a Calvinist pastor. After being trained by the Bernoullis in mathematics, Euler followed Daniel Bernoulli to the newly founded Academy of Sciences in St. Petersburg in 1727, where he became professor of physics in 1731 and then professor of mathematics in 1733 after Bernoulli retired from the position. In 1741 Frederick the Great invited Euler to the Academy of Sciences in Berlin (with Maupertuis serving as President). In 1744 he was appointed the director of the Academy's Mathematical Class. Euler remained in Berlin until 1766, when he returned to Russia after a disagreement with Frederick the Great. He died in St. Petersburg in 1783.

Euler is widely recognized as the greatest mathematician of the eighteenth century, publishing seminal works in algebra as well as differential and integral calculus, and writing on foundational issues in mathematical physics, such as *Mechanica sive motus scientia analytice* (Mechanics or the Analytical Science of Motion, 1736), *Introductio in Analysin Infinitorum* (Introduction to the Analysis of Infinites, 1744), *Reflexions sur l'espace et les temps.* (Reflections on Space and Time, 1748), *Dissertatio de principio minae actionis* (Dissertation on the Principle of Least Action, 1753), and *Vollständige Anleitung zur Algebra* (Elements of Algebra, 1770). While in Berlin Euler wrote, in addition to technical mathematical treatises, works in natural philosophy such as *Recherches sur l'origine des forces* (Inquiry into the Origin of Force, 1750), and, most importantly, *Lettres à une princesse d'Allemagne* (Letters to a German Princess, 1768). This last work consists of well over 200 letters (115 in vol. 1 and 119 in vol. 2) written from April 19, 1760, to May 22, 1762, that were intended to provide instruction in natural philosophy to Frederick the Great's niece, the Princess of Anhalt Dessau.

Published in 1768 only after his return to Russia, the *Letters to a German Princess* gives a nontechnical account of a wide range of topics in natural philosophy, including acoustics, optics, electricity, magnetism, Newtonian gravity, Maupertuis's principle of least action, matter theory, logic, and epistemology. While the bulk of the letters are devoted to presenting standard physical doctrines in a clear and uncontroversial way, Euler develops his own arguments and displays an independent voice on a range of topics. He accepts Newtonian explanations of many particular physical phenomena (Newton's inverse square law, law of inertia, lunar theory, and account of the orbits of the comets), but he rejects Newton's corpuscularian theory of light and the Newtonian commitment to the reality of action at a distance. Though Euler followed Leibniz in advocating mechanism in physics, rejecting atomism, and accepting both a version of the law of continuity and a principle of least action that was Leibnizian in spirit if not in letter, he was highly critical of Leibnizian metaphysics, the theory of monads in particular along with various positions that were alleged to follow directly from it. As a result, he is not properly understood as a Newtonian or a Leibnizian in any straightforward or strict sense.

Euler's *Letters to a German Princess,* which Kant explicitly refers to in his *Inaugural Dissertation* (2:419), occupies an important position in mid-eighteenth-century Germany. For one, Euler's detailed objections to (his understanding of) Leibnizian metaphysics were significantly different from Crusius's criticisms and therefore gave a distinctive flavor to the Academy of Sciences in Berlin, which exercised considerable influence on academics in Prussia and beyond with its Prize Essay questions, publications, and numerous prominent members. For another, the way in which Euler accepted significant aspects of Newtonian science, while developing a non-Newtonian matter theory in terms of impenetrability, inertia, and extension, illustrated one specific way in which a practicing scientist might combine physics and metaphysics and explained how two particularly problematic issues at the time – the infinite divisibility of matter and the role of inertia in the communication of motion – might be understood. It is quite striking that these topics are of central importance to Kant in both his pre-Critical and Critical periods.

Selected Contents of Letters to a German Princess

LETTERS TO A GERMAN PRINCESS (1760–1762)[1]

VOLUME ONE

Letter LXIX[2]
Nature and Essence of Bodies; or Extension, Mobility,
and Impenetrability of Body

The metaphysical disquisition of whether bodies may be endowed with an internal power of attracting each other without being impelled by an external force cannot be terminated until we have examined more particularly the nature of body in general. As this subject is of the greatest importance, not only in mathematics and physics, but in every branch of philosophy, you must permit me to go into greater detail regarding it.

First it is asked: What is body? However absurd this question may appear, as no one is ignorant of the difference between what is body and what is not, it is, however, difficult to ascertain the real characters that constitute the nature of bodies. The Cartesians say it consists in extension, and that whatever is extended is a body. They clearly understand that extension has in this case three dimensions, and that a single dimension, or extension in length only, gives only a line, and that two dimensions, length and breadth, form only a surface, which still is not a body. To constitute a body, therefore, we must have three dimensions, and every body must have length, breadth, and depth or thickness, in other words, an extension in three dimensions.

But it is asked at the same time if everything that has extension is a body. This must be the case if *Descartes's* definition is adequate. The idea of ghosts that the vulgar form does contain extension. It is, however, denied that they are bodies.[3] Though this idea is purely imaginary, it serves to prove that something may have extension without being a body. Besides, the idea that we have of space contains, undoubtedly, an extension with three dimensions. It is admitted, nevertheless, that space alone is not a body; it only furnishes the place that bodies occupy and fill.

---

[1] Originally translated in 1795 by Henry Hunter from the French version (*Lettres à une princesse d'Allemagne*), but significantly revised.

[2] Euler's discussion of the nature of body (or matter) in Letters LXIX and LXX is relevant to Kant's conception of matter in the *Critique*, e.g., as expressed at A848/B876, where Kant characterizes matter as "impenetrable, lifeless extension."

[3] See *Dreams of a Spirit-Seer*, Part One, First Chapter (2:319ff.).

Let us suppose that all those things that are at present in my apartment, air and everything, were annihilated by the divine Omnipotence. There would remain still in the apartment the same length, breadth, and height, but without a body in it. Here, then, is the possibility of an extension that is not a body. Such a space, without body in it, is called a vacuum; a vacuum, then, is extension without body.

It may likewise be said, according to vulgar superstition, that a ghost has extension, but that body or corporality is lacking in it. It is clear, then, that extension is not sufficient to constitute a body – that something more is necessary – hence it follows that the definition of the Cartesians is not exact. But what more is necessary, besides extension, to constitute a body? The answer is mobility, or the possibility of being put in motion; for, even if a body is at rest, whatever may be the causes that preserve it in that state, it would, however, be possible to move it, provided the powers applied to it were sufficient. This excludes space from being included in the class of bodies, as we see that space, which only serves to receive bodies, remains unmovable, whatever motion the bodies that it contains may have.

It is likewise said that by the help of motion, bodies are transported from one place to another, by which we are given to understand that the places and space remain unchangeable. My apartment, however, with the vacuum that I have supposed above, might undoubtedly be moved, and actually is so, as it follows the motion that carries it around the earth itself; here then is a vacuum in motion, without being a body. Vulgar superstition, too, bestows motion on ghosts, and this is sufficient to prove that the power of being moved and extension alone do not constitute the nature of bodies. Something more is missing; there must be matter to constitute a body, or rather, it is this that distinguishes a real body from simple extension, or from a ghost.

Here, then, we are reduced to explain what is to be understood by the term *matter*, without which extension cannot be body. Now, the signification of these two terms is so much the same – that all body is matter, and all matter is body – so that even now we have made no great progress. We easily discover, however, a general character, which is inseparable from all matter, and consequently pertains to all bodies: it is *impenetrability*, the impossibility of being penetrated by other bodies, or the impossibility that two bodies should occupy the same place at once.[4] In truth, impenetrability is what a vacuum lacks in order to be a body.

---

[4] See *Physical Monadology* (1:482ff.).

It will perhaps be objected that the hand may be easily moved through air and through water, which are nevertheless acknowledged bodies; these, then, must be penetrable bodies, and consequently impenetrability is not an inherent character of all bodies. But it is worth noting that when you plunge your hand into water, the particles of the water make way for your hand, and that there is no water in the space that your hand occupies. If the hand could move through the water while the fluid did not make room for it, but remained in the place that the hand occupied, then it would be penetrable, but it is evident that this is not the case. Bodies, then, are impenetrable: a body, therefore, always excludes every other body from the place it occupies, and as soon as a body enters into any place, it is absolutely necessary that the body that occupied it before should leave it. This is the sense that we must affix to the term impenetrability.

21st October, 1760.

Letter LXX
Impenetrability of Bodies

The instance of a sponge will perhaps be produced as an objection to the impenetrability of bodies, which plunged into water appears completely penetrated by it. But the particles of the sponge are very far from being so, in such a manner as that one particle of the water should occupy the same place with one particle of the sponge. We know that a sponge is a very porous body, and that before it is put into the water its pores are filled with air, and that as soon as the water enters into the pores of the sponge the air is expelled and disengages itself in the form of little bubbles so that in this case no penetration takes place, neither of the air by the water, nor of the water by the air, as the latter always escapes from the place into which the water enters.

It is, then, a general and essential property of all bodies to be impenetrable, and consequently the adequacy of this definition must be admitted, *that a body is an impenetrable extension,* as not only all bodies are extended and impenetrable, but likewise reciprocally, as what is at the same time extended and impenetrable is beyond contradiction a body.[5] A vacuum is accordingly excluded from the class of bodies, for though it has extension, it lacks impenetrability, and wherever we meet with a vacuum, there bodies may be introduced without pushing anything out of its place.

[5] See A7–A8/B11–B12 (Introduction).

We must attempt to remove another difficulty raised against the impenetrability of bodies. There are, say the objectors, bodies which admit of compression into a smaller space: as, for example, wool, and especially air, which it is possible to reduce into a space a thousand times smaller than what it occupies. It appears, then, that the different particles of air are reduced in the same place, and that consequently they penetrate each other.

There is, however, nothing in this, for air, too, is a body or a substance full of empty pores, or filled with that fluid, incomparably more subtle, which we call *ether*. In the first case no penetration will ensue, as the particles of air only approach nearer to each other according as the vacuum is diminished, and in the other case, the ether finds a sufficiency of small passages by which to escape as the particles of the air approach each other, but all the while without any mutual penetration. For this reason it is necessary to employ a greater force when we want to compress the air more, and if the air were compressed to such a degree that its minute particles touched each other, we could not carry the compression farther, because, were it possible, the minute particles of the air must mutually penetrate.

It is, then, a necessary and fundamental law in nature that no two bodies can penetrate each other or occupy the same place at once, and it is in conformity with this principle that we must look for the real source of all the motions that we observe in all bodies and of the changes that befall them. As two bodies cannot continue their motion without penetrating each other, it is absolutely necessary that the one should yield to the other. If, then, two bodies are moving along the same line, the one to the left, the other to the right, as it frequently happens at billiards, if each were to continue its motion they must mutually penetrate, but this being impossible, as soon as they come to touch a collision takes place, by which the motion of each body is almost instantly changed, and this collision is produced in nature only to prevent penetration. The motion of each body is precisely changed no further than is necessary to prevent all penetration, and in this consists the real cause of all the changes that happen in the world.

When all these changes are attentively considered, they are found always to take place in order to prevent some penetration, which without these changes must have ensued. At the moment I am writing, I observe that if the paper were penetrable, the pen would pass freely into it without writing, but as the paper sustains the pressure of my pen moistened with ink, it receives from it some particles which form these letters, which could not happen if bodies penetrated each other.

This property of all bodies, known by the term *impenetrability*, is then not only of the greatest importance relative to every branch of human knowledge, but we may consider it as the master spring that nature sets going in order to produce all her wonders. It merits, then, an attentive examination so that we may be able to explain more clearly the nature of bodies, and the principles of every species of movement commonly called *laws of motion*.

25th October, 1760.

Letter LXXIV[6]
Of the Inertia of Bodies: Of Powers

As we say that a body, so long as it is at rest, remains in the same state, so we likewise say of a body in motion that as long as it moves in the same direction and with the same velocity, it remains in the same state. To continue in the same state, then, signifies nothing more than to remain at rest, or to preserve the same motion.

This manner of speaking has been introduced for the purpose of expressing more succinctly our grand principle, that every body, in virtue of its nature, preserves itself in the same state until an extraneous cause comes to disturb it – that is, to put the body in motion when at rest, or to alter its motion.

It must not be imagined that a body, in order to preserve the same state, must remain in the same place: this, indeed, is the case when the body is at rest, but when it moves with the same velocity and in the same direction, we still say that it continues in the same state, though it is changing its place at every instant. It was necessary to make this remark to prevent the possibility of confounding change of place with that of state. If it is now asked: Why bodies continue in the same state?, the answer must be that this is in virtue of their peculiar nature.

All bodies, in so far as they are composed of matter, have the property of remaining in the same state if they are not drawn out of it by some external cause. This, then, is a property founded on the nature of bodies, by which they endeavor to preserve themselves in *the same state*, whether of rest or motion. This quality, with which all bodies are endowed and which is essential to them, is called *inertia*, and it enters as necessarily into their constitution as extension and impenetrability – to such a degree that it would be impossible for a body to exist, divested of this *inertia*.

---

[6] See Kant's Second Analogy (esp. the footnote at A207/B252) as well as his discussion of inertia in the Mechanics of the *Metaphysical Foundations* (esp. 4:543–544 and 4:549–551). See also *Physical Monadology* (1:485ff.).

This term was first introduced into philosophy by those who maintained that all bodies have a propensity to rest. They considered bodies as somewhat resembling indolent persons, who prefer rest to exertion, and ascribed to bodies an aversion to motion, similar to what sluggards have for labor, the term *inertia* signifying nearly the same thing as sluggishness. But though the falseness of this opinion has been since detected, and though it is certain that bodies remain equally in their state of motion as in that of rest, yet the term *inertia* has still been retained, to denote in general the property of all bodies to continue in the same state, whether of rest or of motion.

The exact idea of *inertia,* therefore, is a repugnance to everything that has a tendency to change the state of bodies: for as a body, in virtue of its nature, preserves the same state of motion or of rest, and cannot be drawn out of it except by external causes, it follows that in order for a body to change its state, it must be forced out of it by some external cause, without which it would always continue in the same state. Hence it is that we give to this external cause the name of *power* or *force.* It is a term in common use, though many by whom it is employed have but a very imperfect idea of it.

From what I have just said, you will see that the word *force* signifies everything that is capable of changing the state of bodies. Thus, when a body that has been at rest is put in motion, it is a force that produces this effect, and when a body in motion changes its direction or velocity, it is likewise a force that produces this change. Every change of direction or of velocity in the motion of a body requires either an increase or a diminution of force. Such force, therefore, is always outside of the body whose state is changed, for we have seen that a body left to itself always preserves the same state, unless a force from without acts on it.

Now, the *inertia* by which a body tends to preserve itself in the same state exists in the body itself and is an essential property of it. When, therefore, an external force changes the state of any body, the *inertia* that would maintain it in the same state opposes itself to the action of that force, and hence we comprehend that the *inertia* is a quality susceptible of measurement, or that the *inertia* of one body may be greater or less than that of another body.

But bodies are endowed with this *inertia* in so far as they contain matter. It is even by the *inertia,* or the resistance that they oppose to every change of state, that we judge of the quantity of a body; the *inertia* of a body, accordingly, is greater in proportion to the quantity of matter it contains. Hence we conclude that it requires a greater force to change the state of a great body than that of a small one, and we go on to conclude that the great body contains more matter than the small one. It may even be affirmed that this single circumstance, the *inertia,* renders matter sensible to us.

It is evident, then, that *inertia* is susceptible of measurement, and that it is the same as the quantity of matter a body contains. Just as we similarly call the quantity of matter in a body its mass, so too the measure of *inertia* is the same as that of the mass.[7]

To this then is reduced our knowledge of bodies in general. First, we know that all bodies have an extension of three dimensions, secondly, that they are impenetrable, and hence results their general property, known by the name of *inertia,* by which they preserve themselves in their state; that is, when a body is at rest, it remains so by its *inertia,* and when it is in motion, it is likewise by its *inertia* that it continues to move with the same velocity, and in the same direction, and this preservation of the same state lasts until some external cause intercedes to produce change in it. As often as the state of a body changes, we must never look for the cause of such change in the body itself, since it always exists outside of the body, and this is just the idea that we must call a power or force.

8th November, 1760.

Letter XXVI[8]
System of the Monads of Wolff

Before I attempt to make you sensible of the truth of the principle that all bodies of themselves always preserve the same state of rest or motion, I must remark that if we consulted only experience on the subject, without thoroughly investigating it by the powers of reasoning, we would be disposed to draw the directly opposite conclusion, and to maintain that bodies always have a propensity to be continually changing their state, as we see nothing in the whole universe but a perpetual change in the state of bodies. But we have just shown what are the causes that produce these changes, and we are assured that they are not to be found in the bodies whose state is changed, but outside of them.[9]

The principle, then, that we have established is so far from being contradicted by experience that it is, on the contrary, confirmed by it.

---

[7] See *Physical Monadology* (1:485).

[8] For Wolff's position see his *Rational Thoughts on God, the World and the Soul of Human Beings, Also All Things in General,* in Chapter 1.

[9] This is relevant to Kant's Principle of Succession in *New Elucidation* (1:410–412).

You will easily judge from this how several great philosophers, misled by experience not accurately understood, have fallen into the error of maintaining that all bodies are endowed with powers disposing them continually to change their state.

It is thus that Wolff has reasoned. He says: (1) Experience shows us all bodies perpetually changing their state; (2) Whatever is capable of changing the state of bodies is called force; (3) All bodies, therefore, are endowed with a force capable of changing their state; (4) Every body, therefore, is making a continual effort to change; (5) Now, this force belongs to body only in so far as it contains matter; (6) It is therefore a property of matter to be continually changing its own state; (7) Matter is a compound of a multitude of parts, that are called the elements of matter; therefore, (8) As the compound can have nothing but what is founded in the nature of its elements, every elementary part must be endowed with the power of changing its own state.

These elements are simple beings, for if they were composed of parts they would be no longer elements, but their parts would be so. Now, a simple being is likewise denominated *monad;* every monad, therefore, has the power of continually changing its state. Such is the foundation of the system of monads, which you may have heard mentioned, though it does not now make such a noise as it formerly did. I have numbered the several propositions on which it is established for the purpose of making a more distinct reference in the reflections I mean to make on them.

I have nothing to say about the first and second, but the third is very equivocal, and altogether false in the sense in which it is taken. Without meaning to say that the forces that change the state of bodies proceed from some spirit, I readily agree that the force by which the state of every body is changed subsists in body, but it being always understood that it subsists in another body, and never in what undergoes the change of state, which has rather the contrary quality, namely, that of persevering in the same state. In so far, then, as these forces subsist in bodies, it ought to be said that these bodies, as long as they have certain connections with each other, may be capable of supplying forces by which the state of another body is changed. It follows that the fourth proposition must be absolutely false, and the result from all that went before is rather that every body is endowed with the power of remaining in the same state, which is directly the opposite of the conclusion that these philosophers have drawn.

And I must remark here that it is rather absurd to give the name of *force* to that quality of bodies by which they remain in their state, for if we are to understand by the term *force* everything that is capable of changing the state of bodies, the quality by which they persevere in their state is rather the opposite of a force. It is therefore by an abuse of language that certain authors give the name of force to the *inertia,* which is that quality and which they call *inert force.*[10]

But, not to wrangle about terms, though this abuse may lead to very gross errors, I return to the system of monads, and as the fourth proposition is false, those that follow, which are successively founded upon it, must of necessity be so too. It is false then, likewise, that the elements of matter, or monads, if such there are, are possessed of the power of changing their state. The truth is rather to be founded on the opposite quality, that of persevering in the same state, and the whole system of monads is thereby completely subverted.

These philosophers attempted to reduce the elements of matter to the class of *beings,* which comprehends spirits and souls, endowed, beyond the power of contradiction, with the faculty of changing their state. For while I am writing, my soul continually represents other objects to itself, and these changes depend entirely on my will. I am thoroughly convinced of this, and not the less so that I am master of my own thoughts, whereas the changes that take place in bodies are the effect of an extraneous force.

Add to this the infinite difference between the state of body, capable only of one velocity and of one direction, and the thoughts of spirit, and you will be entirely convinced of the falsehood of the sentiments of the materialists, who pretend that spirit is only a modification of matter. These gentlemen have no knowledge of the real nature of bodies.

15th November, 1760.

Letter LXXVII
Origin and Nature of Powers

It is undoubtedly very surprising that if every body has a natural disposition to preserve itself in the same state, and even to oppose all change, all the bodies in the universe should nevertheless be continually changing their state. We are well assured that this change can be produced only by a force not located in the body whose state is changed. Where, then, must we look for those powers that produce the incessant changes that take place in all the bodies of the universe and that are, nevertheless, foreign to body?

---

[10] Kant criticizes inertia for this very reason in his *Metaphysical Foundations* (4:550).

Must we then suppose, besides these existing bodies, particular beings that contain those powers? Or are the powers themselves particular substances existing in the world? We know of only two kinds of beings in it, the one that comprehends all bodies, and the other all intellectual beings, namely, the spirits and souls of men and those of animals. Must we establish, then, in the world, besides body and spirits, a third species of beings, under the name of power or force? Or do spirits incessantly change the state of bodies?

Both of these views labor under too many difficulties to be hastily adopted. Though it cannot be denied that the souls of men and of beasts have the power of producing changes in their bodies, it would be absurd to maintain that the motion of a ball on the billiard table was retarded and destroyed by some spirit, or that gravity was produced by a spirit continually pressing bodies downward, and that the heavenly bodies, which, in their motion, change both direction and velocity, were subjected to the action of spirits, according to the system of certain ancient philosophers, who assigned to each of the heavenly bodies a spirit, or angel, who directed its course.

Now, reasoning properly regarding the phenomena of the universe, it must be admitted that if we except animated bodies, that is, those of men and beasts, every change of state that befalls other bodies is produced by merely corporeal causes in which spirits have no share. The whole question, then, is reduced to this: Whether the forces that change the state of bodies exist separately and constitute a particular species of beings, or whether they exist in the bodies?

This last opinion appears at first sight very unaccountable, for if all bodies have the power of preserving themselves in the same state, how can it be possible they should contain powers that have a tendency to change it? You will not be surprised to hear that the origin of force has, in all ages, been a stumbling block to philosophers. They have all considered it as the greatest mystery in nature, and as likely to remain forever impenetrable. I hope, however, that I shall be able to present you with a solution of this pretended mystery, so clear that all the difficulties that have hitherto appeared insurmountable will entirely vanish.

I say, then, that however strange it may appear, this faculty of bodies, by which they are disposed to preserve themselves in the same state, is capable of supplying powers which may change that of others. I do not say that a body ever changes its own state, but that it may become capable of changing that of another. In order to enable you to get to the

FIGURE 1.

bottom of this mystery regarding the origin of force, it will be sufficient to consider two bodies, as if no others existed.

Let body A, *Fig.* 1, be at rest, and let body B have received a motion in the direction B A, with a certain velocity. This being laid down, body A is disposed to continue always at rest, and body B to continue its motion along the straight line B A, always with the same velocity, and both the one and the other in virtue of its *inertia.* Body B will then finally come to touch body A. What will be the consequence? As long as body A remains at rest, body B could not continue its motion without passing through body A, that is, without penetrating it. It is impossible, then, that each body should preserve itself in its state, without the one's penetrating the other. But this penetration is impossible, impenetrability being a property common to all bodies.

Since it is impossible that both the one and the other should preserve its state, body A must absolutely begin to move, to make way for body B, so that it may continue its motion, or, body B, having come close to body A, must have its motion destroyed, or, the state of both must be changed as much as is necessary to put them in a condition to continue afterward each in its proper state, without mutual penetration.

Either the one body, therefore, or the other, or both, must absolutely undergo a change of their state, and the cause of this change infallibly exists in the impenetrability of the bodies themselves. Since every cause capable of changing the state of bodies is called *force,* it is necessarily the impenetrability of the bodies themselves that produces the force by which this change is effected.

In fact, as impenetrability implies the impossibility that bodies should mutually penetrate, each of them opposes itself to all penetration, even in the minutest parts, and to oppose itself to penetration is nothing else but to exert the force necessary to prevent it. As often, then, as two or more bodies cannot preserve themselves in their state without mutual penetration, their impenetrability always exerts the force necessary to change it, as far as is requisite to prevent the slightest degree of penetration.

The impenetrability of bodies, therefore, contains the real origin of the forces that are continually changing their state in this world, and this is the true solution of the great mystery that has perplexed philosophers so grievously.

18th November, 1760.

Letter LXXVIII[11]
The Same Subject. Principle of the Least Possible Action

You have now made very considerable progress in the knowledge of nature, which is based on the explanation of the real origin of the powers capable of changing the state of bodies, and you are at present in a condition to comprehend easily why all those of this world are subject to an incessant change of state, from rest to motion, or from motion to rest.

First, we are certain that the world is filled with matter. It is evident that the space separating gross bodies sensible to feeling is occupied by air, and that when we make a vacuum in any space the ether instantly enters, and it likewise fills the space in which the heavenly bodies move. All space being thus full, it is impossible that a body in motion should continue in a single instant without meeting others through which it must pass if they were not impenetrable. And as this impenetrability of bodies exerts always and universally a force that prevents all penetration, it is not at all surprising, then, that we should observe perpetual changes in the state of bodies, though every one has a tendency to preserve itself in the same state.

If they could penetrate each other freely, nothing would prevent any one from remaining perseveringly in its state, but being impenetrable, there must thence result force sufficient to prevent all penetration, and no more results than exactly what is needed.

While they can continue in the same state without any injury to impenetrability, they then exert no force and bodies remain in their state. It is only to prevent penetration that impenetrability becomes active, and supplies a force sufficient to oppose it. When, therefore, a small force suffices to prevent penetration, impenetrability exerts that and no more,

---

[11] The principle of least action was formulated by Pierre-Louis Moreau de Maupertuis, the President of the Academy of Sciences in Berlin from 1746 to 1759 and a close colleague of Euler's. In Maupertuis's formulation of this principle in his "Recherche des loix du mouvement" (1746), it reads: "Whenever any change occurs in nature, the quantity of action employed for this is always the smallest possible." Euler was instrumental in giving this principle a more rigorous mathematical interpretation. Kant refers (approvingly) to Maupertuis's principle of least action in *The Only Possible Argument* (2:98–99).

but when a great force is necessary for this purpose, impenetrability is always in a condition to supply it.

Thus, though impenetrability supplies these powers, it is impossible to say that it is endowed with a determinate force. It is rather in a condition to supply all kinds of force, great or small, according to circumstances. It is even an inexhaustible source of them. As long as bodies are endowed with impenetrability, this is a source that cannot be dried up; this force absolutely must be exerted, or bodies must mutually penetrate, which is contrary to nature.

It ought likewise to be remarked that this force is never the effect of the impenetrability of a single body. It always results from that of all bodies at once, for if one of the bodies were penetrable, the penetration would take place without any need of a power to effect a change in its state. When, therefore, two bodies come into contact, and when they cannot continue in their state without penetrating each other, the impenetrability of both acts equally, and it is by their joint operation that the force necessary to prevent the penetration is supplied. We then say that they act upon each other, and that the force resulting from their impenetrability produces this effect. This force acts upon both of them, for as they have a tendency toward mutual penetration, it repels both the one and the other, and thus prevents their penetration.[12]

It is certain, then, that bodies may act upon each other, and we speak so frequently of this action, as when two billiard balls clash and it is said the one acts upon the other, that you must be well acquainted with this mode of expression. But it must be carefully remarked that in general, bodies do not act on each other except insofar as their state becomes contrary to impenetrability, from which results a force capable of changing it, precisely so much as is necessary to prevent any penetration, so that a small force would not have been sufficient to produce this effect.[13]

It is very true that a greater force would likewise prevent the penetration, but when the change produced in the state of bodies is sufficient to prevent mutual penetration, the impenetrability acts no farther, and there results from it the least force that is capable of preventing the penetration. Since, then, the force is the smallest, the effect it produces, that is, the change of state which it operates, in order to prevent penetration, will be proportional, and consequently, when two or more bodies

[12] See Kant's Third Analogy of Experience (A211–A215/B256–B262).
[13] See *Physical Monadology* (1:484), where Kant argues for a complementary power of attraction. Kant continues to argue for the power of attraction in the *Metaphysical Foundations'* Dynamics.

come into contact so that no one could continue in its state without penetrating the others, a mutual action must take place, which is always the smallest that was capable of preventing penetration.

You will find here, therefore, beyond all expectation, the foundation of the system of the late *Mr. de Maupertuis*, so much cried up by some, and so violently attacked by others. His principle is that of the least possible action, by which he means that in all the changes that happen in nature, the cause that produces them is the least that can be.

From the manner in which I have endeavored to explain this principle to you, it is evident that it is perfectly founded in the very nature of body, and that those who deny it are much in the wrong, though still less than those who would turn it into ridicule. You will already, perhaps, have remarked that certain persons, no great friends to *Mr. de Maupertuis*, take every opportunity of laughing at the principle of *the least possible action*, as well as at the hole continued down to the center of the earth, but fortunately, truth suffers nothing by their pleasantry.

22nd November, 1760.

Letter LXXX[14]
Of the Nature of Spirits

I flatter myself that you are now convinced of the solidity of the reasonings on which I have established the knowledge of bodies, and that of the powers that change their state. The whole is founded on the most decisive experiments and on principles dictated by reason. They involve no absurdity, nor are they contradicted by other principles equally certain. It is not long since any successful progress was made in inquiries of this kind. Such strange ideas were formerly entertained regarding the nature of bodies that all kinds of powers were ascribed to them, of which some must necessarily destroy the others.

Certain philosophers have even gone so far as to imagine that matter itself might be endowed with the faculty of thought. These gentlemen, known by the name of *materialists*, maintain that our souls, and all spirits in general, are material, or rather, they deny the existence of souls and spirits. But when once we have got onto the right road to the knowledge of bodies – the *inertia*, by virtue of which they continue in their state, and *impenetrability*, that quality by which they are subjected to powers capable of changing it – all those phantoms of powers to which I alluded vanish away, and nothing appears a more glaring absurdity

---

[14] Letters LXXX and XCII–III are relevant to the Paralogisms (A338–A405/B396–B432).

than to affirm that matter is capable of thought. To think, to judge, to reason, to possess mental feeling, to reflect, and to ill, are qualities incompatible with the nature of bodies, and beings invested with them must be of a different nature. Such are souls and spirits, and He who possesses those qualities in the highest degree is God.

There is, then, an infinite difference between body and spirit. Extension, *inertia,* and impenetrability – qualities which exclude all thought – are the properties of body, but spirit is endowed with the faculty of thinking, of judging, of reasoning, of feeling, of reflecting, of willing, or of determining in favor of one object preferably to another. There is here neither extension, nor *inertia,* nor impenetrability; these material qualities are infinitely remote from spirit.

It is asked: What is spirit? I acknowledge my ignorance in respect of this, and I reply that we cannot tell what it is, as we know nothing of the nature of spirit.

But it is no less certain that this world contains two kinds of beings, beings *corporeal* or *material,* and beings *immaterial* or *spiritual,* which are of a nature entirely different, as they manifest themselves to us by properties that have no relation to each other. These two species of beings are nevertheless most intimately united, and upon their union principally depend all the wonders of the world, which are the delight of intelligent beings and lead them to glorify their Creator.

It is certain that spirits constitute the principal part of the world, and that bodies are introduced into it merely to serve them. It is for this reason that the souls of animals are in a union so intimate with their bodies. Not only do the souls perceive all the impressions made upon their bodies, but they have the power of acting upon these bodies, and of producing in them corresponding changes, and thus they exercise an active influence over the rest of the world.

This union of the soul with the body undoubtedly is, and will always be, the greatest mystery of the divine Omnipotence – a mystery that we shall never be able to unfold. We are perfectly sensible that the human soul cannot act immediately on all the parts of the body: as soon as a certain nerve is cut, I can no longer close my hand, from which it may be concluded that the soul has power only over the extremities of the nerves, which all terminate and unite in a portion of the brain, the place of which the most skillful anatomist is unable to assign exactly. To this, then, the power of the soul is restricted. But that of God, being unlimited, extends to the whole universe and exerts itself by means that far exceed our comprehension.

19th November, 1760.

Letter XCII
Elucidation Respecting the Nature of Spirits

In order to elucidate more clearly what I have just said about the difference between body and spirit – for it is impossible to be too attentive to what constitutes that difference, as it extends so far that spirit has nothing in common with body, nor body with spirit – I think it necessary to add the following reflections.

Extension, *inertia,* and impenetrability are the properties of body; spirit is without extension, without *inertia,* without impenetrability. All philosophers are agreed that extension cannot occur in spirits. It is a self-evident truth, for everything extended is divisible and you can form the idea of its parts, but a spirit is susceptible of no division and you can have no conception of its half, or of its third part. Every spirit is a complete being, to the exclusion of all parts; it cannot then be affirmed that a spirit has length, breadth, or depth. In a word, all that we conceive of extension must be excluded from the idea of a spirit.

It would appear, therefore, that as spirits have no magnitude, they must resemble geometrical points, the definition of which is that they have neither length, breadth, nor depth.[15] Would it be a very accurate idea to represent to ourselves a spirit by a mathematical point? The scholastic philosophers have professed this opinion, and considered spirits as beings infinitely small, similar to the most subtle particles of dust, but endowed with an inconceivable activity and agility by which they are enabled to transport themselves in an instant to the greatest distances. They maintained that in virtue of this extreme minuteness, millions of spirits might be enclosed in the smallest space; they even made it a question: How many spirits could dance on the head of a pin?

The disciples of *Wolff* are nearly of the same opinion.[16] According to them, all bodies are composed of particles extremely minute, divested of all magnitude, and they give them the name of monads. A monad, then, is a substance destitute of all extension, and on dividing a body until you come to particles so minute as to be susceptible of no further division, you have got to the Wolffian monad, which differs, therefore, from the most subtle particle of dust only in this, that the minutest particles of dust are not perhaps sufficiently small, and that a further division is still necessary to obtain real monads.

---

[15] See Refutation of Mendelssohn's Proof of the Persistence of the Soul (B413–B418), where Kant argues that souls possess an intensive magnitude.
[16] See, e.g., Baumgarten's position on this point in Chapter 3.

Now, according to *Mr. Wolff,* not only all bodies are composed of monads, but every spirit is merely a monad, and the Supreme Being, I tremble as I write it, is likewise a monad. This does not convey a very magnificent idea of God, of spirits, and of the souls of men. I cannot conceive that my soul is nothing more than a being similar to the last particles of a body, or that it is reduced almost to a point. It appears to me still less capable of being maintained that several souls joined together might form a body, a slip of paper, for example, to light a pipe of tobacco. But the supporters of this opinion depend on this ground, namely, that as a spirit has no magnitude, it must, of necessity, resemble a geometrical point. Let us examine the solidity of their reasoning.

I remark, first, that as a spirit is a being of a nature totally different from that of body, it is absurd to apply to it standards that suppose magnitude, and that, consequently, it would be folly to ask how many feet or inches long a spirit is, or how many pounds or ounces it weighs. These questions are applicable only to things that have length or weight, and are as absurd as if, speaking of time, it were to be asked how many feet long an hour was, or how many pounds it weighed. I can always confidently affirm that an hour is not equal to a line of a hundred feet, or of ten feet, or of one foot, or of any other standard of measure, but it by no means follows that an hour must be a geometrical point. An hour is of a nature entirely different, and it is impossible to apply to it any standard that supposes a length that may be expressed by feet or inches.

The same thing holds good as to spirit. I can always boldly affirm that a spirit is not ten feet, nor a hundred feet, nor any other number of feet, but it does not follow from this that a spirit is a point, any more than that an hour must be a point because it cannot be measured by feet or inches. A spirit, then, is not a monad, or in any respect similar to the ultimate particles into which bodies may be divided, and you are perfectly able to comprehend that a spirit may have no extension, without being, on that account, a point or a monad. We must therefore separate every idea of extension from that of spirit.

To ask: In what place does a spirit reside? would be, for the same reason, likewise an absurd question, for to connect spirit with place is to ascribe extension to it.[17] No more can I say in what place an *hour* is, though assuredly an hour is something; something, therefore, may exist without being attached to a certain place. I can, in like manner, affirm

---

[17] See *Dreams of a Spirit-Seer* (2:323–325), where Kant denies that to ascribe place to a spirit is necessarily to ascribe extension to it.

that my soul does not reside in my head, nor out of my head, nor in any particular place, without its being deduced as a consequence that my soul has no existence, just as it may be with truth affirmed of the hour now passing that it exists neither in my head nor out of my head. A spirit exists, then, though not in a certain place, but if our reflection turns on the power that a spirit has of acting upon a body, the action is most undoubtedly performed in a certain place.

My soul, then, does not exist in a particular place, but it acts there, and as God possesses the power of acting upon all bodies, it is in this respect we say He is everywhere, though his existence is attached to no place.

10th January, 1761.

Letter XCIII
The Subject Continued. Reflections on the State of Souls after Death

You will probably be surprised at the sentiment I have just now ventured to advance, namely, that spirits, in virtue of their nature, are in no place. In affirming this, I shall perhaps be in danger of passing for a man who denies the existence of spirits, and consequently that of God. But I have already demonstrated that something may exist, and have a reality, without being attached to any one place. The example drawn from an hour, though feeble, removes the greatest difficulties, though there is an infinite difference between an hour and a spirit.

The idea that I form of spirits appears to me incomparably more noble than that of those who consider them as geometrical points, and who reduce God himself to this class. What can be more shocking than to confound all spirits, and the Supreme Being among the rest, with the minutest particles into which a body is divisible, and to rank them in the same class with these particles, which it is not in the power of the learned term "monad" to ennoble!

To be in a certain place is an attribute belonging only to corporeal things, and as spirits are of a totally different nature, it is not a matter of surprise to say that they are not to be found in any place, and I am under no apprehension of reproach for the elucidations I have submitted to you on this subject. It is thus that I exalt the nature of spirits infinitely above that of bodies.

Every spirit is a being that thinks, reflects, reasons, deliberates, acts freely, and, in one word, that lives, whereas body has no other qualities but that of being extended, susceptible of motion, and impenetrable, from which results this universal quality, namely, that every body remains in the same state as long as there is no necessity of mutual penetration, or of their undergoing some change, and in case of the necessity of their penetrating each other, if they continued to remain in their state, their impenetrability itself supplies the powers requisite to change their state, in so far as it is necessary to prevent all penetration.

In this consist all the changes that take place in bodies: all is passive, and necessarily befalls them in conformity with the laws of motion. There is, in body, neither intelligence, nor will, nor liberty: these are the preeminent qualities of spirits, while bodies are not even susceptible of them.

It is spirit likewise that produces in the corporeal world the principal events, the illustrious actions of intelligent beings, which are all the effect of the influence that the souls of men exercise upon their bodies. This power, which every soul has over its body, cannot but be considered as a gift of God, who has established this wonderful union between soul and body. And as I find my soul in such a union with a certain particle of my body, concealed in the brain, it may be said that the seat of my soul is in that spot, though, properly speaking, my soul resides nowhere and can be referred to that place of my body only in virtue of its action and its power.

It is also the influence of the soul upon the body that constitutes its life, which continues as long as this union subsists, or as the organization of the body remains entire. Death, then, is nothing else but the dissolution of this union, and the soul has no need to be transported elsewhere, for, as it resides in no place, all places must be indifferent to it, and consequently, if it should please God, after my death, to establish a new union between my soul and an organized body in the moon, I should instantly be in the moon, without the trouble of a long journey. And if, even now, God were to grant to my soul a power over an organized body in the moon, I should be equally here and in the moon, and this involves no manner of contradiction. It is body only which cannot be in two places at once, but there is nothing to prevent spirit, which has no relation to place in virtue of its nature, to act at the same time on several bodies situated in places very remote from each other, and in this respect it might be said, with truth, that it was in all these places at once.

This supplies us with a clear elucidation of the omnipresence of God: it is that his power extends to the whole universe and to all the bodies that it contains. It appears to me, of consequence, an improper expression to say that God exists everywhere, as the existence of a spirit has no relation to place. It is more consonant with propriety to say that God is present everywhere.[18]

Let us now compare this idea with that of the Wolffians, who, representing the Deity under the idea of a point, attach Him to one fixed place, since, in fact, a point cannot be in several places at once, and how is it possible to reconcile the Divine omnipotence with the idea of a point?

Death being a dissolution of the union subsisting between the soul and body during life, we are able to form some idea of the state of the soul after death. As the soul during life derives all its knowledge through the medium of the senses, being deprived by death of the information communicated through the senses it no longer knows what is happening in the material world. This state might, in some respects, be compared to that of a man who should all at once become blind, deaf, dumb, and deprived of the use of all the other senses. Such a man would retain the knowledge that he had acquired through the medium of sense, and might continue to reflect on ideas previously formed – his own actions especially might supply an ample store – and finally, the faculty of reasoning might remain entire, as the body in no respect whatsoever contributes to its exercise.

[...]

13th January, 1761.

Letter XCV[19]
Of the Faculties of the Soul, and of Judgment

Had we no other sense but that of smelling, our knowledge would be very limited. We should then have no other sensation than that of odors, the diversity of which, were it ever so great, could not very much interest our soul, being restricted to this, namely, that agreeable smells would procure some degree of pleasure, and such as are disagreeable would excite some disgust.

But this very circumstance carries us forward to a most important inquiry: Whence is it that one smell is agreeable and another disgusting? It cannot be a matter of doubt that agreeable smells excite in the *corpus callosum* a different agitation from what is produced by the disagreeable, but why is it that one agitation in the *corpus callosum* can give pleasure

---

[18] See the *Inaugural Dissertation* (2:414), where Kant approvingly discusses Euler's doctrine of virtual presence.
[19] In this Letter, Euler lays out his epistemological views, which are relevant throughout the *Critique*.

to the soul, while another is offensive, and even frequently becomes insupportable? The cause of this difference resides no longer in body and matter. We must look for it in the nature of the soul itself, which enjoys a certain pleasure in feeling certain agitations, while others excite uneasiness – and the real cause of this effect we do not know.

Hence, we comprehend that the soul does more than simply perceive what passes in the brain, or *corpus callosum;* it adds to sensation a judgment about what it finds agreeable or disgusting, and consequently exercises, besides the faculty of perceiving, another and a different faculty, that of judging, and this judgment is wholly different from the simple idea of a smell.

The same consideration, of the sense of smelling only, reveals to us still other acts of the soul. When the smells are changed, when you apply to the nose a carnation after a rose, the soul has not only a perception of both smells, but likewise notices a difference between them. Hence we conclude that the soul still retains the preceding idea to compare it with what follows. In this consists *reminiscence,* or memory, by which we have the power of recalling ideas, antecedent and past. Now the real source of memory is entirely concealed from us. We know well that the body has much to do in it, for experience assures us that disease and various accidents that befall the body weaken and frequently destroy the memory; it is equally certain, at the same time, that the recollection of ideas is the proper work of the soul. A recollected idea is essentially different from an idea caused by an object. I have a perfect recollection of the sun I saw today, but this idea greatly differs from what I had while I was looking at the sun.

Some authors pretend that when we recall an idea, there happens in the brain an agitation similar to what first produced it, but if this were the case, it would no longer be a recollected idea and I would actually see the sun. They admit, indeed, that the agitation accompanying the recalled idea is much weaker than that from which the original idea proceeded, but still I am not satisfied with this, for it would follow from this that when I recall the idea of the sun, it would be much the same as when I see the moon, the light of which, you will please to remember, is about 200,000 times weaker than that of the sun. But actually to look at the moon and simply to recollect the sun are two things absolutely different.

We may say with truth that the recollected ideas are the same as the actual ideas, but this identity concerns only the soul; with regard to the body, the actual idea is accompanied with a certain agitation in the brain, whereas the recollected one is destitute of it. Accordingly, we say that the idea that I feel or that an object acting on my senses causes in my soul, is a sensation, but it can with no propriety be said that a recollected idea is a sensation. To recollect and to feel always remain two things absolutely different.

When, therefore, the soul compares two different smells, when it has the idea of the one from the presence of an object acting on the sense of smelling, and that of the other from recollection, it has in fact two ideas at once, the actual idea and the recollected idea, and in pronouncing which of the two is more or less agreeable or disagreeable, it exerts a particular faculty, distinct from that by which it only contemplates what is presented to it.

But the soul performs still other operations when a succession of several different smells is presented to it, for while it is struck with each of these in its turn, the preceding are recollected, and a notion is thereby acquired of past and present, and even of future, when new sensations are proposed, similar to those of which it has already had experience. It thence likewise derives the idea of succession, in as much as it under-goes several impressions successively, and from this results the idea of *duration,* and of *time.* Finally, on noticing the diversity of sensations that succeed each other it begins to count *one, two, three,* etc., though this should not go farther, from a lack of signs or names with which to mark numbers. For supposing a man has just begun to exist, and has hitherto experienced no sensations but those of which I have been speaking, far from having created a language for himself, he only knows how to exert his first faculties on the simple ideas which the sense of smelling presents to him.

You see then that the man in question has already acquired the capacity of forming to himself ideas of diversity of the present, of the past, and even of the future, afterward, of succession, of the duration of time, and of number, or at least of the elements of these ideas. Some authors pre-tend that such a man could not acquire the idea of the duration of time without a succession of different sensations, but it appears to me that the same sensation, the smell of the rose, for example, being continued for a considerable time together, he would be differently affected by it than he would if it were presently withdrawn. A very long duration of the same sensation would eventually become tiresome, which would necessarily excite in him the idea of duration. It must certainly be allowed that his soul would be sensible of a very different effect if the sensation were con-tinued for a long time than if it lasted only for a moment, and the soul will clearly perceive this difference. It will accordingly have some idea of duration and of time, without any variation of the sensations.

These reflections, which the soul makes occasioned by its sensations, are what properly belong to its *spirituality*, the body furnishing only simple sensations. The perception of these sensations is already an act of the soul's spirituality, for a body can never acquire ideas.

20th January, 1761.

Letter CII[20]
Of the Perfections of a Language. Judgments and the Nature of Propositions, Affirmative and Negative; Universal or Particular

I have been endeavoring to show you how necessary language is to man, not only for the mutual communication of sentiment and thought, but likewise for the improvement of the mind and the extension of knowledge.

These signs or words represent, then, general notions, each of which is applicable to an infinite number of objects, as, for instance, the idea of hot, and of heat, to every individual object that is hot, and the idea or general notion of *tree* is applicable to every individual tree in a garden or forest, whether cherries, pears, oaks, or firs, etc.

Hence, you must be sensible how one language may be more perfect than another. A language always is so in proportion as it is in a condition to express a greater number of general notions, formed by abstraction. It is with respect to these notions that we must estimate the perfection of a language.

Formerly, there was no word in the Russian language to express what we call *justice*. This was certainly a very great defect, as the idea of justice is of very great importance in a great number of our judgments and reasonings, and as it is scarcely possible to think of the thing itself without out a term expressive of it. They have accordingly supplied this defect by introducing into that language a word that conveys the notion of justice.

These general notions, formed by abstraction, are the source of all our judgments and of all our reasonings. A *judgment* is nothing else but the affirmation or negation that a notion is applicable, or inapplicable, and when such judgment is expressed in words we call it a *proposition*. To give an example: *All men are mortal* is a proposition that contains two notions,

---

[20] Kant discusses the primitive types of judgment in the "Metaphysical Deduction" (A66/ B91ff.).

the first, that of men in general, and the second, that of mortality, which comprehends whatever is mortal. The judgment consists in pronouncing and affirming *that the notion of mortality is applicable to all men.* This is a judgment, and being expressed in words, it is a proposition, and because it affirms we call it *an affirmative proposition.* If it denied, we would call it *negative,* such as this, *No man is righteous.* These two *propositions,* which I have introduced as examples, are *universal,* because the one affirms of *all* men that they are mortal, and the other denies that they are righteous.

There are likewise *particular propositions,* both negative and affirmative, as *Some men are learned,* and *Some men are not wise.* What is here affirmed and denied is not applicable to all men, but to *some* of them.

Hence we derive four species of propositions. The first is that of *affirmative and universal propositions,* the form of which in general is:

Every A is B.

The second species contains *negative and universal propositions,* the form of which in general is:

No A is B.

The third is that of *affirmative propositions,* but *particular,* contained in this form:

Some A is B.

And, finally, the fourth is that of *negative* and *particular propositions,* of which the form is:

Some A is not B.

All these propositions contain essentially two notions, A and B, which are called the *terms of the proposition,* the first of which affirms or denies something, and this we call the *subject,* and the second, which we say is applicable or inapplicable to the first, is the *attribute.* Thus, in the proposition *all men are mortal,* the word *man,* or *men,* is the subject, and the word *mortal* the attribute. These words are much used in logic, which teaches the rules of just reasoning.

These four species of propositions may likewise be represented by figures, so as to exhibit their nature to the eye. This must be a great assistance toward comprehending more distinctly wherein the accuracy of a chain of reasoning consists.

[...]

14th February, 1761.

Letter CXV[21]

The True Foundation of Human Knowledge. Sources of Truth,
and Classes of Information Derived from It

[...]

I shall now have the honor of submitting to your consideration the true foundation of all our knowledge, and the means we have of being assured of the truth and certainty of what we know. We are very far from always being certain of the truth of all our sentiments, for we are but too frequently dazzled by appearances, sometimes exceedingly slight, and whose falsehood we afterward discover. As we are therefore continually in danger of deceiving ourselves, a reasonable man is bound to use every effort to avoid error, though he may not always be so happy as to succeed.

The thing to be chiefly considered here is the solidity of the proofs on which we base our persuasion of any truth whatsoever, and it is absolutely necessary that we should be in a condition to judge if they are sufficient to convince us or not. For this effect I remark, first, that all truths within our reach can be referred to three classes, essentially distinguished from each other.

The first contains the truths of the senses, the second, those of the understanding, and the third, those of belief. Each of these classes requires peculiar proofs of the truths included in it, and in these three classes all human knowledge is comprehended.

Proofs of the first class are reducible to the senses, and are thus expressed:

This is true, for I saw it, or am convinced of it by the evidence of my senses.

It is thus that I know that the magnet attracts iron, because I see it, and experience furnishes me with incontestable proofs of the fact. Truths of this class are called *sensible*, because they are founded on the senses, or on experience.

---

[21] Kant discusses the status of our epistemic attitudes in the Third Section ("On having an opinion, knowing, and believing") of the Canon of Pure Reason (A820/B848ff.).

Proofs of the second class are founded on ratiocination:

This is true, for I am able to demonstrate it according to principles of just reasoning, or by fair syllogisms.

To this class principally logic is to be referred, which prescribes rules for reasoning properly. It is thus that we know that the three angles of a rectilinear triangle are together equal to two right angles. In this case I do not say that I see it, or that my senses convince me of it, but I am assured of its truth by a process of reasoning. Truths of this class are called *intellectual,* and here we must rank all the truths of geometry, and of the other sciences, inasmuch as they are supported by demonstration. You must be sensible that such truths are wholly different from those of the first class, in support of which we adduce no other proofs but the senses, or experience, which assure us that the fact is so, though we may not know the cause of it. In the example of the magnet, we do not know how the attraction of the iron is a necessary effect of the nature of the magnet and iron, but we are no less convinced of the truth of the fact. Truths of the first class are as certain as those of the second, though the proofs that we have of them are entirely different.

I proceed to the third class of truths, that of faith, which we believe because persons worthy of credit relate them, or when we say:

This is true, for several credible persons have assured us of it.

This class accordingly includes all *historical truths.* You believe, no doubt, that there was formerly a king of Macedon called Alexander the Great, who made himself master of the kingdom of Persia, though you never saw him, and are unable to demonstrate geometrically that such a person ever existed. But we believe it on the authority of the authors who have written his history, and we entertain no doubt of their fidelity. But may it not be possible that these authors have concerted to deceive us? We have every reason to reject such an insinuation, and we are as much convinced of the truth of these facts, at least of a great part of them, as of truths of the first and second classes.

The proofs of these three classes of truths are extremely different, but if they are solid, each in its kind, they must equally produce conviction. You cannot possibly doubt that Russians and Austrians have been to Berlin, though you did not see them. This, then, is to you a truth of the third class, as you believe it on the report of others, but to me it is one of the first class, because I saw them and conversed with them, and many others were assured of their presence by means of their senses. You have, nevertheless, as complete conviction of the fact as we have.

31st March, 1761.

VOLUME TWO

Letter VI[22]

Whether the Essence of Bodies Is Known by Us

After so many reflections on the nature and faculties of the soul, you will not perhaps be displeased to return to the consideration of body, the principal properties of which I have already endeavored to explain.

I have remarked that the nature of body necessarily contains three things, *extension, impenetrability,* and *inertia,* so that a being in which these three properties do not meet at once cannot be admitted into the class of bodies, and reciprocally, when they are united in any one being, no one will hesitate to acknowledge it as a body.

In these three things, then, we are warranted to constitute the essence of body, though there are many philosophers who pretend that the essence of bodies is wholly unknown to us. This is not only the opinion of the Pyrrhonists, who doubt of everything, but there are other sects who likewise maintain that the essence of all things is absolutely unknown, and, no doubt, in certain respects they have truth on their side. This is but too certain as to all the individual beings that exist.

You will easily comprehend that it would be the height of absurdity were I to pretend so much as to know the essence of the pen I use in writing this letter. If I knew the essence of this pen (I speak not of pens in general, but only of that one now between my fingers, which is an *individual being,* as it is called in metaphysics, and which is distinguished from all the other pens in the world), if I knew, then, the essence of this individual pen, I should be in a condition to distinguish it from every other, and it would be impossible to change it without my perceiving the change, and I must know its nature thoroughly, the number and the arrangement of all of the parts of which it is composed. But how far am I from having such a knowledge! Were I to rise but for a moment, one of my children might easily change it, leaving another in its room, without my perceiving the difference, and were I even to put a mark upon it, how easily might that mark be counterfeited on another pen. And supposing this impossible for my children, it must always be admitted

---

[22] See On the Amphiboly of the Concepts of Reflection (A260/B316ff.).

as possible for God to make another pen so similar to this that I should be unable to discern any difference. It would be, however, another pen, really distinguishable from mine, and God would undoubtedly know the difference between them. In other words, God perfectly knows the essence of both the one and the other of these two pens, but as to me, who discerns no difference, it is certain that the essence is altogether beyond my knowledge. The same observation is applicable to all other individual things, and it may be confidently maintained that God alone can know the essence or nature of each. It would be impossible to fix on any one thing really existing of which we could have a knowledge so perfect as to put us beyond the reach of mistake; this is, if I may use the expression, the impress of the Creator on all created things, the nature of which will forever remain a mystery to us.

It is undoubtedly certain, then, that we do not know the essence of individual things, or all the characters whereby each is distinguished from every other, but the case is different with respect to *genera* and *species*. These are general notions which include at once an infinite number of individual things. They are not beings actually existing, but notions we ourselves form in our minds when we arrange a great many individual things in the same class, which we call a species or genus, according to whether the number of individual things it comprehends is more or less.

And to return to the example of the pen, as there are an infinite number of things to each of which I give the same name, though they all differ one from another, the notion of *pen* is a general idea, of which we ourselves are the creators, and which exists only in our own minds. This notion contains nothing but the common characters that constitute the essence of the general notion of a pen, and this essence must be well known to us, as we are in a condition to distinguish all the things we call *pens* from those we do not comprehend under that appellation.

As soon as we notice in any thing certain characters, or certain qualities, we say it is a pen, and we are in a position to distinguish it from all other things that are not pens, though we are very far from being able to distinguish it from other pens.

The more general a notion is the fewer it contains of the characters that constitute its essence, and it is accordingly also easier to discover this essence. We comprehend more easily what is meant by a tree in general than by the term cherry tree, pear tree, or apple tree, that is, when we descend to the species. When I say that such an object I see in the garden is a tree, I run little risk of being mistaken, but it is extremely possible I might be wrong if I affirmed it was a cherry tree. It follows, then, that I know much better the essence of tree in general than of the species. I should not so easily confound a tree with a stone as a cherry tree with a plum tree.

Now a notion in general extends infinitely further. Its essence accordingly comprehends only the characters that are common to all beings bearing the name of *bodies*. It is reduced, therefore, to a very few particulars, as we must exclude from it all the characters that distinguish one body from another.

It is ridiculous, then, to pretend with certain philosophers that the essence of bodies in general is unknown to us. If it were so, we should never be in a condition to affirm with assurance that such a thing is a body or it is not, and as it is impossible we should be mistaken in this respect, it necessarily follows that we know sufficiently the nature or essence of body in general. Now this knowledge is reduced to three articles: extension, impenetrability, and inertia.

21st April, 1761.

Letter VII[23]
The True Notion of Extension

I have already demonstrated that the general notion of body necessarily comprehends these three qualities, extension, impenetrability, and inertia, without which no being can be ranked in the class of bodies. Even the most scrupulous must allow the necessity of these three qualities in order to constitute a body, but the doubt with some is: Are these three characters sufficient? Perhaps, say they, there may be several other characters that are equally necessary to the essence of body.

But I ask: Were God to create a being divested of these other unknown characters and possessing only the three mentioned above, would they hesitate to give the name of body to such a being? No, assuredly, for if they had the least doubt on the subject they could not say with certainty that the stones in the street are bodies, because they are not sure whether the pretended unknown characters are to be found in them or not.

Some imagine that gravity is an essential property of all bodies, as all those that we know are heavy. However, were God to divest them of gravity, would they therefore cease to be bodies? Let them consider

---

[23] See the Transcendental Aesthetic (A19/B33ff.) and Axioms of Intuition (A162/B201ff.).

the heavenly bodies, which do not fall downward, as must be the case if they were heavy as are the bodies we touch, yet they give them the same name. And even on the supposition that all bodies were heavy, it would not follow that gravity is a property essential to them, for a body would still remain a body, even if its gravity were destroyed by a miracle.

But this reasoning does not apply to the three essential properties mentioned above. Were God to annihilate the extension of a body, it would certainly no longer be a body, and a body divested of impenetrability would no longer be *body;* it would be a ghost, a phantom. The same holds for inertia.

You know that extension is the proper object of geometry, which considers bodies only in so far as they are extended, abstracting from impenetrability and inertia. The object of geometry, therefore, is a notion much more general than that of body, as it comprehends not only bodies, but all things simply extended, without impenetrability, if any such there be. Hence it follows that all the properties deduced in geometry from the notion of extension must likewise take place in bodies, inasmuch as they are extended, for whatever is applicable to a more general notion, to that of a tree, for example, must likewise be applicable to the notion of an oak, an ash, an elm, etc., and this principle is even the foundation of all the reasoning in virtue of which we always affirm and deny of the species and individuals everything that we affirm and deny of the genus.[24]

There are, however, philosophers, particularly among our contemporaries, who boldly deny that the properties applicable to extension in general, that is, as we consider them in geometry, take place in bodies really existing.[25] They allege that geometrical extension is an abstract being, from the properties of which it is impossible to draw any conclusion with respect to real objects. Thus, when I have demonstrated that the three angles of a triangle are together equal to two right angles, this is a property belonging only to an abstract triangle, and not at all to one really existing.

But these philosophers are not aware of the perplexing consequences that naturally result from the difference that they establish between objects formed by abstraction and real objects, and if it were not permitted to conclude from the first to the last, no conclusion, and no reasoning

[24] See A281/B337 (Amphiboly Chapter) for a discussion of this principle. See also *False Subtlety* (2:49).

[25] Kant discusses philosophers who deny the reality of geometrical properties at *Physical Monadology* (1:480) and *Negative Magnitudes* (2:167–178).

whatsoever, could subsist, as we always conclude from general notions to particular.

Now all general notions are as much abstract beings as geometrical extension, and a tree in general, or the general notion of trees, is formed only by abstraction, and exists outside of our mind no more than geometrical extension does. The notion of man in general is of the same kind, and man in general exists nowhere; all men who exist are individual beings and correspond to individual notions. The general idea comprehending all is formed only by abstraction.

The fault that these philosophers are forever finding with geometers, for employing themselves merely about abstractions, is therefore groundless, as all other sciences principally turn on general notions that are no more real than the objects of geometry. The patient, in general, whom the physician has in view, and whose idea contains all patients really existing, is only an abstract idea, nay, the very merit of each science is so much the greater, as it extends to notions more general, that is to say, more abstract.

I shall endeavor in my next letter to point out the tendency of the censures pronounced by these philosophers upon geometers, and the reasons why they are unwilling that we should ascribe to real extended beings, that is, to existing bodies, the properties applicable to extension in general, or to abstracted extension. They are afraid that their metaphysical principles should suffer in the cause.

25th April, 1761.

Letter VIII[26]

Divisibility of Extension in infinitum

The controversy between modern philosophers and geometers, to which I have alluded, turns on the divisibility of body. This property is undoubtedly founded on extension, and it is only in so far as bodies are extended that they are divisible and capable of being reduced to parts.

You will recollect that in geometry it is always possible to divide a line, however small, into two equal parts. We are likewise instructed by that science in the method of dividing a small line, as *a i, Fig.* 2, into any number of equal parts at pleasure: and the construction of this division is demonstrated there beyond the possibility of doubting its accuracy.

[26] See the Second Antinomy (A434/B462ff.) and Proposition 4 of the Dynamics in the *Metaphysical Foundations* (4:503–508) for the remaining Letters. See also *Physical Monadology*.

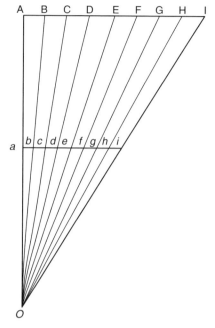

FIGURE 2.

You have only to draw a line A I parallel to *a i* of any length, and at any distance you please, and to divide it into as many equal parts AB, BC, CD, DE, etc., as the small line given is to have divisions, say eight. Draw afterward, through the extremities A *a*, and I *i*, the straight lines A *a* O, I *i* O, till they meet in the point O, and from O draw toward the points of division B, C, D, E, etc., the straight lines OB, OC, OD, OE, etc., which shall likewise divide the small line *a i* into eight equal parts.

This operation may be performed, however small the given line *a i*, and however great the number of parts into which you propose to divide it. It is true that in execution we are not permitted to go too far, the lines which we draw have always some breadth, whereby they are eventually confounded, as may be seen in the figure near the point O, but the question is not what may be possible for us to execute, but what is possible in itself. Now, in geometry lines have no breadth, and consequently can never be confounded. Hence it follows that such division cannot be limited.[27]

---

[27] Compare this demonstration of the infinite divisibility of space with Kant's own at *Physical Monadology* (1:478).

If it is at once admitted that a line may be divided into a thousand parts, by dividing each part into two it will be divisible into two thousand parts, and for the same reason into four thousand, and into eight thousand, without ever arriving at indivisible parts. However small a line may be supposed, it is still divisible into halves, and each half again into two, and each of these again in like manner, and so on to infinity.

What I have said of a line is easily applicable to a surface, and, with greater strength of reasoning, to a solid endowed with three dimensions: length, breadth, and depth. Hence it is affirmed that all extension is divisible to infinity, and this property is called *divisibility in infinitum*.

Whoever is disposed to deny this property of extension is under the necessity of maintaining that it is possible to arrive at last at parts so minute as to be unsusceptible of any further division, because they cease to have any extension. Nevertheless, all these particles taken together must reproduce the whole, by the division of which you acquired them, and as the quantity of each would be a *nothing* or *cipher* o, a combination of ciphers would produce quantity, which is manifestly absurd. For you know perfectly well that in arithmetic two or more ciphers joined never produce anything.[28]

This opinion, that in the division of extension or of any quantity whatsoever, we may come at last to particles so minute as to be no longer divisible, because they are so small, or because quantity no longer exists, is therefore a position absolutely untenable.

In order to render the absurdity of it more sensible, let us suppose a line of an inch long divided into a thousand parts, and that these parts are so small as to admit of no further division. Each part, then, would no longer have any length, for if it had any it would still be divisible. Each particle, then, would consequently be a nothing. But if these thousand particles together constituted the length of an inch, the thousandth part of an inch would consequently be a nothing, which is equally absurd with maintaining that half of any quantity whatsoever is nothing. And if it is absurd to affirm that half of any quantity is nothing, it is equally so to affirm that half of a half, or that the fourth part of the same quantity is nothing, and what must be granted as to the fourth must likewise be granted with respect to the thousandth and the millionth part. Finally, however far you may have already carried in imagination the division of an inch, it is always possible to carry it still further, and never will you be able to carry on your subdivision so far as that the last parts shall

---

[28] See *Physical Monadology* (1:479), where Kant offers a similar line of reasoning.

be absolutely indivisible. These parts will undoubtedly always become smaller, and their magnitude will approach nearer and nearer to 0, but can never reach it.

The geometer, therefore, is warranted in affirming that every magnitude is divisible to infinity, and that you cannot proceed so far in your division as that all further division shall be impossible. But it is always necessary to distinguish between what is possible in itself and what we are in a position to perform. Our execution is indeed extremely limited. After having, for example, divided an inch into a thousand parts, these parts are so small as to escape our senses, and a further division would to us no doubt be impossible.

But you have only to look at this thousandth part of an inch through a good microscope, which magnifies, for example, a thousand times, and each particle will appear as large as an inch to the naked eye, and you will be convinced of the possibility of dividing each of these particles again into a thousand parts. The same reasoning may always be carried forward without limit and without end.

It is therefore an indubitable truth that all magnitude is divisible *in infinitum,* and that this takes place not only with respect to extension, which is the object of geometry, but likewise with respect to every other species of quantity, such as time and number.

28th April, 1761.

Letter IX

Whether This Divisibility in infinitum Takes Place in Existing Bodies

It is, then, a completely established truth that extension is divisible to infinity, and that it is impossible to conceive parts so small as to be unsusceptible of further division. Accordingly, philosophers do not impugn this truth itself, but deny that it takes place in existing bodies. They allege that extension, the divisibility of which to infinity has been demonstrated, is merely a chimerical object formed by abstraction, and that simple extension, as considered in geometry, can have no real existence.

Here they are in the right, and extension is undoubtedly a general idea, formed in the same manner as that of man, or of tree in general, by abstraction, and as man or tree in general does not exist, no more does extension in general exist. You are perfectly sensible that individual beings alone exist, and that general notions are to be found only in the mind, but it cannot therefore be maintained that these general notions are chimerical; they contain, on the contrary, the foundation of all our knowledge.

Whatever applies to a general notion, and all the properties attached to it, of necessity takes place in all the individuals comprehended under that general notion. When it is affirmed that the general notion of man contains an understanding and a will, it is undoubtedly meant that every individual man is endowed with those faculties. And how many properties do these very philosophers boast of having demonstrated as belonging to substance in general, which is surely an idea as abstract as that of extension, and yet they maintain that all these properties apply to all individual substances, which are all extended. If, in effect, such a substance did not have these properties, it would be false that they belonged to substance in general.

If, then, bodies, which infallibly are extended beings or endowed with extension, were not divisible to infinity, it would likewise be false that divisibility *in infinitum* is a property of extension. Now those philosophers readily admit that this property belongs to extension, but they insist that it cannot take place in extended beings. This is the same thing as affirming that the understanding and will are indeed attributes of the notion of man in general, but that they can have no place in individual men actually existing.

Hence you will readily draw this conclusion: If divisibility *in infinitum* is a property of extension in general, it must likewise belong to all individual extended beings; or if real extended beings are not divisible to infinity, it is false that divisibility *in infinitum* can be a property of extension in general.

It is impossible to deny the one or the other of these consequences without subverting the most solid principles of all knowledge, and the philosophers who refuse to admit divisibility *in infinitum* in real extended beings ought as little to admit it with respect to extension in general, but as they grant the latter, they fall into a glaring contradiction.

You need not be surprised at this. It is a failing from which the greatest men are not exempt. But what is rather surprising, these philosophers, in order to get rid of their embarrassment, have thought proper to deny that body is extended. They say that it is only an appearance of extension that is perceived in bodies, but that real extension by no means belongs to them.

You see clearly that this is merely a wretched cavil, by which the principal and the most evident property of body is denied. It is an extravagance similar to that formerly imputed to the Epicurean philosophers, who maintained that everything that exists in the universe is material, without even excepting the gods, whose existence they admitted. But as they saw that these corporeal gods would be subjected to the greatest difficulties, they invented a subterfuge similar to that of our modern philosophers, alleging that the gods had not bodies, but *as it were* bodies (*quasi corpora*), and that they had not senses, but senses *as it were,* and so of all the members. The other philosophical sects of antiquity made themselves abundantly merry with these *quasi corpora* and *quasi sensus,* and they would have equal reason in modern times to laugh at the *quasi extension* which our philosophers ascribe to body; this term *quasi extension* seems to express perfectly well the appearance of extension, without being so in reality.

Geometers, if they meant to confound them, have only to say that the objects whose divisibility *in infinitum* they have demonstrated were likewise only *as it were* extended, and that accordingly all bodies extended *as it were* were necessarily divisible *in infinitum.* But nothing is to be gained with them; they resolve to maintain the greatest absurdities rather than acknowledge a mistake.

3rd May, 1761.

Letter X
Of Monads

When we talk in company on philosophical subjects, the conversation usually turns to such articles as have caused violent disputes among philosophers.

The divisibility of body is one of them, concerning which the sentiments of the learned are greatly divided. Some maintain that this divisibility goes on to infinity, without the possibility of ever arriving at particles so small as to be susceptible of no further division. But others insist that this division extends only to a certain point, and that you may eventually come to particles so minute that, having no magnitude, they are no longer divisible. These ultimate particles, which enter into the composition of bodies, they denominate *simple beings* and *monads.*

There was a time when the dispute about monads employed such general attention and was conducted with so much warmth that it forced its way into the company of every description, that of the guardroom not excepted. There was scarcely a lady at court who did not take a decided part in favor of monads or against them. In a word, all conversation was engrossed by monads – no other subject could find admission.

The Royal Academy of Berlin took up the controversy, and being accustomed annually to propose a question for discussion, and to bestow a gold medal, of the value of fifty ducats, on the person who, in the judgment of the Academy, has given the most ingenious solution, the question about monads was selected for the year 1748. A great variety of essays on the subject were accordingly produced. The president, *Mr. de Maupertuis,* named a committee to examine them under the direction of the late *Count Dohna,* great chamberlain to the queen, who, being an impartial judge, examined with all imaginable attention the arguments adduced both for and against the existence of monads. Upon the whole, it was found that those that went to the establishment of their existence were so feeble and so chimerical that they tended to the subversion of all the principles of human knowledge. The question was therefore determined in favor of the opposite opinion, and the prize awarded to *Mr. Justi,* whose piece was deemed the most complete refutation of the monadists.

You may easily imagine how violently this decision of the Academy must have irritated the partisans of monads, at the head of whom stood the celebrated *Mr. Wolff.* His followers, who were much more numerous and more formidable then than at present, exclaimed in high terms against the partiality and injustice of the Academy, and their chief had well-nigh proceeded to launch the thunder of a philosophical anathema against it. I do not now recollect to whom we are indebted for the care of averting this disaster.

As this controversy has made a great deal of noise, you will not be displeased, undoubtedly, if I dwell a little upon it. The whole is reduced to this simple question: Is body divisible to infinity? Or, in other words: Has the divisibility of bodies any bound, or has it not? I have already remarked that extension, considered geometrically, is on all hands allowed to be divisible *in infinitum,* because however small a magnitude may be, it is possible to conceive half of it, and again half of that half, and so on to infinity.

This notion of extension is very abstract, as are those of all *genera,* such as that of man, of horse, of tree, etc., in so far as they are not applied to an individual and determinate being. Again, it is the most certain principle of all our knowledge that whatever can be truly affirmed of the genus must be true of all the individuals comprehended under it. If, therefore, all bodies are extended, all the properties belonging to extension must belong to each body in particular. Now all bodies are extended, and extension is divisible to infinity, therefore every body must be so likewise. This is a syllogism of the best form, and as the first proposition is indubitable, all that remains is to be assured that the second is true, that is, whether it is true or not that bodies are extended.

The partisans of monads, in maintaining their opinion, are obliged to affirm that bodies are not extended, but have only an appearance of extension. They imagine that by this they have subverted the argument adduced in support of the divisibility *in infinitum*. But if body is not extended, I should be glad to know where we derived the idea of extension from, for if body is not extended, nothing in the world is, as spirits are still less so. Our idea of extension, therefore, would be altogether imaginary and chimerical.

Geometry would accordingly be a speculation entirely useless and illusory, and never could admit of any application to things really existing. In effect, if no one thing is extended, to what purpose investigate the properties of extension? But as geometry is beyond contradiction one of the most useful of the sciences, its object cannot possibly be a mere chimera. [...]

5th May, 1761.

Letter XI
Reflections on Divisibility in infinitum, and on Monads

In speaking of the divisibility of body, we must carefully distinguish what is in our power, from what is possible in itself. In the first sense, it cannot be denied that such a division of body as we are capable of must be very limited.

By pounding a stone we can easily reduce it to powder, and if it were possible to reckon all the little grains that form that powder, their number would undoubtedly be so great that it would be a matter of surprise to have divided the stone into so many parts. But these very grains will be almost indivisible with respect to us, as no instrument we could employ will be able to lay hold of them. But it cannot with truth be affirmed that they are indivisible in themselves. You have only to view them with a good microscope, and each will appear itself a considerable stone, on which are distinguishable a great many points and inequalities, which demonstrates the possibility of a further division, though we are not in a position to execute it. For wherever we can distinguish several points in any object, it must be divisible in so many parts.

We speak not, therefore, of a division practicable by our strength and skill, but of that which is possible in itself, and which the Divine Omnipotence is able to accomplish.

It is in this sense, accordingly, that philosophers use the word "divisibility," so that if there were a stone so hard that no force could break it, it might be affirmed without hesitation that it is as divisible in its own nature as the most brittle of the same magnitude. And how many bodies are there on which we cannot lay any hold, and of whose divisibility we can entertain not the smallest doubt? No one doubts that the moon is a divisible body, though he is incapable of detaching the smallest particle from it, and the simple reason for its divisibility is its being extended.

Wherever we notice extension, we are under the necessity of acknowledging divisibility so that divisibility is an inseparable property of extension. But experience likewise demonstrates that the division of bodies extends very far. [...]

On viewing with a good microscope a single drop of water, it has the appearance of a sea: we see thousands of living creatures swimming in it, each of which is necessarily composed of an infinite number of muscular and nervous fibers, whose marvelous structure ought to excite our admiration. And though these creatures may perhaps be the smallest that we are capable of discovering by the help of the microscope, undoubtedly they are not the smallest the Creator has produced. Animalcules probably exist as small relative to them as they are relative to us. And these, after all, are not yet the smallest, but may be followed by an infinity of new classes, each of which contains creatures incomparably smaller than those of the preceding class.

We ought to acknowledge in this the omnipotence and infinite wisdom of the Creator, as in objects of the greatest magnitude. It appears to me that the consideration of these minute species, each of which is followed by another inconceivably more minute, ought to make the liveliest impression on our minds, and inspire us with the most sublime ideas of the works of the Almighty, whose power knows no bounds, whether as to great objects or small.

To imagine, that after having divided a body into a great number of parts, we arrive at length at particles so small as to defy all further division, is therefore the indication of a very contracted mind. But supposing it is possible to descend to particles so minute as to be, in their own nature, no longer divisible, as in the case of the supposed monads, before coming to this point, we shall have a particle composed of only two monads, and this particle will be of a certain magnitude or extension, otherwise it could not have been divisible into these two monads. Let us further suppose that this particle, as it has some extension, may be the thousandth part of an inch, or still smaller if you will – for it is of no importance – what I say of the thousandth part of an inch may be said with equal truth of every smaller part. This thousandth part of an inch, then, is composed of two monads, and consequently two monads together would be the thousandth part of an inch and two thousand times nothing a whole inch – the absurdity strikes at first sight.

The partisans of the system of monads accordingly shrink from the force of this argument, and are reduced to a terrible nonplus when asked how many monads are requisite to constitute an extension. Two, they apprehend, would appear insufficient. They therefore allow that more must be necessary. But if two monads cannot constitute extension, as each of the two has none, neither three, nor four, nor any number whatever will produce it, and this completely subverts their system of monads.

9th May, 1761.

Letter XII
Reply to the Objections of the Monadists to Divisibility in infinitum

The partisans of monads are far from submitting to the arguments adduced to establish the divisibility of body to infinity. Without attacking them directly, they allege that divisibility *in infinitum* is a chimera of geometers, and that it is involved in contradiction. For if each body is divisible to infinity, it would contain an infinite number of parts, the smallest bodies as well as the greatest, and the number of these particles to which divisibility *in infinitum* would lead, that is to say, the most minute of which bodies are composed, will then be as great in the smallest body as in the largest, this number being *infinite* in both, and hence the partisans of monads triumph in their reasoning as invincible. For if the number of ultimate particles of which two bodies are composed is the same in both, it must follow, say they, that the bodies are perfectly equal to each other.

Now this goes on the supposition that the ultimate particles are all perfectly equal to each other, for if some were greater than others, then it would not be surprising that one of the two bodies should be much greater than the other. But it is absolutely necessary, say they, that the ultimate particles of all bodies should be equal to each other, as they no longer have any extension, and their magnitude absolutely vanishes, or becomes nothing. They even form a new objection by alleging that all bodies would be composed of an infinite number of nothings, which is a still greater absurdity.

I readily admit this, but I remark, at the same time, that it ill becomes them to raise such an objection, seeing they maintain that all bodies are composed of a certain number of monads, though, relatively to magnitude, they are absolutely nothings, so that by their own confession several nothings are capable of producing a body. They are right in saying their monads are not nothings, but rather beings endowed with an excellent quality, on which the nature of the bodies they compose is based. Now, the only question here is about extension, and as they are under the necessity of admitting that the monads have none, several nothings, according to them, would always be something.

But I shall push this argument against the system of monads no farther, my object being to make a direct reply to the objection founded on the ultimate particles of bodies, raised by the monadists in support of their system, by which they flatter themselves in the confidence of a complete victory over the partisans of divisibility *in infinitum*.

I should be glad to know, in the first place, what they mean by the *ultimate particles* of bodies. In their system, according to which every body is composed of a certain number of monads, I clearly comprehend that the ultimate particles of a body are the monads themselves that constitute it, but in the system of divisibility *in infinitum,* the term ultimate particle is absolutely unintelligible.

They are right in saying that these are the particles at which we arrive from the division of bodies, after having continued to infinity. But this is just the same thing as saying after having finished a division that never comes to an end. For divisibility *in infinitum* means nothing else but the possibility of always carrying on the division, without ever arriving at the point where it would be necessary to stop. He who maintains divisibility *in infinitum* boldly denies, therefore, the existence of the ultimate particles of body, and it is a manifest contradiction to suppose at once ultimate particles and divisibility *in infinitum.*

I reply, then, to the partisans of the system of monads that their objection to the divisibility of body to infinity would be a very solid one, if that system were to admit of ultimate particles, but being expressly excluded from it, all this reasoning of course falls to the ground.

It is false, therefore, that in the system of divisibility *in infinitum* bodies are composed of an infinity of particles. However closely connected these two propositions may appear to the partisans of monads, they manifestly contradict each other, for whoever maintains that body is divisible *in infinitum,* or without end, absolutely denies the existence of ultimate particles, and consequently has no concern in the question. The term can only mean such particles as are no longer divisible – an idea totally inconsistent with the system of divisibility *in infinitum.* This formidable attack, then, is completely repelled.

12th May, 1761.

Letter XIII[29]

Principle of the Sufficient Reason, the Strongest Support of the Monadists

You must be perfectly sensible that one of the two systems that have undergone such ample discussion is necessarily true, and the other false, seeing that they are contradictory.

It is admitted on both sides that bodies are divisible. The only question is whether this divisibility is limited or whether it may always be carried further, without the possibility of ever arriving at indivisible particles.

The system of monads is established in the former case, since after having divided a body into indivisible particles, these very particles are monads, and there would be reason to say that all bodies are composed of them, and each of a certain determinate number. Whoever denies the system of monads must likewise, then, deny that the divisibility of bodies is limited. He is under the necessity of maintaining that it is always possible to carry this divisibility further, without ever being obliged to stop, and this is the case of divisibility *in infinitum,* on which system we absolutely deny the existence of ultimate particles, consequently the difficulties resulting from their infinite number fall apart of themselves. In denying monads, it is impossible to talk any longer of ultimate particles, and still less of the number of them that enters into the composition of each body.

You must have remarked that what I have hitherto produced in support of the system of monads is destitute of solidity. I now proceed to inform you that its supporters rest their cause chiefly on the great principle of *sufficient reason,* which they know how to employ so dexterously that by means of it they are in a condition to demonstrate whatever suits their purpose, and to demolish whatever is raised against them. The great discovery made, then, is this, namely, *that nothing can be without a sufficient reason,* and to modern philosophers we stand indebted for it.

In order to give you an idea of this principle, you have only to consider, that in everything presented to you, it may always be asked why it is such, and the answer is what they call the *sufficient reason,* supposing it really to correspond to the question proposed. Wherever the *why* can take place, the possibility of a satisfactory answer is taken for granted, which shall, of course, contain the sufficient reason of the thing.

This is very far, however, from being a mystery of modern discovery. Men in every age have asked *why* – an incontestable proof of their

---

[29] Wolff invokes the principle of sufficient reason in arguing for the necessity of simples at §76 of *Rational Thoughts* (Chapter 1).

conviction that every thing must have a satisfying reason of its existence. This principle, that *nothing is without a cause,* was very well known to ancient philosophers, but unhappily this cause is for the most part concealed from us. To little purpose do we ask *why;* no one is qualified to assign the reason. It is not a matter of doubt that every thing has its cause, but to make [just] some progress hardly deserves the name, and as long as it remains concealed, we have not advanced a single step in real knowledge.

You may perhaps imagine that modern philosophers, who make such a boast of the principle of a sufficient reason, have actually discovered that of all things, and are in a condition to answer every *why* that can be proposed to them, which would undoubtedly be the very summit of human knowledge, but in this respect they are just as ignorant as their neighbors. Their whole merit amounts to no more than a pretension to have demonstrated that wherever it is possible to ask the question *why,* there must be a satisfactory answer to it, though concealed from us.

They readily admit that the ancients had a knowledge of this principle, but a knowledge very obscure, whereas they pretend to have placed it in its clearest light, and to have demonstrated the truth of it, and therefore it is that they know how to turn it most to their account, and that this principle puts them in a condition to prove that bodies are composed of monads.

Bodies, say they, must have their sufficient reason somewhere, but if they were divisible to infinity, such reason could not take place, and hence they conclude, with an air altogether philosophical, *that as every thing must have its sufficient reason, it is absolutely necessary that all bodies should be composed of monads* – which was to be demonstrated. This, I must admit, is a demonstration not to be resisted.

It were greatly to be wished that a reasoning so slight could elucidate to us questions of this importance, but I frankly confess I comprehend nothing of the matter. They talk of the sufficient reason of bodies, by which they mean to reply to a certain *wherefore,* which remains unexplained. But it would be proper, undoubtedly, clearly to understand and carefully to examine a question, before a reply is attempted. In the present case, the answer is given before the question is formed.

Is it asked: Why do bodies exist? It would be ridiculous, in my opinion, to reply: Because they are composed of monads, as if they contained the cause of that existence. Monads have not created bodies, and when I ask why such a being exists, I see no other reason that can be given but this, namely, because the Creator has given it existence, and as to the manner in which creation is performed, philosophers, I think, would do well honestly to acknowledge their ignorance.

But they maintain that God could not have produced bodies without having created monads, which were necessary to form the composition of them. This manifestly supposes that bodies are composed of monads, the point which they meant to prove by this reasoning. And you are abundantly sensible that it is not fair reasoning to take for granted the truth of a proposition that you are bound to prove by reasoning. It is a sophism known in logic by the name of a *petitio principii*, or begging the question.

16th May, 1761.

Letter XIV
Another Argument of the Monadists, Derived from the Principle of Sufficient Reason. Absurdities Resulting from It

The partisans of monads likewise derive their grand argument from the principle of sufficient reason by alleging that they could not even comprehend the possibility of bodies if they were divisible to infinity. Since there would be nothing in them capable of checking imagination, they must have ultimate particles or elements, the composition of which must serve to explain the composition of bodies.

But do they pretend to understand the possibility of all the things that exist? This would savor too much of pride. Nothing is more common among philosophers than this kind of reasoning – I cannot comprehend the possibility of this, unless it is such as I imagine it to be. Therefore, it necessarily must be such.

You clearly comprehend the frivolousness of such reasoning, and that in order to arrive at the truth, research much more profound must be employed. Ignorance can never become an argument to lead us to knowledge of the truth, and the one in question is evidently founded on ignorance of the different manners that may render the thing possible.

But on the supposition that nothing exists but that whose possibility they are able to comprehend, is it possible for them to explain how bodies would be composed of monads? Monads, having no extension, must be considered as points in geometry, or as we represent to ourselves spirits and souls. Now it is well known that many geometrical points, let the number be supposed ever so great, never can produce a line, and consequently still less a surface, or a body. If a thousand points were sufficient to constitute the thousandth part of an inch, each of these must necessarily have an extension, which taken a thousand times would become equal to the thousandth part of an inch. Finally, it is an incontestable truth that take any number of points you will, they can never produce extension. I speak here of points such as we conceive in geometry, without any length, breadth, or thickness, and which in that respect are absolutely nothing.

Our philosophers accordingly admit that no extension can be produced by geometrical points, and they solemnly protest that their monads ought not to be confounded with these points. They have no more extension than points, say they, but they are invested with admirable qualities, such as representing to them the whole universe by ideas, though extremely obscure, and these qualities render them proper to produce the phenomenon of extension, or rather that apparent extension I mentioned above.[30] The same idea, then, ought to be formed of monads as of spirits and souls, but with this difference, namely, that the faculties of monads are much more imperfect.

The difficulty appears to me greatly increased by this, and I flatter myself that you will be of my opinion that two or more spirits cannot possibly be joined so as to form extension. Several spirits may very well form an assembly or a council, but never an extension, since one can abstract from the body of each counselor, which contributes nothing to the deliberation going forward, for this is the production of spirits only; a council is nothing else but an assembly of spirits or souls. But could such an assembly represent an extension? Hence it follows that monads are still less proper to produce extension than geometrical points are.

The partisans of the system [of monads], accordingly, are not agreed as to this point. Some allege that monads are actual parts of bodies, and that after having divided a body as far as possible, you then arrive at the monads that constitute it.

Others absolutely deny that monads can be considered as constituent parts of bodies. According to them, they contain only the sufficient reason. While the body is in motion, the monads do not stir, but they contain the sufficient reason of motion. Finally, they cannot touch each other. Thus, when my hand touches a body, no one monad of my hand touches a monad of the body.

What is it then, you will ask, that touches in this case, if it is not the monads that compose the hand and the body? The answer must be that two nothings touch each other, or rather it must be denied that there is a real contact. It is a mere illusion, destitute of all foundation. They

---

[30] See Volume II, Letter IX.

are under the necessity of affirming the same thing of all bodies, which, according to these philosophers, are only phantoms formed by the imagination, representing to itself very confusedly the monads containing the sufficient reason of all that we call body.

In this philosophy everything is spirit, phantom, and illusion, and when we cannot comprehend these mysteries, it is our stupidity that keeps up an attachment to the crude notions of the vulgar.

The strangest thing about the case is that these philosophers, with a design to investigate and explain the nature of bodies and extension, are at last reduced to deny their existence. This is undoubtedly the surest way to succeed in explaining the phenomena of nature; you have only to deny them and to allege in proof the principle of sufficient reason. Philosophers will rather run into such extravagances than acknowledge their ignorance.

19th May, 1761.

Letter XVI
Continuation [of Letter XV: Reflections on the System of Monads]

The system of monads, such as I have been describing it, is a necessary consequence of the principle that bodies are compounded of simple beings. The moment this principle is admitted, you are obliged to acknowledge the justness of all the other consequences resulting from it so naturally that it is impossible to reject any one, however absurd and contradictory.

First, these simple beings, which must enter into the composition of bodies, being monads which have no extension, neither can their compounds, that is bodies, have any, and all these extensions become illusion and chimera, it being certain that parts destitute of extension are incapable of producing a real extension. It can be at most an appearance or a phantom, which dazzles by a fallacious idea of extension. In a word, everything becomes illusion, and upon this is founded the system of pre-established harmony, the difficulties of which I have already pointed out.

It is necessary then to take care that we be not entangled in this labyrinth of absurdities. If you make a single false step over the threshold, you are involved beyond the power of escaping. Everything depends on the first ideas formed of extension, and the manner in which the partisans of the system of monads endeavor to establish it is extremely seductive.

These philosophers do not like to speak of the extension of bodies, because they clearly foresee that it must become fatal to them in the sequel, but instead of saying that bodies are extended, they call them compound beings, which no one can deny, as extension necessarily supposes divisibility, and consequently a combination of parts that constitute bodies. But they presently make a wrong use of this notion of a compound being. For, say they, a being can be compounded only in so far as it is made up of simple beings, and hence they conclude that every body is compounded of simple beings. As soon as you grant them this conclusion, you are caught beyond the power of retreating, for you are under the necessity of admitting that these simple beings, not being compounded, are not extended.

This captious argument is exceedingly seductive. If you permit yourself to be dazzled with it, they have gained their point. Only admit this proposition, namely, that bodies are compounded of simple beings, that is, of parts which have no extension, and you are entangled. With all your might, then, resist this assertion, namely, that *every compound being is made up of simple beings,* and though you may not be able directly to prove the fallacy, the absurd consequences which immediately result would be sufficient to overthrow it.

In effect, they admit that bodies are extended; from this point the partisans of the system of monads set out to establish the proposition that they are compound beings, and having hence deduced that bodies are compounded of simple beings, they are obliged to allow that simple beings are incapable of producing real extension, and consequently that the extension of bodies is a mere illusion.

An argument whose conclusion is a direct contradiction of the premises is singularly strange. This reasoning sets out by advancing that bodies are extended, for if they were not, how could it be known that they are compound beings, and then comes to the conclusion that they are not so. Never was a fallacious argument, in my opinion, more completely refuted than this has been. The question was: *Why are bodies extended?* And, after a little turning and winding, it is answered: *Because they are not so.* Were I to be asked why a triangle has three sides, should I reply that it is a mere illusion – would such a reply be deemed satisfactory?

It is therefore certain that this proposition, "Every compound being is necessarily made up of simple beings," leads to a false conclusion, however well founded it may appear to the partisans of monads, who even pretend to rank it among the axioms or first principles of human knowledge. The absurdity in which it immediately issues is sufficient to overturn it, were there no other reasons for calling it in question.

But as a compound being here means the same thing as an extended being, it is just as if it were affirmed that every extended being is compounded of beings which are not so. And this is precisely the question. It is asked whether on dividing a body you eventually arrive at parts unsusceptible of any further division, for want of extension, or whether you never arrive at particles such that the divisibility should be unbounded?

In order to determine this important question, for the sake of argument let it be supposed that every body is compounded of parts without extension. Certain specious reasonings may easily be employed, drawn from the noted principle of sufficient reason, and it will be said that a compound being can have its sufficient reason only in the simple beings composing it, which might be true if the compound being were in fact made up of simple beings, the very point in question, and whenever this composition is denied, the sufficient reason becomes totally inapplicable.

But it is dangerous to accept a challenge with persons who believe in monads, for, besides that there is nothing to be gained, they loudly exclaim that you are attacking the principle of the sufficient reason, which is the basis of all certainty, even of the existence of God. According to them, whoever refuses to admit monads and rejects the magnificent fabric in which every thing is illusion is an infidel and an atheist. I am sure that such a frivolous imputation will not make the slightest impression on your mind, but that you will perceive the wild extravagances into which men are driven when they embrace the system of monads – a system too absurd to need a refutation in detail, their foundation being absolutely reduced to a wretched abuse of the principle of sufficient reason.

26th May, 1761.

6

Johann Heinrich Lambert

Johann Heinrich Lambert was born in 1728 in Mülhausen, now Mulhouse, in the Alsace region in France. After receiving very limited formal schooling, Lambert initially held a variety of odd jobs: helping his father (who was a tailor), serving as a clerk in an ironwork, working as a scribe for a law professor in a Swiss Chancellery for five years, and finally acting as a tutor to a private family in Chur (from 1748 to 1758). These last two jobs provided him with the opportunity to read intensively in mathematics and physics and to travel throughout Europe. In 1759, while in Augsburg, he received a position in the newly formed Bavarian Academy of Sciences, in which capacity he worked out his views on photometry and traveled to Erlangen and Switzerland to help with various geological projects. In 1763, after refusing to leave Augsburg for Munich, where the Bavarian Academy was located, his association with the academy there was dissolved. He went first to Leipzig in 1764 and then to Berlin in 1765, where he became a member of the Physical Class of the Prussian Academy of Sciences and remained until his death in 1777.

Although Lambert published two important articles on topics in applied physics in the late 1750s, the majority of his most significant publications came in the 1760s. In addition to further noteworthy articles on mathematics, reflection, perspective, and optics, he published *Cosmologische Briefe über die Einrichtung des Weltbaues* (Cosmological Letters on the Arrangement of the Universe) in 1761, *Neues Organon* (New Organon) in 1764, and *Anlage zur Architectonic* (Appendix on Architectonics) in 1771 (though it had been composed in 1764). Some of Lambert's most original philosophical views and his overall project are helpfully summarized in an article titled "*Abhandlung vom* Criterium veritatis" (Treatise on the *Criterion of Truth*), which he wrote (but chose not to submit) in response to a prize essay question of the Berlin Academy in 1761.

The position that Lambert develops in these works blends Lockean empiricism with a rationalist position that is nonetheless distinct in crucial ways from Cartesian, Leibnizian, and Wolffian versions. In his "Treatise on the Criterion on Truth," for example, Lambert argues that in searching for a criterion of truth, instead of positing some version of clarity and distinctness, one can draw a distinction between concepts that is similar to that drawn between axioms and theorems in, say, Euclidean geometry: axiomatic concepts are immediately justified as soon as they are represented, whereas derivative concepts can be justified by showing how they arise from the axiomatic concepts. Along the way Lambert provides an account of how both the analytic and synthetic method applies to such concepts and how this theoretical apparatus can apply to metaphysics. The two-volume *New Organon* obviously takes on a much larger project, encompassing systematic treatments of what he calls dianoiology, alethiology, semiotics, and phenomenology (which are briefly described in its preface). The focus in the selections in the main text (taken from the Dianoiology) is on the transition between common cognition, which derives directly from experience, and scientific cognition and on how the latter in particular can involve *a priori* cognition.

In mid-November of 1765, shortly after his arrival in Berlin, Lambert initiates a correspondence with Kant, who was four years his senior, but still lacking a permanent position at the university. Lambert was interested in, among other things, Kant's help in finding a publisher for his substantive scholarly works. Although only six letters appear to have been exchanged, they are significant, not only for the now well-known objection that Lambert raised against Kant's position on the ideality of time in the *Inaugural Dissertation,* but also for understanding how Lambert's position might have influenced the development of Kant's thought. Lambert, who expresses admiration for Kant's *Only Possible Argument* (1763), enthusiastically commends his *Organon* to Kant as a work that displays clear parallels with Kant's thinking (a parallel Kant wholeheartedly endorses in a later letter), and describes at length his own take on how their views relate. In fact, the delay between the first four letters (from 1765 to 1766) and the last two letters (1770–1771) was due, so Kant says (10:96), to the importance of the striking thoughts Lambert's letter led him to, especially those regarding the status of metaphysics.

"TREATISE ON THE *CRITERION OF TRUTH*" (1761)[1]

§1. The investigation and knowledge of words that have a correct meaning is indisputably one of the most difficult and most important tasks of logic and the foundation of the certainty of the entirety of human cognition. Every proposition that one issues as true must sell itself to us as true in virtue of the words that express it having a strictly correct meaning, by the concepts that we combine with these words being exactly correct and containing neither confusions nor contradictions within their sphere, and finally by each concept being affirmed or negated of the other just as they are represented in the proposition.

§2. This condition without which no truth can take place is sufficient for definitions, axioms, and postulates, because they attain thereby all the requisite certainty and correctness. And what can in that case be inferred from it according to the rules of syllogisms is brought to the same degree of certainty by these means.

§3. One should pay attention, however, to this difference, which was made only in mathematics for the longest time, if one wants to make the long sought after criterion of truth better known than the sharpest philosophers have been able to do so far.[2] Descartes sought this criterion or sign of demarcation in the clear and distinct perception of a thing, whereas Wolff sought it in the mathematical method that he introduced into philosophy. Both of them can be pretty much equated if one is paying attention to the difference first noted (§2). It is undisputable that if one infers correctly from true propositions, the conclusions are likewise irrefutable. Accordingly, Wolff's criterion of truth in the most proper sense is to this extent applicable to and necessary for theorems, because these must be derived in a mathematical way from definitions and axioms if their certainty is supposed to be apparent to us and be accepted. However, if one asks where the axioms have their certainty from, one must use a criterion that is not very different from the Cartesian one, and it can be reduced at most to the certainty of the correctness of concepts. One calls propositions axioms if one grants, and must grant, their correctness as soon as one understands the words through which they are expressed. However, to understand the words just means to have a

---

[1] Translated from Johann Heinrich Lambert, "Abhandlung zum Criterium veritatis," *Kant-Studien,* Ergänzungsheft 36 (1915): 7–64.
[2] See Kant's discussion of the criterion of truth at B82ff.

clear, distinct, and nice concept of it. Yet this is the Cartesian criterion of truth.

§4. Accordingly, Descartes was mistaken in extending his criterion to all propositions without distinction, as it is valid in the most proper sense only for axioms. I say "in the most proper sense." For one can certainly extend it to all propositions if one counts the distinct concept and representation of its proof among them. A theorem becomes certain only because we represent its proof distinctly and see that it is derived from correct concepts and axioms in the correct way, and whoever produces something mistaken in his inferences will always find that he overlooked something and did not develop the concepts or the proof distinctly enough.

§5. One can see from this that Descartes's criterion extends to all truths mediately, but can be applied immediately only to axioms properly so called. Descartes appears, as it were, to make all propositions into axioms. However, his criterion has yet other holes and deficiencies, among which the most significant is that it cannot be reversed. One cannot say: Whatever I do not have a clear and distinct concept of is not true. Similarly, one also cannot not say: Everything that is true I have a clear and distinct concept of. However, one would have to be able to say both if his criterion were complete and sufficient. For a distinguishing mark must attach to the thing such that it is always posited and removed along with the thing.

§8. I will begin to show that and why the nice and complete enlightenment and development of our concepts has occurred only occasionally and why, as much as they have also been analyzed, the question of whether nothing contradictory remains in them arises again and again. The question is how one can know that there is nothing contradictory in a concept (§7). The path that one has taken so far is the following. One posits a concept. A scholar proposes to investigate it more precisely. He finds that it is composed of several other concepts. He develops these more precisely too and finds that the one has marks that deny precisely what the other's marks affirm in the same sense. He has here an apparent contradiction. Accordingly, he begins either to reject the concept in its entirety, or, if it is an option, takes those marks together that do not contradict each other, separates them from the remaining ones, and takes them individually. Now if the marks are unsuitably confused, he separates them and splits the concept thereby into several more specific ones. If the contradiction arises only in certain cases, he distinguishes these cases from the remaining ones and notes what it is about them that keeps the concept from being applicable and what other concepts must be posited in place of it.

§10. This is the path that has been taken so far, and it is indisputable that it is correct as far as one takes it. The question of whether there is something contradictory in a concept is certainly decided when a contradiction is discovered and this can occur in the manner described. However, whether nothing contradictory remains behind is not thereby determined. One comes closer to the truth, but one cannot say that one has attained it or how far away one is still. However, this is what is required for a complete criterion of truth and one can see from this how much remains. One cannot yet distinguish according to a universal rule those concepts in which a contradiction still lies from those in which no contradiction remains any longer and which are accordingly completely correct. However, this rule would make the sought after criterion of truth complete, because the correctness of the theorems depends on the precise application of the mathematical method and on the correctness of the theorems, which depend, however, on that of the concepts (§3, 4).

§22.[3] Already in the most ancient of times mathematicians realized that one must distinguish between propositions that one admits without proof and those for which one demands a proof for their acceptance, and the difference was so apparent to them that they bestowed special names on them. They also saw that the truth of the latter could be clear only if the latter were deduced from the former, and the way of achieving this through a series of inferences gave them a concept of method that was for a long time called simply the mathematical method, though in fact it can be called the natural method, because it is the soul's true way of thinking and can be utilized in every science. Is it not, however, even more exhaustive than what is required in mathematics, which develops it no further than up to concepts? And might not there be a difference between concepts that is similar to that between axioms [*Grundsätze*] and theorems [*Lehrsätze*]?

---

[3] Compare these next few paragraphs with Kant's discussion of the differences between mathematical and philosophical cognition in the Discipline of Pure Reason in its Dogmatic Use (A712–A738/B740–B766). See also *Inquiry*.

§23. This question is of no small importance if one develops its consequences. To this end we intend to investigate how concepts must appear if such a difference is to take place with respect to them. Retaining the analogy with propositions, we will distinguish axiomatic concepts [*Grundbegriffe*] and derivative concepts [*Lehrbegriffe*] and see to what extent the explanation of them remains similar to the one that is given for axioms and theorems. If this difference works out such that it can be traced back to distinct marks and criteria, it will also not be difficult to carry the similarity further and to define what corollarative concepts [*Lehnbegriffe*], postulated concepts [*Heischbegriffe*], arbitrary concepts, empirical concepts, and problematic concepts [*Übungsbegriffe*] are, whose names we derive from corollaries [*Lehnsätze*], postulates [*Heischsätze*], hypotheses, empirical propositions,[4] and problems [*Aufgaben*], that thereby become individual kinds of a higher genus.

§24. Axioms are different from theorems in that the latter demand proof, whereas the former do not. One admits axioms as soon as one understands the terms, whereas one must similarly understand the terms of a theorem, but it will not be admitted without proof. The necessity of the proof constitutes the difference between these propositions and the proof itself consists of a longer or shorter sequence of inferences through which a theorem is connected with axioms such that one obtains precisely the same certainty with respect to it that one has for the axioms.

§25. Accordingly, if there is to be a similar difference between axiomatic [*Grundbegriffe*] and derivative concepts [*Lehrbegriffe*], it is clear that the former must be such as one admits and accepts on their own, whereas something further must be added to the latter that connects them with the former such that one then admits and accepts them too. It is clear that whatever must be added is similarly a kind of proof, and that inferences too can contribute something, but in particular it will be what one can call the mode of genesis [*Entstehungsart*] of a concept.

§26. Before I proceed further, this is the place to comment in various ways on this observation. Wolff had already shown once several kinds of concepts that had to be proved. Examples of these are when one puts

---

4 Lambert has "empirische Begriffe" (empirical concepts) here, but given the context, he must have meant empirical propositions.

concepts together arbitrarily or adds an arbitrary determination to a concept. One should consult his teachings on the mathematical method and his logic. What I have to remark for the purpose of my observation about it then is that he did not place the importance of the difference that he draws between these concepts in its proper light. We can easily see that precisely those concepts for which he requires a proof are actually only those that we previously (§23) called arbitrary concepts. These are to concepts precisely what hypotheses are to propositions, of which one demands a proof in a completely different sense from that of theorems, despite the fact that a proof is required in both. A hypothesis can become a theorem, but as a hypothesis it is not yet a theorem, and most of the hypotheses thought up so far have eventually been rejected. We infer from this that Wolff either did not notice the concepts that we are calling derivative concepts or at least did not define them and explain their difference from arbitrary concepts, which, however, is important. This remark extends similarly to the remaining differences that we noted regarding propositions (§23).

§27. We can comment further that this great philosopher had similarly already introduced the term 'mode of genesis' into logic, but in fact used it only in definitions. In addition, since he distinguishes nominal from real definitions, he understands the latter as those through which the mode of genesis of a thing is uncovered, and, for that reason, calls such a definition: *definitiones geneticae*. Thus he defines desire [*Lust*] such that it is what arises from the sensation or representation of a good object. It is enough here to comment that there is certainly a difference between the mode of genesis of a thing and that of a concept. In the latter case, the soul just thinks of itself, whereas in the former it thinks about the origin and development of a thing. The real definition may serve to represent the origin and composition of a thing and to bring the thing itself about. By contrast, the explanation of how a concept arises constitutes a way of proving its correctness. For if a derivative concept arises in a correct way from correct axiomatic concepts, sorting out this mode of genesis is a proof thereof, otherwise, however, there arises an illusion and deception that belongs in the same class as incorrect proofs of theorems.

§28. To sort this out in greater detail we shall extend the comparison of concepts and propositions somewhat further. If a proposition is to be proven, it occurs according to either the analytic or the synthetic

method, which are already defined in almost all logics. According to the
analytic method, one starts with a proposition. One proves it through a
syllogism. If the premises are not axioms, they must be proved through
new conclusions until one finally arrives at nothing but axioms, definitions, and experiences. If this happens, one considers the proposition proved. According to the synthetic method, by contrast, one starts
with definitions, principles, and experiences and derives the proof of
the proposition in question from them. The inferences are the same in
both methods, and the difference lies exclusively in the order, which is
completely reversed. All of Euclid serves as an example of the synthetic
method and it has considerable advantages over the analytic method
with respect to presentation and the art of discovery, since the latter
appears almost exclusively in explanatory remarks in logic as an example of the elucidation of a word, in homework examples in school, and
in academic disputations. [...]

§31. After this comment we can return to our main purpose. These two
methods, namely, the analytic and the synthetic, appear in a similar
manner for derivative concepts. The analytic in particular is already
called the dissection of a concept. We have Leibniz to thank for it and
Wolff began to introduce it into logic. In this way a concept receives in
successive stages the name of a clear, distinct, complete, and, after many
steps, extensive concept.

§32.[5] The similarity of these methods for concepts and propositions is
apparent by way of a simple comparison. To prove according to the analytic method, one takes a proposition as it is, provided that it is true,
because a false proposition cannot be proved in any way. One resolves
it [into the propositions on which it depends] by way of syllogisms until
finally one has arrived at nothing but axioms, definitions, and experiences. To dissect a concept according to the analytic method, one similarly takes a clear, but also correct concept. For if it is incorrect, this
dissection will lead to contradictions, as we already explained (§8). This
concept is developed up to the most complete extension [Ausführlichkeit],
and dissected into marks that require no further analysis. What occurs
with respect to propositions through syllogisms occurs here through
the development of the marks out of which the concept is composed
and of which none is already contained in the other, but that, taken

---

5 See, e.g., A727/B755ff.

together, exhaust the concept. The similarity even extends so far that just as one uses one's acuity to discover the intermediate concepts in an analytic proof, about which schoolteachers have previously written entire books *de ineniendo medio termino,* so too for the dissection of a concept one needs just as much acuity to develop all of its marks, to find the proper name for each, and to represent distinctly the combination that they have among each other in the concept.

§33. At the same time, both of these analytic methods have their differences from each other, where that concerning proofs seems to fall behind. If the proposition that one wants to prove analytically and resolve into axioms, etc., is incorrect either in whole or in part, one will not be served by this method, because such a proposition can never in fact be proved. However, one cannot therefore infer to its incorrectness. One cannot infer: I cannot prove this proposition, consequently it is false. [...]

§34. It is different when dissecting a concept with the analytic method. If the concept is in fact incorrect, one can at least frequently discover its incorrectness, [namely] if one develops it until the contradictory marks are brought out, as we already showed at length above (§8). [...]

§36. We can now continue the comparison of concepts and propositions in a more explicit manner, which we accepted previously only as a supposition. Not only does the analytical method or the dissection of concepts actually occur, but one had already recalled that one neither can nor must continue it *ad infinitum,* but rather that it must come to rest at some point. If this doctrine is to be fully clarified, we would necessarily wind up with the proposition: A derivative concept requires [*gebrauche*] nothing more than to be dissected or resolved into axiomatic concepts. If one desires only a nominal definition for these words, then they are completely analogous to those that one provides for axioms and theorems. To dissect here means roughly to explain, to define, to seek out and to determine the scope and the main marks of a concept, and these words are nearly synonymous in logic. A derivative concept is one that requires dissection or a definition. An axiomatic concept is one that requires no further definition, or whose possibility and correctness is immediately evident as soon as one represents it. One will find examples of both in mathematics and logic, and the Cartesian "*Cogito ergo sum*" can be resolved into such simple concepts that provide examples of axiomatic concepts. I shall not yet let myself linger here on this.

§37. Since, therefore, the analytical method not only is possible for concepts, but also has already frequently served for the development of confused concepts, the possibility of the synthetic method can be easily shown and perhaps can already be found in examples. One posits a concept. One resolves it into its marks and at the same time pays attention to how they are combined with each other. All of this is analytic. One then reverses the order. One takes the individual marks and combines them with each other again in the order in which they were found in the concept, and then the concept arises again and this is called the synthetic method. It shows us at the same time how the concept could have arisen naturally from these marks if we had not already known it. Accordingly, it shows what we already required above (§25), namely, the proper and natural mode of genesis of a concept.

§38. Before we proceed to the further dissection of these concepts, we must make several preparatory comments again. So far we have considered these methods only to the extent that they can be compared with those that have long been familiar with regard to propositions. Now the question becomes one of investigating to what extent there is a difference to be found between them. We then decided the question (§22) whether the mathematical method previously used for propositions could also be extended to concepts, to such an extent that now is the time to determine how much or little the consequences thereof are of considerable weight, and whether it is worth the effort to sort it out entirely. Provided that this is possible, we note that the long sought after criterion of truth, which was reduced to axioms through the previous mathematical method and for that reason to the much simpler question about the correctness of concepts, is thereby completely reduced to axiomatic concepts. The nominal definition that we have provided of axiomatic concepts shows that they are such that their possibility and correctness is immediately evident as soon as one understands them. However, this is equivalent to saying that with this everything that would remain deficient in the sought after criteria of truth would disappear completely. The truth of theorems depends on that of the axioms, the truth of the latter depends on the correctness of the concepts, and this correctness depends on that of the axiomatic concepts. The axiomatic concepts, however, are, according to the nominal definition given, intrinsically correct. What is still missing here other than the complete development of the method of tracing each of the derivative concepts back to axiomatic concepts, of making the latter familiar and showing how the former arise from them? It will definitely be worth the effort to work through this investigation completely.

§39. To this end I remark further that in all of the articles that at least I am familiar with in which, in addition to proofs of theorems, concepts are sorted out precisely, the Euclidian form of presentation appears, if not impossible, then so difficult that I would have had to have tackled this treatise twice. First to develop the concepts I was led to by the propositions deduced therein. And then to present everything in such an order that I could have written above each paragraph whether it was a definition, axiom, addendum, problem, or scholium. This is what I am calling the Euclidian form of presentation. For this presentation can certainly exist without this form and writing above the paragraphs does not yet constitute a solid connection between them. [...]

§40. I take note of this in particular because it may serve to elucidate the question of whether the method of building a derivative concept on its axiomatic concepts requires yet other means beyond the inferences that also arise for propositions and in fact exclusively with them, or if the inferences suffice here too if they must be applied in this case. As much as I was still able to comment at the time, in addition to inferences there arise especially for the development of a concept many distinctions, comparisons, remarks and, in particular, also the application of the logical principle that in an affirmative proposition the predicate can be viewed as a property of the subject and the subject can, in turn, be viewed as contained under the predicate, just as a species is under its genus. With the synthetic method, which leads us from familiar concepts to a new concept, I found other means in addition to the comparison of previously discovered concepts, e.g., that such concepts, taken together, represent a special thing, for which one must find a name or come up with a new one. Moreover, that individual new concepts can arise from a confused concept if one lays out the actually different marks. Further, that the concept of a thing can arise just as the thing itself does. Finally, a certain kind of reversed proposition, whose subject is narrower than the predicate, which is very broad, can also offer up very good service. [...] However, this kind of proposition does not occur very frequently.

§42. The analysis of concepts that Leibniz has already introduced shows us that, through correct dissection, concepts that are more composite can be transformed from clear to distinct and, after many steps, to more extensive concepts. At the same time, there are some that must almost necessarily remain clear. Concepts of color and sound, and in general all simple sensations have long been considered to be such, because among them no part can be distinguished from the other, which, however, would have to be the case if the concept is to be distinct.

§43. Concepts of this kind will indisputably be the highest among the axiomatic concepts, and their distinguishing feature is either that they have no recognizable parts and consequently are simple or that their parts are so similar to the whole that one must necessarily attribute the same name to them. The concepts that the soul has of its own thoughts, sensations, and actions belong in this class. We already cited as an example the Cartesian *cogito ergo sum*, which can be resolved into several such axiomatic concepts. The words "to think," "consequently," "to be," "not to be," "not," "impossible," "contradiction," "true," "false," and in general all those that constitute the foundation of logic belong in part to the axiomatic concepts, and in part they can be resolved into such concepts, or are composed thereof, and nowhere will the emergence and sorting out of the mode of genesis of concepts be easier, more proper, and more correct than in logic. For they belong in the most literal sense to subjective reason, which is concerned with itself and with methods, and observes its own operations and at the same time has sensations. Nowhere are observation and experience combined with each other so precisely and indivisibly.

§44.[6] It is sufficiently clear from these examples what axiomatic concepts are and that they exist. This is not the place to seek all of them out, because one would have to go through every science. At the same time it will always be useful to note that since the concepts of logic, which no one will ever call into doubt, are derived from metaphysics, it would always be good to combine metaphysical and especially ontological concepts with axiomatic concepts and to show their mode of genesis as much as can be done, such that they would be connected with them in a necessary way. For only in this way would metaphysics, which has until now had a different form in every country and in every period, become just as immutable as logic has been previously. Wolff had already made

---

[6] Compare the discussion in this paragraph with the Introduction to the Transcendental Logic (A50–A64/B74–B88) and "On the Clue to the Discovery of All Pure Concepts of the Understanding" (A66–A83/B91–B116).

a start with this, and the propositions that he brought from logic into metaphysics are the most indisputable, and find the least resistance. However, it appears that he did not have the patience to bring the remaining ones into connection with it. Yet this can certainly be taken further.

§45. Despite the fact that all axiomatic concepts in general are properly empirical concepts, we will nonetheless have to use this [latter] name for a different kind and, in a certain sense, oppose them to the axiomatic concepts. Almost all of those concepts that arise when one takes the world as it is, and, for that reason, a good portion of those that arise in doctrines of nature, belong to the class of empirical concepts. I qualify this statement deliberately. For in addition to empirical concepts there is yet another kind that we can call derived [*abgeleitete*] or in general derivative concepts. If one represents clearly the difference between axioms, empirical propositions, and theorems, one can easily see the similarity that they have with these kinds of concepts. Accordingly, we draw the following distinction between them. An axiomatic concept is a simple empirical concept that cannot be resolved further or does not require being resolved further, and whose possibility and correctness is admitted as soon as one represents it. An empirical concept here is one that, viewed in itself, can be developed further, but that is accepted absolutely because experience provides it. However, a derivative concept is derived from axiomatic concepts, or from empirical concepts, or from other derivative concepts. This derivation itself consists in the fact that one can distinctly sort out its mode of genesis.

§46. The following propositions can easily be deduced from this. An empirical concept can become a derivative concept if one shows its mode of genesis from axiomatic concepts or simple empirical concepts. In turn, a derivative concept can either be viewed as an empirical concept or resolved into simpler empirical concepts. And if one does this, the experiences that one has with regard to this are, as it were, a test of the correctness of the derivative concept at issue. We would still add that this observation constitutes a considerable part of a still rather undeveloped science, which we call the art of testing human cognition. We showed above that the certainty of the entirety of human cognition depends on the question of the correctness of concepts, and that even in this case it depends only on the method of building them on axiomatic concepts in order to resolve entirely everything that still remains for the criterion of truth. If further means are added to test the concepts through experience, they will thereby be put to the test, and this test will be all the more desirable, the easier it is to become confused in extended inferences or, as it were, to miscalculate thereby.

§55.[7] After these observations, through which we have divided concepts into just as many useful classes as there have been previously for propositions according to the mathematical method, we can now have a look at the sciences and especially at philosophy. Are the derivative concepts themselves built on axiomatic concepts and is their mode of genesis sorted out? How are both of them distinguished from arbitrary and merely empirical concepts? Do not some illicit concepts still remain among the latter? And does one not find concepts that have been improperly borrowed instead of being true derivative concepts? Is it worth the effort to test our cognition against this touchstone, or are the differences we have drawn between these concepts only irrelevant trivialities that do not contribute much to the enlightenment of the sciences and to the certainty of our cognition? I believe that whoever has insight into and feels the excellence and importance of the mathematical mode of presentation will desire that it would also be made completely available for concepts.

The division that we have made therein according to the analogy of propositions determines the intrinsic value of each and every concept with respect to its correctness, certainty, and relevance, the value that it has in each case, and at the same time also the value that it is capable of achieving as well as what is still lacking such that it could be elevated to that state. How does philosophy appear presently if it is tested in this way?

§56. I shall not repeat here what I have already commented above (§44) regarding the purpose of the improvement of this science, but rather make various more general comments that determine somewhat more precisely what is actually to be sought thereby. First, all kinds of concepts defined above occur in philosophy, and indeed indisputable and both good and correct concepts as well as incorrect ones. The point of this would therefore lie only in separating them, of which Leibniz had

---

[7] Compare with "The Discipline of Pure Reason in Dogmatic Use" (A708–A738/B736–B766).

previously made a start. Then we must certainly acknowledge that most of our concepts are empirical and that a good number of illicit and deficient concepts are still mixed in with them. Many of them are also lacking universality, especially where we ourselves cannot inspect all individual objects that belong under a concept. It is clear here that illicit concepts would have to be examined and, if they are erroneous, then changed or rejected. This can happen if one either dissects the concept more precisely or consults experience better.

§57. Further, it will be good, as far as possible, to make the more correct and especially the more composite empirical concepts into derivative concepts, because they become thereby immeasurably clearer, more distinct, and more extensive, and because one thereby comes closer to, or actually finds, the axiomatic concepts. The latter is achieved simply through that dissection through which a concept is divided into its simpler concepts, which will be either axiomatic concepts or empirical concepts. If, however, a derivative concept is to arise, more must be added. One must not only combine these simpler concepts with each other again as they had been, but also prove the possibility of this combination, and this proof must be *a priori*. However, either the proof shows the mode of genesis of the thing itself, and consequently that of the concept along with it at the same time, or else it proves that the path by which we arrived at the concept is correct. Not only does this method work for concepts that are already familiar, but we can also come to entirely new ones according to the very same method. [...]

§66. Most of our definitions are made *a posteriori* and are for that reason hypothetical in a certain sense. One presupposes thereby that words have a simple meaning and express a correct concept. The concepts that are capable of a definition are derivative concepts. Accordingly, one should exhibit their mode of genesis before one accepts them as correct. If one presupposes, by contrast, that they are empirical concepts that can certainly be valid in the stead of derivative concepts, then the question is whether we ourselves or whether only others have them from experience. [...] The proof of universality is lacking for our own empirical concepts and this must for that reason be supplied. Either we must go through all kinds and show that the induction is complete. In this way one knows all kinds and cases of spherical triangles. What one proves of each individual is established in a demonstrative manner in general. However, if this does not work, one must demonstrate the mode of genesis of the concept and show that it is correct. We revealed the means for this above (§57).

§67. However, as long as the universality of a concept rests only on induction that has not yet been completed, one is better off transforming the definition into a proposition whose predicate is the given concept while its subject is what we had wanted to accept in the place of the definition of the concept. One can assure oneself of the truth of this proposition more easily than one can of the completeness of induction. If one can reverse the proposition in this way and find the proof of it, it will function as a definition, e.g., when we say of individuals belonging to the animal kingdom that they are animals, we proceed more correctly than when we want to designate the borders of the animal kingdom, as the definition requires, because to all appearances, the animal kingdom is conflated with the plant kingdom.

§80. If one wants to proceed in metaphysics so strictly, and one must proceed in this way if it is to remain immutable, one must start with what even an egoist must accept and progress with him up through to natural theology. Such an opponent is roughly what the sophists were to Euclid, who wanted to concede nothing to him beyond dialectic. He granted no empirical concepts other than those that he noticed in his soul. One will therefore think: In this manner the main goal, concerning simple and composite things, remains far away. Certainly. For an egoist knows of nothing other than simple and composite thoughts, and for that reason one can only go through the abstract concept of the simple and the composite. He accepts the concepts of change and mutability, the concept of sufficient reason, etc., because he finds change in his thoughts, grants the concepts "impossible," "possible," "necessary," "be," "not be," etc., and presumes the right to demand a sufficient reason for each allegation. And so on. He must first become an idealist, and up to that point it remains undetermined what are simple and composite things, etc. It is true that this order appears somewhat novel. I believe, however, that it is roughly what the Euclidean method seemed to me to be (§78).

This order is different from the previous one in yet another regard. I will elucidate it through examples and remarks that make its advantages clearer. I take the concepts "simple" and "composite" and posit that one need not abstract them from external things in order to apply them correctly at the beginning of metaphysics. An egoist would not concede them in that way. Since one must prove them rigorously and cannot put them off, I have stated that these concepts are to be derived from a *sensu interno,* because they also arise with thoughts, because simpler and more composite thoughts exist. One can inquire whether the determination or definition of these concepts will not be too narrow, because they will not be abstracted in this way from all individual things that are simple or composite, but rather only from thoughts. Various remarks are to be noted about this. For one it would be an apparent mistake contrary to logic if one were to accept a concept of greater scope than one can prove where one is presenting it. It would be hypothetical just to the extent that the proof would be incomplete, and one could otherwise not view it as valid until the proof can be made complete. However, this is always awkward, because one all too easily confuses the hypothetical with what is proven. Accordingly, one does better not to extend the concept right at the beginning further than it has been proven. In that case we have here exactly what I called above the mode of genesis of a concept. The egoist sees it, as it were, arising in his own soul and would have to contradict himself if he did not want to acknowledge it. This has a lot of similarity with Euclid's proof of the possibility of an equilateral triangle and is of the same strength.

§83. We can apply this observation to our question. We have things, concepts, words that can change through all kinds and through countless stages, even if all three are always to accompany each other exactly and have the same scope. There are some that are this way. As long as language remains the same and as long as we can see the sun, one object and one concept will always be represented by the sun. By contrast, it is completely different with the words "influence of the sun." The astrological has pretty much disappeared and the physical is developed more.

§84. Now if one were to ask in which cases thing, concept, and word stay together most consistently, one discovers the following conditions. (1) The thing must also be in the world and easily be distinguished from every other. (2) It must be easily recognizable in itself. (3) No occasion must arise for changing its name. The first one concerns the thing, the second the concept, and the third the word. If both of the first two items are present, the third has nothing to say and merely provides devotees of antiquity with the task of preventing the ancient words from becoming completely unknown. We find both of the first items in our thoughts and in their disposition. We are the most immediate witnesses of their existence and would have to be half asleep if we could not distinguish one thought from another as soon as we represent both of them clearly. Accordingly, all concepts that we derive such that we can put them to the test at every moment, will be of such a kind that nothing in the least will remain that can be objected against them. Logical axiomatic concepts are this way and metaphysical ones are supposed to be too.

§85. By this I do not mean to say that there are not still further concepts of this kind. There is a good number of them in physics and astronomy and even in common life. Thus, e.g., the concept of the elasticity of air, the fluidity of water, and a thousand others certainly belong to them. Each time one can test them again with experience and make them evident. By contrast, one does not know in all cases how far they extend and the inhabitants of hot regions of the earth can easily imagine that water must necessarily be fluid when they have heard or seen nothing about its transformation into ice. How long did one remain in doubt about whether mercury can freeze as well, and one still cannot determine whether air can be frozen! I do not doubt this, but whatever proof I give, one will demand experience. Accordingly, it is more difficult to determine the scope of these concepts, and since metaphysics is supposed to be for everyone, even the greatest skeptic, it is always more prudent and necessary to take its axiomatic concepts from our inner sensations as concepts that we have immediately at hand whenever doubts are raised (§84). The first opponent that one encounters when erecting a metaphysical system [*Lehrgebäude*] is the egoist, and one must make the *utrimque concessa* before one arrives at those who spontaneously concede more without requiring a proof from us. However, we fall back hereby on the inference that we drew at the end of the previous paragraph, and it thus serves as a basic rule if one intends to write a precisely established metaphysics. Further, since concepts that are presupposed according to this rule are of such a kind that they can be put to the test repeatedly and can easily be distinguished from each other, linguistic changes have no influence on it, and the names they bear stay with the concepts and with the language, just as geometrical and logical concepts do.

§86. We have observed here the most extreme precision if one intends to bring forth a metaphysical system [*Lehrgebäude*] *a priori*. This is how Wolff attempted to establish it. The first part of his German metaphysics is a nice example thereof, and it proceeds smoothly until he arrives at the principle of sufficient reason, which has aroused so much dispute. After that he is not as careful to derive concepts from other concepts, but rather takes them as he finds them and is content to explain the up to that point common and most intelligible words. However, in this way he falls back on empirical concepts. At that point his system [*Lehrgebäude*] proceeds *a posteriori*. Aristotle understood his own doctrine in this way right from the start. Wolff, by contrast, derived the concepts synthetically as far as he could, and then used experience. It is also not to be denied that it is difficult to establish the matter completely *a priori,* and if it had come forth in the order that we have sketched above (§80), I believe that Wolff would have caused a much greater sensation with his metaphysics, because it would have been so entirely new.

§87. Still, I do not doubt that metaphysics could be developed *a posteriori* completely and in good order, even if in this case too it would require time and patience. The method in such a case would depend on a store of means for inferring from the appearance [*aus dem Schein*] to the true, from the shadows to the light and the body casting the shadows, and from the part to the whole. Many of these means can already be found in astronomy and the doctrine of nature [*Naturlehre*]. [...] I provide this method here only insofar as it is needed to illustrate its possibility with examples. It is indisputably more general and there should be means to show the idealist, who views everything external to himself as an appearance [*Schein*], what is true from the appearance he has accepted. This would entail establishing metaphysics *a posteriori* as strictly as would be done *a priori* according to the previous observations. Logic and mathematics are presupposed in this, since they are equally independent of every other cognition. And if one wants to proceed according to Wolff's method, one can apply what has been found *a priori* to what one accepts from experience, just as the astronomer applies the basic laws of mechanics to the motion of every celestial body. In this way one can find many propositions and individual parts developed quite properly in Wolff's philosophy.

§88.[8] If we now summarize what has been said so far, we can return to the criterion of truth that we observed at the beginning and speak

---

[8] See A58/B83ff. and "On the Supreme Principle of all Analytic Judgments" (A150/B189ff.).

of it now in a more determinate way. I do not recall that one had yet developed the concept of this criterion distinctly and perhaps it is much too confused to be developed. According to Descartes, it would be, among thoughts, what is evident, *evidentia,* and, so to speak, almost more than the truth itself, because all truths are by no means evident. According to Wolff, it would consist in logic. Accordingly, at the start we take the concept "criterion of truth" only as a hypothetical concept in which we presuppose as a condition that it in fact represents something. However, under this condition, the inference goes through. If the criterion of truth is something actual, it is either mediate or immediate. If it is immediate, then it is in turn either in our soul (*criterium subjectivum*) or in propositions and representations (*criterium objectivum*) or in the relation between the two, e.g., in the impression that the truth makes. These threefold concepts become more familiar now. For (1) Descartes wanted to look for it in the impression that the truth makes, because he held that it consists in thoughts being evident. This is certainly something, but not yet everything. For what should appear to us as true must be evident to us, but not the converse, (§5) consequently it is insufficient. Further (2) if this criterion should lie in propositions so that one could immediately see whether they are true, just as one can recognize the presence of fire from smoke or the presence of light from a shadow, such a criterion would by no means be desirable. There are concepts that are such that they immediately press on us their correctness and truth. However, whether such an immediate criterion would be present in propositions whose truth brings about our approval only after an extensive and profound proof, this is not yet established and it is scarcely to be hoped that it can be found. What I remarked similarly above (§15) defines only the right that we have to give our approval or to withhold it, but not the truth itself. Finally (3) if this immediate criterion were in our soul, we should seek it either in the perception of the harmony of our thoughts or in the laws according to which our thoughts are oriented. Harmony can be acquired through practice and developed considerably (§§12–15), and is good as far as it extends, but it does not reach to infinity and for that reason always has limits and greater and lesser gaps. Additionally, it also serves only whoever has acquired it. By contrast, the laws according to which our thoughts are oriented are certainly laws of the truth and can be used as a criterion with properly so-called axiomatic concepts, because they immediately impress their correctness and truth on us. The ground of contradiction lies high among these laws. However, experience shows us that we cannot extend it immediately to all propositions and truths and it is undecided whether this will ever happen.

§89. From this dissection of the hypothetically accepted immediate criterion we can now see what can be retained from it. (1) The subjective criterion is to be recommended as a very useful exercise, because it is good and useful as far as it goes (§§13–14). (2) The objective criterion applies, at least so far, only to axiomatic concepts, to which those given as examples in §80 can be added. (3) The relative criterion is not a criterion, but rather only a property and a proposition that one cannot reverse.

§90. For that reason we can only retain the objective criterion as far as it extends and it is clear in this case that we must return to the first member of the division and see how the mediate criterion looks. This does not require that one must be able to see at once the truth of every proposition, for otherwise it could not be called mediate. Accordingly, if it is to present a proper concept, it must depend on our recognizing by its means that proposition or concept A is true, because proposition or concept B is true. However, here we certainly have the mathematical method and logic in general, in which Wolff sought his criterion of truth. However, we also see that this mediate criterion is as it were merely a signpost, which helps us along in the realm of truth properly and in a measured order. Yet since one must start somewhere, it is also clear that our immediate objective criterion cannot be absent. We also see the differences between what Descartes and Wolff were seeking. Further, we see that the objective criterion of truth in fact arises, at least for axiomatic concepts, and the method helps us so that we can say not just conditionally: *Si dederis, omnia danda sunt,* but rather categorically: *danda sunt quadam, ergo omnia.* This will always be enough to render superfluous the desire for a universal immediate criterion of truth, which might well be too comfortable for us. For such a criterion would help us only to check, but not to discover, which is just as useful and important. Therefore, since we are sufficient in this way, we also see that whoever might still want to have the objective criterion be completely general, is actually asking for nothing other than a greater shortcut and convenience. I do not believe that it would always be good if we had this. Such a criterion would be about like a table where the food arrived spontaneously prepared. It is of the same sort, because truths, so to speak, are food for the understanding.

§92. Let's now draw together in short sentences what has been presented previously at length in order to present it all in one view and then to see what else remains to be undertaken. There are the following:

1. Axiomatic concepts are those whose possibility and correctness are immediately apparent as soon as one represents them (§36).
2. Accordingly, they are such that one grants them in denying them, should one want to try to deny them. For since they should be immediately apparent, they need not be based on other concepts, but rather can be based immediately on inner sensation (*sensus internus*).
3. For that reason they are, in the strictest sense, those that even an egoist, an opponent who initially borders on being insane, must grant.
4. Logic and mathematics provide concepts of this kind and they also arise in metaphysics (§§ 80, 76, 75).
5. Hypothetically, one can view every empirical concept as an axiomatic concept, as far as experience reaches.
6. To distinguish them, one can call them axiomatic concepts *a posteriori*.
7. Since it is possible to infer from appearance to what is true and to derive actuality from this (§87), the hypothetical too can be elevated in empirical concepts.
8. However, in this way they become genuine derivative concepts.
9. The proof of a derivative concept *a priori* depends on its mode of genesis from axiomatic concepts (§57).
10. An *a posteriori* proof, however, depends on the mode of genesis of the thing.
11. Axiomatic concepts have an immediate criterion of truth (Nr. 2).
12. Derivative concepts, however, have a mediate criterion, because they are provable.
13. Axiomatic propositions have their correctness from concepts (§3), because they arise from their dissection. Their proof is based on empty propositions: e.g., What is contained in a concept is contained therein, etc.
14. Theorems have their correctness from concepts and axiomatic propositions, because they must be proved. Their proof depends on the principle of contradiction and in general on the doctrine of syllogisms. This doctrine is accordingly its mediate criterion of truth. However, it presupposes the immediate criterion (Nr. 4).

§93. From this analysis we see that a more distinct explanation of the method of proving derivative concepts, or showing their mode of genesis, still awaits us. To this end we shall now observe what is synthetic and what is analytic therein in its proper order. Here we have four operations of the understanding, namely, distinguishing, comparing, dissecting, and combining or putting together. Distinguishing primarily is directed at the different kinds that are contained under a genus. For since one has the genus in front of oneself, all that is needed is to determine the difference between the kinds. In that case the concern is with the ambiguity of a word, where one distinguishes from each other various concepts that were conflated with each other there in order to avoid confusion. The same is the case for every other confused concept. One must dissect them and distinguish them properly. Finally, the concern is with the marks that are in a concept that one must distinguish in order to represent them properly and distinctly. And this is then the dissection of a concept: The comparison of concepts and their marks serves not only to find their similarities and differences and for that reason to order their kinds under their genus, but also to see to what extent they are consistent with each other and can be combined. Concepts are thereby combined and the method reveals the mode of genesis of a concept.

§94. Derivative concepts are distinguished from axiomatic concepts by the latter being simple or at least can be assumed to be such, because they have their certainty and correctness intrinsically. The former, however, have their certainty and correctness from the axiomatic concepts and derive their possibility from their composition and combination. Accordingly, they are composite and for that reason can in turn be resolved and dissected into axiomatic concepts as their elements.

§95. The following cases and method can be derived from this:

1. The analytic [method]. Here one assumes the derivative concept as it is or as one has it. One dissects it into its axiomatic concepts, or into those marks of which one is already certain that they arise in the realm of truth. In this way one becomes convinced of the actuality of its elements and parts. What must still be added is that one must become convinced of the possibility of their composition. If this occurs, the derivative concept that one had previously accepted only hypothetically has been established analytically.

2. In this way one can assume a concept hypothetically, of which one does not yet know precisely what exactly belongs within its scope [*Umfang*]. One leaves off what is foreign, useless, and contradictory and takes the items that, taken together, make the concept complete. The investigation of the criterion of truth (§88ff.) provides a distinct example of this.

3. If one binds the true scope of a concept to certain cases where it arises and already constitutes in itself a concept that should precisely not be confused with others, then one must seek it to make it whole and complete in these examples. [...]

4. If one assumes a derivative concept on the basis of its similarity with others, the method may serve as an example for how we, by comparing propositions and concepts, can give the latter a form similar to the mathematical method. We left this similarity hypothetical until we were able to show that the differences of the concepts derived on that basis actually arise in the realm of truth and are useful. One can look back to see how we proceeded piecemeal in this and finally finished (§28ff, 36ff.).

5. If the derivative concept in question is a proper empirical concept, only dissection arises for it. Insofar as this is executed properly, one always arrives at parts that one can view as true because it is an empirical concept and for the same reason the proof of the possibility of its combination too remains absent. For what in fact exists, is already possible in itself. This is then called going *a posteriori,* and it is clear that this procedure does not serve to prove the concept, but rather to use everything that one finds in it for other proofs. Otherwise both of them serve to test each other if one can prove these marks and the possibility of their combination *a priori* or on the basis of other grounds. One should see §57.

6. If one finds in an empirical concept, or even in any derivative concept, such marks that, taken together, already constitute a concept of considerable universality, then it is good to take this one in particular. In this way Leibniz deduced his principle of sufficient reason from an example of Archimedes concerning the scale.

7. This is primarily how it works with relational concepts. E.g., one abstracts a general method from a single case. Since it arises therein, it is possible and its concept is empirical. One turns it into a precise derivative concept if one derives the method from its true grounds and determines the scope of where it can be applied.

8. Concepts that one derives from the mode of genesis of a thing are similarly empirical concepts. One frequently finds later that one could have come across these on one's own. As soon as the path has been pointed out, and it is correct, a derivative concept arises from it.

§96.[9] This is what I was able to find for the analytic method and it is clear that these cases arise often and for that reason are very useful. Let us now observe the synthetic method and see how they can be related to explanations, designations, and inferences. To this end we remark that if one does not want to begin immediately with axiomatic concepts, the use of the analytic method has precedence, because one must have a sufficient store of correct concepts. Since, further, the synthetic method is only a signpost for concepts, just as it is for propositions (§90), we must, at the beginning here, observe only the simple steps, as these always take one farther from any place at which one begins. We remark further that inferences here proceed only through possibilities, because it is not enough to put concepts together as one finds them, for in that case one would often happen upon round squares, wooden iron, and other such absurdities. Rather, one must prove that they can be combined. However, this requires a possibility as an indispensable condition.

§97. Since, therefore, the synthetic method of finding and proving derivative concepts is based on a theory of possibility, its grounds must be taken from this theory. The negative concept of possibility, namely, that what contains no contradiction is possible, is not useful enough here. Similarly, it is not enough to say that what can be thought is what one should call possible. For the word "can" already includes possibility within itself. I believe that if metaphysics, as Wolff initiated it in the first section of his [so-called German] Metaphysics, is to be established according to a strictly synthetic method, one will be able to develop the concepts "being," "not being," "contradiction," "impossible," "opposite," "necessary," "possible" in this order from each other. For that reason we have two theorems: (1) Whatever is, that can be or is possible. (2) Whatever is necessary, that not only is possible, but also cannot be other than possible [*sondern es kann nicht anderst als möglich sein*]. And these two propositions are what we can use for the synthetic method.

---

[9] Compare these next few paragraphs with the "Postulates of Empirical Thinking in General" (A218–A235/B265–B287).

§98. Further we must remark that a derivative concept is at all times a lower concept than the parts of which it consists, excepting the part that distinguishes it from all others. For this part makes it into just what it is and is, as it were, its distinguishing feature *nota, propria, specifica*. If for that reason one has the derivative concept as the subject and one of its parts as a predicate, one then has a universal affirmative proposition. And it can be reversed only if the predicate is either, as it were, the sum of all parts or at least contains the part that is the distinguishing feature of the derivative concept or of the subject. This part may be by itself or it may be contained in the predicate along with others, in which case, it can be reversed, otherwise it cannot. Thus arise two different cases:

1. If the distinguishing feature is in the predicate, one can infer: Where the concept of the predicate appears, the entire concept of the subject must be present as well.
2. However, if the distinguishing feature is not in the predicate, the subject can be present, but it is not necessarily there, but is rather merely possible. It can be the case.

§99. This latter case, which provides only one possibility, is in turn twofold. For the possible in it relates either to the understanding or to the will and its powers. To be possible with respect to the understanding just means undecided, and that is how we take it in theoretical matters, when we say, e.g., it can be, the matter can be true, etc. See §71. By contrast to be possible with respect to the will means that the thing does not exist, but can be made to exist. For in that way it will certainly exist later. This is exactly how it is for things that can occur by themselves and without our aid. E.g., when I say: A comet can appear soon again. It is possible that Caius goes to see Titus. Etc. This, however, is already more theoretical. The undecided or possible with respect to the understanding is in turn of two sorts. For either one has enough insight to see that it would have consequences if one wanted to assert it prior to the decision, as with, e.g., most hypotheses, and there it is better just to let it be. Or one can, where one has let it be, still use it as a hypothesis, and this is always permitted. E.g., one can let it be undecided whether a comet will ever fall into the sun. However, one finds that the calculation of this case can be profitably used for a mass-based scale [*Massleiter*] for the orbits of each and all comets, and nothing prevents us from drawing an advantage from this. The imaginary magnitudes in the analytic are used similarly.

§103.[10] The path indicated here proceeds straight away and is the synthetic method of proving a concept. If it is reversed, it serves to test whether a certain concept is correct or is possible. E.g., we want to assume the concept of a calculating machine as if it were a mere accidental thought just as, say, the concept of perpetual motion was at one time. Accordingly, we provide a nominal definition for it, which remains hypothetical, because we indicate thereby only what the word "calculating machine" could mean in itself. It would be, e.g., a machine by means of which one could make a calculation, as with numbers. In order to develop the possibility of this conception and for that reason also that of the thing, we must ask ourselves: "In which cases can one use machines?" It is clear that this question is an inverse task, *problema inversum,* which is frequently sought after in mathematics in general. The answer or solution says that it occurs whenever an operation always happens according to a single rule. From this the question spontaneously arises as to whether this is also the case in mathematics. And one finds that it does occur. The inference from this is accordingly that calculations could be made with a machine, and consequently the concept of a calculating machine is a true and correct concept. We showed above in a similar way that axiomatic concepts, derivative concepts, etc., can be distinguished from each other with good justification and these differences are correct and considerable (§23ff.). And in precisely this way we have what is correct in the concept of the criterion of truth, separated from the confused concept, and found a fixed meaning in this word, since the concept of this word, if it is to be universal and complete, contains, with respect to the axiomatic concepts, an immediate object criterion, and with respect to every other truth, a method of proceeding from the one to the other; by contrast, however, if one wanted to have thereby a universal criterion, it could be found only in a utopia (§90).

NEW ORGANON (1764)[11]

Preface

The present work which I have written immediately for my own purposes and now deliver to press with the same intent, contains four almost completely distinct parts that necessarily belong together and for which

---

[10] See A57–A59/B82–B83.
[11] Translated from Johann Heinrich Lambert, *Neues Organon* (Leipzig, 1764).

I have not found more proper names than those borrowed from the Greek, namely, of dianoiology, alethiology, semiotic, and phenomenology, and that, taken together, constitute in a more complete way what Aristotle and, after him, Bacon called an organon. And this is also the actual title that I was able to give the present work. The reader expects the reasons for this imposition. Here they are.

It is not necessary to prove at length that one must seek the truth itself, assure oneself of it, and accordingly make himself familiar with and used to the means that serve it. It has already been said countless times. Every human has the requisite powers of the understanding to a greater or lesser degree. It is natural that they are given to him so that he may actually use them. The understanding itself is not content in the face of doubts and uncertainty. It is natural that it seeks to find certainty. One knows that ultimately one is only betrayed by error. It is natural that one seeks to avoid it.

All this is self-evident. However, if one sorts through human cognition, and especially the doctrines of philosophers of every time and place, one finds them in most cases not nearly as harmonious as one would expect given these many motivations. And because the truth is uniform and immutable, one finds, by contrast, that human opinions change almost in spite of the truth, like fashions of clothing, and the history of philosophy teaches us that the doctrines of the philosophers, who, however, make their main occupation the inquiry into truth, fared little better. One can set Aristotle, Gassendi, Descartes, Newton, Leibniz, Wolff, etc., against each other in their main doctrines, and the idealists, materialists, skeptics, fatalists, etc., by contrast, nearly in their entirety.

Observations of this kind very naturally occasion the following four questions:

1. Whether the human understanding is lacking in **powers** to walk safely and with certainty on the path of truth without so much foundering?

2. Whether the **truth** itself is not sufficiently discernible to the understanding in order not to confuse it so easily with error?

3. Whether the **language** in which the understanding adorns the truth makes it, through misunderstanding, indeterminacy, and ambiguity, less discernible and more doubtful, or places other obstacles in its path?

4. Whether the understanding lets itself be blinded by **appearance**, without always being able to penetrate to what is true?

According to these four questions four sciences also arise, which the human understanding must avail itself of as just so many **means** and **tools** if it wants to consciously cognize, present, and distinguish from error and appearance what is true as true.

The first is dianoiology, or the doctrine of the laws according to which the understanding directs itself in **thinking**, and wherein the paths that it must take are defined if it wants to proceed from truth to truth.

Another is alethiology, or the doctrine of the **truth**, so far as it is set against **error**. The truth must be discernible to the understanding, both because to progress further, it must begin with that as well as because this knowledge itself serves the understanding in its progress as a test of whether or not it has foundered.

Both of these sciences would be enough, if the human understanding did not need to bind its cognition to **words** and **signs**, and if the truth did not often show itself to the understanding under a wholly different **appearance**, from which the understanding has to distinguish it, just as from error. This makes still two more sciences necessary for us.

Semiotics, or the doctrine of the **designation** of thoughts and things, is accordingly the third, and should state what sort of influence language and signs have on the cognition of the truth, and how they could be made useful for it.

Finally, phenomenology, or the doctrine of **appearance**, is the fourth, and this is supposed to make appearance discernible, and state the means to avoid it and to penetrate to the truth. It is self-evident that these four sciences are instrumental or just so many tools of which the human understanding must avail itself in the investigation of the truth. The word "organon" means just this, and Aristotle and Bacon took it in this meaning in designating thereby the works that were written with the same intent.

Thus these four sciences also necessarily belong together. For if any one of them is left out, then a gap remains in one's assurance as to whether one has found the truth. That they are almost completely different from each other is immediately clear from the above explanation thereof. I will now add a few more remarks about what I provide here for the purpose of these sciences.

In logic great efforts have already been made to contribute to these sciences. However, they concerned primarily only that which I count here as belonging to dianoiology, except for what Locke says about the use and misuse of words in his work **on the human understanding**, where he dissects concepts somewhat more carefully. Wolff, by contrast, whom we have to thank for the more exact analysis of concepts and method, is very brief in both of his logic textbooks with respect to the use of words, and in general follows a completely different course. I have had to find a middle road in this. In dianoiology, which is primarily concerned with method, I come closer to Wolff. In the first chapter of the alethiology, by contrast, which is concerned with the simple or axiomatic concepts [*Grundbegriffe*] of our cognition, I fall back on those that are such according to Locke, but I must say here that I only reviewed Locke's work after I had already written the first half of this chapter, and that I was thereby led to shorten it. In the second chapter of the alethiology, I combine Locke's simple concepts with Wolff's method, and thereby provide the foundation for various sciences that are *a priori* in the strictest sense. In the fourth chapter, however, this method is applied to the theory of truth itself. And with that I must note here that in §173 and 200 I have used the expression, typical in geometrical demonstrations, of *per constructionem,* in order to point out the similarity of the procedure more explicitly.

In this chapter it was not indeed possible to speak about truth's interconnection without at the same time speaking of **reasons**, at least insofar as they are **reasons of what is true**, and accordingly belong to alethiology. The debates in Germany about sufficient reason are well known. I can leave it up to both parties to judge to what extent they want to agree with me after they themselves have read what I have said about this matter there.

Earlier I said that in the dianoiology I come closer to Wolff and to those who followed him. The theory of **questions**, which I take to be as considerable as the theory of **propositions** [*Sätze*], led me to define the tasks and *postulata* according to the patterns that Euclid gave us and to divide them into theoretical and practical [kinds] as well as propositions can be divided into two such kinds. I depart here from Wolff with respect to the issue itself. With respect to the four syllogistic figures,[12] this philosopher seems to speak of only the first one, because it alone is defined immediately on the basis of *Dicto de omni et nullo.* By contrast, I add to this saying *dictum de diverso, dictum de exemplo, dictum de reciproco,* which give nothing back to the first one, and show that every figure is used specifically and without artifice, and also without one thinking about it, the first with **reasons**, the second with **differences**, the third with **examples**, and the fourth with reciprocal entities. I make note of

---

[12] See Kant's *False Subtlety.*

here only in passing the determination and enumeration of the **next closest paths in inferring** and their formulas and signifying names; the **delineation** of propositions and inferences whereby their permissibility is established, and every conclusion is determined by the mere delineation of the premises; the remarks about the way of **reducing each task taken from the sciences to a logical one**; the comparison of **sentences, rules, conditions, and questions** with the four *modis verborum* of grammar; the theory of **proofs** and **experience**, etc. One can see from this that I was not at all disposed to copy. The exhortation to read and write books, to debate, to refute, etc., I have left out because my intention was directed toward reflection and discovery. Due to what was said previously, I can always recommend **Locke's** and **Wolff's** works for comparison.

In semiotics one will find so many disparate intentions and, if I am not mistaken, all that one can imagine with respect to language and signs. In the first chapter, I establish the entirely natural necessity of speech for the designation of thoughts and things, and after I have provided there the proper mark of **scientific signs**, namely, that the theory of such signs, instead of the theory of things themselves, should be able to suffice, I go through every previously known kind of signs through which we represent something, and evaluate them according to this mark. The cases are at the same time also made more discernible wherever one can more or less apply scientific signs. The remaining chapters are devoted in their entirety to language, indeed to possible and actual languages, often without distinction. It is investigated there what appears **arbitrary, natural, necessary** and, in part also, **scientific**, and how the **metaphysical** is distinguished in languages from what pertains to **characters** and is merely **grammatical**. And this holds without difference for **philology, criticism, linguistic theory**, and **philosophy**, insofar as the subject matter dictates. However, it will be remarked in every place to what extent languages could have been more metaphysical and involved more characters, if they had arisen less haphazardly [*gelegentlich*]. The remark that not all words are equally arbitrary is of importance if languages should be made more scientific or if merely what is scientific therein is supposed to be discovered. If one assumes the root words arbitrarily, the derived and composite words are already scientific according to their **characters**, and all metaphorical meanings are scientific in a **metaphysical** way. With a thoroughly scientific language, however, even the arbitrary root words would themselves be eliminated with respect to the **subject matter** as well as with respect to the **letters** and their **order**. However, since actual languages are not that philosophical, in the last chapter it would remain primarily to seek the hypothetical in the **meaning of words**, and at the same time to attend to how the **meaning** is established, because this is necessary for so-called nominal definitions as something that cannot be continued to infinity. In this respect the sum total of words of a language could be divided into three classes, of which the first one requires no definitions at all, because one can point to the thing itself in its entirety, and consequently can combine word, concept, and thing with each other immediately. The second class, which makes the words of the first metaphorical, uses, instead of a definition, a determination according to *tertii comparationis*. The third class comprehends those words that must be defined and indeed insofar as one can use the words of both of the first two classes for that, and then the words of the third class that are defined in this way are themselves used in turn for definitions. [...]

DIANOIOLOGY OR DOCTRINE OF THE LAWS OF THINKING

Ninth Chapter. On Scientific Cognition

§599. In the previous chapter we have seen to what extent we can obtain concepts and propositions through experience, whether it be that nature speaks to us so loud that we cannot fail to hear it, or that we have to pay closer attention to what it says if we want to hear it, or finally, that we must ask it questions if we want to receive its answer. The first are **common experiences**, the second are **observations**, and the third are **experiments**, and either we have all three ourselves or we get them from others who have had them. In both of these ways we attain cognition of what nature offers us, we learn its **customs**, the **rules** according to which it acts, and enrich ourselves with pictures and concepts of the things that it lays out to our senses or that we bring into view through activities. We learn thereby that something is, that it is **such and not otherwise**, and sometimes also, **what it is**.

§600. If we go no further with this, all cognition that we attain in this way is completely **historical**, and the description of everything that we cognize in this way is merely a **narrative** of what is in nature and what occurs and transpires with the things that nature lays before us. If we stick in this only with what common experience teaches us, we do not exhaust the scope of historical cognition, but rather our cognition will simply be what we call **common cognition**, which every human attains in a similar manner as long as he is not robbed of his senses, because in very many cases nature speaks so audibly that one can hardly fail to hear it.

§601. In this way we attain a certain number of concepts and propositions each of which subsists, as it were, on its own alone, and we assume it because we have seen or perceived it as such or heard of it from others. And this goes so far that people who have nothing further than common cognition, or, in addition to this, a bit of the **more select** historical cognition, form the deeply rooted prejudice that **one can think no further than the senses reach, and what one cannot immediately experience, consequently cannot see or perceive without taking other cognition into consideration, that extends beyond the field of vision of human cognition and is impossible for us to know, etc.**

§602. These prejudices lead us to the difference between historical and scientific cognition and at the same time to **what the latter has in advance [*voraus hat*] and what end [*wozu*] it is actually supposed serve**. We want to begin by illustrating the difference with self-evident examples that we want to take from the mathematical sciences, because they still remain the paradigms of the sciences and proceed the furthest and with the greatest certainty in the discovery and determination of what one cannot **experience**.

§604. [...] It is clear that it depends at least in part on the following: that one finds in another what cannot be found in the one, and that one can in any case spare oneself the effort if it would be too onerous, even if it would be possible in itself. Both are retained through one and the same means. For if A can be found through B, it is irrelevant whether one can find A for oneself, with effort, or not at all.

§605. Accordingly, scientific cognition is based on the **dependency** of one cognition on another and investigates how the one can be determined by the other. In this it is accordingly opposed to common cognition, because the latter views every proposition and every concept as subsisting on its own and without any connection, or at least finds that they harmonize only through individual inferences and comparisons among common experiences [...]

§606.[13] With scientific cognition, by contrast, one makes a **whole** out of this **patchwork**, the truths become dependent on each other therein, one reaches beyond the field of vision of the senses, and receives what

---

[13] Compare the discussion in the following paragraphs with the "Appendix to the Transcendental Dialectic" (A642–A668/B670–B696).

Cicero says of geometry: *In geometria si dederis, omnia danda sunt,* and one can add, *et ultra quam quod credideris.* This is no exaggerated praise of scientific cognition. For countless examples show, e.g., that geometry teaches us to find what can be found through no experience or actual measurement, that it saves us countless measurements and among these the impossible and most cumbersome ones, and reveals more to us than we could have believed it possible to find. The single proposition that one can find the third angle of a triangle from the other two, and that if the length of one of the sides is given, the other two are as well known as if they had been measured, saves us half of the six measurements. According to common cognition, however, all six would necessarily have to be undertaken individually. It is clear in this that if the actual measurement of all six items is even doable, geometry would still save us half of the trouble. [...] And in this way something can be measured in the heavens because something can be measured on the earth. For geometry shows us the connection and the relation between the two.

§609. Now these observations make apparent the difference between common and scientific cognition and the cited examples establish that the concept of scientific cognition is certainly a real and not a completely impossible concept. They also show that its renowned advantages are consistent with each other and consequently, if taken together, contain nothing contradictory. We will not yet determine the true scope of the concept of **scientific cognition**, but rather take up the noted properties as we have found them, and see in part what is the case with it and in part also what we know at the same time thereby without having distinct insight into it.

§610. Scientific cognition is distinct from common cognition first in that where the latter views every concept or every proposition as subsisting on its own, the former, by contrast, determines how they depend on each other (§605). Since common cognition has its concepts and propositions thanks only to the senses and consequently both are from common experience, in the beginning we want to go no farther and consequently to grant to scientific cognition only so much as that it is concerned to compare empirical concepts and empirical propositions with each other and to look around as to how they depend on each other, that is to say how, if one knows or can assume as familiar some things, the remaining ones can be found on that basis. E.g. the first inventor of geometry took, say, three lines and sought to put them together into the shape of a triangle.[14] The attempt succeeds, the lines meet and he notes that the angles are now already present and that if he wants to change the one, or two or three, something about the length of the sides must be changed as well. The matter makes him take note. He takes other lines and finds that there are cases where they do not meet and that he must lengthen one of the shorter ones, etc. One easily sees that a brief experiment of this kind leads to further observations and that one is imperceptibly led to seek reasons for this.

§611. However, we do not want to go this far here, but rather only observe somewhat more closely our admitted proposition. It consisted in scientific cognition being concerned to compare experiences with experiences. This first step already removes it from common experience, because the mere consciousness of these experiences is transformed into a more precise **observing** and frequently into actual **experiments** (§557). For since common cognition exhibits such experiences only as broken off pieces or as individual fragments, it is clear that one would have to view them with greater awareness if one wants to find what they contain in themselves through which the one can be compared with the other or lets itself be determined by the other. For one investigates to what extent they are similar to and different from each other or in what relations they stand in to each other. However, in order to find this, one must certainly **seek to enlighten the concept of each one individually**.

§629. The remarks made in the last two §§ indicate at the same time where one is still held back in the transformation of a bit of common cognition into scientific cognition and what else must still be added. We called such a bit of common cognition chaos and must view it as such because one is not assured (§611) on the basis of a more precise investigation and observation whether there is confused material in it and because the suspicion is that the answer is more likely yes than no (§618). Now if we undertake to go through such a chaos more precisely and sort it out, regardless of how obscurely we still perceive it, we already represent it in itself as a whole that is capable of development, dissection, and a nicer ordering of its parts. Whether we capture right at the start everything that belongs to this whole, that is not provided by common cognition, because it does not take the thing that precisely (§618). Accordingly, this must be considered and ascertained through

---

[14] See Kant's discussion of Thales in the B-Preface (Bvii–Bxliv).

a more precise investigation and one saves oneself much effort if one can determine even roughly which parts of common cognition must be taken together so that one has gathered either what is set out in advance [*das Vorgesetze*] or the whole that lies therein, albeit still in rough and raw materials. This is especially necessary and useful where such materials still have to be gathered together through observation and experiments. [...] The selection of observations and the arrangement of the experiments depends on it, and if some are forgotten, it is certainly possible to bring forth several rules, propositions, relations, etc., out of them, but they constitute no whole and gaps remain in it whose size and importance is still indeterminate. [...] We do not yet have the knack for finding the integral from such differential magnitudes.

§630. If one does not undertake, however, such extensive wholes, one also does not need as many materials, and one can be satisfied in taking those together that have a closer similarity and resemblance with each other. Closer observation of each one (§611) and their comparison provides in that case a certain number of combinations through which their **similarities**, **differences**, and **relations** can be determined and the remaining gaps can be discovered. Such an investigation of the similarities, differences, and relations between **related concepts** is, in addition, particularly beneficial in bringing about light and order in the first foundation of the theory being undertaken, and to avoid in part the ambiguity of words, in part the conflation of things and conceptions, and in general the confusion in them (§618) and their dissonances (§620).

§632. [...] For in fact it is much more useful for us and for others if, instead of rushing immediately to definitions and ordering them according to our frequently still confused concepts, we first look around somewhat more precisely where we have these concepts from, whether nothing in them could be sorted out more carefully and whether others have nothing to sort out in the concept that they form of the thing and of the words, before they can agree with us? [...]

§633. Up to now we have observed in great detail the *requisita* of sorting out the elements of historical cognition and at the same time have provided the order according to which one can bring such elements together so that one follows from the other and can be determined thereby. In this way the cognition of such a fragment becomes **scientific**, because one then knows each part more precisely and has more distinct insight into its relations with the others. Further, since one of the main aims of scientific cognition is supposed to be that one is thereby put in a position to render experience superfluous or even to derive from it those propositions and concepts that one would otherwise have to find by experiments or could not even be found at all, (§604) we have also already shown what this is all about and what is required for it (§612ff.) and one can similarly consider here what we had said in the first chapter (§§64–78) about the composition and discovery of new concepts, where we specifically had the intention of showing how such concepts can be found without beginning with the things themselves, (§64) and for that reason without looking to see whether these things already exist or would still have to be made. Now this is called rendering experience superfluous in the proper sense to the extent that if one still wants to do it, it serves only as a test, (§573) or if it is something that one can use, it is undertaken for the sake of this use. [...]

§634. Now insofar as one can find propositions, properties, relations, concepts, etc., on the basis of what one already knows without first needing to take these immediately from experience, to that extent we say that we find such propositions, properties, etc., *a priori* or **from the front** [*von fornen her*]. However, if we have to use immediate experience in order to know a proposition, property, etc., we find it *a posteriori*, or **from the back** [*von hinten her*].[15] What this difference, which is mentioned quite often with respect to our cognition, brings with it, we must develop somewhat more precisely and to this end use as an aid in part words and in part the thing itself.

§635. For one, the words *a priori* and *a posteriori* reveal in general a certain order according to which one thing in a series is before or after another. And here in particular they relate to the difference concerning which one we begin with and whether we proceed from the last ones to the first ones or the reverse, from the former to the latter. Now such orders are in the things of the world insofar as they follow each other, and if we know that something **will** happen, then we certainly say that we know it **in advance** [*voraus wissen*], especially if we can infer it from what

---

[15] Compare the discussion of the terms *a priori* and *a posteriori* in these sections with Kant's remarks on the topic in the A and B versions of the Introduction (A1–A16 and B1–B30).

precedes it. By contrast, if we experience what has happened only later, **knowledge in advance [*Vorauswissen*]** is eliminated and one says eventually at most only that **one could have known it in advance**. Experiencing this **only later** or *post factum* is for that reason the opposite of **knowledge in advance** or **foreseeing** and it is so by the **time** at which a thing occurs separating the one from the other. If one sees only in retrospect that one **could** have known the thing, this just reveals that one did not think about it or did not immediately remember everything from which one could have found it. Now since this did not happen, one had to **let it depend on experience**. And this is necessary as often as one does not actually or *ipso facto* know it in advance, regardless of whether or not one could have known it in advance. For in this way it is determined only after the fact whether it would have been possible for us. [...]

§636. In such special cases we just do not use the modes of speaking *a priori* and *a posteriori,* in part because they are not well known in regular life and in part also because they refer in general to the order in the connection of our cognition. For since we must have the premises before we draw the conclusion, the premises precede the conclusion and accordingly this is certainly called to **precede** *a priori.* By contrast, if we do not have the premises, or are not immediately aware of them in order to be able to draw the conclusion, we have no means other than experience that represents each proposition, as it were, as subsisting on its own, (§605) and we must let it depend on experience in order to know the proposition. Now since this is not *a priori,* one called it *a posteriori* and thereby made it a *Terminum infinitum* (§89) out of the latter concept.

§637. However, one easily sees that these two concepts must be taken **reciprocally.** For if one wanted to infer that not only immediate experiences, but also everything that we can find on the basis of them is *a posteriori,* the concept *a priori* would be used in few of those cases where we can determine something through inferences in advance, because in such a case we would have to thank experience for none of the premises. And in that case nothing at all would be *a priori* in all of our cognition.

§639. Accordingly, we want to let it be valid that one can call something *a priori absolutely* and in the strictest sense only if we have nothing at all to thank experience for. Whether in such a case this kind of thing is to be found in our experience, that is a completely different, and in part really unnecessary question. By contrast, we have no difficulty in calling *a priori* in the **broadest sense** everything that we can know **in advance** without first letting it depend on experience.

§640. After this definition of both of the extreme meanings it can easily be discerned that something is more or less *a priori*, according to how we can derive it from more [or less] distant experiences, and that, by contrast, something is **completely not** *a priori* and consequently is **immediately** *a posteriori* if we must **experience** it immediately in order to know it.

§641. Meanwhile, a certain means can be found in this that brings both *extrema* closer together. For one can draw a distinction among what we have to thank experience for, whether it be merely concepts or propositions. In this way one calls *a priori* what can be derived from the concept of a thing and, by contrast, *a posteriori* where one cannot use the concept of the thing to that end or where one has to take, in addition to what it provides us, several propositions from experience in order to be able to draw the conclusion, or finally, where one does not make any progress with it at all, but rather must take the proposition itself immediately from experience.

§642. Now from this it follows on its own that our common and historical cognition is *a posteriori* with respect to us insofar as we acquire the same through the use of the senses. Further, that scientific cognition is *a posteriori* insofar as we use propositions of experience for it and, by contrast, one can call it *a priori* insofar as we derive it from the concepts of things and without enlisting several propositions of experience.

§643. We offer this distinction because *a priori* cognition is preferable [*vorzüglicher*] to *a posteriori* cognition. For the less one is allowed to rely on experience, the further one reaches with cognition, because that from which something else can be derived is always higher and more universal, or at least cannot be lower and more limited.

§644. Now we primarily have to investigate here whether and to what extent a cognition can be acquired merely on the basis of the concept of the thing and for that reason be scientific *a priori*. If this can be found, we extend thereby the concept of scientific cognition that we had accepted above (§610) only insofar as it was concerned with bringing experiences into connection [with each other] and deriving the one from the other.

§645. Accordingly, in order to take up the investigation that arises here, we will have to begin by sorting concepts out with respect to this and bringing them into proper classes. And this difference therein depends primarily on the way **in which we acquire or can acquire concepts**. For it is clear that the more we ourselves can have concepts without taking experience into account, the more our cognition becomes *a priori*. With this we fall back on the difference between concepts indicated above (§185), which we now want to develop more precisely.

§646. For one, that we have and can have concepts from experience requires no further proof, because common cognition has no other insofar as it depends only on sensations. Accordingly, **concepts of experience** are intrinsically possible concepts and, in fact, those for which we have to thank immediate perception. [...]

§647. Immediate concepts of experience are individual, both with respect to the thing that we perceive and with respect to the consciousness of each individual impression that the thing makes on the senses. Now in spite of the fact that we cannot express with words in detail what is individual, especially where the thing is much too composite, so much still remains in the picture of it that we often [*mehrenteils*] recognize the thing itself when it appears again and, in fact, the easier, the more frequently and the more precisely we perceived it, and that we can compare them with those that awaken more or less similar perceptions in us. This brings it about that with common cognition we are often able to sort out the things that act on our senses into genus and species, and to place each individual into its class. In this way common cognition also gives us universal and abstract concepts, in part of those things that nature itself has distinguished into genus and species, such as that of animals, plants, metals, stones, etc., in part of more general concepts of relations, as, e.g., cause, effect, change, [and] magnitude are.

§649. We have already provided in detail above (§§35–64) the determination of the scope [*Umfanges*] of a concept, whereby both thing and word are given and where consequently the concept itself is a **concept of experience** and for that reason we will no longer linger on this, but rather seek out the remaining kinds of concepts.

§650. To this we have similarly (§64) remarked that the **composition** of individual marks is a means of attaining concepts and that one can proceed **arbitrarily** insofar as the possibility of such a concept can be proven later (§65ff.). Now as long as the possibility has not yet been proved, the concept remains **hypothetical**, and we noted at the same time (§68) that physical hypotheses are such concepts. [...]

§651. Since hypothetical concepts must be proved, this occurs either from experience (§§65–66) and there it transforms itself into a **concept of experience**, because it is in fact unimportant in this case whether we begin with what is arbitrarily composed or with experience, without which the concept cannot yet be viewed as possible (§645).

§652. However, if the possibility of a hypothetical concept is established on the basis of reasons without letting it depend on experience, one can call it a derivative concept [*Lehrbegriff*], just as one calls propositions that are proved theorems [*Lehrsätze*] (§148, 154). And again it is unimportant whether one begins with composition or with the concept, because the proof must still first make the concept into a **derivative concept**. We already showed in the first section (§§67–78) the various ways of attaining derivative concepts and for that reason shall not repeat them here, but rather only remark that derivative concepts and concepts of experience can be transformed into each other, namely, when one finds the **proof** of the latter, but, as it were, **tests** the former with experience.

§653. Since composite concepts can be resolved into simpler ones as its marks, one can conceive of completely simple concepts that cannot be resolved further, but that can be determined or denoted [*angezeigt*] through relations to other concepts. Such simple concepts constitute the foundation of the entirety of our cognition and one can justly and in the most proper sense call them **axiomatic concepts** [*Grundbegriffe*] in order to contrast them with derivative concepts [*Lehrbegriffe*]. Since they have no parts, nothing is to be distinguished in them, and for that reason its representation and perception remains absolutely clear. We shall not decide here whether the concepts of **color, sounds, space, time, existence**, etc., are such simple concepts. This much is certain, namely, that we can define them at most only through relations because the representation or perception thereof is thoroughly uniform. Therefore, since we do not have to set up many comparisons of its marks in order to perceive its difference, because it is itself its mark, they serve, by contrast, to indicate to us the difference between composite concepts, because the latter can be resolved into the former and consist in a certain number and modification thereof.

§654. Since at least two elements are required for a contradiction, because the one must cancel out the other, axiomatic concepts necessarily possess nothing contradictory. For since they are not composite, there is nothing in them that could cancel out anything else in it. Accordingly, the mere representation of a simple concept constitutes its possibility and this forces itself on us along with the representation.

§655. From this it follows that an impossible concept cannot be simple. For it is impossible because it contains in itself both A and not-A, and for that reason is composed of representations that cannot coexist with each other, because one cancels the other. E.g., wooden iron, round square, etc.

§656. Since in the dissection of composite concepts we approach the simple or axiomatic concepts when we resolve them into their internal marks, it is clear that the farther we can proceed *a priori* in scientific cognition, the farther we go in this resolution and that our scientific cognition would be *a priori* completely and in the strictest sense (§639), if we were cognizant of the axiomatic concepts in their entirety and could express them in words, and knew the first foundation of the possibility of their composition. For since the possibility of an axiomatic concept forces itself on us along with the representation (§654), it arises thereby completely independently of experience such that even if we already have to thank experience for it, experience provides us, as it were, only the occasion for consciousness of it. However, once we are conscious of it, we have no need to procure the ground of its possibility from experience, because possibility is already present with the mere representation. Accordingly, it becomes independent of experience. And this is a *requisitum* of cognition [that is] *a priori* in the strictest sense (§639). Now if we are conscious of each simple concept on its own, the words are only denominations thereof whereby we distinguish each one from the others, and combine **intuitive** [*anschauende*] with **figurative** [*figürlichen*] cognition. Finally, if we are familiar with the foundation of the possibility of their composition, we are also in a position to form composite concepts from these simple ones without procuring them from experience. Accordingly, here too our cognition becomes *a priori* in the strictest sense (§639).

§657. We can cite circumstances that show that we are conscious, at least in a still confused way, of the truth and actuality of what we have first established under the assumed conditions, because we frequently and without noticing view very many universal propositions and concepts as completely independent from the actual world. To this belong all propositions that are necessarily true in themselves and that we consider among the **eternal** and **immutable** truths that can never be otherwise. [...] We may have experience to thank for these concepts, but it is only as an occasion, because we can abstract from it completely afterwards.

§658.[16] If we view the concept of **extension**, both according to space and time, or immediately view the concepts of **space** and **time** as completely simple concepts, we have three sciences that are *a priori* in the strictest sense: namely, **geometry**, **chronometry**, and **phoronomy**. And if one conversely admits that these three sciences are *a priori* in the strictest sense, then the concepts of **space** and **time** are simple concepts. For geometry demands no other possibility than that of a straight line and that of its position around a point such that it immediately constructs angles, circles, spheres, and with these, all figures and bodies. Chronometry requires nothing beyond the uniform course of time and obtains therewith cycles, periods, etc. Phoronomy takes space and time together and erects thereby the theory of motion, velocity, and translation of moved points, etc. Accordingly, if one assumes that the concepts of time and space are simple, they are independent of experience (§656) and consequently, since these three sciences use nothing beyond these concepts, they are *a priori* in the strictest sense. However, if one assumes conversely that these sciences are thoroughly *a priori*, it similarly follows that the concepts of space and time must be simple concepts, because they are laid at the foundation of these sciences without any further development. It is worth remarking as an aside that we are not counting dynamics here as falling under phoronomy, and similarly we are not counting the chronology of the actual world, or historical chronology, as falling under chronology mentioned here, because we are not extending these three sciences here farther than the extent to which they necessarily and indisputably belong among the **eternal** and **immutable** truths (§657).

---

[16] See the Transcendental Aesthetic (A19/B33ff). See also Kant's remarks on the concept of space in *The Only Possible Argument* (esp. 2:71) and *Inquiry* (esp. 2:278–2:282).

§659. Simple concepts can be used only for comparison and composition. The former provides relational concepts, the latter, by contrast, derivative concepts. For since simple concepts have no internal marks, but rather are themselves their own marks (§653), they have no internal predicate other than themselves, e.g., what is, is; to exist is to exist, etc. They can certainly become predicates, by contrast, because they either do or do not occur in every other concept. Further, their comparison makes a certain impression on the soul and this impression provides a relational concept (§59) that serves, as it were, as a bridge for moving from the one to the other. That is how relations are in geometry, and the relations between **time** and **space** are determined in phoronomy through the concepts of **motion** and **velocity**.

§660. Since experience provides occasions for concepts, it is clear that if we remain only by the mere possibility of these concepts, the determination of existence, which is peculiar to experience, is kept separate. And to this extent we take the concept as subsisting on its own, and it will be able to be viewed as *a priori* as soon as we can secure its possibility without [having to depend on] experience (§656).

§684. One easily succumbs to a circle if one wants to define concepts that are intrinsically simple, because one naturally uses such concepts in defining more composite ones. E.g., space is the order of things that exist at the same time and are external to each other [*außereinander*]. The concept of **externality** [*außereinander*] already includes within itself the concept of space and would not be defined properly without a circle.

§685. Those circles that arise in this way through relational concepts have no necessary influence on the truth of the explanation. They provide propositions that are identical, but both cannot be viewed as definitions at one and the same time. Accordingly, one must investigate which of the two can be retained as a definition and the other can then be derived from it as a consequence. Thus when one says, e.g., that an hour is one-twenty-fourth part of a day, one can certainly infer that a day must consequently have 24 hours or that it is divided into 24 hours. By contrast, if one wants to define what a day is, it must occur through the time within which the sun must circle the heavens once.

7

Marcus Herz

Marcus Herz was born to a poor Jewish family in Berlin in 1747 and was first educated there according to strict Talmudic tradition. In 1766, four years after moving to Königsberg at the age of fifteen to undertake an apprenticeship in business, he matriculated at the "Albertina" as a medical student – its faculty of medicine was the only one in Prussia at the time that would accept Jewish students. As was customary for medical students, Herz began the university with a series of courses in the so-called *humaniora* (modern languages, philosophy, and mathematics), where he became especially enamored with philosophy as taught to him by Kant. (That Kant had a unique relationship to Herz as well is clear from his decision to have Herz defend his *Inaugural Dissertation* publicly, a decision that met with some resistance among the faculty.) Because of financial circumstances, Herz left Königsberg to attend medical school first in Berlin and then in Halle, where he received his medical degree in 1774. He then returned to Berlin to practice medicine, where his patients included several high-ranking families, and he, along with his notable wife, Henrietta Herz, maintained a popular salon that functioned as a center for leading young intellectuals such as Wilhelm and Alexander von Humboldt, Friedrich Schleiermacher, and Friedrich Schlegel.

Though he was employed full time as a physician, Herz was able to complete several works in the natural sciences (especially medicine) and philosophy. He published *Briefe an Ärzte* (Letters to Physicians) in 1777 and, based on lectures he gave at his salon, *Grundriß aller medizinischen Wissenschaften* (Outline of All Medical Sciences) in 1782 along with *Grundlage zu seinen Vorlesungen über die Experimentalphysik* (Foundation for His Lectures on Experimental Physics) in 1786. In philosophy he authored *Betrachtungen aus der spekulativen Weltweisheit* (Observations from Speculative Philosophy) in 1772 and *Versuch über den Geschmack und die Ursachen seiner Verschiedenheit* (Essay on Taste and the Causes of Its Differences) in 1776, which was revised and enlarged in a second edition that came out in 1790, the same year as Kant's *Critique of the Power of Judgment*. He also penned several works aiming at reform within the Jewish community at the time.

Herz's personal correspondence with Kant, however, is also of significance. After Herz left Königsberg for Berlin, Kant wrote letters to Lambert, Sulzer, and Mendelssohn, providing Herz with an entrée into the learned circles of Berlin, an opportunity that Herz, along with his wife, made the most of in the following decades. Herz wrote Kant many letters thereafter, and while Kant did not always respond – a fact that he repeatedly excused with his being fully occupied reformulating his own views throughout the 1770s – when he did write, it provides one with extremely helpful clues as to the state of his views at the time. Kant's letter to Herz from February 21, 1772, has thus rightly become famous for its explanation of what he was finding problematic in his own previous works.

Herz's *Observations from Speculative Philosophy* was written shortly after Kant's *Inaugural Dissertation* and as a commentary on that work. While it is therefore a self-avowedly derivative tract, it is none the less instructive insofar as it illustrates (1) how one intimately familiar with the general intellectual context in which Kant was working and lecturing understood Kant's position in the *Inaugural Dissertation*, (2) what challenges Kant's views at this time might face, and (3) what opportunities would have been available for further development. What one finds is that Herz is especially interested in three specific issues. First, Herz formulates and applies to the subject matter of the *Inaugural Dissertation* a certain understanding of transcendental philosophy, distinguishing sharply between sensible and pure rational cognition. Second, accepting Kant's account of sensibility (along with his account of space and time) from the Dissertation, Herz clarifies (1) how this conception is distinct from the Wolffian account (2) how it does not devolve into an illegitimate subjectivism, and (3) how it relates to certain views of relations under discussion at the time. Third, Herz provides an insightful discussion of how someone committed to the essential features of Kant's view in the *Inaugural Dissertation* might react to Crusius's distinctive position by showing what the liabilities of Crusius's basic epistemological principles might seem to be and how these issues bear on the distinction between real and logical essences. Though the self-effacing tone of

Herz's personal remarks might lead one to expect few novel insights into deep philosophical truths, he reveals himself throughout to be a subtle thinker, very much capable of appreciating Kant's position and thinking through where it might lead.

This chapter contains five of the most salient letters from Kant's and Herz's correspondence from 1770 to 1776 and well over half of Herz's *Observations from Speculative Philosophy.*

First Letter: From Herz to Kant,
September 11, 1770

Eternally unforgettable teacher,
Esteemed Herr Professor,

Forgive me, dearest Herr Professor, for only now paying my respects to you, though I have been here since last Thursday. The unusual wakefulness, the five days' journey and the uninterrupted agitation that one experiences on the stage coach had so weakened my body, spoiled as it is by comfort, that I was unfit for any other important business, and how much more unfit for communication with you! [...]

My first visit here was to Herr Mendelssohn. We conversed for four whole hours over certain things in your Dissertation. We have very different philosophies; he follows Baumgarten to the letter and he gave me to understand very clearly and distinctly that he could not agree with me on a number of points because they did not agree with Baumgarten's opinions. On the whole he likes the Dissertation and he only regrets that you were not somewhat more expansive. He admires the penetration shown in the proposition that, if the predicate of a proposition is sensible, it is only subjectively valid of the subject, while, on the other hand, if the predicate is intellectual, etc.[1] Similarly the development of the infinite, the solution to Kästner's problem.[2] He is about to publish something in which, as he says, it will look as though he has simply copied your whole first section; in short, he thinks the whole Dissertation an excellent work, though there are certain points with which he does not totally agree. One of them is that in explaining the nature of space, one must use the words "at the same time" [*simul*], and in explaining time the word "after" [*post*]; he also thinks that "at the same time" should not be put into the principle of contradiction.[3] [...]

> Your must humble pupil and
> most obedient servant
> Marc. Herz
> Berlin
> *The 11th of Sept. 1770*
> [P.S.] My compliments to Herr Kanter.

---

[1] *Inaugural Dissertation*, Section V.
[2] 2:399–400, and Moses Mendelssohn, *Philosophische Schriften*, Parts 1 and 2 (Berlin, 1771).
[3] See *Inaugural Dissertation* (2:416) and Mendelssohn's letter to Kant, 25 December 1770.

SECOND LETTER: FROM KANT TO HERZ, JUNE 7, 1771

Dearest Friend,

[...] You understand how important it is, for all of philosophy – yes even for the most important ends of humanity in general – to distinguish with certainty and clarity that which depends on the subjective principles of human mental powers (not only sensibility but also the understanding) and that which pertains directly to the facts. If one is not driven by a mania for systematizing, the investigations which one makes concerning one and the same fundamental principle in its widest possible applications even confirm each other. I am therefore busy on a work, which I call "The Bounds of Sensibility and of Reason." It will work out in some detail the foundational principles and laws that determine the sensible world together with an outline of what is essential to the Doctrine of Taste, of Metaphysics, and of Moral Philosophy. I have this winter surveyed all the relevant materials for it and have considered, weighed, and harmonized everything, but I have only recently come up with the way to organize the whole work. [...]

I am delighted to learn that you intend to publish a work on the nature of the speculative sciences. I anticipate your book with pleasure and since it will be finished before mine, I will be able to take advantage of all sorts of suggestions, which I shall surely find in it. [...]

Your sincere, devoted friend,
Immanuel Kant

THIRD LETTER: FROM HERZ TO KANT, JULY 9, 1771

Most Esteemed Herr Professor,

Aside from the usual pleasure of seeing that my dear teacher's memories of me have not yet been extinguished, your last letter had another effect on me of much greater importance than you might have imagined. My friend Herr Friedländer said to me on his arrival that you are no longer such a devotee of speculative philosophy as you used to be. What's that I am saying – "not a devotee"? He said that you had told him explicitly on a certain occasion that you took metaphysics to be pointless head scratching, a subject understood only by a handful of

scholars in their study chambers but far too removed from the tumult
of the world to bring about any of the changes that their theorizing
demands. Since most of the rest of the world has no comprehension of
metaphysics at all, it cannot have the slightest effect on its well-being.
You supposedly said to him that moral philosophy for the common man
is thus the *only* appropriate subject for a scholar, for here one may penetrate the heart, here one may study human feelings and try to regulate
them by bringing them under the rules of common experience. How I
trembled at this news! What? I thought, was it all just deception when
my teacher on so many occasions extolled the value of metaphysics? Or
did he then really feel what he claimed to feel, though time has given
him a more penetrating insight into the essential nature of science, an
insight that has all at once converted his warmest dispositions into cold
aversion? So the fate of all our enjoyments is the same, be they physical
enjoyments or mental, call them what you will – they all intoxicate us
for a few moments, agitate our blood, allow us for a little while to be
Children of Heaven, but soon afterwards we experience the most pain-
ful torments of all: disgust, which imposes penance after penance on
us for our transitory moments of delight. Why then all that shouting
about the pleasures of the mind, all that noise about the happiness that
springs from the works of the understanding, happiness which is closest
to that of the gods themselves? Away with that rubbish, if theorizing can
accomplish nothing more than can the fulfillment of any other desire –
or indeed far less, since the disgust that follows, disgust over wasted
time and effort, necessarily awakens in us an unending regret! I was
really prepared to accept this fate and renounce all the sciences, even
to smother my "child," already half-born; but your letter called me back
in the nick of time from my rashness: You are still the same devotee of
metaphysics as ever, it must have been only a bad mood that made you
say otherwise. You are once again engaged in producing a great work
for the public, and you still maintain that the happiness of the human
race depends on the truths that you are going to demonstrate concerning the bounds of knowledge! O what a secure pledge has been put into
my hands by this confession from the greatest friend of humanity: that
he can never cease to treasure the subject which constitutes the only
remedy to bring about human happiness!

You will receive my book by regular mail and I suspect you will find
little in it that should cause you to make any changes in the work you
have at hand. I need hardly tell you, dearest Herr Professor, how little
I deserve credit for my book. I have merely had your own book before

my eyes, followed the thread of your thoughts and only here and there have I made a few digressions, things that were not part of my original plan but that occurred to me while I was working. I hope you will therefore be kind enough to share in whatever applause I may expect to receive. It is all due to you, and the only praise I deserve is for being a conscientious auditor. But let me be disgraced, eternally disgraced, if I have misunderstood you, if I have substituted inauthentic wares for the genuine article, let the whole world's censure be upon me! I could use this opportunity to discuss various matters in my book, but I shall wait until you have read it and written me your opinion. In developing the concepts of space and time I digressed to discuss the nature of the principles of the beautiful; my investigation of relations led me to a proof of the reality of the soul, a proof that perhaps deserves attention; in the second part of the book I merely followed you and only made a small gesture in the direction of further progress.

[...]

I have only started to read Lambert's *Architektonik* so I cannot make any judgments about it. Besides, I have only a few spare hours to devote to non-medical studies.

I have chattered long enough. Be well, unforgettable Herr Professor, and write to me soon and at length about my book. For, I swear to God! your judgment alone will determine its worth for me. In the meantime think of

your most obedient servant and pupil
Marcus Herz

OBSERVATIONS FROM SPECULATIVE PHILOSOPHY (1771)[4]

FIRST DIVISION

[14] The concept that we have of a world, like any other concept, can be considered from two different points of view. Either according to its actuality, insofar as it is a complete object of our cognition, or according to how it arises, insofar as we arrive at it through our sensible cognitive faculties or through pure reason. In the second case, the form or the way that is necessary for us to form the concept can, in turn, be abstracted

---

4 Translated from Markus Herz, *Betrachtungen aus der spekulativen Weltweisheit* (Königsberg: Kanter, 1771). Page numbers from this edition have been inserted in brackets.

from the concept itself and become a special object of observation, or the concept does indeed remain our object, but we do not consider it as it is outside of us independently of our cognitive faculties, but rather only how it can be represented through them as actual.[5]

These various ways of investigating our concepts are so very different from each other that each one of them not only requires an entirely [15] special method, but also presupposes principles that are unique to them and that can be conflated with those that are unique to the others, [but] seldom without cost to the truth, and never without running the danger of being led far astray in the course of our thinking. I believe, dearest friend, that the causes of the disputes into which philosophers have forever been drawn concerning the most important objects of metaphysics, are sought in the neglect of this very distinction and not in the vicissitudes of science; and, in my opinion, their efforts to convince each other of their different systems can never cease to be in vain as long as they do not distinguish properly these different ways of philosophizing and speak with one voice about their different principles.[6] There are a number of examples that I could offer to you as proof of how often, in investigating the source of different confusions, one ultimately realizes that [16] the principles [at issue] have not been properly distinguished and the boundaries that limit our cognition have been mistakenly adapted to external objects, and of those that Herr Kant discusses in his treatise, I shall select only the first one I happen upon to confirm this truth.

Some explain, e.g., the mathematically infinite by a *multitude* [*Menge*] than which no greater can be thought.[7] Now since in the doctrine of magnitudes this is just like a number [*Zahl*] to which no more units can be added in thought, which we can represent to ourselves as little as it is possible in and of itself, the entire concept must necessarily be a mere fiction for them, and as soon as an infinite series of simultaneously existing or successively actual things is being discussed, their mistaken explanation of the infinite lends them the most disputable weapons for denying the possibility of such things. However, if the infinite is taken in its true meaning, then it expresses such a multitude [*Menge*] [17] whose relation to every other number that is taken as a unit of measurement cannot be expressed through any number, but it then follows that such an infinite, viewed as a *whole,* cannot be an object of our representation, but not at all that it is impossible in itself. We, who cannot form

---

[5] See A11/B25.
[6] See A1–A16/B1–B30 (A and B Introductions).
[7] Kant discusses this example in the *Inaugural Dissertation* in a note (2:389).

a concept of a *whole*, except by a continual addition of parts, must at some point come to an end with this addition if we want to conceive the whole as determinate. But after having completed the collection [*Zusammensetzen*], there is nothing that should keep us from adding in thought yet further parts to this whole, however large it may be; but the infinite permits no end to addition, because it could otherwise be conceived to be larger than it actually is, and is for that reason precisely contrary to the procedure that is necessary for us to form a whole; however, for such a being that does not require the difficult means that we must use to obtain the concept of a whole and whose infinite understanding cognizes intuitively [18] the innermost [features] of things, the representation of an infinite whole costs it far less than does us the thought of an ever so small magnitude. For the present I have produced this example to show you how those who start from a false explanation of a concept and those who, not heeding the correct explanation, do not properly distinguish its subjective from its objective possibility, are rushing toward error in lockstep. However, merely look at these concepts that are so fruitful in metaphysics, at space and time, and you will find that the notorious difficulties about the location of the soul, the omnipresence of God, infinite divisibility, etc., which are dangerous cliffs for many philosophers, are all grounded in the fact that the limits of the actuality of external things are taken to be the same as the limits of our cognition, and for that reason conditions that are prescribed to this [cognition] according to the pleasure of a highest wisdom have been carried over to the state [*Verhalten*] of external things themselves; so it is likewise impossible to have insight into the [19] necessary connection between them and our cognition of them. Weigh carefully, dearest friend, what difference there is between both of these sentences: *This object cannot be otherwise; I cannot represent this object to myself otherwise.*[8]
[...]

[20] We obtain the concept of a simple thing as well as the concept of a world by means of two different paths, which we must distinguish from each other with care.[9] We obtain them either through pure reason or through the sensible cognitive faculty. In the first case only the concept of *composition* [*Zusammensetzung*] is needed for our purpose. We add this in thought to all actually present things, however many there are, and in that case we have a *largest whole*, which for that reason cannot

---

[8] See B410–B411.
[9] See A418/B446 and A487–A489/ B515–B517.

be conceived as larger, because nothing is left that would have been excluded from this universal composition. By contrast, if we entirely remove just this concept in a thing that has already been composed, the pieces we are then left with are completely simple parts, each one of which no longer constitutes a whole, because by the universal removal of all composition nothing manifold remains that could still be *one* by means of [21] a connection.[10] In the latter case, however, where we are tracking the mode of origin of both these concepts through the sensible cognitive faculty, a universal adding in thought or removal of composition is not sufficient, but rather we must follow these concepts starting from their origin, continuing through their entire formation, so that we are able to cognize intuitively in a sensible manner the way in which we get to them. For that reason, in order to obtain the concept of a *whole*, we must gradually order and connect with each other those simple parts that are given to us, and conversely, we must gradually separate the parts in a composite thing, until the whole is completely dissolved if we want to arrive at simple things. This gradual connecting and separating can occur only in a series of successive moments, and we can, for that reason, represent neither an analysis nor a synthesis, unless we are already in possession of the concept of time, a concept that, as I shall show you below, is presupposed by all of our sensible cognitions, [22] but must be completely dismissed from cognitions of pure reason.[11]

Now you will already see somewhat more distinctly how important this precise distinction between the different modes of philosophizing is in investigations of the truth. For we presuppose the concept of time in analysis as well as in synthesis and in our activities regarding both we must go, so to speak, parallel with the flow of time, yet time itself neither consists of simple parts that cannot be divided in turn, nor encompasses a determinate set of parts within itself to which, after they have been exhausted, yet further ones cannot be added in thought to infinity. For this reason, we will be able to form a complete concept of neither a *continuous magnitude* nor an *infinite whole* by means of our sensible epistemic faculty, because in both cases we have no boundaries where we can finally stop with the division or composition so as to have brought forth a simple part through the former [23] and such a whole that cannot be conceived of as larger through the latter.[12] By contrast, not only does nothing stand in the way of pure reason that could keep

---

[10] See A434/B462ff. (Second Antinomy).
[11] See A497/B525ff. (Section Seven of the Antinomy of Pure Reason).
[12] See A169–A171/B211–B213 (Anticipations of Perception).

it from thinking of both of these concepts as possible, but it can even be proven *a priori* with absolute rigor that they must necessarily occupy a place among actual things.

We therefore have to pay attention to the following three items for a complete explanation of a world, which, taken together, sufficiently distinguish this concept from every other.

First, *matter* in a metaphysical sense, or the given parts in which the connection takes place that transforms it into a single *whole*. These must be substances in order to constitute the component parts of a world. Everything else besides these is merely a determination of them and concerns their state more than them.

[24] Second, the *form* or the connection itself, which makes the manifold items into one single [whole]. This [connection] must be reciprocal and homogeneous.[13] Reciprocal, because every one-sided connection can bring about at most only an ideal whole; homogeneous so that the entire combination can be derived from a single ground at all. Due to this condition we will not be able to view the connection that exists between a ground and its consequent as identical to the one that makes different substances into a *whole*. For although the consequent stands in a real dependency on an active cause and cannot be thought without it, the ground itself is still connected only ideally with the consequent, that is, insofar as it is to be thought as such, but nothing contradictory is to be found in and of itself in the concept of its existing without a consequence. Now since we must have the *principium* of an objective whole, we will seek the form that constitutes the essence of this whole in a set of substances that are next to each other [25] and stand in a combination by means of some ground or other (I let it be undetermined what this actually consists in) such that each of them relates to all the others taken together like the complement of a whole to the whole itself. Once this *principium* of the world-whole has been determined, one will have to assert of it what is valid of the essence of each and every other thing, [namely] that it is eternal and immutable and, irrespective of all mutations to which this whole is subject in light of its changing states, still never ceases to be the same as long as its existence is not completely taken away.

Finally, third, the *greatest perfection* of a whole.[14] This determination is necessary because it is actually this through which the whole of a

---

[13] See the Third Analogy (B256/A211ff.).
[14] See B114–B115 (Metaphysical Deduction).

world is distinguished from every other whole in which form and matter are indeed likewise present, but to which the appellation of a whole is ascribed only relatively, since matter comprehends within itself not everything actual, but rather only some of it. By contrast, the matter of the world-whole consists in everything [26] created, consequently there is no more matter that can still be added to this so as to constitute an even larger whole by means of combination. And for that reason real totality must be ascribed to the concept of a world in the highest degree.

This is not the place to determine whether this totality consists in a finite or infinite amount [*Menge*] of matter. However, you must not fail to notice that, in the latter case, it can be an object of our sensible cognition as little as can a series of successive things that are infinite regarding time. It is easy to see that if we could represent an infinite multitude [*Menge*] of things existing next to each other even without the help of pure reason, we would also actually have a [sufficient] supply for a series that would be temporally infinite, because we would simply be able to think these different items in just as many different moments and view them as a whole. Yet I have shown you that an infinite series that is supposed to be represented as a whole through our sensible epistemic faculty [27] even seems to have something contradictory about it and for that reason can be merely an object of pure reason.

Now let us characterize one primary difference between sensible and pure rational cognition in order to investigate it all the more clearly and to be able to develop the makeup of each in particular.

What is sensible in our cognition is that by means of which our state behaves passively in the presence of external objects; what is intellectual [in our cognition] is the faculty to represent such things to which, due to their makeup, no access is permitted through the senses. For that reason sensible cognition does not have external objects as its immediate object, but rather has the changed state that has been brought about through its impressions. With rational cognition, by contrast, there is no means between the external objects and the cognition of them, for which reason the former is the immediate object of the latter. Now if every cognition is directed [28] toward its closest object, is different if this [object] is different, and is immutable if it remains constantly the same, then sensible cognition, too, which has only the changed state of a subject as an object, will be different in different subjects as long as its state is not similarly modified by the impressions of external things. Since pure rational cognition, by contrast, relates immediately to external objects, it can be subject to a change only insofar as the external objects themselves take on a different figure or are observed from a different perspective, but as long as these remain the same, cognition of them must also be identical in all subjects.

I have said that sensible cognition expresses something subjective.[15] The following consideration, which seems to me to be of importance, will show you that this is true only of a part of sensible cognition, namely, insofar as it is undetermined. However, to the extent to which sensible cognition is restricted to a [29] special object, it is constantly involved with what is objective. [...] [30] The impressions that our sensible instruments [*sinnliche Werkzeuge*] receive from present, external objects, or rather the changed state of our soul that stands in the closest connection with them, can be called cognition only in a very improper sense, since it constitutes only the matter of cognition, whereby the soul behaves merely passively. But it becomes active only when it orders the received impressions with respect to each other according to a rule or law that is prescribed to it in its process, and compares them to each other in different ways. I will call this law according to which it undertakes comparison and subordination the *form*, in contrast to the matter, in the cognition, and, indeed, *the form of sensible cognition*, when the matter is given through the [31] senses, and *the form of pure rational cognition*, when it has its origin in pure reason. It is apparent that with respect to sensible cognition something objective is contained in both the matter and the form, but that there is a determinate result only when it is compared with something subjective. In the matter the impression of the senses and the state of the soul that follows it is something objective and must be present in all subjects as soon as an external object that acts on it is there, because otherwise an active cause would have to be conceived without an [attendant] effect. By contrast, the kind of effect, or its special determination, depends on the passive part and must, for that reason, be diverse in different subjects. The opposite is the case for the form. The law that is prescribed to the soul in representing sensible objects is the *objective* in cognition. This must be thought of as real [*reell*] in the soul if one wants to represent it with all of its properties. [32] However, since a universal law delivers a determinate result only by being applied, a more precise determination of the form likewise depends on the result of the matter to which it is applied; and since something subjective is contained in these, as I have established, so, too,

---

[15] See A29/B44–B45 (Transcendental Aesthetic).

something subjective is similarly contained in the determinate result of the form of sensible cognitions, and the result itself will have to be diverse in different subjects.

It is completely different, by contrast, with pure rational cognition. For in that case its immediate objects are external objects so that the matter in cognition is completely free from everything subjective, and for that reason the laws of pure reason, which constitute the *form*, must also have an objective validity in their application.[16] However, one must guard against taking them to be the only ones that external objects are subject to, as long as one can definitively establish that matter does not completely exhaust the objects in our rational cognition as well, but rather leaves parts in them behind that are matter for [33] a higher understanding and must be treated according to a higher form that is inconceivable to us.

[...]

[40] I return now to observing the different kinds of our cognition. Pure reason can be applied in a two-fold way. Either it observes concepts of things or of relations that are present between [42] them, or else it is concerned merely with inferences, i.e., with the subordination of more specific concepts under more general ones. In the former case Herr Kant calls its use *real*, and in the latter *logical*. The real use [of reason] seems to be especially proper to metaphysics, whereas the logical use is common to all sciences, because every cognition that we have of any thing can be viewed either as contained under a more general one or as opposed to it, and must be viewed in this way if it is to be more than a merely intuitive cognition and if we want to make progress with a more precise determination of its makeup. If the objects to which this logical use of reason is applied are constituted such that we obtain them by means of the senses, the result of cognition still does not cease to be sensible, even though reason helped us to [attain] it. For what shows us to which class our cognition belongs is its origin, and not the way in which it is treated. For that reason [42] the real use of reason, which is pure rational cognition in the strictest sense, does not have objects that are derived from a sensible source as its object at all, but rather only those on which reason itself bestowed their original existence.

[...]

[44] You have now seen how different sensible and rational cognitions are from each other. I have shown you that, since in the former case the

---

[16] See A89–A90/B122 (Transcendental Deduction).

matter, whose precise determination depends on the determination of form, is not external objects themselves, but rather their impressions on our senses, or the change that they bring about in our state, and consequently must be diverse in different subjects, the result will never express something purely objective. By contrast, in the latter case there is nothing subjective in the matter, for which reason in rational cognitions the subjective [part] of the form must collapse into what is objective, and every result must also be objectively necessary. We now need to consider specifically [45] *both kinds of forms* in order to cognize in what way they must be applied so that we obtain the concept of the world as a result.

I trust myself to assert, with Herr Kant, that the form of our sensible cognition consists in the concepts *space* and *time,* and that they have their origin neither in experience nor through abstraction from other concepts, further, that they neither are themselves universal concepts under which other, more specific concepts are contained, nor have their intrinsic reality such that they can be thought without all remaining concepts, but rather that they reside in the soul as conditions that are prescribed to it for the representation of sensible objects by the highest wisdom such that such a representation is thoroughly impossible for it without it being the case that the soul combines it with these two concepts and determines the objects according to them. [...]

[46] Since it is now clear that we can sensibly represent to ourselves no external objects, unless we think of them as next to each other or as occurring in succession, that is, that we insert them into the concept of time, the [47] concept of time itself will also be no abstraction from sensible cognition, because we must already be in possession of it if we are to be capable of sensible cognition, which is precisely contrary to the nature of the act of abstraction.[17] Accordingly, we should view the Wolffian definition of time, that it be *the order of successive things,* not as a real definition of the way in which we obtain this concept, but rather as a mere nominal definition. For *succession* means in fact nothing other than being actual at different times, and hence the concept of time must already be presupposed if we want to comprehend the explanation of it. Similarly, *being simultaneous* is nothing other than being present at one and the same moment of time, and we cannot in turn bring this into the explanation as a criterion of time without going in a circle. You see quite distinctly that, if we hope to obtain the true nature of this concept, one

---

[17] Compare these next few sections with A30/B46ff. (Transcendental Aesthetic).

should certainly not begin with [48] external objects, the cognition of which is the ground of the precise determination of the concept of time found within us, instead of it being presupposed by the latter.

[...]

[54] Above I mentioned to you the deficiency of the definition of time, which is unavoidable if one explains time by means of the order of successive things. I add the following observation, [55] which seems to me to be of considerable importance. If any determination is abstracted from a thing and is viewed separately, a concept emerges that has greater scope than the subject in which it had inhered, because in that case other subjects fall under it as well that, in light of all remaining determinations besides this one, can be different from the previous [subject]. One knows that all of our inferences of reason are based on this, because everything that one necessarily finds in this abstracted concept applies with the greatest certainty to both the object from which it was abstracted and all remaining objects of which it is a predicate. However, in light of the universal validity [of such a concept] one should not neglect the following difference. Either the determination is grounded in the essence of the thing from which it was abstracted, or one does not have insight into its necessary connection, in which case induction teaches us only that it is found in different things of the same kind. In the first case, [56] after abstraction it becomes a universal concept that has greater scope than does the prior concept of objects, because it not only extends over all of these, but can also comprehend under itself others in addition to these, for which everything that is claimed with respect to it must hold as well. In the latter case, by contrast, it will be a universal concept too, but one cannot say with certainty that it has greater scope than the entire kind of thing from which it was abstracted, and as long as induction is not such that it completely exhausts the entire kind, then all inferences from the universal concept will extend no further than to the individual objects of which experience has taught us that this determination is connected with it. Let us now turn to its application. If we view the concept of time as something abstracted from external objects, we will not be able to count it [as belonging] to the first class, for this concept cannot be derived at all *a priori* from the essence of external things, [57] and if it were necessarily connected with that essence, then one would have to concede that God, too, could have represented it in no other way than in time. We shall therefore have to count it as being among the second class of abstractions, as a concept that we find bound up with individual changes of bodies. Now because no changes can be

thought in the corporeal world except motions, you see distinctly in that case how variable the laws of motion would have to be, because they are based on the concept of time according to whose constitution they are oriented, although this concept itself is derived from the motions that we have [cognition of] from experience.

According to my account of the concept of time, by contrast, it has its existence not through abstraction, but rather I view it as a condition that has its actuality in the soul, that it must constantly use in sensibly representing changes and that is hence inseparable from sensible representation. Now although the concept does not have [58] greater scope than sensible cognition, it constantly runs parallel to it, and the changes of *sensible* objects must be oriented toward the makeup of that without which it cannot be represented.

[...]

[60] Now since all external objects, as many of them as there are, can be known sensibly only if we represent them to ourselves as next to one another or following upon one another, space and time, the two supports of our entire sensible cognition, constitute at the same time the ground of the connection by means of which everything actual, taken together, becomes a whole that is not, in turn, part of a greater whole.

The question of whether space and time are innate or acquired concepts will be resolved according to the previous account, [61] which is perhaps the only one that can decide the whole notorious quarrel over innate truths. The principle of contradiction as well as the remaining principles of reason that are capable of no further proof, are indisputably of such a nature that they cannot be abstracted from the objects that are present, for to treat them and abstract from them, the use of reason itself is already required, which necessarily presupposes these principles. They also cannot be innate in the soul as determinate, because they in fact first occur only when actual objects are given to which they can be applied, just as every form contains something determinate only insofar as matter is present, to which it is fitted. As form, they are therefore necessary laws, which are indispensable to the soul in judging truth and falsity in the objects; however, as soon as one wants to view them *a priori* as innate in the soul, and attribute to them a determinate, objective reality, without looking to [62] objects, for whose cognition they are really only the conditions, then one is necessarily drawn into countless complexities, and the objections which Locke raised against innate truths are in that case irresistible.

Just as these are principles of the soul in light of its pure rational cognition, so [too] space and time are [principles] in light of cognitions that take the senses as their origin either immediately or mediately. If they were determinate innate concepts, then they would have an absolute reality in the soul that would have to precede sensible cognition; and if they had their existence in the external objects themselves, then one would already have to have a previous cognition of them to be able to abstract space and time from them; that is, we would have to be able to represent sensible objects to ourselves without thinking of them somewhere and at some time. Now since both are directly contrary to experience, only the one case remains of viewing space and time as concepts that are, though innate [63] in the soul, merely present in it as forms that are only completely determined when they are applied to objects of sensible cognition.

The soul will therefore be related to both, to the principles of pure reason as well as to space and time, neither as a *blank* nor as an *imprinted* slate, but rather, as Leibniz holds on another occasion, as a tablet on which is drawn the outline of a picture that is to be sketched on it, to which the objects of cognition that actually constitute the picture must be made to fit. However, you should not overlook this distinction [namely] that since the pure cognitions of reason have external objects as their immediate object, whose objective designation coincides with the one that is found in the soul in order to receive them, and nothing is for that reason subjectively true that is not objectively necessary, the immediate object [64] of our sensible cognition, by contrast, is our changed state that is brought about through sensible impression, and not the external object itself, from which these impressions stems. For this reason the subjective designation in the soul will also be identical with the objective designation insofar as it refers to its immediate object, namely, to sensible impressions, or the changed state [of the subject]; with respect to external things themselves, however, it can decide nothing, because the impressions of a single object can take on very different forms in different subjects.

Therefore when I claim, along with Herr Kant, that space and time are nothing real, I am merely denying their objective reality, but this should in no way be understood to hold for subjective reality, because they do not in fact relate to the impressions of external objects otherwise than the pure truths of reason do to the external objects themselves, and no one will likely call into doubt that these have a reality in the soul. You see now completely [65] distinctly the important point in which my explanation of these concepts is different from Wolff's.[18] If space is the *order of things existing next to each other* and time the *order of successive things,* they are nothing but relations, and indeed relations that are merely ideal and are grounded nowhere in our representation. However, if they are necessary conditions of sensible cognitions in our soul, then they admittedly remain similarly something only subjective, but not mere *idealia,* but rather realities grounded in the essence of our soul. However, when I deny them external validity, then this brings along with it the nature of the relation. Objective reality is absolutely not a predicate that can be attributed to any arbitrary relation. For since in every relation two or more things that are being compared with each other must be present, the result that arises from this comparison (which in algebra one calls the exponent) must necessarily be grounded either in one of these things that are being compared or [66] in both taken together. In the first case the result would have to be present even if this thing in which the relation is grounded were there all by itself, provided also that the other completely lost its existence or would at least not be taken into consideration at all; however, it is evident that this is precisely contrary to the nature of a relation, which consists merely in the comparison of two things. In the latter case, by contrast, the result cannot possibly be a simple predicate. Therefore, for any relation some subject must necessarily be presupposed that compares these objects with each other and actually highlights a simple result from among the differences that it perceives in the effects of both. Every relation can in turn either be so constituted that the ground of the result is contained in one of the two things that are to be compared with each other, as something positive, which, however, cannot be represented by us other than as a ground, unless we view it in relation to the other thing [67] as, e.g., the relation of an efficient cause to its effect, where a force is necessarily contained in the former as an absolute determination – only we cannot conceive of it as a force, unless we also represent a passive object on which it expresses its effect. Or it [i.e., the relation] is such that the ground of the result is not contained as a positive determination in either of the things to be compared, but rather depends merely on the representation of the subject that, so to speak, receives the effects of both and compares them with each other as, e.g., the relation of *larger* and *smaller, more* and *less composed,* etc. And hence the important difference between *real* and

---

[18] Compare this discussion of space and relations with that in the Amphiboly (A260/B316ff.). It is also relevant to the Transcendental Aesthetic.

ideal subjective concepts arises. Both presuppose a subject, but only the former are actually contained in the object as proper determinations and require the existence of a subject only when they are to be viewed as the grounds of a relation. By contrast, the latter do not inhere in the object in any way, [68] but rather are only actual as relations and can for that reason be sought only in a subjective representation.

When we apply this observation to the material in front of us, the great difference between the Wolffian and Kantian explanation of space and time becomes even clearer. If space and time are necessary principles in our soul, they have an objective reality in it, and an omniscient mind that represents the soul with all of its predicates must at the same time cognize these laws that inhere in it as objective determinations. However, because we cannot think them except in relation to sensible objects, they are subjective concepts such as have a subjective reality. However, if they are, according to Wolff, merely *the order of external things,* then they must necessarily belong to that kind of subjective concept that must be merely ideal relations, because they can be grounded as proper determinations neither in one of the two objects that are to be compared nor in both [69] at the same time.

I have shown you that relations that are merely ideal, and have their reality only in the representation of a subject, are possible. Perhaps the following observation, if you deem it worthy of some attention, will even convince you that such relations must necessarily be present. The acute Lambert shows very distinctly that our judging, inferring, and all laws of thinking in general merely show us the way that we have to take to get from one concept to another as the objects of our thinking. They concern, therefore, only the form that takes place between the concepts, which must, however, themselves necessarily be presupposed as true if we want to be assured not only that we have taken the correct path, but also that the result that ensues agrees [70] with the truth. As long as we are not convinced that the matter that is given to us contains nothing contradictory in itself, we can never raise a justified claim to the truth of the inferred result by means solely of the most rational treatment thereof. The practice of refuting one's opponent, which logicians call a *deductio ad absurdum,* where on the basis of a false premise that he assumes as true and by means of a series of inferences one ultimately forces on him a proposition whose falsity is readily apparent, [that practice] proves distinctly that we can be led by the most proper rational inferences from error to error as well as from truth to truth. The form of both is completely the same, and the difference lies only in the matter to which it is applied. Now since the truth and falsity of a concept depends only on the fact that its determinations can subsist with or contradict each other, we are also only assured of its truth and of the concept we derive [71] from it when we have dissected it until its components are no longer capable of further contradiction, that is, [not] until we have obtained concepts that are not in turn gathered from various determinations, but rather are simple and have only themselves as signs. As long as our analysis has not gotten down to simple components, we have no guarantee that the concept does not contain yet more unknown determinations that cancel each other out and thereby make the concept impossible.

However far we may carry out our analysis of a concept, we can certainly never obtain such simple concepts in which not even different relations could take place. Even simplicity, conceivability, and degrees of intensive magnitudes are qualities that supply material for countless comparisons of a simple concept with our cognition or with other concepts of a similar kind. Now if these relations were contained in the [72] concepts themselves independently of all representation, then they would constitute special determinations as something positive in them, and since we, consequently, could never completely come to an end with our analysis in this way, we would have to relinquish completely the total conviction of the truth of a sentence brought about by reason, because concepts are certainly always presupposed of whose truth we can in no way be assured at the start. In fact, however, the relations mentioned above, which take place with simple concepts, are only ideal, are grounded merely in the subjective representation of whoever compares the simple property of a simple concept in different ways with others, and do not, for this reason, constitute special determinations in the concept itself that could contribute anything to its impossibility.

If I have tired you, dearest friend, with numerous subtleties, you should attribute this merely to the nature of the subject matter in front of us. The study of [73] relations is so complicated that it has been sorted out properly only by very few. Nevertheless these are of such importance that the understanding and misunderstanding of their true nature has as a consequence truths and errors that have no small influence on the happiness of humankind. According to my previous observation, if one had never let this truth out of one's sight [namely] that every relation presupposes some subject or other in the representation of which two or more objects are compared with each other and deliver a simple result, then one would become acutely aware that the subject that undertakes the comparison would necessarily have to be a simple substance.[19] For if it did itself in turn consist in different parts of which each one were capable only of receiving a simple effect or of having a part of a whole representation, then in the representation of a relation one would have to assume in turn another subject in which the individual representations of these different parts of the first subject coincide and constitute [74] a single representation if a result is to arise that cannot be grounded in those representations that are themselves now the objects that were compared with each other by the second subject. One may push this subject off as far as one likes, but we must ultimately arrive at a simple being that is in a position to represent different objects at once and to bring about a single result through their comparison. Therefore one would have been able to establish with less effort and greater ease the error of those who believe that thought is a property that God could have bestowed on matter no less than he could have on the soul, insofar as we do not even have to call upon the pure truths of reason, but rather even the perception of a single sensible relation proves to us sufficiently that there must be a simple substance in us that is essentially different from the constitution of matter. You know how much one has gained from the materialists when one has gotten to [75] this point with them, and how prepared the transition is, then, to that great and important truth [namely] that the existence *of ourselves* does not end at the same time with the dissolution of our body.[20]

[...]

[79] I believe that I have presented you with the different constitutions of our sensible and pure rational cognition and the different influences that they have when applied to the concept of a world from a more illuminating perspective than you have perhaps observed up to now. However, I flatter myself that I have shown you no unpleasant service if, before concluding this observation, I draw your attention to several remarks that Herr Kant touches on [80] only in passing, but that doubly illuminate the profundity that is, according to the judgment of our greatest minds, proper to this man in all of his writings, and that open up a perspective to philosophers that nearly borders on the sublime.

According to the preceding observation, the unity of the world depends on the reciprocal interaction of substances that constitute the elements of the world, and this [interaction] depends on what is common

---

[19] See A351–A361 (Second Paralogism).

[20] Herz adds a lengthy discussion of this topic in an appendix, a portion of which is translated below.

to its ground. This must be no less true for our soul as an element of the world. It will be able to express its proper efficacy [*Wirksamkeit*], which consists in representing itself as well as all remaining parts of the world, only to the extent that an infinite power is present to it along with all external things, [an infinite power] that is their common cause, due to whose unity alone it is possible that what follows can act on each other reciprocally and constitute a whole. Now since space is the condition under which the soul, by means of the sensible cognitive faculty, may represent that as a whole [81] which is objectively a real whole through reciprocal activity, this concept necessarily presupposes an objective connection. The possibility of different places, that is, of the relations of substances to each other insofar as they can be sensibly cognized, occurs therefore only because objectively the universal cause is internally present to the substances that are, due to their reciprocal dependency, combined with each other and transformed into a real whole. For that reason, according to Herr Kant space would be omnipresence in appearance (*omnipraesentia phaenomenon*), i.e., omnipresence, viewed as a phenomenon, yields infinite space.

The same application can be made for the concept of time. This concept, as a subjective law of our sensible cognition insofar as we represent different states (for it is thoroughly necessary that you not disregard this circumstance, [namely] that although space and time are equally conditions of our sensible [82] representations, the difference between them is that the former is necessary for the intuition of the object itself and the latter is necessary for the representation of its states), presupposes an enduring existence of the object whose determinations succeed one another and change its state. Were there not in everything that changes something constant to which the changing marks are successively attributed, one would say very improperly that the same [thing] *changes,* but rather [one should say] that it would completely cease at each moment and exchange its existence with another.[21] Now if, as can be proven on the basis of other reasons, the duration of a changeable and hence contingent thing is possible only to the extent that it is conserved by a *necessary* and *eternally enduring essence,* the concept of time will also take place only under the condition that some eternal duration is present, that is, so to speak, the foundation of the states that flow from it and that must not be represented in turn through a series of moments, but rather through an [83] intuition as a continuous line. Consequently, time, as

---

[21] See the First Analogy (A182/B224ff.).

opposed to space, will be *eternity in appearance* (*aeternitas phaenomenon*), or the infinite and immutable eternity provides us with the concept of an infinite time within appearance.

Herr Kant, who proceeded on this subtle path with more than philosophical caution, finally takes leave of this observation since he believes with considerable modesty that it is better to keep us in the not at all too spacious realm of our reason than to trespass its limits and, according to the example of one like Malebranche, to let his imagination graze unbridled on mystical pastures. However, I do not believe that you as well as any other philosopher will count this observation as useless speculation, because it appears not only to contain a fruitful seed for the development of the nature of space, time, motion, divine omnipresence, etc., but also can perhaps [84] be a path in all of metaphysics on which one may be able to arrive at many hidden truths very quickly.

If I were permitted to venture a supposition, I would find this idea of space and time to be most similar to the one that Newton had of it, and through a small adjustment that one makes to it they can perhaps be brought completely into agreement. You will be able to recall how often the concept that this great man had of space and that appeared so paradoxical to many philosophers, was the subject matter of our discussions; and I have never been able to convince myself that this great mind should have had as coarse a concept of God as his opponents wanted to foist upon him with his *sensorio communi*. However, one must maintain, with Clark, that when talking about God it is nearly impossible to express oneself properly in any language. And in fact, when the greatness of reason, the strength of mind, and the deep cognition of God's works are the sole guides that lead us to the true and correct cognition of divinity [85] itself, of whom, O dearest friend, has one less reason to suspect such a low and bodily representation of the infinite being than of a Newton, the pride of human reason, whose mind seemed to be so much closer to that state into which we all hope to be placed at one point, than he was elevated above the present state of so many mortals!

[86] SECOND DIVISION

If the method of every science consists in the order in which its propositions are developed from each other and these depend on principles that are specific to each science, after the previous discussion of our sensible and pure rational cognition you will not be able to object in the least that sciences that are concerned with two so very different objects cannot at all be treated according to a single method. The procedure of whoever wants to convince [us] of the beauty of some object is completely identical to that of whoever demonstrates for us the properties of a triangle or of any other such geometrical truth, to the extent that both have our cognition of objects and not the objects themselves as their subject matter. For every step that they take with us, both of them depend on [87] necessary laws that reside in our soul to which they attempt to accommodate their results. For this reason when the former adds nothing else to the impressions that we have received from external objects through the senses (which constitute the matter in our cognition), but rather, by dissecting it into the clearest [elements], laying it open to observation from all sides, and not letting the smallest of their relations to each other escape our attention, shows us that they are in agreement with the eternal laws that reside in all of us, he has completed his task. And when the latter develops for us from an arbitrarily formed idea countless others that we must have thought along with it on account of the intuitive principles of space, he has likewise completed his task. [...] [88] Unconcerned with the external reality of things both of them bestow the greatest certainty on their doctrines by basing them on the eternal laws of our cognition and view *us* alone as the world in which their objects may have reality. By contrast, we would thank only half-heartedly whoever established, e.g., the existence of God or the immortality of the soul in no other way than as agrees with the basic laws of *our* cognition, as long as these basic laws are not such that external things must agree with them independently of all representation as well. We want to be convinced that a god must necessarily exist, not that it is necessary for us to think him; that our soul is incapable of mortality *according to its nature,* not that it *appears this way to us.*

From this observation arises the important difference between the two main sciences to the extent to which the synthetic or analytic method is specific to them. The former occurs in the [89] doctrine of magnitudes, for since an arbitrary idea is assumed in it and a plurality of other ideas contained in it are gradually developed, with every step forward it actually extends its scope and our cognition of it is increased through synthesis to the same degree. For that reason one can always start with the definition of a concept in order to derive the remaining theorems from it without having to be concerned about their correctness; because the explanations are arbitrary, they also cannot be false. In philosophy, however, where every object must be present along with everything that can be cognized in it, we can obtain cognition only by dissecting what is contained in it by means of analysis, and climbing from the particular to the universal. Therefore, definitions cannot be the beginning, but rather must be the end of it, as the results of our entire cognition.[22]

[90] In all sciences whose principles are given by experience or can be intuitively cognized from such concepts that contain the form of sensible cognition, as, e.g., the concepts of space, time, and number, all *a priori* investigations into the method that is specifically proper to each one of them is completely superfluous, for since the principles, as intuitive cognition, already have the greatest certainty in and of themselves, they can be subject to no errors, and the use of reason in this case is merely logical, by more specific concepts being subordinated to more general ones and the properties of the one being derived from the constitution of the other by means of the principle of contradiction. Thereupon, for that reason one first abstracts the method that best agrees with the science after it has already matured. Only in metaphysics, in which the use of reason is real and whose first concepts and principles themselves are given through pure reason, the way in which our reason proceeds must first be investigated and properly [91] taken apart if one wants to take a secure step in the science itself. The laws that logic prescribes for us presuppose without investigation the principles as the standpoint from which reason takes its course, and for that reason they are equally valid of all disciplines, but a science in which the principles themselves are to be developed must to that extent have a method completely specific and proper to it, since its object is essentially different from the object of every other science.

My purpose here is not to dissect a matter of such importance. I am all-too cognizant of the insufficiency of my powers to dare to strike out brazenly on a path on which I discover so few previous footprints. I will simply point out to you several propositions that have mistakenly been carried over from our sensible cognition to the cognition of pure reason, from which numerous difficulties and errors can be derived that one finds spread out liberally in many systems, and [92] I will, in turn, contrast these sentences with others that can serve as rules in this process for very different kinds of cognition in order at least to avoid this deceptive fallacy that has the most important consequences in all of philosophy.

In every judgment a predicate is a mark of the subject and for that reason a condition without which the subject cannot occur in any way.

---

[22] See the Discipline of Pure Reason in Dogmatic Use (A712/B74off.).

I do not utilize the expression that Herr Kant uses somewhere,[23] that the predicate is an *epistemic ground of the subject*, because, in my opinion, no epistemic ground can have greater extension than the thing that is supposed to be cognized through it, so that one can in all cases safely infer the existence of this wherever one encounters it. But it is completely different with propositions [*Sätzen*]. Every predicate has greater extension than the subject, or rather its extension is not determinate at all, and there can therefore be cases where the predicate is present, and yet the subject is still deficient – a circumstance [93] that is diametrically opposed to the nature of an epistemic ground. [...] If, however, the predicate is viewed as a condition, it must immediately be conceded that it can also have a greater extension than the subject. For if it is the condition of the subject, it already follows immediately that the predicate, as condition, must always be present where the subject is present as the [94] conditioned object, but by no means the reverse.

According to this presupposition I propose the following universal rule: *Every predicate must be of the same kind as the subject whose condition it is, and if they are different from each other in their nature, the condition obtains only insofar as the subject is viewed in the makeup of the predicate.* This, dearest friend, is the main rule whose violation I take to be the mother of uncountably many errors that one is subject to in metaphysics and especially in the development of its principles. [...]

[103] [This mistake is made by Crusius when he asserts that everything that is, must exist somewhere and at some time. However, there are further aspects of Crusius that require clarification.] Crusians place the supreme *principium* of possibility in what can be thought, and three further propositions are subordinated to it, namely, the principle of contradiction, the principle of the inseparable, and the principle of the uncombinable. Therefore, the principle of contradiction does not exhaust entirely the impossible; rather, there can also be things in which nothing contradictory can be found that, however, are nonetheless impossible, merely because *we* cannot think them, for it is agreed once and for all that everything incomprehensible to *us* is also not intrinsically possible, unless, as Herr Crusius carefully adds, a revelation or a duty commands us that it should still be held to be possible. Because, however, the conceivable is offered as the supreme criterion of possibility, and one will undoubtedly not be satisfied with that, but [104] rather will ask yet further: "What is the criterion of the *conceivable?*" or: "What

---

[23] See *Inaugural Dissertation* (2:411).

is, in that case, properly conceivable and what not?," Herr Crusius is forced to take refuge in sensation or an internal drive [*Trieb*], and thus this latter [criterion] is, in the end, the most supreme arbiter that passes judgment about possibility and impossibility, and how arbitrary it must appear to undertake investigations about truth and falsity, since we must in each individual case approach our sensation and interrogate it concerning how external objects are supposed to be situated.

You see, dear friend, how little more is required in the way of principles to construct individual doctrines on it that are precisely opposed to the true laws of the understanding. Granted that one is supposed to investigate the existence of the soul, the Crusian infers, according to his principles, in the following way: "The existence of a thing and its presence in space are two concepts that our sensations combine together. Now because we cannot separate them and it is not opposed to any explicit command [105] or duty not to separate them from each other, the principle of the inseparable teaches us that existence without any space cannot take place. Further, our internal sensations want to have existence and time combined. Therefore, according to the principle of the inseparable, God cannot be present if he is not in time." [...] I proceed now to present to you the rules that one should follow in the *method of metaphysics*.

The first rule is: *The principles of our sensible cognition may never transgress its boundaries and be conflated with those that are prescribed to our pure rational cognition.* This is clear all by itself, as soon as one distinguishes properly between what is objective in an object and what is subjective [106] and compares them, as I showed you above, as something universal and something particular.

The second rule is: *If something that stands under the condition of space and time is affirmed or denied of any concept of reason, the judgment can never be expressed objectively, but is rather true only insofar as the subject becomes an object of sensible cognition.*

[...]

[111] As far as the false consequences that arise from this mistaken principle [i.e., that everything is possible only under the conditions that make cognition of it possible] with respect to the constitution of things, I refer you to most of the propositions that Herr Crusius derives from his *principle of the inseparable*, several of which I have already presented to you [112] above. It is as clear as the light of day that as soon as one does not recognize the principle of contradiction as the sole criterion of possibility, and leaves it to our sensation or a certain I know not what

to decide truth and falsity, then one must also view everything separate that can be represented in our sensations none other than in a certain way, as an objective impossibility.

Herr Kant adds to this kind of fallacious proposition the following, that *everything impossible cannot be a and not-a simultaneously,* and consequently, *that in which not-a and a are present simultaneously, is possible.* I must admit, dearest friend, that although I am completely of his opinion about the falsity of this proposition, I nevertheless depart from him with respect to the kind of prejudices to which he thinks this one belongs. Herr Kant maintains that the concept of time is necessary for the principle of contradiction.[24] A and *not-a,* he says, contradict each other only if they exist at *one* time, but they can certainly take place at different times. [113] Therefore, since a concept of sensible cognition must be combined with the concept of contradiction, it [i.e., this proposition] belongs to this class and consequently, according to the rule that has been established, if it constitutes the predicate in a judgment, it can have only subjective validity for the subject. However, it does not appear that the concept of time is completely necessary for the principle of contradiction if it is expressed in the following way: *No subject a can be not-a.* At the same time, it is no less universal in this form than in any other, for if one wanted to object, say, that a subject *a* could certainly become *not-a* at another time, one must keep in mind that the subject in that case is no longer *a,* but rather an entirely different one, and the proposition: No *a* can be *not-a,* does not suffer the least restriction.

Now if it is beyond all doubt that in the proposition: *No a is not-a,* where one of the contradictory concepts constitutes the subject, then the concept of time is not at all contained in it, because if *not-a* takes place, it never occurs in the subject *a.* Thus it is also undeniable that [114] the proposition: "*Not-a* cannot be ascribed to a subject to which *a* is ascribed," has unrestricted validity and can do entirely without the concept of time. For if the determination *a* ceases and leaves its place in the subject for the *not-a,* the *not-a* does not thereby become a predicate of a subject in which *a* inheres as a determination. Therefore if it is said in metaphysics that nothing is *a* and *not-a,* this proposition expresses nothing more than that *not-a* cannot be attributed to a subject that has *a* as a mark and vice versa, and the condition *simultaneous* (*simul*), which one commonly finds added to this principle in textbooks is completely superfluous. If we assert, consequently, of a square circle,

---

[24] See B191–B192/A152–A153.

e.g., that it cannot be, because it contains something contradictory, the *can-be* cannot be viewed as a special predicate that is denied of its subject, the square circle, because in that case one would really have to assume one subject with two contradictory determinations. [115] Rather, it expresses that no square can be attributed to a circle, or that no circle can be thought of as square. You see now that the principle of contradiction is an entirely pure concept of reason and we will not be able to count the mistaken uses of it as one of the prejudices according to which a condition of sensible cognition is taken to be an objective condition of external things.

Similarly, you must concede to me that the proposition "Everything impossible contains a contradiction," is false as soon as you consider the following. First, I claim that one cannot establish *a priori* the impossibility that something can not be possible, even though it contains nothing contradictory. For if one wanted to prove this, one would have to use, in turn, the principle of contradiction and place the possible in opposition to what is not possible. [...]

[116] Second, one can demonstrate quite rigorously that there is an intuitive impossibility without thereby perceiving something contradictory. To this end, simply take a look at the concept of the necessary, and you will find complete confirmation of what I have claimed.

All philosophers agree it is beyond all doubt that there is no completely contingent thing, but rather that every actual thing presupposes a ground that determines it and in such a way that if it were to be otherwise than it actually is, it would contradict the original ground. From this it follows quite distinctly that since that is necessary whose opposite contradicts something, every actual thing in nature must also be necessary. One says, in fact, [117] that everything is necessary, but because the necessity of contingent things is constituted such that its opposite contradicts an external thing, namely, its ground, metaphysicians call it a hypothetical or rather an extrinsic necessity. However, if we represent such a thing that is not necessary due to an external condition, but rather contains the determination that its opposite contradicts, then we have an internally necessary thing. You will not find it difficult to appreciate why I depart from the usual denominations for both of these kinds of necessities (namely, *hypothetical* and *absolute*) and replace them with external and internal necessity. According to the laws of our understanding we can represent nothing as impossible except for when we conceive of some determination that it contradicts, and because that is necessary whose opposite is impossible, the necessity of each thing will also depend on those determinations with which its opposite is in conflict, i.e., [118] it will be only hypothetical, because it completely ceases, as soon as the necessitating condition has been removed. The difference between both of the conceived kinds of necessity thus does not consist in [the idea] that the former presupposes a hypothesis, whereas the latter does not, but rather merely in [the idea] that the former has the hypothesis outside of itself, while the latter has it internally as a determination.

If the necessitating condition constitutes an internal determination of what is necessary, we are to attend to the following difference. Either it is arbitrarily combined with the subject, or it is itself in turn a necessary determination thereof. In the former case that determination whose opposite contradicts it can still be called necessary only in a very improper sense, since it is so because its opposite removes another such determination that is not necessary as such. In the latter case, where the necessitating condition is itself a necessary determination, the same inference can be applied to it. Either its opposite [119] contradicts an external or an internal condition. In the former case it would, along with everything that is necessary due to it, be only externally necessary, and in the latter case the necessitating conditions would have to be multiplied to infinity. You see, dearest friend, that we can twist and turn as much as we like, but the concept that we have of impossibility accompanies us at every step, and our concept of what is internally necessary can never become complete until we arrive at some absolute determination, i.e., such a determination that is [internally necessary] not because its opposite contradicts some other determination, but rather that is cognized intuitively as necessary. Mathematical truths, which are the model of internal necessity, belong all the same to that kind of internal necessity whose necessitating condition is arbitrarily combined with the thing and are for that reason vastly different from absolute necessity. The necessity that a triangle is half of a parallelogram having the same height and base as it depends, [120] if we pursue the series of inferences that have led us to this truth, on the mere definition of a triangle, i.e., on the combination of the three sides which would not occur if the contrary of this proposition were true. Similarly, the necessity of the proposition that the square of the hypotenuse in a right triangle is equal to the square of its remaining sides is based on the combination of the right angle with a triangle that exactly contradicts the opposite of this proposition. However, if we wanted to go further and investigate what actually renders necessary the combination of the three lines or of the right angle with the triangle, we no longer find any necessitating conditions in the things themselves, but rather these [conditions] must be found externally in the choice of whoever decides to bring about this combination.

It is clear that mathematics requires no greater evidence, for, because it is concerned only with possible things, we are finished with the analysis of conditions as soon as we arrive at [121] definitions, i.e., arbitrary presuppositions. However, if we move on to the realm of actuality and want to demonstrate there the necessity of properties or of the things themselves, it does not depend on how we prefer to combine determinations with each other arbitrarily, [determinations] that are to serve hereafter as necessitating conditions that make other determinations necessary. And since therefore the necessitating conditions in something necessary cannot be pushed off to infinity, the necessity of the existence of God must be conceived of *absolutely*, i.e., the necessity does not occur because its opposite, non-being, is contrary to some determination, but rather because it posits existence per se independently of all conditions. In his exceptional work, which we once read with such great pleasure, Herr Kant attempted to derive the necessity of the divine existence not from the principle of contradiction, but rather from another principle that [122] is no less certain. But with all the praise that this work has received from philosophers, it has not yet, I do not know the cause, enticed any of them to enter onto this charted path. A path that seems to be nearly the only one for the achievement of the most important purpose of man.

Now if the principle of contradiction contains in itself no sensible concept and consequently the principle that *everything that contains no contradiction is possible* cannot be brought under the universal prejudice due to which sensible cognition is conflated with rational cognition, we will have to seek another productive source from which this erroneous principle, along with its consequences, takes its origin. Perhaps I will have success, dearest friend, in discovering it through the following observation. Herr Kant is trying primarily to analyze the difference between sensible and pure rational cognitions. Thus it was enough for him to show that the former has as an object only something [123] subjective and the latter has what is objective about the objects, and to provide the principles that are proper to each according to their different natures. However, I believe that I can claim, with much probability, that there is all-too great of a distance even between the objective behavior of things insofar as it is determined by us according to the laws of pure reason, and what takes place in them independently of our cognition, in order to infer from the former to the latter with confidence in all cases. I base my conjecture on nothing less than the nature of our cognition in general. *Locke* shows clearly that this never extends further than to the properties that are ascribed to it. Every part of our cognition is a judgment in which we attribute some determination to a thing as a predicate to a subject. However, that which constitutes the foundation on which all determinations depend, that is, that to which everything we cognize of it is ascribed, cannot, in turn, [124] be a determination in and for itself, because otherwise it would have to presuppose in turn a subject to which it is attached, but rather it must be such that it can be cognized only intuitively and never through a judgment. Consequently, it ceases to be an object of our cognition, at least as long as we are in our current state and cognize only the surface of things. But when we want to determine the properties of an object, we take those that must necessarily be ascribed to it, and from which all of the rest can be derived with good reason, to be its essence and judge these according to the extent to which they are grounded in or contradict it. Thereupon we transfer with the greatest certainty the results onto the thing itself in which our assumed essence is itself only a predicate. The difference between the true essence of a thing and that which is only taken as such by us will henceforth be so apparent to you that I take it to be superfluous to make it even clearer. [125] But so that we do not conflate them with each other in the future, I will call the former the *real essence* and the latter the *logical essence*. In the parlance of the Crusians the former would be a *subjectum quod* and the latter a *subjectum quo*.

Now since it is possible, indeed even very probable, that the real essence of a thing, viewed in itself, is not indifferent to each property that can be attributed to it, but rather is, according to its internal nature, capable of accepting the one and incapable of the other, without their compatibility with the remaining determinations being able to render a verdict about this, nothing is clearer than that our judgments and inferences, which all underlie the logical essence, and are grounded merely on the correspondence or the conflict of one property with the others, are in no way able to exhaust the entire constitution of the object, but rather leaves much still undecided, which, however, is determined down to the smallest detail by the real essence. I believe one can set forth the following principle as established: "That which is determined by the [126] fundamental determinations of a thing, which we call its logical essence, that is, which is either grounded in them or contradicts them, must similarly either be attributed to the real essence necessarily or cannot [possibly] be one of its predicates; by contrast, what remains undetermined by the logical essence must still be determined exactly in the real essence." You must not conflate this proposition with what is presented in metaphysics, namely, that every actual thing must be determined on all sides. This concerns merely actual things, which must be determined in light of all contradictory predicates, because it is in fact just as contradictory [to say] that neither of the two contradictory predicates be ascribed to one thing as that both should be found in it. However, in light of possible things this proposition decides nothing, and it is not thereby established that if a thing has *a* as a predicate, *not-a* could not have taken its place, unless *not-a* contradicts the essential determinations of the [127] thing. However, according to my previous proposition I believe the real essence itself is able to determine the possibility and impossibility of each predicate without the fundamental determinations so that the highest understanding, which penetrates into the inner-most reaches of things, must intuitively recognize in these [things] which properties can be taken up into in them and which are incapable of this, without it first needing to undertake comparisons with the remaining determinations and to judge their agreement with each other according to the principle of contradiction.

We can now easily proceed to apply [this] to our present purpose. The proposition that "everything that contains a contradiction is impossible" is valid for the logical as well as the real essence. For since the former is necessarily contained in the latter, nothing that contradicts it [i.e., the former] can occur in it [i.e., the latter]. However, the converse proposition that "everything impossible must contain a contradiction, and consequently, where one is not found, there is also no impossibility present," can be valid merely for the logical essence, because we have no [128] other criterion for possibility and impossibility, but if this proposition is applied to the real essence and one attempts to impose whatever does not contradict the former, as possible for the latter, one commits a fallacy in any case.

This observation seems not to have eluded the acuity of Herr Crusius, for he does not hold the principle of contradiction to be the universal judge of everything possible and impossible; however, on the other hand, he apparently restricted its scope far too much, since even within the boundaries of *our* cognition, where merely the logical essence is at issue, he adds to it further principles other than the principle of the inseparable and that of the uncombinable, which, however, can be understood only as consequences derived from them.

From this perspective, too, the great difference between mathematical and philosophical evidence is easily seen. The difference between [129] logical and real essence does not occur at all in the doctrine of quantity, which is not concerned with the existence of objects, whose properties it develops. For since its object is an arbitrary idea, it [i.e., the object] arises entirely within the boundaries of our cognition and both essences coincide. For this reason I do not say, in the strictest sense, that *this triangle* is half of a parallelogram that has the same height and base, nor that *this sphere* is two thirds of a cyclinder, but rather the space that is enclosed by three lines and what arises when a semi-circle rotates around its diameter, is etc. Matters are different, however, for the study of the constitution of things. As long as consequences are derived from an assumed definition, that is, from the logical essence of a thing, the philosopher walks in step with the geometer, although this is not yet sufficient for him; it must first be shown, then, that the assumed definition is not merely arbitrary, but is rather the only one that completely agrees with the true constitution of the object. And this is the path that still [130] lies ahead of him, after he has completed this task.

I have dared, my dearest friend, to blaze a path from which you will judge many a system with entirely different eyes than you may have done up until now; [you will so judge] when you see with little effort what influence on all of metaphysics this difference between the laws of pure rational cognition and the objective relations of things must have, if it is, as I suspect, something more than mere speculation, and [when you see] which changes one must undertake in its principles and method, if one ever intends to raise it to the highest level of its perfection. [...]

APPENDIX

[...]

[153]²⁵ *Kant* and *Moses* [Mendelssohn], you who taught me to use my reason, led me, by humane hand, to divine philosophy, and honored me as well with the acquaintance of those you trust, are whom I also have to thank for this kind deed [namely] that all terrible doubts about my future happiness have been entirely banished from my breast. The proof

²⁵ See the Paralogisms of Pure Reason, especially the Second Paralogism (A351ff.).

that leads me to the existence of a soul shows me the flibbertigibbet of a Voltaire and Lamettrie in their true guise and not only allows me to surmise with the highest probability, but [also] convinces me with mathematical certainty, that something simple resides in me whose property it is to think and to will. At all moments I experience that I perceive external objects, compare them among each other, and observe their relations to each other. – I perceive the pleasant odor of a rose, immediately thereafter I also open my sense organs to the fair emanations of a narcissus, both have put my olfactory nerves into a harmonious motion, albeit in different ways; I look into what is farthest within, hold both impressions up against each other, perceive that my state was changed a bit more by the one [154] and a bit less by the other, and look!, it is not my body that perceives this, it is a soul, an immortal soul in me that alone is capable of initiating this comparison of both of my states. For, I repeat it once again, no relation takes place if no subject is present to perceive it. The release of the fleeting parts would certainly have been in the rose as well as in the narcissus even if there never were a perceptive being whose senses would have been touched by it; but this property, that the latter smells more pleasant, [and] places me in a more joyful state than the former, would have to have been lost from them entirely if no perceiving being were present to compare their impressions to each other. But how, of what makeup is this perceiving *I* in me? Perhaps no less corporeal than this machine that comes before my eyes – perhaps the machine itself – perhaps it consists of more delicate parts than these, of parts that indeed escape from our coarse senses, but still are subject to corruption no less than each ethereal mist? There is nothing that I am less concerned about. Even before I compare to each other the different releases of these two flowers, I had the rose alone and my [155] friend had the narcissus, and each breathed a special stream of voluptuousness, but as much as we convinced ourselves of our pleasure, it was still impossible for both of us together to determine which stream affected our irascible nerves more softly, which one did so more mildly. Imagine we had then switched our containers of air [such that] he had the rose and I the narcissus, and we now happily looked at each other, compared both effects, and judged unanimously which one was more refreshing for us. What is the source of this change? This reversal added nothing to both of our impressions, taken together, that was not already in them previously, and yet we are now capable of a new judgment that we were not in a position to make before. Nothing makes better sense, for as soon as one realizes that the expressions "more pleasant" and "more unpleasant," "more refreshing" and "less refreshing" are merely relations between two objects with respect to the changes that they bring about in a state, it is clear that one can make use of them only when both objects act on a single subject that is able to compare its various modified states to each other; but we were not in a position to do this [156] as long as each of us had received only the impression of his own object and could have no representation of the changed state of the other. I apply it now to my own self. If that in me which perceives external objects and compares them to each other were to consist of different parts, e.g., of *a* and *b*, either each part would have to have both representations, of the rose and of the narcissus, or they would have to divide the whole representation among themselves, and *a*, e.g., perceive only the impression of the rose and *b* only the effect of the narcissus. In the first case I would have in me two complete perceiving substances, two souls, of which the one would be completely superfluous; and even if one did not take such eliminability to be enough of a reason to consider the soul not to consist in more than one substance, I can still endorse this opinion without detriment to [the doctrine of the soul's] immortality. For since each part is capable of as much as the whole, taken together, the latter can still be subject to dissection, though each individual piece of me that is left over still does not cease to have representations, to think and to will. And in the latter case, where each part, unaware of the representation of the other, has only its own representations, it is [157] impossible that a judgment could arise in the whole that relates to both of them together, and after I had perceived the effect of the rose and of the narcissus, there would be as little [occasion] for me to indicate a relation between the two of them as my friend and I were able before we switched flowers with each other. Now if I assumed in me yet a third substance, *c*, that, in turn, compared both representations *a* and *b* to each other, the aforementioned inference holds of it, and I may think this through as much as I like, but ultimately I must still arrive at a simple being that is capable of bringing about the amazing appearance of thinking.

Perhaps one arrives at the same result if one proceeds from the other end, namely, from simple representations that cannot be dissected into parts, in order to take place in a composite soul. However, this route does not seem as secure to me as the preceding one, and I view it as superfluous to abandon a proven path and to work through new twists unnecessarily. [...]

FOURTH LETTER: FROM KANT TO HERZ,
FEBRUARY 21, 1772

Noble Sir,
Esteemed friend,

You do me no injustice if you become resentful at my total failure to reply to your letters; but lest you draw any disagreeable conclusions from it, let me appeal to your understanding of my turn of mind. Instead of excuses, I shall give you a brief account of the sorts of things that have occupied my thoughts and that cause me to put off letter-writing in my leisure hours. After your departure from Königsberg I examined once more, in the intervals between my professional duties and my sorely needed relaxation, the project that we had debated, in order to adapt it to the whole of philosophy and the rest of knowledge and in order to understand its extent and limits. I had already previously made considerable progress in the effort to distinguish the sensible from the intellectual in the field of morals and the principles that spring therefrom. I had also long ago outlined, to my tolerable satisfaction, the principles of feeling, taste, and power of judgment, with their effects – the pleasant, the beautiful, and the good – and was then making plans for a work that might perhaps have the title, *The Limits of Sensibility and Reason.* I planned to have it consist of two parts, one theoretical and one practical. The first part would have two sections, (1) general phenomenology and (2) metaphysics, but this only with regard to its nature and method. The second part likewise would have two sections, (1) the universal principles of feeling, taste, and sensuous desire and (2) the first principles of morality. As I thought through the theoretical part, considering its whole scope and the reciprocal relations of all its parts, I noticed that I still lacked something essential, something that in my long metaphysical studies I, as well as others, had failed to consider and which in fact constitutes the key to the whole secret of metaphysics, hitherto still hidden from itself. I asked myself this question: What is the ground of the relation of that in us which we call "representation" to the object? If a representation comprises only the manner in which the subject is affected by the object, then it is easy to see how it is in conformity with this object, namely, as an effect accords with its cause, and it is easy to see how this modification of our mind can *represent* something, that is, have an object. Thus the passive or sensible representations have an understandable relationship to objects, and the principles that are derived from the nature of our soul have an understandable validity for all things insofar as those things are supposed to be objects of the senses. Similarly, if that in us which we call "representation" were active with regard to the object, that is, if the object were itself created by the representation (as when divine cognitions are conceived as the archetypes of things), the conformity of these representations to their objects could also be understood. Thus the possibility of both an *intellectus archetypus* (an intellect whose intuition is itself the ground of things) and an *intellectus ectypus,* an intellect which would derive the data for its logical procedure from the sensible intuition of things, is at least comprehensible. However, our understanding, through its representations, is neither the cause of the object (save in the case of moral ends), nor is the object that cause of our intellectual representations in the real sense (*in sensu reali*). Therefore the pure concepts of the understanding must not be abstracted from sense perceptions, nor must they express the reception of representations through the senses; but though they must have their origin in the nature of the soul, they are neither caused by the object nor do they bring the object itself into being. In my dissertation I was content to explain the nature of intellectual representations in a merely negative way, namely, to state that they were not modifications of the soul brought about by the object. However, I silently passed over the further question of how a representation that refers to an object without being in any way affected by it can be possible. I had said: The sensible representations present things as they appear, the intellectual representations present them as they are. But by what means are these things given to us, if not by the way in which they affect us? And if such intellectual representations depend on our inner activity, whence comes the agreement that they are supposed to have with such objects – the objects that are nevertheless not possibly produced thereby? And the axioms of pure reason concerning these objects – how do they agree with these objects, since the agreement has not been reached with the aid of experience? In mathematics this is possible, because the objects before us are quantities and can be represented as quantities only because it is possible for us to produce their mathematical representations (by taking numerical units a given number of times). Hence the concepts of the quantities can be spontaneous and their principles can be determined *a priori.* But in the case of relationships involving qualities – as to how my understanding may, completely *a priori,* form for itself concepts of things with which concepts the facts should necessarily agree, and as to how my understanding may formulate real principles concerning the possibility of such concepts, with which principles experience must be in exact agreement and which nevertheless are independent of experience – this question, of how the faculty of the understanding achieves this conformity with the things themselves is still left in a state of obscurity.

As I was searching in such ways for the sources of intellectual knowledge, without which one cannot determine the nature and limits of metaphysics, I divided this science into its naturally distinguished parts, and I sought to reduce transcendental philosophy (that is to say, all the concepts belonging to completely pure reason) to a certain number of categories, but not like Aristotle, who, in his ten predicaments, placed them side by side as he found them in a purely chance juxtaposition. On the contrary, I arranged them according to the way they classify themselves by their own nature, following a few fundamental laws of the understanding. Without going into the details here about the whole series of investigations that has continued right down to this last goal, I can say that, so far as my essential purpose is concerned, I have succeeded and that now I am in a position to bring out a critique of pure reason that will deal with the nature of theoretical as well as practical knowledge – insofar as the latter is purely intellectual. Of this, I will first work out the first part, which will deal with the sources of metaphysics, its method and limits. After that, I will work out the pure principles of morality. With respect to the first part, I should be in a position to publish it within three months.

In an intellectual project of such a delicate nature, nothing is more of a hindrance than to be occupied with thoughts that lie outside the field of inquiry. Even though the mind is not always exerting itself, it must still, in its quiet and also in its happy moments, remain uninterruptedly open to any chance suggestion that may present itself. Encouragements and diversions must serve to maintain the mind's powers of flexibility and mobility, whereby it is kept ever in readiness to view the subject matter from other sides and to widen its horizon from a microscopic observation to a general outlook in order that it may see matters from every conceivable position and so that views from one perspective may verify those from another. No other reason than this, my worthy friend, explains my delay in answering your pleasant letters – for you certainly don't want me to write you empty words.

With respect to your discerning and deeply thoughtful little book, several parts have exceeded my expectations. However, for reasons already mentioned, I cannot let myself go into discussing details. [...]

[...] A single letter from *Mendelssohn* or *Lambert* means more to an author in terms of making him reexamine his theories than do ten such opinions from superficial pens. Honest Pastor Schultz, the best philosophical brain I know in this neighborhood, has grasped the points of the system very well; I wish that he might get busy on your little essay, too. According to him, there are two mistaken interpretations of the system lying before him. The first one is that space, instead of being the pure form of sensible appearance, might very well be a true intellectual intuition and thus might be objective. The obvious answer is this: there is a reason why space is claimed not to be objective and thus also not intellectual, namely, if we analyze fully the representation of space, we find in it neither a representation of things (as capable of existing only in space) nor a real connection (which cannot occur without things); that is to say, we have no effects, no relationships to regard as grounds, consequently no real representation of a fact or anything real that inheres in things, and therefore we must conclude that space is nothing objective. The second misunderstanding leads him to an objection that has made me reflect considerably, because it seems to be the most serious objection that can be raised against the system, an objection that seems to occur naturally to everybody, and one that Herr Lambert has raised. It runs like this: Changes are something real (according to the testimony of inner sense). Now, they are possible only if time is presupposed; therefore time is something real that is involved in the determinations of things in themselves. Then I asked myself: Why does one not accept the following parallel argument? Bodies are real (according to the testimony of outer sense). Now, bodies are possible only under the condition of space; therefore space is something objective and real that inheres in the things themselves. The reason lies in the fact that it is obvious, in regard to outer things, that one cannot infer the reality of the object from the reality of the representation, but in the case of inner sense the thinking or the existence of the thought and the existence of my own self are one and the same. The key to this difficulty lies herein. There is no doubt that I should not think my own state under the form of time and that therefore the form of inner sensibility does not give me the appearance of alterations. Now I do not deny that alterations have reality any more than I deny that bodies have reality, though all I mean by that is that something real corresponds to the appearance. I cannot even say that the inner appearance changes, for how would I observe this change if it did not appear to my inner sense? If someone should say that it follows from this that everything in the world is objective and in itself unchangeable, then I would reply: Things are neither changeable nor unchangeable, just as *Baumgarten* states in his *Metaphysics,* §18: "What is absolutely impossible is neither hypothetically possible nor impossible, for it cannot be considered under any condition";[26] similarly here, the things of the world are objectively or in themselves neither in one and the same state at different times nor in different states, for thus understood they are not represented as in time at all. But enough about this. It appears that one doesn't obtain a hearing by stating only negative propositions. One must rebuild on the plot where one has torn down, or at least, if one has disposed of the speculative brainstorm, one must make the understanding's pure insight dogmatically intelligible and delineate its limits. With this I am now occupied, and that is the reason why, often contrary to my own resolve to answer friendly letters, I withhold from such tasks what free time my very frail constitution allows me for contemplation and abandon myself to the drift of my thoughts. So long as you find me so negligent in replying, you should also give up the idea of repaying me and suffer me to go without your letters. Even so, I would count on your constant affection and friendship for me just as you may always remain assured of mine. If you will be satisfied with short answers then you shall have them in the future. Between us the assurance of the honest concern that we have for each other must take the place of formalities. I await your next delightful letter as a sign that you have really forgiven me. And please fill it up with such news as you must have aplenty, living as you do at the very seat of learning, and please excuse my taking the liberty of asking for this. Greet Herr *Mendelssohn* and Herr *Lambert,* likewise Herr *Sultzer,* and convey my apologies to these gentlemen with similar reasons. Do remain forever my friend, just as I am yours,

I. Kant
Königsberg
February 21, 1772

FIFTH LETTER: FROM KANT TO MARCUS HERZ, NOVEMBER 24, 1776

Dear Herr Doctor,
Worthiest friend,

[...]

As a matter of fact I have not given up hopes of accomplishing something in the area in which I am working. People of all sorts have been

---

[26] Kant's rendition of this § of Baumgarten's *Metaphysics* is not a literal translation. See Chapter 3.

criticizing me for the inactivity into which I seem to have fallen for a long time, though actually I have never been busier with systematic and sustained work since the years when you last saw me. I might well hope for some transitory applause by completing the matters I am working on; they pile up as I work on them, as usually happens when one is on to a few fruitful principles. But all these matters are held back by one major object that, like a dam, blocks them, an object with which I hope to make a lasting contribution and which I really think I have in my grasp. Now it needs only finishing up rather than thinking through. After I acquit myself of this task, which I am just now starting to do (after overcoming the final obstacles last summer) I see an open field before me whose cultivation will be pure recreation. I must say it takes persistence to carry out a plan like this unswervingly, for difficulties have often tempted me to work on other, more pleasant topics. I have managed to recover from such faithlessness from time to time partly by overcoming some difficulty that comes along, partly by thinking about the importance of this business. You know that it must be possible to survey the field of pure reason, that is, of judgments that are independent of all empirical principles, since this lies *a priori* in ourselves and need not await any exposure from our experience. What we need in order to indicate the divisions, limits, and the whole content of that field, according to secure principles, and to lay the road marks so that in the future one can know for sure whether one stands on the floor of true reason or on that of sophistry – for this we need a critique, a discipline, a canon, and an architectonic of *pure reason,* a formal science, therefore, that can require nothing of those sciences already at hand and that needs for its foundations an entirely unique technical vocabulary. I do not expect to be finished with this work before Easter and shall use part of next summer for it, to the extent that my incessantly interrupted health will allow me to work. But please do not let this intention arouse any expectations; they are often troublesome and hard to satisfy.

And now, dear friend, I beg of you not to be offended by my negligence in writing, but I hope that you will honor me with news, especially literary, from your region. My most devoted regards to Herr Mendelssohn, and also to Herr Engel, Herr Lambert, and Herr Bode, who greeted me via Dr. Reccard.

Your most devoted servant and friend,

I. Kant

8

Johann August Eberhard

Johann August Eberhard was born in Halberstadt, Lower Saxony, in 1739, the son of a teacher and choral director. After studying theology, philosophy, and classical philology at the University in Halle, he became a tutor for Baron von der Horst's eldest son back in Halberstadt. In 1763 he followed the Baron to Berlin, where he met Moses Mendelssohn, Friedrich Nicolai, and other leading proponents of the Enlightenment. While employed first by the Baron and then as a pastor in Charlottenburg, he wrote two works, in 1772 and 1776, that garnered widespread attention and led to his appointment in 1778 to a professorship of philosophy in Halle, where he remained for the rest of his life, publishing prolifically in philosophy, aesthetics, and theology. In 1786 he was elected an external member of the Academy of Sciences in Berlin, while the theology faculty in Halle awarded him a doctoral degree in 1808 for his theological writings. He died in 1809.

Eberhard's first publication, in 1772, was titled *Die neue Apologie des Sokrates* (The New Apology of Socrates) and supported the Enlightenment cause by criticizing, among other things, the doctrine of the damnation of the heathens, the orthodox Lutheran interpretation of original sin, and the notion of eternal punishment. His next writing, *Allgemeine Theorie des Denkens und Empfindens* (Universal Theory of Thinking and Sensing), was selected by the Academy of Sciences in Berlin as the winner of its annual Prize Essay question in 1776. As a professor in Halle, his rate of publication accelerated, just as the scope of topics he treated increased. Most notable are his *Vorbereitung zur natürlichen Theologie* (Primer on Natural Theology, on which Kant commented extensively; cf. 18:491–606) in 1781, *Theorie der schönen Künste und Wissenschaften* (Theory of Fine Arts and Sciences) in 1783, *Allgemeine Geschichte der Philosophie* (Universal History of Philosophy) in 1788, *Versuch einer allgemeinen-deutschen Synonymik*

(Essay on a Universal German Synonymy) in 1795–1802 (6 vols.), and the *Handbuch der Ästhetik* (Handbook of Aesthetics) in 1803–1805. He also served as the editor of two important, even if relatively short-lived journals: the *Philosophisches Magazin* (Philosophical Magazine) from 1788 to 1792 and the *Philosophisches Archiv* (Philosophical Archive) from 1792 to 1795.

Eberhard's *Universal Theory of Thinking and Sensing* is an attempt at accommodating central elements of the empiricist tradition that was increasingly important in Germany in the 1770s, within an essentially Leibnizian metaphysical and epistemological framework. Thus after arguing for the necessity of a single basic power of representation for simple substances in the first section, Eberhard considers in the long second section the conditions under which this power can be exercised in both thinking and sensation and the laws that it operates according to in each case. In thinking the basic power is active in representing an external unity distinctly according to marks, whereas in sensing it is passive with respect to the plurality it represents confusedly as not distinct from itself, but as occurring next to each other as parts. In the third section Eberhard uses these laws to explain how to develop the understanding and "heart" in light of his account of thinking and sensing. In the fourth section, he provides a brief sketch of how a person's intelligence and moral character are to be evaluated.

Eberhard's importance for Kant's theoretical philosophy is evident in at least two fundamental ways. First, Eberhard's allegation (in an article that he published in one of the journals he edited) that the *Critique of Pure Reason* contained nothing that was not already in Leibniz's philosophy provoked Kant to write *On a Discovery Whereby Any New Critique of Pure Reason is Made Superfluous by an Older One* in 1790, in which he defended his claims to originality. Second, Eberhard's project of reconciling two apparently distinct faculties of thinking and sensing provides important points of comparison and contrast with Kant's own general undertaking in the first *Critique*.[1]

---

[1] In this respect Eberhard's views are similar to Tetens's, who is the subject of Chapter 9.

Contents of Universal Theory of Thinking and Sensing

UNIVERSAL THEORY OF THINKING AND SENSING: A TREATMENT THAT RECEIVED THE PRIZE ANNOUNCED IN THE YEAR 1776 BY THE ROYAL ACADEMY OF SCIENCES IN BERLIN (1776)[2]

[3] INTRODUCTION

Speculative philosophy has long been accused of its investigations being of little use for practical life. The opposition between the science of the schools and that of life has become a saying with respect to philosophy as well. Taking into account that much ignorance and some ill will [4] may have contributed to the contempt of science, one could well have expected more accommodation and willingness on the part of many philosophers to direct their investigations toward the benefit of life. The first and most advantageous step that has been undertaken through recent efforts to draw philosophy down from its ivory tower and to introduce it into human society, has certainly occurred by philosophers becoming better acquainted with the sensations of the human soul and rendering these observations fruitful by combining them [5] with a straightforward and illuminating theory.

For this reason, if one wanted to characterize the most recent speculative philosophy properly, one would look especially to its discoveries in the theory of sensation. By paying some attention to the progress being made in gathering useful doctrines one can quickly see that this theory

---

[2] Translated from Johann August Eberhard, *Allgemeine Theorie des Denkens und Empfindens* (Berlin, 1776).

is a conquest that is to be ascribed to the realm of philosophy. Ancient philosophy concerned itself at most with several attributes of outer sensation, to the extent that it had to deal with them in logic, in the [6] discovery of the sources of certainty. A universal prejudice against the faculty of human sensation caused philosophers of antiquity to neglect the remaining parts of that theory almost entirely. An ancient tradition subjected its changes to the rule of the body, whose origin most of them derived from a hostile principle. This idea is a spring whose waters flowed in a thousand branches almost through the entirety of ancient philosophy, occasioned copious Roman institutions [*tausenderley roman-hafte Einrichtungen*], and is still preserved in our eyes in many adventurous cultural forms, practices, and ways of life among [7] mystics and ascetics. Finally, in the lap of such morals and ways of life, scholastic metaphysics, which drove speculation to a sophistication and subtlety in which these ideas lost their visibility for our practical understanding and were no longer tangible, never allowed itself to be brought down to the level of observation or to the constitution of those mental capacities which it looked down on with proud disdain, under the name of the lower faculties of the soul.

Two events in the history of philosophy provided an occasion to open the way for a better constitution of the theory of sensation. The first was [8] the discovery of the nature of several derivative properties (*qualitates secundariae*) of bodies, namely, of colors. It was noticed that they were not anything actual and independent in things, but rather that as sensible impressions they were perceived in the way in which they appeared through the senses. One thus felt compelled to become better acquainted with this still very foreign part of the human mind and to investigate its nature. If Leibniz thereby had the opportunity to take note of the difference between representations with respect to their clarity and distinctness, and in this way to unlock perspectives [9] on the intellectual and sensible world, that does not diminish the honor of his discovery. He carried what Newton had noted only about the derivative properties of bodies, over to the first and primitive properties, extension, impenetrability, shape, and motion, and thereby led psychology several significant steps further than Locke.

The second event was observations about moral sense that several philosophers were initially directed to in their investigations about the actuality of natural law. They could [10] not progress far along this path without quickly discovering the intimate connection of the fine arts with the moral sciences – noting how the sensitivity [*Empfindlichkeit*] mentioned above drove the soul to a love of beauty, by means of which it inclined toward a love of the good. From then on the fine arts received dignity even in the eyes of the philosopher and a utility that had previously been felt only very dimly. The poet carried the rose of pleasure in his hand, the philosopher showed where it was grown and how one could promote on this field not only the flower of delectation, but also the fruit of utility for further progress and proliferation.

[11] In these investigations they thus noted that certain unconsidered [*unüberlegte*] sensations of the morally good and of the intellectually beautiful were present that harmonized with natural law and the rules of taste. To give a reason for this harmony they had to seek the various universal determinations through which sensing can be brought under a predicament along with thinking. They had to discover the source from which the various appearances of both effects of the soul could be derived so as to sketch the basic outlines of a theory of sensation by means of the *principii reductionis* and several fruitful directive notions [12] (*notiones directrices*). It was therefore the need for a metaphysics of critique and morals that ultimately forced philosophers to dissect inner sensations into their basic materials and to derive them from the simple power of the soul along with the remaining thoughts and sensations.[3]

The fortunate connection in which the study of philosophy and aesthetics has been pursued by several very accomplished recent philosophers has finally brought us closer to the secure prospect of promoting the intellectual and moral formation of man with better success [13] through the impartial and well-ordered processing of all powers of the soul – bestowing vim and vigor to his considerations through the arts of the imagination, attributing propriety, security, scope, and order to his taste and sensation through reflection, and applying both for the animation and direction of his moral powers. It is superfluous to remark that the execution of this plan would reveal the utility of philosophy and aesthetics in their greatest triumph. The Royal Academy of Sciences took a step closer to this execution by calling for a [14] more precise theory of thinking and sensing. It rightly demands that one look to the following three elements, that one namely:

(1) Develop precisely both the basic conditions of this two-fold power of the soul and its universal laws;

---

[3] For Kant's opinion of attempts to explain the various activities of the soul in terms of a fundamental power, see A648/B676ff. (in the Appendix to the Transcendental Dialectic).

(2) Thoroughly investigate how both of these powers of the soul depend on each other reciprocally, and what kind of mutual influence they have on each other;

(3) That one point out the principles according to which one could evaluate [15] how far the mental capacities (genius) and moral disposition (character) of a human being depend on the strength and liveliness, as well as the increase of both powers of the soul, and what kind of relation the latter stand in to each other.

A proper account of the universal principles on the basis of which answers to these three elements of the task could be derived in a satisfactory manner, would provide useful information for psychology, critique, morals, and pedagogy, and shed advantageous light on the [16] investigation of the purpose of the fine arts and their application to the moral development of man, of the grounds of natural law, and on the rules for the evaluation of human character.

[17] First Section

On the Basic Power of the Soul in General

To be able to represent both powers, the power to think and the power to sense, as standing in reciprocal influence, we must seek to understand their relation to the original primitive power of the soul.[4] A common point of unity for both must be indicated in this primitive power, if they are to be reciprocally dependent on each other. Were they to lie separate and isolated in the soul such that the one could not reach the other, interact with it [18] and be penetrated by it, it would be in vain to seek rules through which one could conceive of them as being maintained in reciprocal limitation and have a healthy influence of the one on the other. For this reason if one were to represent the soul as an ever so subtle matter, if one were to assign the power of cognition to one part of the matter and the power of sensation to another part, there would be no intelligible way to explain the possibility that the one might improve and heighten the other. Human beings do not always think and act coherently, they often do not see – perhaps fortunately – the consequences of their own principles, for otherwise the materialists would have to consider it superfluous to animate our cognition through

---

[4] Kant's discussion of a "common root" of understanding and sensibility at A15/B29 (Introduction) is relevant here, as is his (previously mentioned) discussion of powers of the soul at A648ff./B676ff. (in the Appendix to the Transcendental Dialectic).

sensation, and to want to steer our sensation through proper cognition. That intention is consistent only if one assumes the most precise simplicity of the soul.

[19] Assume that this simplicity of the soul is extended to the unity of its power. With respect to the representation of the simple nature of the soul it is not enough if one removes all composition from extension. The highest perfection of a transcendental psychology requires that one also acknowledge the unity of its power and be convinced that the composition of extension follows from the composition of powers. Before philosophy made it this far, it had to resort to making up a special power for every expression of the primitive power that could not be united with other expressions thereof and had to be traced back to one basic source. One could not determine to what number one should restrict these divisions of the soul and under how many denominations of powers one should bring them. The divergence of philosophers' opinions on this is quite natural. If it is consistent with the simplicity of the soul that it be composed of [20] three powers, it can just as easily have, according to several more recent Platonists, seven, or, according to Chrysippus, nine. With time one can excuse the philosophers of antiquity that they took recourse to this not very philosophical proliferation of the soul's powers, since it can be established by way of a rather complete induction that not a single philosophical school, except for Descartes's, came to know the perfect immateriality of the soul, or of any other spirit, including that of the most perfect one.* However, ever since [21] one got to know the essence of the mind better and determined more precisely the essential difference between spiritual and bodily substances, the plurality of the soul's powers was retained only in name among the more thorough group of philosophers, as it was protected by linguistic usage, which was not always taken from the nature of the thing. For only a few have carried over to the issue itself what was a mere way of speaking that cannot subsist with scientific precision. For on closer investigation the result must be established very soon that the plurality of powers in the soul cannot be assumed without some extension therein.

---

* One posited spontaneity as the essence of a spirit, and the lack thereof as the essence of matter. One derived this lack of spontaneity in matter from the heterogeneity of the parts out of which it was composed. One inferred from this heterogeneity the inertia of bodies for external motion, its origination through composition, and its destruction through dissolution. By contrast, the homogeneity of parts renders an extended spirit suitable for spontaneity and incapable of all natural origination and destruction. The doctrine of the simplicity of spiritual substances went no further, even with Plato and Aristotle.

[22] If a primitive power must be that in a thing which contains in itself the sufficient reason of all a thing's accidents, it can be nothing other than a substance. Otherwise, if it were an accident, it would not subsist on its own, but would rather have its subsistence in another, and the accidents would also have to be grounded in this other, the reason of which one had sought in it, but not found sufficient, i.e., it would not be a primitive power. Therefore, if a is supposed to be a distinct basic power, b another distinct basic power, c yet another, etc., then a, b, c would each be the source of certain accidents, without being grounded, in turn, in another power, x, in common, [and] therefore they would have to be substances. These powers that exist distinct from each other would therefore be, in the proper sense of the term, parts of the soul that exist externally to each other, for which reason they would necessarily make the soul be extended. It will be shown below that the appearances of both faculties of the soul, which are so dissimilar, [23] can still be explained on the basis of one basic power, and that by comparing them, one arrives at something more general into which they can be resolved such that it becomes the universal sufficient reason from which one can derive all changes and appearances of derivative powers, regardless of how heterogeneous they are. Now if this universal basic power suffices to provide a satisfying reason for all psychological phenomena, it would be very unphilosophical to take refuge in the proliferation of primitive powers, with which one attempted to help oneself in the early days of psychology.

One can give this proof even more support by turning our attention to our consciousness.[5] For we feel that our soul is not only one, but also constantly the same. It belongs to the former that the being that thinks in us is represented as the sole subject of all its changes, of its [24] thinking, sensing, acting, suffering, etc. This cannot happen if it is not one [thing] that contains the ground of all of these indivisible determinations that coalesce in one [thing]. It would be just as impossible if these different determinations were scattered in various subjects without being ultimately gathered together in a single [thing], as it would be if all of these changes of thinking, sensing, etc., ended in different powers that were independent of each other and of one first basic power. Power a would know nothing of what became actual through power b, power b would know nothing of the changes that were brought about by powers a, c, etc., they would therefore not be able to think as one as

---

5 Compare the following with the Transcendental Deduction (A95ff./B129ff.) and the Paralogisms, particularly the Third Paralogism (A361–A366/B408ff.).

long as they were not modifications of one universal basic power x that everything resolved into, that unifies everything, from which everything can be explained, and that, by virtue of being the origin [25] of all changes, becomes the most solid tie in nature through which a thing is one and that can be separated neither by the power of nature nor by that of the almighty.

Relatedly, the soul cannot think of itself as one and the same being throughout the entire duration of its existence without this intimate and essential simplicity of the basic power. The soul cannot remain the I, one and the same person, without the most precise simplicity of its power. For the conservation of the I and of personhood depends simply on the consciousness of its uninterrupted persistence. To cognize this self-identity it must think itself as the subject of all of those changes of which it is conscious up to the present moment of its thinking. For this reason, if, through a displacement that is not without precedent, a human being took himself to be someone other than he was several years before, he would also believe that his present substance [26] has not had the thoughts and sensations or has not undertaken the actions that he had had or had undertaken prior to the point in time of his transformation. Such an incident can be explained in no other way than by positing that in such a soul certain representations have been extinguished in such fashion that the transition from the one state into the other is destroyed and the tie that holds them together is ripped apart completely. For this reason one easily sees that it is merely the consciousness of the continuity in our representations through which our soul recognizes its numerical identity and assures itself that it still persists as the same I or moral individual. It will suffice initially to state only in general why this cannot be maintained without the simplicity of the power in the soul. Namely, it must very quickly find that insofar as different changes in the soul have their origin in different separated powers, consciousness [27] of the universal connection and of the constant flow of these changes cannot take place in the soul. If a change proceeds through one power, that will be an occurrence that is not noticed outside of this power, whereby therefore the universal band that unifies all the soul's representations into one power, and thus the recognition of personal identity, cannot possibly subsist. Now all of this does not agree with universal experience at all. Every human being is conscious that he can hold onto the thought of certain sensations, remember different accompanying circumstances, analyze them into several component parts, and compare those parts with each other, and finally, through reflection, form a distinct representation of his state during the sensation, hold this idea up against the sensation itself, and make sure of its correctness. If [28] this were not the case, it would be pointless to think about a theory of sensations; we would be able neither to make observations of this faculty in the soul nor to compare with experience the doctrines that consideration has brought forth. It is just as typical that our considerations are disturbed by intervening sensations, and therefore the state of thinking is interrupted by a state of sensing; however, also that sensations can, in turn, be weakened, diminished, or directed somewhere else. All of these appearances can easily be explained if the soul is only one single power that, after it has been modified in different ways, expresses itself either as a sensation or as a consideration.

Now, as easy as this explanation is on the presupposition of the complete simplicity of the soul, it is just as impossible if one assumes several distinct powers. For [29] in that case one cannot at all explain how a modification of the soul transitions into another one, and how a state of cognizing can follow a state of sensing, a state of willing can follow a state of deliberating and vice versa. So that the one power can express itself in such a case, it would have to be able to hold another back for that long and stem its expressions; when, later, the mechanism had run its course and completed its role, it would have to impart an impulse to another so that the latter could begin its business in place of the former. One can easily see how poorly one can cope with the explanation of the transition of one modification of the soul into another on this presupposition, and how difficult it becomes to render intelligible in what manner one state or change proceeds from another in a natural way. By contrast, if the soul has only one original power, there is not the least difficulty. Therefore one can [30] justifiably claim that psychology first attained the form of a science by more recent philosophy having sought to trace all changes of the soul back to one primitive power. Why should one now eschew it in this science, when one would have to view it as an imperfection in the doctrine of nature and in all other sciences, if one were forced to assume a new independent principle for each kind of appearance? Instructors of nature will believe that events in the corporeal world can be brought into a completely coherent system only when they can trace all of the apparently different laws and appearances in the corporeal world, on both the large and the small scale, in chemistry, astronomy, vegetation, mineralogy, with magnetic, electric, and cometic matter, back to the laws of a universal driving force, which they intend to discover in the matter of light.

[31] Second Section

On the Original Determinations and Laws of the
Powers of Cognition and Sensation

We must now seek out the basic power of the soul of which the powers of cognition and sensation are modifications, [and] we must distinctly state

(1) under what conditions this basic power appears in the form of cognizing at one time and of sensing at another, and
(2) what laws they follow together as well as each separately, and how these laws can be explained on the basis of the nature of the soul itself.

I

The following will establish that I had to submit in advance the observations on the unity of the power in the soul [32] that were contained in the first section. The effort of convincing one of this unity would hardly have been worth it if what is essential to this power could not itself be determined precisely. This essential [feature] can be nothing other than what is common to all expressions of this power, regardless of how different they are otherwise, that into which they can all be resolved, and on the basis of which an account can be given of all of its determinations. Now if one resolves all of the ever so intricate appearances in the soul into their first components, one must always arrive at representations.* The [33] human soul's primitive power can thus be nothing other than the striving to have representations. These will also infallibly proceed at all times from dissimilar appearances, if we first learn to classify them in the different mixtures in which they typically hide their original form, and to separate these blends into their original materials. What ensues in all such close combinations of several original materials in the corporeal world occurs here as well, namely, that in the intermingling each element in particular is typically lost and a third, completely foreign matter arises in which the original elements can no longer be [34] identified, until one catches a glimpse of them again in their true form through separation.

---

* Just as matter and motive force is what is apparently substantial in bodies, the power of representation is the same in simples. The scientific doctrine of nature proceeds from the former, psychology from the latter. [...]

For objects of a spiritual nature we miss this convenience of following their composition back to the original material. We cannot dissect a sensation into its first fibers or resolve it into its first elements. However, once we have assured ourselves of the main element and can trace it even to a limited extent through various dead ends and in various transformations, we can still provide information about why it must have such a shape with this modification; in this way we have done everything that science can demand of us.

Now precisely that is the case here. That is exactly what matters in this observation, namely, that one demonstrate how two things that appear as different as thinking and sensing can still consist of one original material, [and] how this [35] common original material must be modified such that two seemingly contrasting appearances can result from it. Circumstances arise in the case of sensing that are so unique to it and so distinctive, that after we have derived them from the soul's original power, there can be no difficulty with the remaining ones.

(1) The first appearance that is especially unique to the state of sensing consists in the fact that the soul views itself as passive in sensing, but as active in the state of thinking.[6] To be able to explain this circumstance, we must investigate what must be the case if our soul is to represent itself as active. As long as it finds itself in a state of distinct representations, it is exactly aware of how one representation arose in it from another. It distinguishes from each other every division that lies in front of it on the entire field of its present ideas, [36] and places one foot in front of the other on this field with full awareness so that with each and every new step it retains in view the previous one that led it to the next one. The distinctness of cognition entails that it sees lying in front of it the manifold directions of each concept. It could pursue any one of them, but by taking only one from among the many paths, it is conscious of its arbitrary choice [*Willkühr*], and the feeling of activity depends solely on the feeling of this arbitrary choice.

This allows us to remove several difficulties that arise with regard to the doctrine of the freedom of the will. Why does one say that one is conscious of one's freedom only in a state of distinct representations, even if these representations proceed, just as others do, according to the principle of sufficient reason and determine the will? For no other reason than that we are conscious in that case of our own activity. And we find a way here of uniting the freedom of the [37] will with the connection of

---

[6] See A50ff./B74ff. (Introduction to the Transcendental Logic).

changes in the world. Our free actions have their certainty and necessity insofar as they are well-founded, but we feel our freedom thereby insofar as we have, among distinct representations, most parts of a total representation clearly in front of us and intuit therein the unconditioned and physical contingency of an action. That is how far consciousness extends with a free action. Therefore, since this consciousness does not encompass all of its parts, it is to that extent an appearance that corresponds with the object only in part. By contrast, its moral necessity is visible, which is strengthened by the wise ruler of the world by being connected with punishments.

It is completely otherwise with the state of sensing, whether it be that of outer or [38] inner sensations. If we are conscious of the transition from one idea to another in the case of distinct thinking, and if we feel our own activity by means of this consciousness, this is all entirely lacking for sensing. It is evident with outer sensations that as soon as our sense organ is in an appropriate position to sense an object, it no longer depends on us whether we want to sense it or not. It is apparent here that in the transition from thinking to sensing as well as in the transition from one sensation to another, the intermediary ideas that would allow us to be conscious of this transition are entirely absent. For that occurs with inner sensations, especially when they have a degree of strength and clarity that is fairly considerable. And this circumstance has bestowed the name of [39] passions, affects (from *afficere*), "*Leidenschaften*" in almost all languages that encompass the original philosophy of common human understanding. One can strengthen this opinion by taking note of the circumstance that one cannot change, direct, interrupt, and obscure a sensation on the spot however one likes. Now what the soul judges with regard to external sensations leads it astray with regard to inner sensations. [...]

[45] (2) If we follow the clue provided, it will also be easy to provide an account of the other phenomenon in the case of thinking and sensing, namely, that in thinking the soul views the object with which it is concerned as located outside of itself. By contrast, with the use of the power of sensation it believes that it has to do with its own state.[7] This psychological deception is unavoidable according to the nature of both states. If in a state of distinct thinking I see the objects themselves distinctly, and distinguish their parts properly from each other, this distinctness must also extend to me, the thinking subject. I must

---

[7] See A320/B376–B77.

also distinguish myself, what is thinking, from the objects as what is thought. That is sufficient. Because I think both myself, the subject, and the objects of thought that concern me, as distinct, my soul represents them as external to each other. This must [46] be otherwise in the state of sensing, according to its nature. Since the number and strength of representations in this case that come together in one sensation and coalesce into one central point do not permit the time and freedom for dissecting and distinguishing, I also cannot distinguish myself, as the *subjectum inhaesionis,* from the representations.

By means of this observation a misunderstanding can be avoided that has led to a confusion in morality for a long time. Several philosophers from the Epicurean school, who believed that they could not deny the existence of altruistic sensations in human beings, noticed, in order to derive such a sensation from their principle as well, that we have ourselves as our intention when we satisfy these desires. [...] [47] It can already be enough to cognize that there are sensations that have as their object the well-being of others immediately and that of ourselves mediately, and that one calls the former altruistic, which also have their own special obligation. However, how does it happen that we conflate ourselves with the object in the former case and that we believe that we enjoy ourselves in other cases?

That can be explained completely naturally from the nature of sensations as it was attempted above. As correctly as we distinguish our mediate pleasures, in reflection, from the immediate pleasure external to us, so too, in sensation, both are blended with each other such that they cannot be distinguished. From these premises it also follows yet further: (1) that the more confused a sensation is, the less the sensing substance distinguishes itself from the [48] cause of its sensation. Now since the representations of the state of our body are the most confused, we also represent its changes mostly as in us. This is also the case (2) for the difference between the senses in light of the greater or lesser degree of the distinctness of their representations. The sensing subject distinguishes itself less from the sensation itself with those sensations that we obtain through the sense of smell, taste, and feeling, than it does with those that we receive through hearing and sight, because there is more distinctness in the representations that we obtain through these senses, and for that reason they also provide us with the first materials for intellectual sensations. The greater the liveliness and strength of the altruistic or moral sensations, the more exact is the confusion of our self with the objects. The melding of our own pleasure with [49] those pleasures that are to be caused in others external to us, far from being sufficient to become an objection to human nature, is its greatest honor. The greatest degree of inwardness in this mixture proves nothing other than the greatest degree of liveliness of the sensation of foreign well-being. Blessings to this divine rapture! Blessings to every heart capable of it.

Further, one can determine from this law what sensation represents as subjective and what as objective. The stronger the sensation of a perfection or imperfection is, the more the sensation represents it as subjective. For this reason, with mixed sensations the representation of perfection must be stronger than that of imperfection if it is to remain pleasant. If the representation of imperfection is stronger than that of perfection, the sensation becomes unpleasant. [...]

[54] These remarks are not actually supposed to explain our present psychological tasks themselves. Philosophers who are concerned only with the body in their psychological experiments have not actually done anything if they do not use their observations of bodies as indications of how to pursue the soul itself. And if they are useful to this end, what must proceed from them is that for a sensation according to the different degrees of its strength and liveliness, the correspondingly greater or smaller number of individual representations must be combined in a single One. However, why they should all meld together in a Single One, the reason for that we can find only in the limitation of our soul. This will explain why (1) in the direct ratio of the number of representations and (2) the inverse ratio of time, the sensation must increase in strength and liveliness, and the fire that distinguishes everything around it [55] with its luster, engulfs the other powers of the soul, and leaves it life and activity only for this one sensation. [...] For this reason it happens that we (1) can give no nominal definition of the sensible properties of bodies, but rather must make, e.g., colors knowable through immediate intuition, and (2) can provide no noticeable transition therein from real definitions to the sensible impression that these sensible properties make. [...]

[58] We can now bring the difference between thinking and sensing back to the following main marks. It is obvious that for every limited power thinking can never be completely pure, and that therefore the designation of thinking and sensing is set merely according to the feature that dominates in each state. Now these marks are

(1) In thinking, *unity;* in sensing, *manifoldness* [*Mannichfaltigkeit*].[8]

---

[8] See A107 (in the A-Deduction).

[59] (2) In thinking the manifold are represented *within each other;* in sensing *next to each other.*

(3) Consequently, in thinking as marks, in sensing as parts.

Consequently, the more distinct, the less next to each other; consequently, the more external and next to each other, the more confused. That follows immediately from the mode of efficacy of the outer senses and of bodily motions. In the world all parts are connected to each other in the most perfect way. Therefore, the manifold that is represented as one through a confused representation is a continuum of which our body and its changes are the closest medium through which we intuit the rest of the world and represent the manifold in it. Further, since the motion of all of its elementary parts belongs to the motion of our body, in virtue of the precise bond between body and soul the total motion must not ensue where its partial motion [60] is not depicted in the soul. Therefore, if a representation is supposed to move the will and accordingly the body, it must be put together and confused such that according to the harmony between the soul and the body, all partial perceptions are contained in it unnoticed. Experience agrees with this exactly. For the motion of the faculty of desire and of the body must ensue most rapidly after a strong sensation has occurred.

A power can be measured by the number of accidents grounded in it or by the effects that are possible through it. Therefore, a power of representation can be measured through the sum of the manifold that it can represent all at once. With respect to this manifold, no other difference can arise than either that the one is thought in the other or that they are all thought as external and next to each other. Since every greater degree of power can be thought as the sum of several smaller ones and therefore the greater degree presupposes the smaller one, [61] it is natural that the ideas of genus and species that are formed through analysis must be abstracted from the individual, because our cognition begins with the senses and the senses represent nothing other than individuals. The representations of the senses must for that reason be prior in time[9] to the understanding's concepts, since the law of development intends that the power progresses from the less perfect to the more perfect and since distinctness is certainly a perfection of cognition. [...]

[66] Now if this difference [between thinking and sensing] consists in general, on the one hand, in the number and, on the other hand, in

---

[9] See B1 (B-Introduction).

the clarity of the representations, it follows that both powers must come together in something common and deviate from each other through their peculiarities, and that both what they have in common and what is specific to each must have its consequences.

(1) The first thing that they have in common is that they are possible through representations. Now since the human soul is a power to have representations, they must be mere modifications of this primitive power or, to adhere to the linguistic usage of other philosophers, derivative powers of this primitive power. What was adduced only in general for the simple [67] and limited power of the soul can now be applied more concretely and made fruitful. As a limited power the soul is suited for the expression of this power only to a certain degree, thus either for the combination of a certain number of small representations to a larger main perception, or for the elevation of one single perception to a certain degree of clarity and distinctness. The comparison of degrees of these representations among each other according to its original material would lead us to a mathematics of the soul. However, the selection of the unit of measure will already indicate whether one has reason to hope for such a science. In the comparison of sensations among each other the measuring unit would have to be an unnoticeable representation that will be useless for this purpose precisely because it is unnoticeable and in the comparison of sensations with thoughts we have completely [68] heterogeneous magnitudes that are not at all commensurable with each other.

(2) From the simple and limited power of the soul it also follows: that if the soul is hindered in its operations, it is the soul itself that is hindering itself. [...]

[70] (3) It follows from the limited nature of the soul that it must be able to gather together the manifold individual representations under one main representation if it is to be pleasant to it. The development of this law will lead us to the point where the borders of thinking and sensing [71] coincide. It will indeed be impossible to provide that point in concrete terms. For in nature nothing is cut off and isolated [*insculiret*], the gradations blur amongst themselves unnoticeably, and the words of all human languages indicate only the outermost lines of demarcation of the properties of things, but not at all the unnoticeable nuances of the sensible as well as the intellectual world. We can gradually indicate the noticeable degrees in the force of the simple, and classify things accordingly; we can distinguish obscure, clear, and distinct perceptions abstractly; but what uncountable diversity is not still grasped

under this general expression, obscure, clear, distinct. If the law of continuity requires that each perception must have gone through all of these imperceptible degrees if it is to move from the lower to the higher levels, from the obscure to the clear and from the clear to the distinct; and if we are permitted to apply the [72] laws that experience lets us perceive in the clear field of the soul, to its unfathomable depths, then we must be willing to permit these degrees in obscure perceptions as much as in clear and distinct perceptions.[10] If to this end one assumes only the state of a completely apparent lack of sensation, where the soul seems to have lost its inner and outer consciousness, because no point is illuminated more than any other on the surface of the soul [...], in this state all of our representations seem to be completely balanced, in view of the intensity of their light. Now in this obscure chaos, if any representation becomes attractive to us and clear [such] that our attention grasps it, and [73] separates it from the remaining ones, the following must occur:

(1) This representation that has become clear must proceed through all intermediate degrees from its obscurity up to its clarity just as the rays of light that are brought into a dark room by a light, must run through all the points of the line that are conceivable in all directions in the empty space of the room. As quickly as this might happen, it can still happen only successively; the greater degree of illumination therefore presupposes the lesser ones at all times.

(2) The smaller perceptions that link up with each other for the clarification of a main perception and that constitute its proximate components, no longer need to remain completely in the same degree of obscurity in which they were in the immediately preceding state of the soul. [...] [74] This is precisely the essence of the analysis of representations and for that reason the law of the power of imagination helps us thereby.

(3) To precisely the same degree in which the main perception becomes clear, the degree of obscurity of the remaining ones, which do not belong to this main perception, increases. However, that too occurs only according to the indestructible laws of order. [...]

[77] If we take these two elements, unity and manifoldness, as the ground for the division of all kinds of pleasure, it thereby allows one

---

[10] See the Anticipations of Perception (A165ff./B207ff.). See also B414 for a discussion of clarity and "degrees of consciousness" (in the Refutation of Mendelssohn's Proof of the Persistence of the Soul).

to notice a law of the operation of the soul that [78] I want to provide in advance in order to compare it with the following classification and thereby to create an *a posteriori* proof for it through induction.

This law is: for a limited being in the precise ratio in which the manifold, the warmth and the strength increases in a total representation, the intensity of the unity or the distinctness decreases, and vice versa, or the intensity of the unity is inversely related to the manifoldness and vice versa.

We notice primarily that where the sum of partial representations alone exhausts the power of a given soul, we cannot pay special attention to any part thereof. This state is, in a sense, pleasant to the soul, but it cannot remain so for long. It is pleasant to it insofar as it feels its activity in it, but it cannot occur without a certain exertion, and these two sensations of its activity and exertion, or, which [79] is the same, of its realities and limitations, merge together into One mixed main sensation, but it will make this main sensation pleasant or unpleasant according to whether the sensation of activity or exertion dominates. [...] This unification of the lesser perceptions occurs only through the representation, in that the soul represents the agreement, or that in which they agree, more clearly than their differences. The lowest stage of this unity must therefore arise from the least ground of unification, namely, from the representation of their mere existence next to each other, whether it be in space or time, and the obscurity of their differences. [...]

[93] With sensation therefore a sensible judgment conforms to the different limitations and modifications of the sensing subject, and this law must be an ample source of differences in taste. Depending on whether the soul, according to its ability, collects together more or less parts of the manifold, or finds more or less facility to hold tight to the one or the other parts through its talents and training, its estimation and judgment will occur [94] differently. This is the original source of all of the infinite differences in taste and judgment among human beings.

The good, therefore, can be sensed, and then it appears to us in the form of the beautiful insofar as the sensible [*empfindbare*] expression of proficiency, temperance [*Ebenmaaß*] and propriety will exist. However, the good can also be thought, and that occurs through the analysis and the ascent to the simplest and most general concepts thereof. The more the representation of the good approaches the simple, the more it becomes an object of thought. [...]

[95] Finally, the most perfect unity of all in concepts is created for us by cognition of the true. We attain this unity by analyzing a concept into its marks.[11] The more precisely this analysis occurs, the more fortuitously, in turn, the most correct composition in judgments and propositions can be undertaken later. For to affirm or deny something correctly, one must assure oneself whether a representation is a mark of another. If one views this mark as the higher concept from which, along with its specific difference, the lower one [96] is composed, then it must, according to the principle of contradiction, be the predicate of the latter. One typically proceeds this way in the mathematical sciences, where one abstracts from all other properties of bodies and proceeds from the mere concept of extension. We therefore have the greatest unity here, namely, the identity of the concept itself, which is taken by itself and separated from everything foreign to it. The source of truth cannot lie higher than in this identity; it must be prior to all else in judging – the idea predicated of itself, not yet combined with anything else. And this predicating a representation of itself is so necessary because it is the activity of the understanding itself. In the representation of two contradictory propositions the understanding destroys its own operation by attempting to think the two together.

And therefore the soul's kinds of production follow in descending order from the simplest to the most composite, [97] or from the most distinct thinking to the most confused sensing, as follows:

(1) Pure thinking, or the simplest idea predicated of itself. $A = A$.

(2) As a mark of another idea, $A = A + C - C$.
   This mark can first be cognized in the subject of a proposition through more or less intermediary ideas. The idea of this subject is thereby more or less composite.

(3) The one idea is contained in the other, not as a mark, but as a sufficient ground of a reality that can be thought through it. Since everything actual can become actual only through a power, this gives us the idea of power, and since, further, power is measured by the actions that can be actual through it, it is known in these actions.

---

[11] See Kant's discussion of philosophical method in the Discipline of Pure Reason in Dogmatic Use (A713ff./B741ff.). See also Kant's discussion of the use of the principle of contradiction in cognition (e.g. A150ff./B189ff. – On the Supreme Principle of All Analytic Judgments).

[98] As far as the manifold can be thought in each other, that is therefore as far as the realm of thinking goes. If it is thought as external to each other, we enter the realm of sensing, and the manifold is unified

(4) through similarity,
(5) through proportion,
(6) through continuity.

The laws that the soul follows in thinking are distinguished much better in logical treatises than are those laws in accordance with which sensations act. One can explain this on account of the very understandable reason that with thinking the soul is more conscious of its operations and of the rules that it follows than with sensing. In the state of sensing, it is incapable of reflecting on its changes; as soon as it became capable, the impressions of the sensation would be extinguished. Therefore nothing remains for the soul [to do] except to gather together again in memory the scattered elements of its [99] state of sensing, to observe them in others, and to compose a theory gradually on the basis of these collected observations. One can easily see how complete these observations can be, how precise the memory, how penetrating the observations of others, and how universal the laws abstracted from them. Compared with what I have indicated about the primitive power of the soul up until now, they will certainly lead us in the meantime to several certain and fruitful principles. The more confused and violent the sensation is, the harder it will be to explain its modifications and transitions.

Since the most violent sensation contains the most manifold, the least and most inconsiderable degree of unity will take place with it, and that is the mere existence [of things] next to each other, whether it be in time or space.[12] This is enough to wake one representation through the other, and [100] to blend both with each other. This is how it commonly happens, when the thinking understanding does not instruct the sensation that one representation is thought as the mark of the other. The entire philosophy of the common man, according to which everything that is sensed as [existing] next to each other belongs to each other, and everything that is sensed in succession, is grounded in each other, consists largely of such fraudulent moves. All this is the felt presuppositions of astrology and magic, whose power is inevitably destroyed with the development of concepts.

---

[12] See the Transcendental Aesthetic (A19/B33ff.).

The external determinations of place, time, shape, color, etc., provide sensations with just as unreliable marks when it transitions from one representation to another through the same, or throws them together with what is within. [...]

2

[110] If we are in a position to derive from the concepts provided above concerning the difference between thinking and sensing the laws that we notice, through experience and observation, as being specific to both states, we will be able assure ourselves of the truth of such concepts by way of a kind of psychological test. Since this test must obtain its material from experience, one will never be in a position to undertake induction completely for such laws. New and strange situations in which human beings are thinking and sensing will provide an occasion for new observations that, with time, can be brought under [111] new laws. Therefore, initially it must be enough to have derived the most universal laws from the theory with the help of already made observations and to have classified them such that the new ones can easily be brought under the already properly ordered rubrics.

(1) Insofar as the state of both sensing and thinking contains representations, the replacement of the one state with the other can occur only according to the law of the imagination, or by means of the association of ideas. In the one case, when thinking passes over into sensing, the soul must come upon a partial idea in the flow of its thoughts that awakens all at once a considerable sum of individual representations. These flow together into one sensation that from then on occupies the field of the soul all by itself, and rules that field until, according to the same law, one of the many small partial ideas gains the upper hand with respect to [112] clarity and attracts the soul's attention such that it allows itself to pursue this one over others, to analyze it, to compare its parts and thus to reflect on it. [...]

[115] (2) In the state of thinking, cognition is intuitive, in the state of sensing, it is symbolic. In the former case the representation of the sign is clearer than the representation of the thing, whereas in the other case it is reversed. This phenomenon was easily noticed in experience, and a brief comparison with the nature of the thing derives it from the limitations of the power of representation. One cannot penetrate deeply into an idea otherwise than by holding onto its separated parts by means of signs and assuring oneself of its marks through signs. The further that one proceeds in the analysis, the more the number of deep-seated distinguishing

marks increases, the less, therefore, the soul's power suffices to hold onto the preceding ones in intuition, the more its attention is drawn away from the intuition of the things toward the representation of the signs. Until finally the soul is no longer conscious of anything beyond the signs and proceeds in the deep paths of truth with a blind operation.

[116] This kind of blind operation has been viable so far only in the mathematical sciences, and one has to ascribe it primarily to the application of this method that one has made more progress in the mathematical sciences than in the metaphysical sciences. This circumstance has long ago roused the attention of philosophers. They would very much like to have garnered this convenience for philosophy to the extent that the impossibility of separating metaphysical concepts and of expressing their combinations with signs such that the combination of the notions itself was depicted in the combination, was not culpable for having to place this invention in the same class as the philosopher's stone, the *perpetuum mobile*, etc.

With sensations, by contrast, one sees the thing itself. It is livelier for us when we see it immediately than when we experience it in succession through signs, and then have to take the trouble [117] to put them together as best we can. [...]

[123] (3) Each sensation is connected with a desire and an aversion.

Sensations have this in common with all representations, but just because a large number of obscure and confused representations come together into a unity in each sensation, the desire or aversion that accompanies them must also be larger and more noticeable. Therefore, whatever occurs with all representations on a small scale, also occurs here on a grander scale. [...]

[130] Amidst all of the differences of opinion concerning the combination of the body and the soul, all philosophers still agree that the most precise tie is found between them when the changes of both parts mutually accompany each other without interruption, and that the reason why a soul and a body belong together such that they constitute one human being lies in this correspondence of both of their changes. Those who have considered the consequences of these principles more fully then proceed to extend it down to the smallest moment of each change as well. They say: when the soul represents, by means of the senses, all larger and noticeable changes in the body, will that not also be true of smaller ones? When it [131] feels the piercing of a sword that tears its fibers, will it not also have to represent the ever so subtle motion of each blood globule, every elementary fiber?

The larger motions are to all intents and purposes nothing other than the sum of all smaller ones that are contained in it, just as the motion of fire is nothing other than the motion of all particles constituting the fire. Now if, on the one hand, the body is supposed to be the most complete corporeal automaton and the soul the most complete spiritual automaton, all the larger more noticeable motions should correspond in the former by means of smaller ones; similarly, they must also be represented in the soul by means of corresponding unnoticeable representations, in order to bring about the combination of all changes in one power as well as the most precise tie between the body and soul. Now just as a large, noticeable motion arises from the summation of infinitely many smaller motions in an organic body, [132] so too an infinite number of unnoticeable representations, to each of which some infinitely small motion corresponds, exists in each sensation. One must acknowledge that these [smaller ones] follow the same laws that one notices for the larger ones. This infinite sum of small representations thus also has its infinite sum of small blind incentives that function in the principle of our soul all the more securely and unreachably, the less we come by them immediately and can work against them. As certain and as unavoidable as our inhaling and exhaling, our hunger and thirst are accompanied by such blind representations and are composed of them, and for precisely that reason proceed without interruption and act irrepressibly, the efficacy of all such highly complex and confused sensations is just as secure. It alone therefore must provide the best analysis of the origin of all actions that not only did not arise through a desire [133] of which we are conscious, but also had our express aversion against it. [...]

[135] One could easily bring these remarks closer to the various branches of the moral sciences, if it did not lead us too far off. At least this much is immediately obvious at first sight, namely, that the cultivation of our faculty of sensing is of the greatest importance for us. We thus know what obstacles the exercise of virtue finds in man and how one would need to come to its aid if one wants to establish its principles against the underlying drive for self-preservation and sensual pleasures. As much [136] as its principles may be impressed on our original form, it still first costs the effort of establishing light for ourselves through the fog of sensible impressions in order to change in the sunshine. It made things quite difficult for many a serious moralist that it noticed, as if in a moment of tranquility, how a young uncorrupted mind expired amidst pure heavenly love against its divine form, which, as soon as it

was to come to act, also succumbed to the worst temptation. The same sensibility, still free of guidance from reflection and not yet strengthened by being inculcated in the good, gave in to impressions that found no sufficient counterbalance in those principles that were not yet firmly rooted to sensations. One must thus presuppose among those who stay true to the highest rules of right against corporeal martyrs and the fear of death, nothing less than a state of virtuous enthusiasm [*Schwärmerey*], in which principles [137] have turned into so many and such strong sensations as is needed to retain the constantly ruling state of the love of law in them.

With the help of these remarks one is in a position to say in advance with some certainty which principle someone would decide in accordance with if his heart is divided by a battle of a selfish passion with a moral sensation. If the latter does not immediately determine the decision on the spot, then the former has won everything. The passion has time to find strength through ancillary ideas, which do not remain absent when the soul is occupied for a long time with intuiting an object from all sides; by contrast, the sensation already loses its power by becoming older and having once had to follow the passion. [...]

[138] (4) The state of sensing extinguishes the state of thinking.

That will already be clear enough from the preceding. If the great number of smaller partial representations that come together in a lively sensation occupy the entire attention of the soul, and direct this attention at all times to the largest representation, in order to be able to do that, it will have to make more obscure the less lively ideas that follow individually and especially in succession in the state of thinking. [...]

[140] (1) Thus to put oneself in a position to reflect, no preparation is more rational and more needed than to go to a quiet place and to foster calm within one's inner and outer sensations. [...] [141] For that reason, a dominating passion gets along very poorly with the pursuit of truth; just as every abrupt motion of the soul puts an end to all reflection.

This is a circumstance that makes cognition of the truth incredibly difficult. The most important study that man can undertake is man himself, his inclinations, his passions. The most important observations that he could make regarding himself would be precisely those that he could make regarding his sensations and his passions, about their origin, their similarities, their transformations, growth, and demise; for our entire self-cognition depends mostly on this insofar as it can be useful for our moral formation, for the guidance of our will. And we are not at all in a position to observe ourselves precisely in this state of passion. [...]

[143] (2) According to precisely that law, according to which the state of thinking yields to sensations, weaker sensations are also extinguished in favor of stronger ones. For that reason if one investigates all paths through which a sensation can receive a greater [144] degree of strength, one will know how one should guide the mind from one sensation to another, which is of the greatest importance for the soul's rule. [...]

[149] However, in order to be able to state more precisely how sensations obscure or clarify each other, weaken or strengthen each other, one must pay attention to their specific kinds. I will seek (1) to order together, (2) to trace the appearances that arise in this context back to a few simple laws, and (3) to derive them from the essential limitations of the soul's primitive power. I hope thereby to extend somewhat further the enlightenment in this matter that various recent philosophers have brought about therein.

Sensing is, as was already noted above, originally different from thinking in that with sensing a [150] larger sum of smaller partial representations crowd together into a total representation. These partial representations are woven together into a total representation in such a way that they do not let themselves be differentiated distinctly in any specific way therein, but rather contribute only in an obscure way within the total representation. The limitation of the soul's primitive power is at fault in this. It is precisely from this limitation that one must thus also explain which partial representations are compatible with each other such that they can be melded together in a total representation, and after they have been melded together, it must actually increase its strength. The most general law that the soul follows here can be none other than this:

> Its total sensations are increased by all of those partial sensations that have enough common determinations to be grasped under one main representation, but also enough specific [151] determinations to increase the number of partial sensations in the total sensation.

One can classify sensations accordingly. Those sensations that belong together under the same closest genus and thus have certain determinations in common, are homogeneous, the rest are heterogeneous. The homogeneous ones thus agree with one another regarding certain determinations, and with respect to others they are different. If those with respect to which they are different, differ from each other not merely according to the degree, but also according to their kind, then they are opposed to each other; however, if they are different merely according to degree, then they are related. This classification gives us three kinds of sensations, the homogeneous opposed, the homogeneous related, and the heterogeneous, all of which, after they have been combined in different ways to the whole sensations can also have different effects, either [152] strengthening or weakening each other. For they are combined with each other either merely temporally and spatially, or they flow together in one idea and are thus united. The homogeneous opposed sensations strengthen each other, if they are combined with each other. *Opposita juxta se posita magis elucscunt.* That is the reason why contrast has such a great effect in the fine arts and sciences. Black and white, red and green, next to each other, dissonance and consonance, pain and pleasure when they succeed each other strengthen each other mutually. If they are unified in one idea, they weaken each other. The examples provided prove that. Contrasting sensations, if they flow into one [sensation], must cancel each other mutually.

If homogeneous sensations are related to each other, the effect is the opposite. Here they weaken each other, if [153] they are combined, and strengthen each other if they are united. Two equal degrees of warmth, sensed in combination with each other, incite a stronger sensation of warmth; however, if they succeed each other, the sensation of the latter is weakened by the sensation of the former. This is how it is with one kind of color, sound, pain and pleasure, etc.

All heterogeneous sensations weaken each other mutually, because they destroy each other.

These remarks can easily be compared with the noted universal laws of the strengthening and weakening of sensations among each other, if one combines the law of the relations of sensations among each other with respect to the reason for their strength. As a result of this latter law, a sensation is stronger, (1) the more it represents (2) in a smaller measure of space and time, or [153] this strength is stronger in a direct ratio [*in ratione directe*] to the number of parts and in an inverse ratio [*inversa*] to time and space.

Heterogeneous sensations would have to cancel and weaken each other, as they have nothing in common through which they could be brought together into one sensation, and contrasting homogeneous sensations could not be united, because they likewise destroy each other. By contrast, the related sensations could strengthen each other only if they gain through the reduction in time and space what they lost through the lack of manifold in their parts. [...]

[158] [...] And the following main rules apply:

(1) External sensations weaken internal sensations, and vice versa.
    [...]
[159] (2) Pleasant sensations weaken unpleasant sensations and vice
    versa; only that the sensation that is to win out should also be het-
    erogeneous and have a significant degree of strength, or that sev-
    eral thereof should follow each other until they bring about their
    effect. [...]
[160] (3) Everything that gives strength to a partial sensation, such
    as novelty, something interesting in its content, the speed with
    which it acts, will also give it emphasis, according to the above
    laws, either to strengthen a sensation all the more or to extinguish
    it all the more quickly.

By contrast, the strengthening of a sensation is brought about through
the incitement of other sensations such as are subordinated to the main
sensation and homogeneous with it. The ruling representation obtains
even more clarity and life by having several others be associated with it
that can be united with it in a focal point, and, instead of dispersing the
soul's attention, attract it even more strongly in one direction. For that
reason, [161] in a state of joy the mind is inclined to lose itself in the most
amusing hopes and to overflow with tenderness, friendship, benevolence.
In a state of dejection and despondence, a cheery or lavish music would
be offensive, since a slow, soft, and sad music that is so to speak amalgam-
ated with our main sensation, would leave us with a kind of enjoyment.

Ultimately, the soul does nothing here other than to follow a propensity that becomes all the more powerful and gripping, the more its force
is increased through an added weight.
    [...]

[165] (5) The state of sensing depends only mediately on our freedom.

The feeling of freedom can take place in the soul in no way other than
through the consciousness of spontaneity. However, this consciousness
presupposes that we notice the transition from one state to another, that
we notice how we pursue the one by rejecting and obscuring the other,
that we thus have more of them in front of us where we give ourselves
over to the most striking. This is how we act in a state of distinct thinking,
as we are irresistibly pulled along by the sensation. Therefore we are left

with no room to choose, which requires a calm overview of several representations, among which one can, through a conscientious reinforce-
ment, incline the will in the direction of where calm [166] consideration
takes note of the best. [...]

[167] The next inference from this law is that the more confused a
sensation is in its kind, the less free it will be, the less it will be under
our control. According to the classification of sensations provided above
corporeal sensations must for that reason be harder to rule and to suppress than are the intellectual and the moral sensations. And in fact
we have more power to suppress our anger, our curiosity, our ambi-
tions than our hunger and thirst; granting that these affects can have
a degree of strength for a while, but they can diminish, and over time
cannot withstand the feeling of corporeal needs. Ambition, curiosity,
etc., may paint ever so attractive prospects of future pleasures: *ventre
affamé n'a point d'Oreilles.*[13]

[168] THIRD SECTION

On the Formation of the Understanding and the Heart
through the Power of Cognition and Sensation

The previous observations of the power of cognition and sensation must
have a two-fold use, the one of applying the most suitable mode of formation of the understanding and heart, and the other of simplifying
thereby the judgment of genius and of character, by bringing forward a
certain mode of understanding and disposition [*Gemüthsart*] from the
different mixtures and modifications and from the different mutual
influences, of both powers on each other.

I must immediately recall here at the start that I often take the word
"sensations" in the broadest sense. The French language has the advantage that [169] it can distinguish between "*sensation*" and "*sentiment.*"
It understands by both noticeably clear representations. However, the
former encompasses only external sensations and the felt perfection of
the body. Besides this feeling of the perfection of the body the soul also
feels its own perfection and imperfection: in particular, it feels certain
properties and changes in the objects outside itself as perfect and imperfect. The latter are not immediate objects of the senses, but rather are
abstracted from the sensible sensations and are brought before intuiting
in this new form of the imagination. [...]

---

[13] The hungry stomach has no ears.

[170] *1*

In view of formation the most universal rule is this:

Both powers, that of cognition and of sensation, must be [171] exercised and built up with proper industry.

The correctness of this rule results from the most perfect unity of the basic power of the human soul. With this presupposed, it is self-evident that the entire soul cannot possibly obtain its greatest possible construction and development without the use of all partial powers. The most intimate connection of all of its representations also entails that each proper exercise of the one power must have its salutary influence on the other. However, the limited nature of the soul does not allow that we are obliged to one manner of representation to the neglect of the others without the whole thereby suffering. For that reason one should not think that any partial estimation of a power with the formation thereof that is based on it could be faultless. That will be shown even more clearly when one observes the matter from the following two perspectives.

[172] The proper use of the power of cognition and sensation is needed, first, insofar as both are capacities that require exercise for their development, and second, for the perfection of those kinds of representations that are possible through them.

(1) Through the exclusive production of one kind of representation we must obtain a facility for such representations according to a primitive law in the soul. That holds both with respect to the power itself and for the objects with which it is concerned. One can make oneself both physically and mentally so sensitive, one can acquire such a propensity to introspection, one can, in time, indulge so habitually in pleasant or unpleasant sensations that the soul becomes obedient to such a special propensity alone. Through the disruption of this balance of the soul's facilities, the soul loses the requisite mastery over itself. And this mastery is [173] of the greatest importance for its well-being. In light of the harmonious replacement of its changes the soul does not stand under the undivided rule of a bright and free faculty of reason: if through a disproportionate exercise some power that no opposite force is capable of affecting should become strengthened. For that reason just as a properly induced distraction by the pleasure of company and the enjoyment of scenes of nature, or by the observation of works of art and attention to the products of the imagination can ward off aridity [*Trockenheit*] and apathy, which would otherwise be a consequence of

abstract observations, so too being occupied with serious sciences can lessen the sensitivity to irregular passions. [...]

[174] The unobstructed correct progress of the soul's productions depends in general on the order in its representations. However, this order depends on each kind having the degree of clarity and distinctness that adheres to it. Accordingly, external sensations must have a greater degree of clarity than the images of our fantasy. That is the sole means through which we can distinguish the former from the latter. As soon as the images of the imagination become clearer and livelier than sensible sensations, and this becomes the accustomed state, the soul mixes the external sensations with the imaginings, and that is precisely the state of a deranged person, whom one calls insane, as soon as one sees him act according to such incorrect sensations. The [175] cause of such a sad occurrence can lie in the fact either that sensations have been weakened too much or that the imaginings have been strengthened beyond their proper measure. [...]

[176] In such a miserable state of mind there are intermediary degrees, even if they cannot at all times be noticed externally and cited. At the lowest level of mental disorder they are representations that have obtained a noticeable degree of clarity, that is fervor [*Begeisterung*], or enthusiasm, a state that, if it becomes dominant and habitual, lays the ground for excessive enthusiasm [*Schwärmerey*] or fanaticism. In this state representations become increasingly confused so that the soul easily takes its imaginings to be sensations. However, it does not yet noticeably confuse these with external sensations, at most it takes them to be the effects of a supernatural cause, because it is conscious of neither its connection with external sensations nor with a preceding series of thoughts or sensations. [...]

[180] [...] That is the one side that we must observe in the regular exercise of the soul's powers. The effort of the understanding does indeed have its salutary consequences, even if we do not in all cases find the truth, just as the enterprise of the hunt is useful, even if we do not bag any wild prey, insofar, namely, as bodily exercise has health and strength as consequences. It is the same with all of the soul's powers.

(2) The other side that one can observe with respect to this object are the representations themselves that are possible through both of these powers, the power of cognition [181] and that of sensation. These cannot have their greatest possible perfection without the proportionate use of both powers. However, that is their highest perfection, that they have not only the highest degree of liveliness and strength, but also the

highest degree of dignity, extent, truth, and certainty. Cognition will be lacking in one of these merits whenever the latter qualities are not bestowed on it through distinct thinking and the former through the promotion of their clarity. [...]

[184] Whatever one can understand is true, whatever one cannot understand is false. If one wants to explain this intelligibility, it will become evident that one cannot assure oneself thereof except by going back step by step to indisputable principles.

Therefore it follows from this that cognition of the truth is not a product of sensation, that a certain feeling can thus not be the failsafe sign of the truth. This principle extends not just to theoretical cognition, but also to practical cognition. Moral propositions must be [185] recognized through precisely the same kind of argumentation as the theorems of other sciences because they contain judgments whose truth one can confirm only by showing the connection of their components. Thus, just as there are truths that are beyond the horizon of the healthy understanding, so too there are moral objects whose evaluation is beyond the horizon of moral feeling. The neglect of this remark has brought considerable confusion into the moral sciences as well as into the sciences that are immediately adjacent to them. One turned a certain feeling of the true and the good, a feeling for truth and a moral feeling, into a criterion of the true and the good. One therefore gave the faculty of sensation a standing that it does not have according to its nature. Showing the consequences of this reversal in the use of the soul's powers in the history of the sciences, specially the moral sciences, would lead us too far astray at the moment. However, it is [186] the duty of philosophy to ban this feeling from science itself and to provide instruction as to its proper definition. This is not to be a source of truth, but rather a defeat of all clear judgments that are retained in the soul through consideration or unnoticed abstraction, in order to express itself in all cases with a speed that is specific to sensation. It is not to be denied that there is, in this sense, a moral sense and it is also to be distinguished from conscience, because it senses morality in general first and also in the actions of others second, as conscience is concerned only with the evaluation of its own actions so that one can say that the former serves as the legislator, the latter as the judge. In this manner one avoids both ways out, on the one hand, an exaggerated respect [*Achtung*] for the moral feeling, according to which one makes it into a first principle independent of reason, [187] a highest judge in all moral matters, and, on the other hand, an equally exaggerated contempt [*Verachtung*], through which one denies it all existence and all benefit. [...] [188] It follows from the nature of clear representations that this feeling of truth must act with a liveliness that cold contemplation does not and cannot have. And the conviction in such cases typically increases and decreases according to the degree of this liveliness, and is also measured in this way. Such a conviction can have a strength as great as can ever be expected for any other conviction that rests on such firm grounds.

The cause of this is the internal immediate intuition of truth that is inseparable from the clarity of representations and [189] remains precisely in step with this clarity. With respect to the certainty that arises through reasoning, one can come nowhere close to this evidence, especially in new, unfamiliar matters. What is derived through correct inferences and from undeniable principles must indeed be just as certain, therefore effect just as much conviction, as the first principles themselves. However, what experience teaches is completely contrary to this equality of this evidence. [...]

[194] From all of this it follows that a proportionate exercise of the faculties of cognition and sensation alone can bring about the highest perfection of our cognition through the correction and animation thereof.

2

The power of sensation must be built up through a proportional pleasure of the various kinds of sensation.

Corporeal sensations, from the most confused kind [195] up through those that are least confused, with all of their related drives, have an equal claim on a measured exercise. Only this exercise must be measured if it is to be reliable, and one wants to avoid, to the same degree, a too prim [spröde] and stoic contempt of the former, and a bestial opulence through a disregard of the latter. Nothing other than nature can provide us with this path between both extremes, under the direction of a bright and unbiased faculty of reason. A more precise familiarity with our sensations, with their nature and both their corporeal and spiritual effects, must in that case provide reason with principles according to which it determines the measure of pleasure for each kind. The restriction among them according to such rules is that wise measure that is so benevolent, and can easily be distinguished from an irrational and baseless abstemiousness of excessively [196] enthusiastic [schwärmerischen] Encratites. According to this law of measure one must also immediately determine what kind of sensations are capable and in need of a special strengthening by means of the art of the imagination. And it is soon clear that merely corporeal sensations and the sensual pleasure to be enjoyed therein have no need of being promoted by any means other than the natural need proper to it. [...]

[209] FOURTH SECTION

On the Evaluation of Genius and Character

The powers of sensation and cognition admit of an infinite manifold of reciprocal limitations and mixtures, both in themselves and in their different sub-species on both sides. However infinitely manifold the heads and the kinds of minds among humans may always be, they can all certainly be derived from the various relations of the skills and tendencies that arise from the faculty for thinking and sensing. I can do nothing about this here other than provide the roughest outlines of such a complex and until now so little worked out discipline [210] as the doctrine of the evaluation of the human genius and character is. Nothing further can happen right now than to bring about the most universal derivations from their sources and to order them under and next to each other. If a science that rests on theory and observation at the same time is yet to be constructed, then the putting together of the framework by proper classification is the first and most necessary task that can be undertaken to that end.

I

In no human soul is there any faculty that is entirely ineffective. However, one says that man is advantageously equipped for that performance at which the relation of his cognitive faculties makes him better skilled than others. If the ground of this relation lies in its original set-up, then it is *talent*. If it lies in the additional practice of one or the other faculty, whether one undertakes this practice with conscious intention or not, it is an *acquired skill*. It is natural that a certain talent leads to the practice corresponding to it and to [211] the skill that arises from it rather than to any other, but it is not necessary. One can even work against a talent, however well endowed, and a thousand circumstances that the education of man depends on can provide occasion for this. The more outstanding the talent is, the greater the ruling ability is, the stronger it will be determined to the practice corresponding to it. One typically calls it genius in a special sense when it makes human beings suited and determines them with a noticeable strength to a certain kind of accomplishment, and one understands it in this way when one attributes such an irresistible power to a genius.* This power acts through nothing else [212] than the indescribable pleasure that the soul enjoys in the easy expression of its powers. [...]

[215] [...] A human being is predisposed either more to distinct thinking or more to sensing. I understand sensing to be all clear representing, whether it is immediately through the outer senses or not. One can call the latter a sensible genius, the former an intellectual genius.

An intellectual genius has as its objects (1) thoughts, (2) sensations, (3) actions. In the first class it sees the true and the false, and that is the introspective philosophy, in the second class it senses [216] the pleasant and the unpleasant, that is the poetic, and in the third, it suspects the useful or the harmful, and that is the bustling genius. This latter class has two spheres, the planning and the executive. Since strength of soul belongs to the latter, it also requires a certain quality of the heart, which must be provided in greater detail in the estimation [*Würdigung*] of characters. [...]

[233] 2

Order and regularity in the faculty of desire constitutes a virtuous character, the opposite a vicious character. This order and regularity can be inculcated and retained through nothing other than following the faculty of reason. [...]

[254] I cannot pursue the previous observations in all of their different tributaries. Otherwise it could now be investigated how they must be applied in aesthetics, morals, pedagogy, and politics, which way of living, which constitution, which stage of perfection and refinement of civil society, would be best suited to the expressions of one of [255] the soul's two powers, or to their different subordinate kinds and modifications, which one has to judge with respect to the perception of the excellent exercise of one among them, or one of their subordinate kinds, about the morals and way of thinking of an individual human being or an entire nation. As instructive and pleasant such digressions might be, I would certainly transgress therewith the borders that an illustrious Academy has prescribed for the treatises.

---

* In a general sense genius is called the cognitive faculty in general insofar as it is opposed to the faculty of desire, and then it can be called "head" [*Kopf*] in German. One notices about human beings the head and the heart. However, when a particularly high degree of intellectual ability is indicated that is opposed to what is more common, then it is as little the same as "head" as a specific difference is with its genus. [...]

9

Johann Nicolaus Tetens

Johann Nicolaus Tetens was born in Tetenbüll, Schleswig, in 1738; he studied first in Rostock in 1755–1756 and then in Copenhagen after 1757, receiving his master's degree (*Magister*) in physics in Rostock in 1759. In 1760 he moved to the newly formed Academy in Bützow, where he became professor of physics and philosophy in 1763. He accepted an ordinary professorship of philosophy and mathematics at the University of Kiel in 1776 and was elected to the Royal Danish Scientific Society in 1787. Far from being an academic who would pursue only scholarly ends, Tetens was also interested in a variety of practical endeavors, from the administration of insurance plans to the functioning of dikes. From 1789 until his death in 1807, Tetens was a high-level financial administrator for several private and government institutions in Copenhagen.

Tetens published on a wide range of topics throughout his career in German, Danish, and Latin: in natural philosophy (on *vis viva,* the force of cohesion, friction, the effects of climate, the curative powers of magnets, and magnetic metal in Mecklenburg), mathematics (on the functions of curves, the principle of least difference, the formulae of polynomials, and the properties of the number nine), economics (on the national debt of England, the calculation of pensions, and Danish monetary policy), philosophical theology (on proofs of God's existence and the reality of our concept of God), and miscellaneous philosophical topics (on the differences between human beings, the rank ordering of the sciences, the various uses of human knowledge, the principles and uses of etymology, and the history of tolerance). While the vast majority of his sixty-eight publications are short contributions to regional journals, his works include several substantive philosophical tomes. Of particular note are his *Über den Ursprung der Sprache und der Schrift* (On the Origin of Language and Writing, 1772), *Über die allgemeine speculativische*

Philosophie (On General Speculative Philosophy, 1775), and especially his *Philosophische Versuche über die menschliche Natur und ihre Entwicklung* (Philosophical Essays on Human Nature and Its Development, 1777).

While Tetens is sometimes referred to as a "German Locke," it is clear that despite significant overlap in their ultimate positions, his primary philosophical project (which he carries out at length in *Philosophical Essays on Human Nature and Its Development*) is very different from Locke's. For, using a Lockean method (which he calls the method of observation), Tetens addresses a question that he takes to be central to the efforts of a broad range of eighteenth-century philosophers (including Leibniz, Wolff, and Eberhard): Is there a single faculty or cognitive power that is responsible for our knowledge of the world, or are there several heterogeneous principles at work? This question dictates that he first carefully observe and describe the various kinds of representations that we have so as to determine whether the differences between them are differences in kind or merely of degree. Tetens pursues this goal in the first four essays of *Philosophical Essays* by distinguishing between impressions, conscious states, and thoughts.

Armed with this analysis of our basic kinds of mental states, Tetens can then turn (in the fifth through ninth essays) to the different kinds of knowledge that we have – empirical (or sensible) knowledge of contingent things and rational knowledge of necessary truths – and the nature of the distinction between them so as to determine how the basic kinds of representations are employed in such knowledge. Based on such analyses, Tetens can then conclude that there is but one fundamental principle or faculty that is simply active in different ways at different times (in different "directions" and on different "sides"). The final essays in the *Philosophical Essays* concern how human beings can develop their powers, whether these powers are consistent with free will, and what such development means for man's "perfectibility."

Along the way, moreover, Tetens discusses several issues that extend beyond Locke's position. For one, Tetens devotes considerable attention to Hume. In a detailed discussion of Hume's account of causality, Tetens argues that Hume is wrong to think that causality is nothing more than constant conjunction (or succession) plus the imagination's purely subjective expectation to find them together. For this overlooks the crucial ideas that a cause brings about its effect with objective necessity and that an effect should be intelligible on the basis of its cause. While Tetens's ultimate position is closer to Locke's insofar as he thinks that our understanding (rather than our imagination) gives us familiarity with causality from our own case (in the form of volition) and that we do not have the kind of insight required for knowledge of causality in many other instances, he clearly associates the necessity and intelligibility of causality with the processes of inferring and deriving conclusions in logic and suggests that the justification for some causal laws is not based on induction but is rather *a priori*. Nor is Tetens's interest in Hume restricted to causality; he discusses Hume's position on the self and on external objects at length and with a critical eye.

Another striking feature of Tetens's *Philosophical Essays* is that he is extremely interested in providing a coherent and comprehensive account of sensible and rational cognition. One important feature of his analysis of cognition in general stems from his distinction between what is absolute (which is derived from impressions) and what is relative (which stems from our power of thinking). Tetens explicitly allows that there need be no similarity between our impressions of what is absolute about an object in knowledge; knowledge pertains only to the relations that hold between what is absolute. As a result, Tetens is concerned with providing an exhaustive list of the basic different kinds of relations that we can represent. Also of note, however, is the way in which Tetens defines objective necessity (as opposed to purely subjective necessity of the kind to which Hume, in his eyes, reduced causality) in terms of what any being endowed with similar faculties would perceive. Moreover, it is in this context that Tetens explicitly considers the possibility of beings possessing other or greater cognitive faculties, what "things in themselves" must be like (for any being that thinks at all), and how to understand the contrast between the sensible and intellectual world.

In light of the many interesting points that Tetens raises, points that draw on Kant's own position in his Inaugural Dissertation in 1770 and anticipate views that would be developed more fully in the *Critique of Pure Reason* in 1781, it is clear that Kant ought to have been quite interested in Tetens's *Philosophical Essays* when it was published in 1777. Fortunately there is ample historical documentation that Kant actually read Tetens. For example, in a letter to Herder in May of 1779, Hamann claims that Kant always had Tetens's book open on his desk, and Kant himself mentions the importance of Tetens in a letter to Marcus Herz in 1778 (10:232). Moreover, after the publication of the first *Critique,* Kant explicitly mentions Tetens as one who is especially well suited to understanding, and perhaps even continuing to fill out, his own project (10:341). At the same time, Kant was at least implicitly critical of some of Tetens's views (10:270). For example, Kant makes clear that his objection to Locke applies to Tetens just as much, since both investigate the nature of our cognitive faculties empirically rather than transcendentally. Also, Kant asserts much more clearly a decisive difference in kind in accounting for the differences between reason (or the understanding) and sensibility, while Tetens still attempted to explain both in terms of a core notion of activity that would simply be applied in different ways. Still, on balance, it is clear that Tetens occupies a central place in the historical context of Kant's first *Critique*.

Contents of Philosophical Essays on Human Nature and Its Development

Preface

First Essay: On the Nature of Representations

Second Essay: On Feeling, on Impressions and Sensations

Third Essay: On Awareness and Consciousness

Fourth Essay: On the Power of Thought and on Thinking

Fifth Essay: On the Origin of Our Cognition of the Objective Existence of Things

Sixth Essay: On the Difference between Sensible and Rational Cognition

Seventh Essay: On the Necessity of the Universal Truths of Reason, Their Nature and Grounds

Eighth Essay: On the Relation between the Higher Cognitions of Reason and Those of Common Human Understanding

Ninth Essay: On the Basic Principle of Sensing, Representing, and Thinking

Tenth Essay: On the Relation of the Power of Representing to the Soul's Other Active Faculties

Eleventh Essay: On the Fundamental Power of the Human Soul and the Character of Humanity

Twelfth Essay: On Spontaneity and Freedom

Thirteenth Essay: On the Soul's Essence in Man

Fourteenth Essay: On Man's Perfectibility and Development

PHILOSOPHICAL ESSAYS ON HUMAN NATURE AND ITS DEVELOPMENT (1777)[1]

Preface

The following essays concern the effects of the human **understanding**, its laws of thought and its basic faculties, also the active **power of the will**, the **basic character of humanity**, **freedom**, the **nature of the soul**, and its **development**. These are undoubtedly the most essential points in our nature. I admire the great men who have already applied their keen intellects to these objects, and I have sought to make use of their efforts. But I do not believe that for this reason a prejudice arises against me, should my efforts not also equal theirs. Humanity is still very much a mine from which every inquirer has prospects for a good yield, and this is the case, I would like to add, even if he only undertakes anew paths that are already well trodden. For the complete evidence that would exclude all rational doubt is still lacking here and there even for the most urgent of truths, on which much light has already been shed.

I think it necessary to explain in advance the **method** of which I have availed myself. It is the **observational** method that Locke employed with the understanding and that our psychologists have followed in experimental psychology [*Erfahrungs-Seelenlehre*].[2] Taking the modifications of the soul as they are cognized through a feeling of the self [*Selbstgefühl*], becoming aware of and observing them with careful repetition and under changed conditions, then comparing and analyzing these observations and seeking out the simplest faculties and the [various] kinds of effects and their relations to each other; these are the most essential tasks if one intends to undertake a psychological analysis of the soul that relies on experience. This method is the method of the doctrine of nature [*Naturlehre*], and the only one that reveals to us the effects of the soul and their interconnections as they really are, then gives us hope of finding principles from which one can reliably infer their causes, and, finally, allows us to determine something about the nature of the soul, as the subject of the expressions we observe of its power, with a certainty that is more than mere guesswork.[3]

---

[1] Translated from Johann Nicolaus Tetens, *Philosophische Versuche über die menschliche Natur und ihre Entwickelung* (Leipzig, 1777).

[2] See Aix (A-edition Preface) and A86/B118–B119 (Transcendental Deduction) for a mixed evaluation of Locke's project.

[3] See A341–A348/B399–B406 (Introduction to Paralogisms) for Kant's doubts about developing a science (either empirical or rational) of the soul. See also A848–A849/

What recent psychologists have called the **analytical** or also the **anthropological method** is an entirely different process. One observes changes in the soul from the perspective that they are something in the **brain** as the internal organ of the soul, and attempts to explain them as states and changes in the brain. Materialists dissolve everything into bodily changes that are a consequence of the brain's internal organization. It is true that **mechanical** psychologists distinguish between the immaterial soul, the **I**, and the corporeal organ, and then allow the former its own share in the soul's expressions, one that is distinct from what the [corporeal] organ has, but the analyses of the latter just as much as the explanations of the former all attempt to show how far feeling, representing, consciousness, pleasure, pain, desire, and action not only depend on the organization of the brain, but themselves consist in its changes and states. And if something cannot have its seat in a bodily organ, then its seat will be in the immaterial soul for those who accept such a thing. The organ of thought is a machine for which the soul is its motive force. What is attributed to the soul in its typical meaning, or to the essence of the soul, is something in this ensouled organ, as in its subject. Thus the crucial point for these analytical explanations of the soul's changes lies in determining more precisely the way in which they occur in it. One can justly call these resolutions [*Auflösungen*] **metaphysical**. They lie entirely outside the limits of observation and ultimately consist in a reduction of what is observed in the soul to modifications of the brain, modifications, however, that an immaterial I can both have a share in and modify, as an active and moving force, at the same time that the brain does. [...]

First Essay: On the Nature of Representations[4]

Section I: On philosophers' efforts to derive representations,
impressions, and thoughts from one basic power

The soul has **impressions**, it has **representations** of things, of their features and relations, and it **thinks**. These expressions of its power are represented by the common understanding as different effects it

---

B876–B877 (Architectonic of Pure Reason) for Kant's views on the relation of empirical psychology to metaphysics.

4 The selections from this essay and the next are relevant to the opening of the Transcendental Aesthetic (A19/B33ff.) and the Introduction to the Transcendental Logic (A50/B74ff.), where Kant discusses the relations of the different varieties of representation to each other. See also On the Concepts of Pure Reason (A319–A320/B376).

has, and for which reason each of them also has its own denomination. Viewed superficially, up to where common observation reaches, **impressions** are not **representations** and both of them are not **thoughts**. Each of these expressions of our power is revealed in its own way, with its own character and as having its special effects that are different from the effects of the others. Thus to this extent these activities, and their faculties, appear to be different.

But if a philosopher now engaged in inquiry seeks to analyze these different appearances, delves a bit deeper below the surface of the soul, and traces the way in which the different expressions of our powers arise from an inner active principle of the soul, how far do their superficial differences extend in this case, and how deeply do they go into its internal [constitution]? There is one and the same being, the common source, from which all activities of the soul arise. Where and in what way do they get divided into the different branches [*Ausflüsse*] that our observations of our self let us become aware of?[5]

Is the entire difference between them perhaps merely **superficial**? [...] Or does this difference consist only in a difference in the **tools** with which the inner principle of the soul works? [...] Or is it merely an inner **difference in degree**, a more or less?[6] [...]

Instead of becoming entangled in trying to determine what others may have overlooked, I am willing to concede that all of them have, for the most part, taken the proper path, namely, the path of observation and analysis, but I must also admit at the same time that, despite the effort that I have given in following them, especially the path of the keen and deep investigations of Mr. Bonnet and our Wolff, I have not been so satisfied with their procedure that I did not think it necessary to repeat the entire inquiry on my own. [...]

The path that I have taken toward my goal may deliver me there or it may not. I have still thought it necessary, prior to all else, to investigate separately at the start each of these effects of the soul, **impressions**, **representations**, and **thoughts**. Perhaps one had not yet observed them enough before comparing them, due to which many obscurities must have remained after making such a comparison. I have made a start with representations.[7]

---

[5] See A15/B29 (Introduction).

[6] In the following Tetens discusses the views of Condillac, Bonnet, Leibniz, Wolff, Helvetius, Search, and Sulzer.

[7] In the rest of the First Essay, Tetens provides a characterization of what representations are. He argues that representations have two characteristic features: "The first

SECOND ESSAY: ON FEELING, ON IMPRESSIONS
[*EMPFINDUNGEN*] AND SENSATION [*EMPFINDNISSE*][8]

Section I: Determination of what having feelings and
impressions [is like], and what feelings, impressions,
and sensations are called

After the faculty of representation, it is feeling that belongs to the
simplest basic expressions of the soul, and the latter perhaps even more
than the former. My intention in this second essay is to investigate this
in a way that is similar to how the power of representation was treated in
the first essay. Wherever it is revealed most clearly, that is where its characteristic features should be noted from its effects, and then pursued
further in its connections with other faculties to the extent that doing
so seems necessary to me to cognize the relations between the simplest
principles that are the first developments that we can observe of the
basic nature of the soul.

In an impression a change of our state, a new modification in the
soul, arises. I direct my eyes toward the sun. Something happens. I **feel
something**, have an impression of it. The impression [*Eindruck*] is gotten
in this case from without. At least that is what I believe. I feel by means
of outer sense or, **I have an impression of something external**. Such
a feeling is sometimes neutral, sometimes pleasant or unpleasant. The
felt change is the **impression**. [...] **An impression is a perception of an
object that is present**.[9]

---

essential character of representations is that they are **residual enduring consequences**
of other, earlier changes in the soul" (p. 28). The second feature of representations is
that "they **refer us to** other objects and features of which they are signs in us" (p. 76).

[8] Tetens uses "*Empfindung*" to refer either to an impression itself or to the activity of
having an impression, while he typically employs "*Empfindnisse*" to indicate the content
of the impression. Because English does not have cognates for "impression" that correspond to the German usage and because Tetens uses "*Empfindung*" much more often
than "*Empfindnisse*," we shall use "impression" for the former and "sensation" for the
latter.

[9] In ensuing discussions in the second essay, Tetens defines feeling and having impressions in terms of three features. "**First**, it is easy to observe that we feel and have
an impression of nothing other than what is **present**" (p. 170). "**Further, the act of
feeling is capable of different degrees**" (p. 172). After analyzing various kinds of
feeling, Tetens notes: "Regardless of what differences there are in impressions, closer
attention reveals that **what we immediately feel and have impressions of is never
something relative, neither relations nor relations of things, and that, by contrast,
only the absolute in things outside and inside us is an immediate object of feeling**.
This is the third characteristic feature of feeling as a special faculty of the soul"
(pp. 191–192).

Third Essay: On Awareness [*Gewahrnehmen*] and Consciousness[10]

Section I: Determinate concept of awareness and consciousness
Our typical ways of speaking, as when we say that we are **aware of something**, **become aware of it**, **notice it**, **become conscious of it**, **are conscious**, **cognize it**, etc., do not have exactly the same meaning, but they are certainly all related to a simple basic generic concept of an expression of our cognitive powers that, as most psychologists now are accustomed to say, is designated in its purest and simplest form by the term **awareness**. [...]

Being aware is a **distinguishing**. [...] **Noticing** says more than awareness. Whoever **notices** something seeks out a feature of the object of awareness by means of which one can become aware of and distinguish the object again. **Being conscious of something** expresses a lasting state in which one feels [the act of] distinguishing an object, or its representation, and one's own relation to it. Consciousness is [...] a feeling, but a clear feeling, a clear impression, a feeling that is connected with distinguishing between the felt object and the self. Feeling and awareness are the two components of consciousness.

Section III: Awareness brings forth the thought of a relation. Comparison of the thought of a relation to the feeling of the absolute

[...] Two objects that we cognize as **identical**, as the same, as similar, have, as things, their absolute features [*Beschaffenheiten*]. Every egg has its size, shape, color, and weight objectively in itself. These are its absolute features. But what is it that we call its **similarity**, identity, sameness? Where is its sameness? It is apparent that it is present only **subjectively** in the understanding, which adds the predicate of similarity to the ideas of things after comparing them. The thought of the relation is produced by the power of thought and is nothing outside of the understanding, but rather is an *ens rationis* [a being of thought]. [...]

The question is more complicated for another type of relation [*Verhältnissen*], namely, those relations [*Beziehungen*] that we represent to ourselves only for **actual** things and that depend on the different way in which the things are **actually** present with each other, on the way,

---

[10] The selections from this essay as well as Section III in the next are relevant to the Transcendental Deduction (A84–A130/B116–B169).

namely, in which they can be **next to each other** at the same time, or how they follow **upon one another**, in one word, on the modes of their co-actuality. Are these too a mere product of the understanding, just as was the case for the relations mentioned above, and do they arise in a similar way from comparison, and are they only something **subjective** in us? Leibniz and his followers, and, among more recent philosophers, Mr. Mendelssohn, Kant, Ulrich, and others have answered this question in the affirmative, though not entirely in the same way, while others have denied this.[11] [...]

These observations draw one into the most intricate metaphysical investigations concerning the nature of space and time, which I do not want to go into here, though I will have to do so more on another occasion, when the various modes of efficacy of the power of thought come under closer scrutiny. For all of the speculation about the general concepts of the understanding mentioned above ultimately depend on psychological investigations into the way in which they arise and into their subjective nature in the understanding.[12] [...]

FOURTH ESSAY: ON THE POWER OF THOUGHT AND ON THINKING

Section III: The origin of concepts of relations
(1) On the first original thoughts of relations.

(1) [...] In investigating **awareness** we established that the thought that arises when what we are aware of is a separate thing is a thought of a relation that the soul adds by means of its action, and that must not be conflated with the feeling of the absolute in things.[13] Whatever the objective aspect of things may be like that constitutes the basis of the **conceived relation, awareness** is still an effect of a certain expression of the power of thinking that combines itself with impressions and representations.

The way in which this happens for awareness is how it happens for the remaining concepts of relations. When we view two things as **identical**, when we think of them as standing in **causal** relations, when we

---

[11] See Kant's Transcendental Aesthetic (A19–A49/B33–B73) and the Amphiboly (A260–A292/B316–B349).

[12] Presumably Tetens has in mind the generic concepts of identity, similarity, diversity, and modes of co-actuality, i.e., space and time.

[13] See B130 (Transcendental Deduction) for a similar claim.

represent one thing in another as a feature in a subject, or both of them at the same time next to each other or as following each other, there is a certain **act of thinking**, and the relation in us that we are thinking is something **subjective** that we attribute to the objects as something **objective** and that arises from the thinking. These acts of thinking are the **first original thoughts of relations.** [...]

Section IV: On the concept of a causal connection[14]

(1) The Humean explanation of this concept.

(2) Examination of this explanation. The concept of a causal connection [*Verbindung*] represents more than a mere connection [*Verbindung*]. It also contains the idea of the dependency of the one on the other.

(3) The idea of dependency, which is more than a mere connection, derives from initial causal relations [*Beziehungen*] and from the impressions of those actions that relate them to each other.

(4) What "conceiving of the one from the other" is and what inferring and drawing conclusions are.

(5) Determining the origin of the concept of a causal connection. The way in which this concept is applied.

(1) I shall use the concept of a **causal connection** to elucidate by way of example what was said in the previous section about the origin of relational concepts [*Verhältnißbegriff*] from the initial relations [*Beziehungen*] of representations in us. And I shall use this concept all the more, the more extensive the consequences are that depend on its proper determination in an overview of the nature of human cognition. Hume overlooked one of its essential components, which at the same time served as the primary occasion for his making the same mistake with respect to the entirety of human cognition, and, because he was not aware of its inner strength, he believed that he could make it topple through his skeptical sophistry.

Hume believed he had found that the concept of the **dependency** of an effect on its cause, or, of **causal** connection, of **causality**, etc., whatever one wants to call it, is ultimately nothing other than an effect of the imagination and that its entire mode of origin can be explained according to the law of the association of ideas. The observations that this

---

[14] This entire section is directly relevant to Kant's Second Analogy of Experience (A188–A211/B232–B256).

philosopher calls on in defending his opinion prove how acute his eyes are in seeing into the nature of human understanding. None the less, I hold that he himself would have found his explanation insufficient if he had not been held up by one side of the operation of the understanding alone, if he had not overlooked others, or at least had not noticed them less distinctly.[15]

We have – such is his reasoning and that of those who have followed him in this – **constantly** found two objects conjoined [*in Verbindung*] in our impressions, of which we call the one the **cause** and the other the **effect**. The **impression of what** we call the **cause** comes first and the impression of the **effect** follows. The ideas of them thus arose in this order and in this connection, are reproduced again in the same [order], and are present to us in this order in almost every case. We have seen, e.g., one ball approaching another with a certain velocity and strike it; then we have an impression of a new motion in the second ball. Everyday we have seen it get light as the sun rises. Such ideas that constantly accompany each other and follow each other are placed so closely together in the imagination and are connected so intimately that as soon as the one is present in us again, the second one also arises as its consequence or as its companion. If we happen, by some chance, to come upon the following idea of the effect first, then the imagination, in turn, puts the preceding idea in its proper place, of which it has had impressions that were followed so many times before by impressions of that effect. Finally, by habit, this combination of ideas becomes so necessary for us that we can no longer separate them and are forced to proceed from the one to the other. Now when we transfer this succession of ideas over to objects outside of us, the thought arises: "if one of those objects is actually present, the second one will also accompany it," that is, we represent the one as the cause and the other as the effect and conceive of a **causal** connection between them.

It was not so hard to discover a host of examples where the thought of this causal relation of things was ultimately based on nothing other than such a combination [*Verbindung*] of representations that are derived from impressions, especially when composite causes are resolved into simple ones. In most cases we are incapable of any other cognition of this kind of combination of actual things. The simple principles of the doctrine of nature, on the basis of which the causal combination [*wirkende Verbindung*] of bodies is understood, are collections of a set of

---

[15] See B19–B20 (B-version Introduction) for a similar explanation of Hume's error.

corresponding and similar experiences. [...] And thus it happens that the idea of a cause, if we represent it distinctly, draws forth the idea of an effect with a kind of **necessity**. We thus move, driven by force, from the thought that the former is really present, to the consequence that the effect exists as well.

There is much that is correct in this Humean explanation. The thought, "one thing is a cause of another," requires that the ideas of the cause and its effect either have already been or are presently conjoined, as a result of which one leads back to the other; and due to this conjunction, if we pursue the representation of the cause and the thought that it is present, the thought of the existence of the effect is forced on us with a certain necessity. Further, it is true that we use the **constant succession** of things as a **character** [or sign] of their causal relation, which is also in that case a completely reliable characteristic [or sign] of it if what we call its **activity** is found in the cause and if nothing except for such a cause is present that could bring about the effect that occurred. It is due to this final circumstance that we are most often in doubt. For who can be sure that nothing is present in what is hidden, and acts when our impressions reveal nothing to us? For this reason we attend to whether what follows the action of the cause persists whenever the action itself is obstructed or stops.

(2) Even granting Hume this much, we are still not yet beyond everything that is questionable in his explanation. From the representation of a **constant succession** [*einer beständigen Folge*] of the one upon the other he derives our entire concept of the causation of the one **through** the other? But we represent it to ourselves as if **the effect depended on the cause**, were **produced** by it, and made actual **through** it.[16] Does not this last way of representing it contain further ideas beyond constant succession? We view the effect as something that is **intelligible** [*begreiflich*] on the basis of its cause! Is [the] **intelligibility** [of one thing] on the basis of something else nothing more than the fact that the idea of the one occurs in us when the idea of the other is present, regardless of the way in which the former draws the latter along after it within us? And is **intelligibility** merely a consequence of a previous association of ideas?

Let me first give this preliminary reminder. In such cases where the connection between the ideas of the cause and the effect is based only in the **association of the imagination** – to which most judgments of the

---

[16] See A91/B124 (Transcendental Deduction).

kind that lie in the simple principles of the doctrine of nature belong – it is certain that we represent their **causal connection** as amounting to more in our judgment about their **dependence** on each other than the association of our ideas and the mere co-presence of their objects. Warmth is the cause of the expansion of bodies. It may be that we have no other ground for this assertion in front of us than the constant conjunction of warmth in the body with that of the expansion of the body in our impressions. It may be that this enduring conjunction, which has turned into a habit in us, is the only thing that pushes us from one representation to the next and transfers the thought of its existence, so to speak, from the idea of what has gone before to the idea of what follows. None the less, we presuppose in ourselves that yet another real connection exists between the objects. We see, namely, the ideas in us [as standing] in a **necessary** succession. For whatever reason this connection may have become necessary in this way, we do take it into consideration and assume that a necessary connection [*Zusammenhang*] corresponding to it is present in the objects. The **necessary** connection [*Verknüpfung*] of ideas in their succession in us is actually our **representation** of the **causal connection** [*Verbindung*]. For as soon as we attain the insight that the latter connection of ideas is nothing more than an association of the imagination, and that one follows upon the other merely with a **subjective** necessity, the understanding's judgment that declares the objects themselves to be dependent on each other ceases.[17]

From this it is clear that even if Mr. Hume had proven that none of our assertions about the causal connection [*Verknüpfung*] of things has a basis [*Grund*] that is more real than the one given, there is still another ingredient in the concept of this connection [*Verbindung*] that stems from the way in which ideas are connected and made into a sign of the objective causal relation between objects. Now if it is assumed that this additional ingredient is something imaginary, then the entire concept, and what is **real** in it, would be distinguishable from it. But if one is investigating its inner content and sense, it must be taken in its entirety at the start.

(3) Now let's continue. Is what lies in the concept beyond what Hume found in it really something made up? Are there not many examples in which the subjective connection [*Verbindung*] of ideas arises from a **necessary** mode of action of the understanding and has a completely different basis from its association in the imagination? Are there not

---

[17] See B5 (B-edition Introduction) and B168 (Transcendental Deduction).

examples in which the understanding, to conjoin all at once the idea of the effect with that of the cause as closely as is required for the thought of a causal relation, needs nothing more than that both ideas lie in front of it and are held up against each other without it ever having previously experienced them in such a connection? [...]

If we investigate the source of our conviction regarding the first fundamental laws of motion, we find several examples of this kind. Is it a case of induction that a body, once placed in motion, retains its motion unchanged as long as no external cause changes it? That a body at rest will forever stay at rest as long as no foreign cause drives it away? Is it a case of induction and only induction that the action of a body is in every instance combined with a reaction? If one counts up the individual cases of the first law in particular, in which one has had the occasion to observe it, and compares them to others that seem to depart from it, one will hardly be convinced that we view the latter law as a universal law of nature because our imagination has, on the basis of our impressions, only gotten used to connecting the idea of an external cause with the idea of a change in the state of rest or motion of the body. There were undoubtedly impressions that provided the first occasion for discovering the law, but an act of reasoning was added, an inner spontaneity of the understanding, by which the combination [*Verknüpfung*] of ideas was brought about. The idea of a body that has been set in motion and that neither acts nor is acted on by any other leads the understanding to the representation that its motion will continue unchanged, and although this latter idea must also have been derived from impressions, its combination with the former is still a product of the power of thinking, which, **according to its nature**, brings about this relation between ideas, and the combination of the predicate with the subject that it brings about in us by means of this operation is much more the ground of our conviction that our judgment is a true judgment than is the association of ideas based on impressions. I do not intend to claim thereby that one could establish any one of the general principles of the doctrine of nature in its **complete determinacy** *a priori* on the basis of mere concepts. In my opinion they are contingent truths. There is no absolute necessity in the understanding to connect the subject and the predicate in such a way as is required here. But the understanding combines them according to a habitual law of thinking that it follows, although it does not follow it [i.e., this law] with the irresistible force had by those [laws] that the understanding assumes in thinking the necessary truths of reason, e.g., the principle of contradiction. Such general thoughts are true thoughts, prior to all experience. We do not cognize them on its basis by means of abstraction, and that such connections of ideas become established also does not depend on iterated repetition. [...]

(4) **Fourth**. Let us also observe the connection of thoughts when we say: "We understand a consequence from its principles." Is it not clear that **deriving**, **drawing a conclusion**, and **inferring one truth from another** is a connection of ideas that is essentially distinct from associations in our fantasy? [...]

(5) Now, the result of these reminders. **First**, it is probably not the **mere succession of impressions** upon each other from which the conception of a **causal** connection [*Verbindung*] is derived. Rather, there are certain special kinds of associations of ideas from which it is abstracted, and, in fact, those in which something more is noticed than that one idea occurs and that the other then follows it. Undoubtedly we initially get this concept from the feeling of our own striving and its effects. [...]

Second, we transfer this concept, which we have gotten from our feeling of ourselves, to external objects. [...]

Third, the understanding can derive the concepts of a **ground** [*Grunde*] (*ratio*) and of **what is grounded** in it and of the **intelligibility** of the latter on the basis of the former only from the activity of its understanding, of inferring and deriving. "Understanding one on the basis of another" does not mean seeing one thought succeeding the other. [...]

Section V: On the difference between relations and
general concepts of relations

(1) Not all relations can be reduced to identity and diversity.
(2) Classes of general simple relations.[18]

(2) Leibniz, whose keen and penetrating insight into the general kinds of thinking in human understanding is also apparent here, distinguished two classes of simple relations. To the one belong relations proper, namely, those that arise from the comparison of things – identity and diversity, similarity and dissimilarity, with all their kinds – which he called relations of comparison. To the other, however, he counted those

---

[18] See Kant's Amphiboly and On the Clue to the Discovery of all Pure Concepts of the Understanding, esp. the Second and Third Sections, On the Logical Function of the Understanding in Judgments and On the Pure Concepts of the Understanding (A70/ B95–A76/B101 and A76/B102–A83/B109).

relations that have their ground in an actual connection of objects, such as dependency, order, the combination of things into a whole, their position, etc. He called them relations of combination (*relations de concours*). This division already sheds some more light on matters. But is it exhaustive? How can a causal connection [*Verbindung*] be brought under a common genus with inactive relations, which depend on a different kind of mere co-presence and are consequences of the simultaneous existence of several things, since both of these latter classes are different from each other just as essentially as they are from the first class of relations, that of comparison? [...] Accordingly, to classify simple relations in general exhaustively, which are also simple modes of thinking and thus also simple effects of our power of thought, I distinguish three kinds. One kind arises from the comparison of representations. This is the class of identity and diversity and its kinds. [...] Another kind arises from collecting and dividing, combining and separating representations, and from the various ways in which that can occur. [...] Distinct from this is the third general kind, which contains the relations of dependence, the combination of what is grounded with its ground, and of an effect with its cause.

Fifth Essay: On the Origin of Our Cognition of the Objective Existence of Things

Section V: On the origin of the fundamental concepts
of the understanding that are required for judgments about
the existence of things. Concept of a subject and its features.
Concept of the self as a thing

[...] Hume, as the author of a famous treatise on human nature declared the idea that we have of our **self**, or of our soul, "to be a collection of several particular impressions that follow each other, but that are separate and scattered, from whose connection in the imagination the idea of **one** whole, as a subject, was made, which views the content of each individual impression as its feature."[19] He inferred from this that we can claim nothing more about the soul than that it is a bundle [*Inbegriff*] of qualities and changes, which, since they are immediately sensed, actually exist, but not that it is **one thing**, a **complete unity** [*ein Ganzes Eins*], an actual **thing**. And this is what his opponents objected to, namely,

---

[19] This passage seems to be a paraphrase rather than an exact translation of any passage in Hume's *A Treatise of Human Nature*.

that he explained away even the **existence of the soul** and admitted only the **actuality** of its thoughts and changes. However, this was the outermost limit in rational skepticism [*raisonnierenden Skepticismus*].

It is well known what Mr. Reid and Beattie objected to it, namely, that it goes against common sense. Their answer is not incorrect, [but rather] only unphilosophical as long as another answer is possible, one that would at the same time cite the reason for his error as well.

The matter is not as Mr. Hume says it is, and one can assert this without assuming that something more is actually present than what he himself recognizes, namely, only as much as we are aware of **immediately**. But Mr. Hume overlooked one important circumstance.

I feel one representation, and another, also an activity of thinking, an expression of the will, etc., and these impressions are different and actual. But I have even more impressions.

As often as I have an impression of, am aware of, or become immediately conscious of a representation, I am to that extent also conscious that this feeling of my modification is only a prominent aspect of a much larger, more extensive, stronger feeling, though one that is, in its other parts, obscure or at least less clear. And I am just as conscious of this latter [feeling] and in the same way that I can always be with respect to each individual feature of which I become aware, in the same way, namely, that one can ever become immediately conscious of something. Thus I have such an impression that carries me to the thought that a **thing** and a **feature** in this thing is present, in the very same way that I can arrive at this thought according to Mr. Hume's own explanation: a **feature** is actual.

And in this whole impression the **obscure [back-] ground** for it is always **the same**, if I am aware of one aspect of it as presently actual in me instead of another that has faded away. This [back-]ground for the whole impression, which is related to its prominent feature as flatland is to the foot of a towering mountain, is **the same** throughout **all** of the particular changes that occur in the impression and the representation. For that reason the concept of the **identity of our I** [comes] from comparing the present feeling of our I, as a subject with the features that are present in it, to a similar feeling that was reproduced from the past. But this just in passing. Another of its consequences is that the idea or representation of my **I** is not a **collection** of individual representations that our imagination might have turned into a whole just like it unifies the individual representations of soldiers into a representation of one regiment. That unification lies in the **impression** itself, in nature, and not in a combination that it makes itself. For this reason a representation of **one** subject with **different** features arises, that is, a **representation** that immediately arises from the **impression**, must be **thought** in this way and turned into an **idea** such that the common understanding of man actually does form it in this way.[20] The understanding could have formed this idea in Humean fashion only if it had overlooked this much of it in its natural observations and grasped it only on one particular side, as this fine metaphysician [did] in his speculation, since he wanted to discharge [*ablösen*] one part of it after another in distinct [or orderly] fashion.

Section VII:[21] A remark against idealists based on the origin of our judgments about the external actuality of things, from which impressions the idea of external existence is initially derived

Now if these abstractions [i.e., the general concepts of an object, of actuality, and of substance] are present by means of the combined activity of feeling, the power of representation, and the power of thinking, we can pass judgments about the **existence** of things within us and outside us. But to cognize completely distinctly [both] the way in which our power of thinking operates and the grounds of the reliability of its judgments, the following must be taken into consideration.

A judgment – e.g., what I feel with my finger and call a **body**, is an actual thing and object that is present outside of me as a soul or a human being – contains the following thoughts. I feel or have an impression. Further, what I feel is an actual thing, an object, substance. And it is different from myself. [...]

Neither Hume nor Berkeley would, I think, object to the reliability of our judgment in the example given above if they were to acknowledge as obvious that my present feeling of an external body, when viewed as material for the notion of an external, actual thing, is completely similar to other impressions from which the general concept in question has been formed. [...] [The only thing that one could have reservations about] ultimately amounts to this: that if we attribute an objective actuality to external things in the sense that we attribute it to our self and its features, then a merely apparent or imperfect [*mangelhaft*] similarity of subjects would have to blind us in our representations, a similarity that

---

[20] These remarks are relevant to the Transcendental Deduction (esp. A107 and B134–B135), the Paralogisms (esp. the Third Paralogism), and the Refutation of Idealism (B272–B279).

[21] This section is relevant to the Refutation of Idealism (B274–B279).

is not in fact present and that would not be found in a careful investigation [of these matters]. [...]

The question here, in our present investigation, is not about the correctness or incorrectness of our judgments about the existence of external things, but rather about the way in which these judgments arise and about the order in which they arise. Does an understanding that develops itself chart its course such that all impressions were first taken to be features of our self and only later, after much reasoning, could a more correct cognition be attained? Or was the latter cognition just as natural and instinctive in just the same sense as judgments are about our existing self and about what exists in it?

By returning to our previous remarks about general concepts and about the way in which they are combined with our impressions and bring about judgments of the existence of things, one can see that there is still much that ought not to be overlooked if the natural path of the understanding is to be observed distinctly. [...]

If we thus presuppose that the whole sum of impressions and representations is already divided into different groupings and separate wholes, that the soul's inner feelings of itself are distinguished from the feelings of its body, and that these, in turn, are distinct from the impressions of external objects, of a tree, a bird, a mountain, a river, etc., and are all represented as different wholes and subjects, [then] from which of these separate groupings could and must the materials for the general concept of an **actual object** be drawn? Those from which the abstraction occurred must necessarily have the predicate of being actual objects as soon as reflection sets in. Thus if the impression of a tree has something in common with the impression of a self, which is turned into the idea of an existing object, then it is just as necessary to think that the tree is an actual object as it is to think that I myself am something actual. It is thus apparent how involved this question is and what the reason is why Hume and Berkeley did not answer it as other non-idealistic philosophers have. [...]

If an impression is to belong to those from which the idea of an **object** that is **present for itself** is drawn or certainly **could** have been drawn just as well as from others, then the following is a requirement for it: "It must be present in the soul alone, separate from all others, and it must subsist for a while in this way, and it must then also be represented in this way alone again as separate." But for this it is required that during the time when it is present, it **alone** occupies the faculty of impressions, to the extent, namely, that it permits no other simultaneous feeling in addition to itself that would be strong enough to be perceived and that it alone occupies the soul of the being that feels during its act of awareness.

Every **external** impression that is of some strength and duration possesses the power, at least for a while, to draw the soul outside of itself, to the extent that it forgets itself as a reactive, representing, thinking, and desiring being, and occupies itself alone with the modifications brought forth in it without thereby being aware of its own activities. This is experience.

And the occasion for placing such impressions inside oneself is absolutely lacking. They are impressions separate from the others and present all by themselves. For that reason we also place all of them outside of ourselves, for we must become aware that they are things distinct from our self. [...]

Sixth Essay: On the Difference between Sensible and Rational Cognition

Section I: On sensible cognition and the cognitive faculties that are active with respect to it

(1) The difference between sensible and rational cognition.

(1) All previous observations still lead to the result in question. A being that can feel, bring about representations, and grasp or be aware of relations is capable of everything that a human soul can accomplish when it creates cognitions for itself. All activities of the understanding consist of these elementary actions. Part of my goal in the last two essays was to show this. Now yet another [goal] reappears, namely, to seek out, on the basis of observation, the relation that the basic activities and faculties have to each other and their reciprocal dependencies. I ask for no light here other than what experience gives: no hypotheses, no speculation based on concepts. What should be done in case that torch goes out must be determined if it comes to it.[22]

Every cognition is, as cognition, a product of the **power of thinking**. But we have **sensible** cognition and we have **rational** cognition. Common experience notes this difference. The power of thought is less in the former and more in the latter. Thus there are always two sides to our cognitive powers that stand apart from each other. The relations of these two sides to each other and the **difference** in the relations that arise

---

[22] See The Discipline of Pure Reason with Regard to Hypotheses (A769–A782/B797–B810).

when each simple faculty contributes its own part to sensible and rational cognition can bring us one step closer to the relations of these faculties themselves. So much has been said about both in new investigations by Locke, Condillac, Bonnet, Hume and others and, in fact even more by Leibniz and Wolff, that in most cases I can simply refer to them. However, they left something behind that is not pure chaff if it is gathered together. The foreigners mentioned, and Bacon not excepted, have seen only from a distance and rather obscurely what concerns the nature of our **rational** insight, the course of the understanding in speculation, and the establishment of **general theories**, in particular. Most often the understanding comes under observation when it gathers [its various] experiences and forms its first sensible ideas from impressions, as occurs in natural science and in psychology. But when the same power of thinking takes a higher path in general theories and brings truths together to form sciences – on this path, which is as slippery in philosophy as it is secure and smooth in mathematics, one did not spy as keenly, as intimately, as intuitively [*anschauend*] how it should proceed and what the guiding rule of its procedure should be. And this is the source of many one-sided judgments. Whether the power of thought is perhaps occupied with something that is not quite natural for it when it speculates? Whether general abstractions and their connections perhaps lie outside of its [proper] atmosphere? Whether it is not in air that is too rarified for it or surrounded by fog and clouds such that it can never attain secure cognitions? These are, I think, no longer questions, and thanks go to the mathematical sciences for making it so. I do not propose to rely on a general **fundamental science** that is supposed to have the standing of algebra in philosophy, because questions still remain about its status.[23] Hume proclaimed his judgment about it in advance, and after the powerful attempts that many metaphysicians – Leibniz and Wolff among them – have undertaken in trying to establish it, perhaps the majority of recent philosophers would prefer that it be stricken from the list of possible sciences. But geometry, optics, astronomy – these products of the human spirit and irrefutable proofs of its greatness – are certainly real and established cognitions. According to what basic rules should human reason erect this colossal building? Where does it find solid ground for this goal, and how can one draw from its individual impressions general basic ideas and principles that are to serve as the unshakeable foundation for such lofty constructions? The power of thought must employ its greatest strength to prove itself in this endeavor.[24]

---

[23] See A734/B762.
[24] See the second edition Preface (especially Bvii–Bxxiv).

I repeat: Every cognition, as cognition, is a product of the **power of thought**. Neither **feeling** nor the **power of representation** can distinguish, bring awareness about and cognize. The power of thought does this. But that does not capture what is unique about **sensible cognition** and **cognition based on impressions**. What is this difference?[25]

Seventh Essay: On the Necessity of the Universal Truths of Reason, Their Nature and Grounds

Section I: On the subjective necessity of awareness, judgments, and inferences in general

One of the most distinguished and difficult investigations concerning the more general principles of reason focuses on their **necessity**. What does it consist in and what is its ground? To what extent and why are they of a different nature from that of the individual judgments of impressions?

Nothing can be said about the **objective necessity** of propositions until one investigates the kind of **subjective necessity** with which our understanding thinks them, observes the nature of general propositions in us as products of the power of thinking, and notices its features. [...]

Section II: On the subjective necessity of the modes of thought insofar as their form is determined necessarily by their grounds

(8) In what cases there is an inner absolute necessity.

(8)[26] But there are other cases where the relational thought "that one thing is the cause of another" is **absolutely necessary** as soon as one compares the cause and the effect.[27] [...]

We see possible cases where the thought of a **causal connection** [*Verbindung*] would be a subjectively **absolutely necessary** thought according to its form, but at the same time one also sees the reason why

---

[25] In the rest of this section of this essay, Tetens describes two kinds of sensible cognition. The one, which he calls "pure experience," are impressions and whatever is immediately based on such impressions. The second kind of sensible cognition contains both impressions and images produced by the imagination. In the second section of this essay, Tetens explains how rational cognitions require general concepts and how the warrant for such cognitions is not based on the impressions that are required for the formation of the abstract concepts they involve; they are not grounded on experience by means of induction.

[26] This section is relevant to Kant's Second Analogy of Experience (A189–A211/B232–B256).

[27] As opposed to cases where something is merely subjectively necessary, which Tetens discusses earlier in this essay.

so few or even none of our relational thoughts about **actual** connections in the world belong to that class.

We understand quite a bit about **actual** cases of causation, but none of them exhaustively. If a ball set in motion is headed toward another one at rest, at least one of them, if not both, must change its state. I say that we **understand** the latter on the basis of the former. But how? We have an idea of one ball approaching the other, we have an idea of this motion and its direction, and we also have an idea of the ball that is lying at rest in its path. Now the idea of the change of place of one of the two stems from these thoughts. However, this idea does not arise from these thoughts except by means of another thought, namely, "that these two balls are impenetrable and thus cannot occupy one and the same space at the same time." Insofar as this last thought, which helps us in guiding our reflection, is nothing other than an association of ideas obtained from impressions, the thought process that depends on it is not absolutely necessary. [...]

Section IV: On objective truth and on
objectively necessary truths

(1) What the truth of our cognition of objects depends on.
(2) What it means to say: objects are as we represent them to ourselves.

(1) We cognize how we think **subjective necessity** according to the general laws of the understanding from observation. We feel that we cannot represent to ourselves a squared circle and cannot maintain that a thing is distinct from itself. **Objective** necessity is based on this subjective necessity.[28] The impossibility of thinking of things otherwise is attributed to things external to the understanding. Our ideas are now no longer ideas in ourselves; they are things outside of ourselves. The features and relations that we are aware of in them are represented to us as features and relations of the things themselves that they would have even outside our thought and that every other thinking being would have to cognize as being in them. This is how instinct does it. This is an effect of common human understanding, and the metaphysics of old saw something correct in this procedure and took as an axiom that **truth is something objective**.

---

[28] See B166–B168 (Transcendental Deduction), where Kant dismisses such a claim.
* Lossius, *Physische Ursachen des Wahren* [Lossius, *Physical Causes of What Is True*].

Considerable effort has been expended for a long time about whether beauty is only something relative to us or whether there is also something **absolute** in beautiful objects. [...] And as a result one compared truth with beauty and held that the parallels between both of them extend so far that one could also say of truth: "It is nothing at all other than a relation for the person who is thinking it," a proposition that one recent philosopher extended to its greatest scope and attempted to prove as having such a scope.* It may not even be impossible that there be thinking beings that can also represent what **is contradictory** for us. This last thought is the most radical attack that skepticism can level against human reason. [...]

Yet one must first determine what is actually important with respect to truth and what it means when we believe that things in themselves are also as we represent them to ourselves. And then the way in which we reach this judgment and the grounds that lead us to it must be considered.

If **truth** is declared to be the **correspondence of our thoughts with things**, this **correspondence** can be nothing other than an **analogy** according to which an **idea** is supposed to be related **to another idea** just as one **thing** is supposed to be related **to another thing**. To compare **objects** with **ideas** means nothing other than to compare representations with representations or one representation that is derived from an impression with another one that I already have. If the **objects** are identical or diverse just as the **ideas** of them are, then **the relations in the former are just like the relations in the latter.**[29] [...]

The nature of our thinking and our judgments teaches this as well.* An impression is red with respect to the makeup of a body that is thus colored, [in the way] that a word is with respect to the thought that it signifies. These impressions depend on the nature of the being receiving the impressions and on other circumstances such that one cannot possibly assume that every other being with other tools, under other circumstances, would be modified by the same object in the same way as I am. Such impressions are only something **subjective**. They are what they are only for whoever receives them. But there is no thought and no truth in these impressions, even if they can be mistaken. Thinking consists in being aware of the **relations** of representations and in these only can truth and error arise. Whatever impression it is that I receive of the red color, it is still the portion of the book that lies in front of me that is

---

[29] See A57–A60/B82–B84) (Introduction to Transcendental Logic).
* Fourth Essay, [Section] VII, 5.

red, namely, it is the same impression that I have had in other cases and called red. A thing is round, has corners. These expressions say nothing more than that something that is the same as what I call round and having corners is attributed to the thing. Nothing hinges on it if someone else has the impression of corners that I have of something round. The correctness of the thought depends only on my judgment being correct, and judgment is a relational thought. [...]

(2)[30] The second initial issue that we must determine is what the **objectivity** of our cognition might really mean. A certain set of relations are attributed to the objects, are in them outside of the understanding, and are the same here as the relations of ideas are in the understanding. [...]

The idea of the common understanding that we have when we view something as an **object** or as **objective** and that we express when we say "The matter is thus" contains in fact the thought that the matter both would and would have to be perceived just as we represent it to ourselves by everyone else who has the same sense for it that we do. "The matter is constituted such" just means: "It can be perceived [*empfindbar*] in this way."

A **constant appearance** [*Schein*] is reality for us, as several philosophers put it, and is tantamount to being and actuality. This is to a certain extent correct, because we do not know how to distinguish in our impressions between an **appearance** that always remains completely the same and what is **real**. But it is none the less true that if we grasp the thought "A matter that constantly appears in the same way is a **real** thing and is constituted in itself as it appears," we certainly want to say something more than just this, namely, that it **seems** such to us. It will and, according to its nature, must also appear such to every other being that feels and has impressions. This is a further feature that is contained in that predicate.

The same concept of the objective is retained in philosophy. [That] things are constituted in this or that way **for themselves** [*für sich*] means in this case as well that every being that has an impression of it or represents or thinks of it must have such an impression of it, must represent and think of it in such a way if this being is considering it in the same way as we do when we ascribe an objective reality to our cognition. For it is implicitly assumed that the same requirements that

---

[30] The following discussion is relevant to the Transcendental Deduction (A84–A130/ B116–B169, especially B140–B143).

move us to view our own cognitions as objective – since we presumably know that they are at times only subjective appearance – must also be present for other cognitive beings for whom cognition is supposed to be objective. We have a representation of the most perfect understanding according to which we must believe that it thinks objects such as they are in themselves.[31] For this reason we view it as a principle that when we represent things to ourselves as they are in themselves, our representations of them correspond to those in the divine understanding. I am speaking here in the sense of those who claim such an objective reality for our cognition. [...]

Now we have the proper sense of the question of whether **truth** is only something **subjective** for whoever is thinking it or whether it is also something **objective**. Thoughts consist in relations of impressions. Thus, are those relations that we are aware of in our impressions the same as those that any being thinking of objects would have to find in its own impressions, assuming that its cognition has the status of real cognition, which ours has and which we are still calling on? Regardless of what the impressions of things are like, or of what take the place of our impressions as signs of the individual actual objects in a thinking being – since we can certainly not attribute [our impressions] to the divine understanding – the question concerns their relations. If those relations that we find in our own impressions are bound to this kind of impression alone, then their entire analogy with objects is nothing other than a subjective mode of cognizing the relations of things and, for example, being square and round are uncombinable in a single figure only for us. If, by contrast, these relations are independent of the nature of the impressions and are the same as what every other thinking being must be aware of in its own impressions, the impossibility of a square circle is an **absolute objective impossibility**.

The question cannot, I think, go further. Should one say that all thoughts, as thoughts of relations, are something merely subjective and that relations as their objects are nothing external to the understanding? This is beyond doubt for relations based on comparison. For similarity and diversity are only thought in the understanding. It is not as obvious with respect to relations concerning the mode of coexistence of things and causal connections. But granted that this

---

[31] See A26–A30/B42–B45 (Transcendental Aesthetic), B138–B139 (second edition of the Transcendental Deduction), and Phaenomena/Noumena.

were the case, what would follow is only that all thoughts and thus also all truths in us would be something subjective to the extent that a power of thinking is receptive to them. I believe that this is not at issue.

The following can still be said. Relations that our understanding is aware of in the things may perhaps themselves be other kinds of relations than those that another power of thinking might grasp. Similarity and diversity, being next to each other, and depending on each other, those are the modes of thinking of our understanding. Are they also the modes of thinking of every other understanding? Is it thus impossible to figure out whether our modes of thinking about objects are also the modes of thinking of an angel or even of the divine understanding? Thus the relations that we are aware of in our impressions are simply thoughts for us and only truths for us.

One can respond to this [as follows]. The first goal will be abandoned and another set. We have no concept of an understanding that is not aware of such relations [as exist] among the ideas of which we are aware. Thus if there is a power of thinking that is so completely heterogeneous from ours that the relations it brings about are incommensurable with ours, then it is something that can be viewed as analogous to an understanding or, if it is an excellence greater than our power of thinking, as an understanding *per eminentiam*. But it is not an understanding proper or a power of thinking of which we have a concept. And such powers of thinking proper are presupposed if the question is whether the relations of objects we are thinking are the same as those that all other powers of thinking must have of them. Things **in themselves** are either identical or diverse, but that means nothing more than that they are identical or diverse for every kind of being that can think the relations of identity and diversity.

One should not infer from this that the question does not make sense and belongs to an antiquated scholasticism. If one replaces the words **objective** and **subjective** with the words **unchangeably subjective** and **changeably subjective**, it is not necessary to take into account the powers of thinking of other beings of which we have no concept, and what the question means is still apparent. It is the same as if we were to ask what depends on the special configuration of our organs and on our current makeup, and what is, by contrast, necessary and always such, and remains such, however much the corporeal tools of our thinking may have changed, as long as our I remains a thinking being.

Eighth Essay: On the Relation between the Higher Cognitions of Reason and Those of the Common Understanding

Section I: What is higher cognition of speculative reason [*raisonnierenden Vernunft*]? On the nature of general theories

In previous times **sensible** cognition was contrasted with **rational** cognition. The world as it is presented to the senses (*mundus sensbilis*) was contrasted with the world as it is revealed to the understanding (*mundus intellectualis*), that is, the **confused** representations of things and their relations to each other, as one initially receives them through the senses, was contrasted with the **distinct** ideas that one forms by developing them and thinking about them according to **general concepts and principles**.[32] And philosophers investigated how both of these kinds of representations are related to each other. We see almost the same questions and the same observations, only that they arise in a different form, since recent philosophers have investigated how **common human understanding** and its cognitions relate to **higher speculative** reason and its **scientific** insights. The skeptics maintained and their opponents have admitted that the two are inconsistent with each other. The former propose that reason should be the deciding judge in such cases, while the latter prefer that it be **common understanding**, which should also be there to correct its own initial missteps. Speculative reason cannot and should not do that.[33] [...]

Ninth Essay: On the Basic Principle of Sensing, Representing, and Thinking

Section I: Determination of the point under investigation

On the basis of the preceding investigations I feel justified in assuming as a principle of experience that no more than these three faculties of the soul, **feeling**, the **power of representing**, and the **power of thinking**, are required [to account] for the effects of human cognitive powers. All

---

[32] See Kant's Phaenomena/Noumena (A235–A260/B294–B315) and Amphiboly (A260–A292/B316–B349).

[33] Tetens goes on to argue that a proper account of reason and common sense reveals how the two do not really stand in conflict with each other, because they stem from one and the same faculty. Any conflict between the two must in fact be merely apparent and due either to a misapplication of reason or to coming to believe that a *subjective* connection of impressions that the imagination brings about by means of its principles of association is actually an *objective* connection.

activities of our cognitive powers, from our first sensible expressions to our finest and highest speculations, consist in feeling, in representing, and in thinking. These faculties are already efficacious in our first and simplest awareness, that is, in the first expressions of the understanding, but one also finds none other than these in the highest effects of the most enlightened reason.

But one cannot now immediately infer from this that every being endowed with **awareness** also contains within itself all of the capabilities [*gesammte Anlage*] of the human understanding. For it is also apparent from the previous observations that each of these simple faculties must also be endowed with a degree of **perfectibility**, which could perhaps be absent even if the faculties were still present. Perhaps the power of thinking that animals have can attain apperception of **things**, objects, sensible objects, but not the awareness of the **relations** between the objects, without which judgments proper and inferences are not at all possible. [...]

Can one say that the matter will not be completely illuminated, but rather only clarified somewhat here and there, if we can determine with sufficient evidence whether the three faculties mentioned, [that is, the faculties] of feeling, making representations, and thinking, arise from a single basic power and are only higher aspects of it on different sides? Or whether they themselves are **basic principles** in the soul that are already intrinsically different and separable? [...] Without saying a word about how Condillac, Bonnet, and later figures have proceeded in their analyses, I intend to forge my own path and, once again, to compare with each other the nature of these kinds of effects [as ascertained] from observations of them, and only then to provide the concept of a basic principle of human cognitive power that seems to suggest itself spontaneously upon comparing these experiences.[34]

---

[34] In sections two, three, and four of this essay Tetens turns to describing several essential similarities between feeling, representing, and thinking. In section five he then considers the apparent disanalogies between these cognitive activities. At the end of this section Tetens describes the process of cognitive activities in terms of the following sequence: "Feeling, representing, and thinking can be presented in this order. First, the power of representing made representations [after impressions were received or "felt"] and placed them in preliminary fashion in a certain order and connection. Then a feeling of transition and relations followed. After that [came] the act of thinking and its effects, thought of a relation, namely, separating representations and relating them to each other, and the awareness of these relations insofar as it brings about the thought of a relation. This thinking has, in turn, its consequences for the representations. The mere representations are turned into ideas [...] and stand out from others more distinctly now than before."

Section VI: The result of the previous experiences is the following.
The first part of the act of thinking, relating representations to
each other, is a spontaneous effect of the power of representing.
The second part, becoming aware of the relations, is a new
spontaneous expression of feeling

(1) What kind of concept of an inner relation of the three basic activities of feeling, representing and thinking is contained in what has been described up to now? I am in search of a concept of their origin in a single basic principle according to which they are as similar and as diverse, as intimately connected and as dependent on each other, and as separable from each other as our observations represent them as being.

One cannot easily doubt that those acts that belong to the relations of representations are not finer and new expressions of the same faculty that is called the power of representing. This is one of the essential parts of thinking.

But [what of] the second, the act of awareness, by means of which the proper thought of a relation or a subjective relation is brought forth in us?

Is this act something other than an expression of **the same power** to which the feeling of relations is attributed? Is it not the effect of this faculty insofar as it is an active power, namely, insofar as it does not merely accept and feel modifications and react to it, but rather insofar as a **new activity** is connected with this relation? **An active faculty of impressions** is thus the faculty that brings about the thought of relations and the second and most prominent ingredient of the power of thought. [...]

(2) [...] Feeling, having representations, and thinking are capacities of one and the same basic faculty and are distinct from each other only in that this principle acts in different directions on different objects and with greater or lesser spontaneity when it reveals itself sometimes as a feeling being, other times as a representing being, and yet other times as a thinking being.[35] [...]

TWELFTH ESSAY: ON SPONTANEITY AND FREEDOM[36]

Section XV: Unification of the universal propositions
of reason with the concept of freedom

(1) The connection between causes and effects is not in all cases a
necessary connection.

---

[35] See A648–A649/B676–B677 (Appendix to the Transcendental Dialectic).
[36] This entire essay is relevant to the Third Antinomy.

I am convinced that the preceding investigations have put beyond doubt that in our impressions and observations of freedom everything is very much internally consistent. For if we determine ourselves, on the one hand, independently of external circumstances and by internal motives, and feel that this is how it is for us, yet, on the other hand, seem to be subject to these motives, then both of these [claims] can be reconciled with each other by noticing that our internal power is independent and is set up internally to will just as much as not to will, to act just as much as to refrain from acting, when it determines itself with the motivating representation, just as it does with an object that comes before it in the appropriate way, and applies its efficacy to it. Therefore, viewed from this perspective, the doctrine of freedom is, I maintain, free of difficulties as a part of observational psychology.

But now a second issue reappears, with respect to which so much obscurity and confusion has always been found. If free causes act and contingency is supposed to take place in their expressions of efficacy and actions, how can the universal connection between cause and effect be present and how can the effect be determined in every respect, or completely, in advance by its preceding causes and circumstances? That is, in a case where free causes are active and bring about contingent effects, how can the universal principles of reason be applied to a causal combination, which does not appear to admit of any exception at all?

Without getting involved in lengthy explanations of metaphysical doctrines that would be appropriate here, I merely want to point out briefly how I myself reason about this. It is certain that there must be a conceptual confusion somewhere here, and one can surmise in advance that the knot is not only very complicated, but also must be at a location, perhaps at the level of fundamental concepts, where one can get at it only with great effort. For those who are not at all familiar with metaphysical speculations about necessity and contingency, the following addendum will be useless, which I would have left out in any case, if quite a lot did not hinge on the attentiveness of speculative philosophers and, if this were possible, on their conviction and agreement. [...]

The **effect** is **necessarily** connected with **its cause**, says Mr. Hume and others along with him. Therefore, the dependence of the latter on the former is **necessary**, that is, the effect must follow and cannot fail to occur if the entire cause is completely present. For that reason, they now infer further, the impression too that makes us believe regarding our free actions that under the same circumstances under which we perform them we could have refrained from acting or acted differently, is an empty appearance and a fallacy of inner sense, as optical illusions occur with our outer, visual sense.

The impression does not deceive us, the indeterminist answers, and I agree with him. But when he adds: "the dependence of the effect on the cause is binding with **necessity** only if the cause is a **completely determining cause**, a **Wolffian sufficient ground**, and not all causes are of this sort, nor even can be, because not everything has or must have such a sufficient reason," this addition contains a line of reasoning to which I cannot assent.[37]

The proposition "that every effect that is brought forth, every thing, every modification, every action that arises, has its completely determining sufficient reason on which it depends in order to arise and with respect to all of its qualities and relations to become such as it actually is and none other," this proposition is a principle that I consider to be an axiom without it being necessary to prove it by means of induction on the basis of experience.

However, even if it were not such an axiom, viewed as a universal principle of the understanding in metaphysics, I would have to assume immediately on the basis of experience that actions of the human soul and also those that are most indifferent and free in the highest degree, are constituted such that each and every thing that comes to be and everything that is contingent should adhere to this principle. Not a single one of them is lacking in such a complete and determining ground as to why they proceed in such a manner and not otherwise. [...]

But if the **effect** is combined with a **sufficient cause** that **determines it completely**, one must still locate a **two-fold** makeup [*Beschaffenheit*] within this combination, one that distinguishes them from each other by real marks [*reelle Merkmale*], of which the one makes it into a **necessary** connection, while the other turns it into a **contingent** connection. If one prefers not to call it by this name, because, say, the metaphysical lexicon that one is using as a guide is against it, one can choose another. It is enough if a real difference that can be cognized distinctly is found in this case.

Let the completely determining cause of an effect be present, then it is indeed an axiom: "If that cause is present, the effect also occurs" (*posita causa ponitur effectus*), but there is a qualification here, or there must be one, namely, this: **insofar as no obstacle is present**. The wind will turn

---

[37] Tetens is distancing himself from Crusius's position, albeit without mentioning him by name.

the moveable weathercock around, but only under the condition that it was not stuck, or that the weathercock was, say, not being held by someone's hand or had not otherwise lost its mobility through rust. In these cases it does not turn. [...] In general the actual occurrence [of the effect] presupposes the condition that the currently present complete cause, which immediately precedes the effect, remains the same in the next moment, or that some foreign object that separates the latter from the former does not intercede between it and the effect. [...]

It is therefore clear that in addition to the completely determining efficacious cause that the effect depends on for all of its qualities and relations, the **absence of intervening obstacles** is always presupposed as well.

And in that case it follows **necessarily**, or, to use standard metaphysical concepts that can be retained here unchanged, in such a way that **it cannot fail to occur**. If the completely determining cause and the absence of all obstacles occur together, and if one adds the proposition "the effect does not occur," a contradiction arises. The proposition "the effect occurs" is a necessary consequence of the previous propositions just as the three angles in a triangle are a necessary consequence of its three sides. Whoever leaves something to chance denies this and the indeterminist denies this as well. He claims that he is forced to it [i.e., this denial] because of what experience teaches about freely acting causes. I do not make such a claim and if they view this as the shibboleth of their opponents, the determinists, I assume that I should be counted among the latter.

However, if the condition that no obstacle is present cannot be assumed, if it still holds, and if one has **only** the presupposition "that the completely determining cause is present" by which I understand both the actual efficacious cause with its active power and the remaining positive requirements and circumstances that contribute something to the determination of the effect, then two very different cases take place and everything depends on the important difference between them.

(2) Under which presuppositions is the causal connection **contingent?**

[...] We represent the **cause**, its **action** and **the effect becoming actual**, in a certain **temporal sequence**, as close and contiguous as their individual moments may be to each other. According to this idea, one can also even connect up with the presupposition of a positive ground the condition that no obstacle is present in the first moment, and two very different cases still remain, which are both possible. In the one case, an obstacle of some sort can still arise in the following moments, but not in the other.

The connection between a cause and its effect is thus contingent when the entire positive ground can exist and remain as it is along with all remaining positive requirements when the effect is caused, and a new obstacle can nonetheless intercede that holds up its achievement [*Ausrichtung*] or causality. This is a contingency that, in the proper sense, takes place in the dependence of the effect on the **present** and also **enduring** cause.

But if it is the case that the actual prevention [of the effect] is possible only by some change in the positive sufficient ground, whether it be in the active power or in the external requirements and circumstances, it is nonetheless contingent that the effect results when the sufficient ground is currently present. For the effect can also fail to occur in this case too, although the ground is present **now** and is changed when the obstacle arises. When, e.g., a ball approaches a container and the latter moves out of the way, one can then say that the container did not stay in the same place that it was at before, and this circumstance belonged to the total sufficient ground. Therefore the entire cause did not remain unchanged when the obstacle arose. One could therefore say that if the effect could be absent in this case although the cause was present, this is not because the effect could be separated from the cause and the projected circumstances, but rather because the cause or the circumstances, even though they are this way right now, can be changed so that they no longer remain the way they are now. The contingency that takes place here thus lies in the **contingency of the causes and of the circumstances**, or in the contingency of the present, positive, sufficient ground itself. However, from whatever perspective one views the matter, it is always the same. "Although everything is currently present on which the effect depends, [i.e.] the entire cause with all of its circumstances, the effect does not follow except under the presupposition that no obstacle arises and that everything could subsist as it is and remain unchanged without any additions until the effect is brought about, and the present state of things does not itself make this condition superfluous."

The causal connections of actual things in the world are, according to Leibniz and Wolff, contingent in the sense in which it is defined here. One cannot demonstrate, Leibniz said, in physics as one can in geometry, a saying whose true and complete meaning is not always grasped. Active causes in nature have their effects under the circumstances noted, but it is not for that reason a contradiction if the latter are absent even if the former are present with all of their requirements and circumstances. One can in that case demonstrate only that the effect follows if one assumes beyond the existence of the causes also the condition that no obstacle arises to block its path, but otherwise the conclusion that the effect is brought about does not follow from the previous premises, according to which the cause and its circumstances exist. This is without doubt an extremely important **internal** contingency within the world that the philosophers mentioned above set in opposition to the Spinozistic and stoic necessity.

(3) Under which presuppositions is it [i.e., the causal connection] **necessary?**

What occurs is, by contrast, **necessarily** bound to its sufficient ground, if the latter, once it has been assumed as it is, contains within itself the second condition that no obstacle arises such that this condition can be derived from the former as one of its consequences. If the efficacious cause cannot be robbed of its efficacy during its action or even weakened therein, if the object cannot be taken away from it, if the cause acts irresistibly and the requirements of action are immutable – when all of this is gathered together, the effect becoming actual is a necessary consequence of the actuality of the complete ground. Omnipotence would **necessarily** act at all times if it were not the omnipotence of a **free** being that can pose an obstacle to itself through its own inner power and check, so to speak, its omnipotence.

(4) The contingency of the connection, if free causes act.

There is quite a difference between this universal contingency of efficacious connections in the world and the internal contingency that takes place in cases where the active [*thätige*] cause acts [*wirket*] with freedom. When wind blows the clouds, lightning strikes, and water breaks through the dams, it is indeed possible that these effects could also have been prevented under the same circumstances, but on what basis and which cause would have had to produce this obstacle? The causing of the effects was contingent either because the efficacious causes are contingent on their own and, although they were there, could have been removed previously, before they had their effect, or because their activity was surmountable and resistible. However, if an actual obstacle is to have arisen, then an external cause would have been required that would have been associated with it and been involved in its activity. The contingency of the connection itself is indeed, considered from one perspective, internal and has its ground in the way in which the nature of the efficacious powers is constituted. For the interceding cause may or may not actually interfere, but the effect is still linked to the supposed cause by a connection that could be absent, changed, or removed. However, this contingency also contains an indication of an external cause that is present beyond the one that acts here, and beyond the circumstances under which it acts, that is, beyond the individual sufficient ground. As we view a certain thing as something that can be brought about, its emergence must not only be free from internal contradiction, but it is also assumed that a power really exists that possesses the capacity required to bring it about. One can certainly also view this absolute possibility, namely, that the thing can **come to be** if only a power **were** present that **had** the capacity to bring it about, as its absolute possibility of becoming, or as its internal **feasibility** [*Machbarkeit*]. However, the **more proximate possibility** [namely] that it can be done and brought about, presupposes that the power required for this already exists. Therefore, if the causal combination should be viewed, according to this account, as contingent only in cases where actual powers are present with a capacity sufficient to intercede in the circumstances assumed and to prevent the effect, then the contingency that is found in the connections of the corporeal world is nothing more than an external contingency that refers to an external cause that can intercede in this case from somewhere else.

For this reason this contingency is also no longer present in the connection if the condition is merely added that nothing from without gets in the way. Throw a spark in dry powder and assume that nothing else is present beyond these two interacting things and the other typical circumstances that would be contrary to the incendiary power of the fire and to the powder catching fire and exploding, then enough has been assumed. The effect follows, and does so necessarily under these presuppositions.

By contrast, when a free cause acts, it is possible that the action be interrupted or prevented due to the capacity to do the contrary that is to be attributed to the acting being itself. Let the free cause act, the effect can still fail to occur, not only because the cause itself can be impeded, but also because it can interrupt its action through its own internal power, and has the complete capacity to do so, even if the latter lets it take its course. Therefore, there is an internal contingency in free actions that does not require the existence of external causes and that can also not be removed by any external power except insofar as the action is also coerced and would cease being a free action.

Therefore, in order to derive the effect of a freely acting power from its sufficient cause, it is not enough to assume the latter along with all of its requirements. What must be added as well is that no obstacle is involved from without. And this is not yet enough; it must be added further that nothing from within gets mixed up in this, namely, that the active power does not hold itself back or determine itself in some other way.

These differences, based on universal concepts, are still at least real differences which even the indeterminist does not deny, or at least may not deny, in order to maintain his system. He denies only that this contingency suffices for free actions. But this had to be posed anew as a question.

The contingency that is explained here is the same one that we meet with in our experiences with the soul. The impression of our freedom contains exactly this, neither more, nor less, than what is contained in the former concept. Reason and experience are in harmony with each other. I act as I do according to sufficient reasons, but I **can** also act otherwise, through myself and on my own [*durch mich selbst und aus mir selbst*] if I am in control of myself [*wenn ich meiner selbst mächtig bin*]. [...] Leibniz said, quite rightly: **nothing occurs** without a sufficient reason. But who gave philosophers the license to say: nothing **can** occur without a sufficient reason. [...]

The indeterminist is not content with any possibility of the contrary and thus not with any possibility of the thing itself insofar as a completely sufficient or determining ground of it is assumed. In his eyes, contingency is not a truly complete contingency unless the prior active cause and all of the requirements of the action, and even the condition that no obstacle interferes, are still nevertheless compatible with the effect not occurring. If this is the essence of contingency, then contingency requires **blind chance** with respect to what happens. There is a principle of reason at play here, where we part ways. However, nowhere have I found that anyone has established, on the basis of experience, a [notion of] contingency that posits more in free actions than does what was explained above. One merely inferred that such contingency must be present, because otherwise none would be present. But which one is supposed to be the authentic contingency? The **internal indeterminacy** of the principle in the soul that decides for itself? This is certainly present, but it is completely consistent with the principle of internal sufficient reason. I can will and not will, and will as it pleases me; and if it pleases me that I will, I retain my capacity not to will just as much as I did beforehand. But isn't some example present where I would have willed without it being the case that this self-determination was especially pleasing to me or that there was something in the preceding circumstances why I willed more than not willed, or more this object rather than another? For that reason this ground not should not be called a **determining** ground, because it actually makes the acting power no longer internally sufficient for the action as it was beforehand, but rather represents only an object of power, and I would be very much in agreement, and would wish that it not be called determining.

Concordance

Section of Critique of Pure Reason	Page Reference	Wolff, *Rational Thoughts*	Knutzen, *System of Efficient Causes/ Imm. Nature of the Soul*	Baumgarten, *Metaphysics*
Preface A	Avii–Axxii			
Preface B	Bvii–Bxliv			
Introduction A	A1–A16			
Introduction B	B1–B30			
Transcendental Aesthetic				102
On Space	A22/B37–A30/B45	14–15	61	102
On Time	A30/B46–A49/B73			
Transcendental Logic	A50/B74–A704/B732			
Introduction	A50/B74–A66/B91	22–36		
Transcendental Analytic				
On the Clue (Metaphysical Deduction)	A66/B91–A83–B116	22–36		
Transcendental Deduction	A84/B116–A130/B169	27, 46–47		89–90

Crusius Sketch	Euler, Letters	Lambert, "Treatise on Criterion"/ New Organon	Herz, Observations	Eberhard, Universal Theory	Tetens, Philosophical Essays
					357–359
138		264–265			374–375
	185–187	267	281–282	323, 333	360
137, 138	185–187	267	281–282	323	360, 363–369
145–146		273	286–287, 289–290, 292–293	338	360, 360–361, 362–363
146, 51	211–213				377–381
149					
138		233, 242–243, 249–251, 257		329	359–360, 360–361 377–381,
162	198–200	242–243	285–286		367–371
173			287–288	325, 332	357–359, 361–362, 362–363, 363–369, 370–373

(continued)

(continued)

Section of Critique of Pure Reason	Page Reference	Wolff, Rational Thoughts	Knutzen, System of Efficient Causes/ Imm.Nature of the Soul	Baumgarten, Metaphysics
Schematism	A137/B176– A147/B187			
Supreme Principles of Analytic & Synthetic Judgments	A148/B187– A158/ B197	9–10		
Axioms of Intuition & Anticipations of Perception	A161/B202– A176/ B218			
First Analogy of Experience	A182/B224– A189/ B232	18–19	78–79	98–99
Second Analogy of Experience	A189/B232– A211/ B256	11–12, 18, 19–20, 37–38, 40, 42, 45		99
Third Analogy of Experience	A211/B256– A215/ B262			
Postulates of Empirical Thought	A218/B265– A235/ B287			107, 108
Refutation of Idealism	B274–279	23		
Phaenomena/ Noumena	A235/B294– A260/B315			
Amphiboly	A260/B316– A292/B349	10–11, 39–40, 41–42	59	89–91
Transcendental Dialectic				
Introduction	A293/B249– A309/B366	29, 30		
On the Concepts of Pure Reason	A310/B366– A338/B396			

Crusius Sketch	Euler, Letters	Lambert, "Treatise on Criterion"/ New Organon	Herz, Observations	Eberhard, Universal Theory	Tetens, Philosophical Essays
137, 140, 143			302–303	337	
138, 164	211–313		284–285	335	
141–142			297		
142, 143–144, 149–150, 152–161, 172, 174	187–189				363–367, 376–377
161, 171–172	194–196		285		
140–141, 150–152, 174		255			
					370–373
162					377–381, 381–382
	209–213		292–293		362–363, 369–371, 381–382
				330–331	360, 360–361

(continued)

(continued)

Section of Critique of Pure Reason	Page Reference	Wolff, *Rational Thoughts*	Knutzen, *System of Efficient Causes/ Imm. Nature of the Soul*	Baumgarten, *Metaphysics*
The Paralogisms of Pure Reason	A338/ B396–A405/ B432	7–8, 22, 24, 46–50	54–56, 58–59, 66, 67–69, 70–72, 76–83	115–117, 125, 127–129
1st Substantiality	[A348–A351]	48–49		112, 123, 125–126
2nd Simplicity	[A351–A361]	47–48	79–80	124–125, 125–126
3rd Personal Identity	[A361–A366]			118, 125–126
4th Ideality	[A366–A380]			111, 114
The Antinomy of Pure Reason	A405/ B432–A567/ B595			95, 102, 103, 104, 105–106, 106–107, 108, 109–112
1st Size	[A426/ B454–A433/ B461]			95, 97–98, 102, 105, 106
2nd Composition	[A434/ B462–A443/ B471]	16–17, 38–39, 39–40, 40–44	60, 63	97–98, 101–103, 109–112
3rd Freedom	[A444/ B472–A451/ B479]	33–34, 34–36	54–56	105, 107, 108, 120–122, 129–130
4th Necessary Being	[A452/ B480–A460/ B488]	51		105–106
The Ideal of Pure Reason	A567/ B595–A642/ B670	52–53		95, 97
On the Ontological Argument	[A592/ B620–A602/ B630]			

Crusius *Sketch*	Euler, *Letters*	Lambert, "Treatise on Criterion"/ *New Organon*	Herz, *Observations*	Eberhard, *Universal Theory*	Tetens, *Philosophical Essays*
172–173, 174–176	196–197, 198–202		283	325, 335	357–359, 370-373
177–178					
177–178			295–296, 309–310		
				325	370–373
138–139, 170–173			283–284		
163					
163	213–226, 228–230		284		
157–160, 177					384–391
165–169					
168					

(continued)

(continued)

Section of Critique of Pure Reason	Page Reference	Wolff, *Rational Thoughts*	Knutzen, *System of Efficient Causes/ Imm. Nature of the Soul*	Baumgarten, *Metaphysics*
On the Cosmological Argument	[A603/ B631–A614/ B642]	51		103–104
On the Physico-theological Argument	[A621/ B649–A630/ B658]			
Appendix to the Transcendental Dialectic	A642/ B670–A704/ B732	48–49		124
Transcendental Doctrine of Method	A707/ B735–A855/ B883	9, 32, 33		90–91

Crusius *Sketch*	Euler, *Letters*	Lambert, "Treatise on Criterion"/ *New Organon*	Herz, *Observations*	Eberhard, *Universal Theory*	Tetens, *Philosophical Essays*
166					
167					
		263–264		322, 323	383
137, 138, 178–179	183–187, 202–205	235, 238, 244	299–300	337	357–359, 374–375

Bibliography

Ameriks, Karl. *Kant's Theory of Mind.* New York: Oxford, 2000.

Baumgarten, Alexander. *Acroasis logica in Christianum L. B. Wolff.* Halle, 1761.

Aesthetica. Frankfurt, 1750–1758.

Ethica philosophica. Halle, 1739.

Initia philosophiae practicae primae. Halle: Hemmerde, 1760.

Meditationes philosophicae de nonullis ad poema pertinentibus. Halle, 1735.

Metaphysica. Reprinted in Immanuel Kant's *Gesammelte Schriften,* vols. 15,1 (pp. 5–54) and 17 (pp. 5–226). Halle, 1739, Frankfurt, 1757, Rpt. Berlin: de Gruyter, 1902–.

Crusius, Christian August. *Anleitung über natürliche Begebenheiten ordentlich und vorsichtig nachzudenken.* Leipzig: Gleditsch, 1749.

Anweisung, vernünftig zu leben. Leipzig: Gleditsch, 1744.

Dissertatio de usu et limitibus principii rationis determinantis vulgo sufficientis. Leipzig, 1743.

Entwurf der nothwendigen Vernunft-Wahrheiten. Reprinted in Christian August Crusius, *Die philosophischen Hauptwerke,* ed. G. Tonelli, vol. 2. Leipzig, 1745. Rpt. Hildesheim: Georg Olms Verlag, 1964.

Weg zur Gewißheit und Zuverläßigkeit der menschlichen Erkenntnis, reprinted in Crusius, *Die philosophischen Hauptwerke,* ed. G. Tonelli, vol. 3. Leipzig, 1747. Rpt. Hildesheim: Georg Olms Verlag, 1964.

Eberhard, Johann August. *Allgemeine Geschichte der Philosophie.* Halle: Hemmerde, 1788.

Allgemeine Theorie des Denkens und Empfindens. Berlin, 1776.

Handbuch der Ästhetik. Halle: Hemmerde, 1803–1805.

Die neue Apologie des Sokrates. Berlin: Nicolai, 1772.

Theorie der schönen Künste und Wissenschaften. Halle: Waisenhaus, 1783.

Versuch einer allgemeinen-deutschen Synonymik. Halle: Ruff, 1795–1802.

Vorbereitung zur natürlichen Theologie. Halle: Waisenhaus, 1781.

Euler, Leonard. *Dissertatio de principio minae actionis.* Berlin: J. G. Michael, 1753.

Gedancken von den Elementen der Körper. Berlin: Haude, 1746.

Introductio in Analysin Infinitorum. Lausannae: Bousquet, 1744.

Lettres à une princesse d'Allemagne sur divers sujets de physique et de philosophie. St. Petersburg: Royal Academy of Sciences, 1768–1772.

Mechanica sive motus scientia analytice. St. Petersberg: Academy of Sciences, 1736.

Recherches sur l'origine des forces. Berlin, 1750.

Réflexions sur l'espace et le temps. Berlin, 1748.

Vollständige Anleitung zur Algebra. St. Petersburg: Academy of Sciences, 1770.

Friedman, Michael. *Kant and the Exact Sciences.* Cambridge, MA: Harvard University Press, 1992.

Guyer, Paul. *Kant and the Claims of Knowledge.* New York: Cambridge University Press, 1989.

Herz, Markus. *Betrachtungen aus der spekulativen Weltweisheit.* Königsberg: Kanter, 1771.

Briefe an Ärzte. Mitau: Hinz, 1777.

Grundlage zu seinen Vorlesungen über die Experimentalphysik. Berlin: Voß, 1786.

Grundriß aller medizinischen Wissenschaften. Berlin: Voß, 1782.

Versuch über den Geschmack und die Ursachen seiner Verschiedenheit. Mitau: Hinz, 1776.

Kant, Immanuel. *Correspondence.* Ed. A. Zweig. New York: Cambridge University Press, 1999.

Critique of Pure Reason. Ed. P. Guyer and A. Wood. New York: Cambridge University Press, 1998.

Gesammelte Schriften. Berlin: Königlich-Preussischen Akademie der Wissenschaften zu Berlin, 1902–.

Lectures on Metaphysics. Ed. K. Ameriks and S. Naragon. New York: Cambridge University Press, 1997.

Theoretical Philosophy 1755–1770. Ed. D. Walford with R. Meerbote. New York: Cambridge University Press, 1992.

Knutzen, Martin. *Commentatio philosophica de commercio mentis et corporis per influxum physicum explicando.* Königsberg: Langenhemium, 1735.

Commentatio philosophica de humanae mentis individua natura sive immaterialitate. Königsberg: Reusner, 1741.

Elementa philosophiae rationalis seu logicae. Königsberg: Hartung, 1747.

Philosophische Abhandlung von der immateriellen Natur der Seele. Königsberg: Hartung, 1744.

Philosophischer Beweis von der Wahrheit der christlichen Religion. Königsberg: Hartung, 1740.

Systema Causarum Efficientium. Leipzig: Langenhemium, 1745.

Vernünftige Gedanken von den Cometen. Frankfurt, 1744.

Kuehn, Manfred. *Kant: A Biography.* New York: Cambridge University Press, 2001.

Lambert, Johann Heinrich. "*Abhandlung vom* Criterium veritatis." [1761] in *Kant-Studien,* Ergänzungsheft 36 (1915): 7–64.

Anlage zur Architectonic. Riga: Hartknoch, 1771.

Cosmologische Briefe über die Einrichtung des Weltbaues. Augsburg: L. Klett, 1761.

Neues Organon. Leipzig: Wendler, 1764.

Leibniz, Gottfried Wilhelm. *Die Philosophischen Schriften von Leibniz.* Ed. C. I. Gerhardt. 7 vols. Berlin: Weidmann, 1875–1890.

Longuenesse, Béatrice. *Kant and the Capacity to Judge*. Princeton, NJ: Princeton University Press, 1998.

Lossius, Johann Christian. *Physische Ursachen des Wahren*. Gotha, 1774.

Mendelsssohn, Moses. *Philosophical Writings*. Ed. D. Dahlstrom. New York: Cambridge University Press, 1997.

Philosophische Schriften, Parts 1 and 2. Berlin: Voß, 1771.

Newton, Isaac. *Mathematical Principles of Natural Philosophy and His System of the World*. Trans. A. Mott, rev. F. Cajori. Berkeley: University of California Press, 1934.

Tetens, Johann Nicolas. *Philosophische Versuche über die menschliche Natur und ihre Entwicklung*. Leipzig: Weidmanns, 1777.

Über den Ursprung der Sprache und der Schrift. Bützow: Berger & Boedner, 1772.

Über die allgemeine speculativische Philosophie. Bützow: Berger & Boedner, 1775.

Watkins, Eric. *Kant and the Metaphysics of Causality*. New York: Cambridge University Press, 2005.

Wolff, Christian. *Vernünftige Gedancken von Gott, der Welt und der Seele des Menschen, auch allen Dingen überhaupt*. Reprinted in Abt. 1, Bd. 2 of Christian Wolff's *Gesammelte Werke* [Halle, 1720]. Hildesheim: G. Olms Verlag, 1983.

Vernünfftige Gedancken von den Würkungen der Natur. Reprinted in Abt. 1, Bd. 6 of Christian Wolff's *Gesammelte Werke* [Halle, 1723]. Hildesheim: G. Olms Verlag, 1981.

Wood, Allen. *Kant's Rational Theology*. Ithaca, NY: Cornell University Press, 1978.

Index